Voices of Torah
Volume 2

A Treasury of Rabbinic Gleanings
on the Weekly Portions, Holidays,
and Special Shabbatot

Voices of Torah

Volume 2

A TREASURY OF
RABBINIC GLEANINGS
ON THE WEEKLY PORTIONS,
HOLIDAYS, AND
SPECIAL SHABBATOT

Edited by
Rabbi Sonja K. Pilz, PhD

Introduction by Rabbi Amy Scheinerman

CENTRAL CONFERENCE OF AMERICAN RABBIS

5780   NEW YORK   2020

Library of Congress Cataloging-in-Publication Data
Voices of Torah : a treasury of rabbinic gleanings on the
weekly portions, holidays, and special Shabbatot / edited by
Hara E. Person ; introduction by Kenneth J. Weiss.
   p. cm.
ISBN 978-0-88123-159-5 (pbk. : alk. paper) 1. Bible. O.T.
Pentateuch--Commentaries. I. Person, Hara.
  BS1225.53.V65 2011
  222'.107--dc23   2011019258

Voices of Torah, Volume 2
ISBN: 978-0-88123-341-4 (pbk.) | ISBN: 978-0-88123-342-1 (ebook)

    Copyright © 2020 by Reform Jewish Publishing, a division of CCAR Press.

Printed in U.S.A. All rights reserved. No portion of this book may be copied in any
form for any purpose without the written permission of the Central Conference of
American Rabbis.

                    10 9 8 7 6 5 4 3 2 1

        CCAR Press, 355 Lexington Avenue, New York, NY 10017
                         (212) 972-3636
                      ccarpress@ccarnet.org
                       www.ccarpress.org

Contents

Introduction	vii	**LEVITICUS**	181
Acknowledgments	xi	Vayikra	183
		Tzav	191
GENESIS	1	Sh'mini	197
B'reishit	3	Tazria/M'tzora	203
Noach	9	Acharei Mot/K'doshim	211
Lech L'cha	17	Emor	219
Vayeira	25	B'har/B'chukotai	227
Chayei Sarah	33		
Tol'dot	41	**NUMBERS**	235
Vayeitzei	49	B'midbar	237
Vayishlach	57	Naso	243
Vayeishev	65	B'haalot'cha	249
Mikeitz	73	Sh'lach L'cha	257
Vayigash	79	Korach	265
Va-y'chi	87	Chukat/Balak	273
		Pinchas	287
EXODUS	95	Matot/Mas'ei	295
Sh'mot	97		
Va-eira	105	**DEUTERONOMY**	305
Bo	113	D'varim	307
B'shalach	121	Va-et'chanan	315
Yitro	129	Eikev	323
Mishpatim	137	R'eih	331
T'rumah	147	Shof'tim	339
T'tzaveh	155	Ki Teitzei	347
Ki Tisa	163	Ki Tavo	355
Vayak'heil/P'kudei	171	Nitzavim/Vayeilech	363

Haazinu	373	Purim	419
V'zot Hab'rachah	379	Pesach; the Time of the Omer, including Yom HaShoah, Yom HaZikaron, Yom HaAtzma-ut; and Shavuot	423
ADDITIONAL READINGS	381		
The High Holy Days	383		
Sukkot, Sh'mini Atzeret, and Simchat Torah	395	Tishah B'Av	449
		Elul	457
Chanukah	409		
Tu BiSh'vat	413	Glossary	459

Introduction

Rabbi Amy Scheinerman

Judaism has, from its inception, embraced textual interpretation as a practice. The texts of our Torah have sparked and fueled an ongoing, evolving conversation about the salient concerns of Jewish life and thought: the nature of God, Israel's relationship with God, our obligations to God, Jewish ethics, and Israel's relationships with other peoples. Our library of textual interpretations, expounding our stories and sacred laws, has grown over the millennia. Jews have continuously returned to the texts of the Torah to draw guidance from it, but also to breathe new life into it.

Even within the Pentateuch (the Five Books of Moses) itself, we see evidence of intertextual commentary as a fundamental mode of Jewish theological expression and engagement with the Sacred: "These are the words that Moses addressed to Israel on the other side of the Jordan [River]. . . . On the other side of the Jordan, in the land of Moav, Moses undertook to expound the Torah" (Deut. 1:1, 1:5). Long before the Rabbis inherited the Torah and created a formal technique of biblical textual interpretation and commentary, biblical authors read and responded to the stories and texts they knew. Judy Klitsner, in *Subversive Sequels in the Bible: How Biblical Stories Mine and Undermine Each Other*, demonstrates that the Book of Jonah confronts and overturns some of the basic assumptions implicit in the story of the Flood (Gen. 6:9–9:28), that the tale of the midwives in Exodus 1 is a powerful polemic against the failure of the city-state as described in the tale of the Tower of Babel (Genesis 11), and that the stories of Sarah and Rebekah counter the vision of women presented in the first three chapters of Genesis. "Sequels" are voices interpreting and commenting on the texts of the Torah. And this happened within the Hebrew Bible itself!

In *Mishnah Pirkei Avot* (*Ethics of the Sages*), which functions as an introduction to the Talmud, Ben Bag Bag opines on behalf of all the sages, "Turn [the Torah] and turn it, for everything is in it. Scrutinize it, grow old and gray in it, do not depart from it. There is no better quality than it" (5:24). The early Rabbis elevated Torah study and interpretation to a central, formal, and sacred undertaking, assuring that the tradition of reading, interpreting, challenging, and expounding holy texts would remain an integral intellectual and spiritual practice for the generations to follow them. All reading is an act of interpretation; no text has only one literal meaning. Our Rabbis not only understood this truth; they celebrated and reveled in the human capacity for "turning Torah over and over" to find ever-new meanings in it.

Studying and interpreting the texts of our Torah guides us to the questions we need to ask and helps us find our answers. Rabbi Akiva is credited with teaching that the Torah's meaning goes beyond the *p'shat* ("the direct, contextual meaning of the text") and extends into the realms of *remez* ("the symbolic or allegorical meaning"), *d'rash* ("homiletical meaning"), and *sod* ("esoteric or mystical meaning"). Each mode of interpretation contributes its own dimension of meaning to the sacred texts of our Torah. Through interpretation and commentary, Torah has become an ongoing process of inquiry that invites new voices—yours included—to join the conversation, generation upon generation.

Becoming a part of the conversation of interpreting the texts of our Torah brings inspiration, comfort, instruction, moral insight, and hope. This is the power of Torah, "a tree of life to those who hold fast to it" (Prov. 3:18). Each generation is blessed by the interpretations it inherits. Each generation contributes its own understanding to the growing library of interpretive texts, passing them on to succeeding generations. Those whose commentaries are offered in this volume have absorbed the learning of preceding generations, and share their ideas with you and with generations to come. This volume of *Voices of Torah* contributes to the ever-flowing river of Torah.

These "Voices of Torah" were originally written by Reform rabbis wishing to share short commentaries on the weekly Torah reading in the bimonthly newsletter of the Central Conference of American Rabbis. These pieces are gifts to our treasured colleagues around the world. As the editor of the *CCAR Newsletter*'s "Voices of Torah," it is my privilege to solicit and edit each piece, which often affords me an opportunity to engage the writers, my colleagues, in conversations about the texts of our Torah.

The pieces are short, averaging 250 words. Mark Twain famously quipped, "I didn't have time to write a short letter, so I wrote a long one instead." Indeed, this captures the challenge of presenting in a short, concise piece the kernel of an idea that can be expanded into a full-length sermon or Torah study, suggesting directions for elaboration.

The group of our authors is diverse. It spans three continents. Some of our authors are mid-career; others are retired. Men and women, LGBTQ and straight, community rabbis, chaplains, and congregational rabbis all contributed to this volume. New people join the group periodically.

Since I came on board as the editor of the *CCAR Newsletter*'s "Voices of Torah" in 2007, we have lost two precious colleagues and superb rabbis who were close personal friends: Rabbi Janice Garfunkel, z"l and Rabbi Jeffrey Ballon, z"l. This volume of *Voices of Torah*, which contains some of their Torah—their legacy—is dedicated to them.

The contributing authors in this volume are as follows:

Rabbi Ruth Adar
Rabbi Tom Alpert
Rabbi Jeffrey Ballon, z"l
Rabbi Michael Boyden
Rabbi Fred Davidow
Rabbi Rabbi Janice Garfunkel, z"l
Rabbi Norman Hirsh
Rabbi Mark Levin
Rabbi Charles Middleburgh, PhD
Rabbi Joshua Minkin, DMin
Rabbi David Novak
Rabbi Louis Rieser
Rabbi Gila Ruskin
Rabbi Amy Scheinerman
Rabbi Bill S. Tepper
Rabbi Pamela Wax
Rabbi Stephen Wylen
Rabbi Israel Zoberman, DMin

You might enjoy reading these *d'rashot* ("interpretations", "short sermons") in conjunction with the Torah reading on Shabbat or as quiet readings for Shabbat afternoon. They might serve those of you who lead or participate in Torah study groups or who are preparing a *d'rash* (short sermon). Students of Torah will appreciate the spectrum of ideas inspired by each *parashah* ("Torah portion") and the wide array of ancillary texts cited to comment on the biblical text itself.

Allow me to close with an ancient "voice of Torah" from *Midrash B'midbar Rabbah* (13:16) affirming the polyphonic nature of Jewish textual interpretation. After Moses consecrates the Tabernacle in the wilderness, the twelve tribal chieftains contribute offerings that include "one silver basin of seventy *sh'kalim*" (Num. 7:19). The midrash explains that the silver *mizrak* ("basin") is an allusion to the Torah and that the "seventy *sh'kalim*" hints that there are "seventy faces of Torah"—seventy different ways to understand each passage. Textual interpretation allows us to see the many facets of Torah, our sparkling jewel and ever-flowing fountain of wisdom that speaks to every generation. May it sustain, challenge, and inspire us all.

On behalf of us all, we are delighted and privileged to share with you these *divrei torah* ("words of Torah"). We hope that you, like us, find wisdom, meaning, intellectual challenge, and spiritual comfort in the infinitely responsive "voices" of our Torah.

Acknowledgments

The first thank-you goes to all of the rabbis whose contributions of Torah, writing, time, and patience make up this book. From 2010 to 2018, these *d'rashot*, published in the bimonthly *CCAR Newsletter*, made not only commentaries on the weekly *parashah*, but also reflections on Jewish life in the U.S., and voices of personal and lived theologies accessible to our members. Voices of Torah is an inspirational gift to our members and beyond, and as such, a warm thank-you goes to Rabbi Ruth Adar; Rabbi Tom Alpert; Rabbi Jeffrey Ballon, z"l; Rabbi Michael Boyden; Rabbi Fred Davidow; Rabbi Janice Garfunkel, z"l; Rabbi Norman Hirsh; Rabbi Mark Levin; Rabbi Charles Middleburgh, PhD; Rabbi Joshua Minkin, DMin; Rabbi David Novak; Rabbi Louis Rieser; Rabbi Gila Ruskin; Rabbi Amy Scheinerman; Rabbi Bill S. Tepper; Rabbi Pamela Wax; Rabbi Stephen Wylen; and Rabbi Israel Zoberman, DMin.

More than anyone else, Rabbi Amy Scheinerman and her careful and tireless work as the editor of the original contributions to the *CCAR Newsletter* contributed to this book. If, almost ten years after the publication of the first volume of *Voices of Torah*, we are able to publish a second volume today, it is due to her wisdom and dedication as an editor, rabbi, and member of the CCAR.

The support of Hara Person, publisher of the CCAR Press, her guidance and trust, were vital for this publication; as well as the ongoing encouragement of Rabbi Steven A. Fox, CCAR Chief Executive. Our rabbinic interns Vanessa Harper and Jessica Kerman, as well as summer intern Kobi Appel-Bernstein, all played important roles in compiling the *d'rashot* included in this project. Debbie Smilow and her careful work and advice turned a manuscript into a book, and the thorough eyes of Debra Hirsch Corman, Otto Barz, and Michael Israelwitz moved the project toward publication. To Ortal Bensky, Raquel Fairweather, Carly Linden, Rabbi Dan Medwin, and Sasha Smith: *todah*.

Genesis

בראשית *B'reishit*
(Genesis 1:1–6:8)

B'reishit
Rabbi Stephen Wylen, 2011

"Let us make the human [*adam*] after our own image" (Gen. 1:26).

It is possible that the word *adam* derives not from *adamah* (earth), but from *dimyon* (imagination, resemblance), and that the initial *alef* is prefixed. The distinction of the human being from all other creatures lies in the power of imagination. All other creatures perceive only what is, but the human being, who is created from a mixture of above and below, divine and animal, sees with the power of imagination. The human perceives that which is beyond the senses, that which could be. The human being can deduce one matter from another and draw conclusions beyond sensory perception. Few today would contend that the resemblance of the human being to the Divine lies in its form, as visualized at the Sistine Chapel ceiling. Modern philosophers have tended to focus on reason as aspiring to the Divine, thereby setting science over against faith; but historically, religious rationalists like Maimonides, and even the nineteenth-century Romantics, described reason and imagination as complementary and cooperative powers of the human soul. Imagination was not relegated to the realm of fine arts and belles lettres.

Arthur Green has called for a new theology that integrates our new scientific knowledge into received spiritual wisdom. Can the reintegration of imagination assist with this endeavor? Can we make such a theology emotionally relevant in the lives of our people, such that they will not have to turn to a fundamentalist rejection of reason as they seek spiritual warmth and meaning?

B'reishit
Rabbi Janice Garfunkel, z"l, 2012

I was surprised to learn that although the Hebrew words used for both Adam's and Eve's punishments are the same, they are nearly always translated differently.

In both the 1962 and 1967 JPS translations we find for Eve: "I will make most severe your pangs [*itzvoneich, ayin-tzadi-bet*] in childbearing; in pain [*b'etzev, ayin-tzadi-bet*] shall you bear children" (Gen. 3:16). For Adam we find: "By toil [*b'itzavon, ayin-tzadi-bet*] shall you eat of it" (Gen. 3:17).

Why did translators use "pangs, pain"'for Eve but "toil" for Adam? I further find it interesting that Eve's "punishment" is giving birth to children (the word translated as "toil" might also be translated as "labor" in both cases), and at the conclusion of Adam's punishment, mortality is introduced: "Until you return to the ground—for from it you were taken. For dust you are, and to dust you shall return" (Gen. 3:19). Of course, the creation of new life via the birth of babies does necessitate mortality. While this consequence is phrased in the masculine singular, we know that both Adam and Eve share equally in it, as do the animals.

Perhaps these words are neither punishment nor consequence, but merely a description of what life is like, as a parent might say to a child: I brought you into this world and taught you right from wrong, good from evil. Now, you must grow up, labor to have children, labor to earn a living, and eventually return to dust.

B'reishit
Rabbi Michael Boyden, 2013

One of the lessons that we all have to learn in life is that nothing is perfect. That may seem like a human problem, but it is also God's. Having made a world that was meant to be good, at the end of our *parashah* we read that "Adonai regretted having made human beings on earth, and was heartsick" (Gen. 6:6).

In *B'reishit Rabbah* 8:3, Rabbi Berechiah says that God is like a king who engages an architect to design a palace for him. When he sees it, he doesn't like it. But who could he be angry with, if not with the architect? So, how strange it is that God was saddened in God's own heart!

God's world is an imperfect place. Indeed, Rabbi Avahu tells us in the same midrash (*B'reishit Rabbah* 9:2) that God created many worlds and destroyed them. While our world was meant to be *tov m'od* (very good), one of the interpretations of those two seemingly harmless words is *tov mot* (good to die). The world can be a good place, but death is also part of the package.

And what brought Cain to murder Abel? One explanation attributes his action to envy. Cain and Abel tried to divide up the world between them, with Cain taking possession of the land and Abel of the movable chattel. However, Cain was never satisfied with what he had and sought to drive Abel out of the world.

There is enough in this *parashah*—as indeed in this world—to make one despair. And yet its concluding words give us cause to believe that not all is lost: "But Noah found favor with God" (Gen. 6:8). Even when today seems hopeless, there is always a tomorrow "when the sun of righteousness will rise with healing in its wings" (Mal. 3:20).

B'reishit
Rabbi Stephen Wylen, 2014

Why does the Torah begin with the letter *bet* and not with *alef*? To teach us that just as the *bet* is closed before, above, and below, we should not inquire into what is before or above or below, but only into what is open to us—the Torah (*B'reishit Rabbah* 1:10). This midrash teaches us two things: first, it teaches us that religion is about human behavior and the study of Torah more than it is about answers to ultimate questions (one good response to the popular atheists of our time!); second, the midrash teaches us about the limits of human knowledge. The *Zohar* makes a similar point when it states that the *"reishit"* of Creation is the initial material point of Creation. "Beyond that point nothing is known" (*Zohar* to Gen. 1:1).

The big bang theory of Creation makes the same contention. We can study the big bang up to billionths of a second after its beginning. Of the actual moment of Creation and the time before, nothing can ever be known.

Does this mean that the authors of *B'reishit Rabbah* and the *Zohar* were theoretical physicists who knew of the big bang long before Einstein and Heisenberg? No, of course not. But we might entertain the possibility that the truth might be known and described from different perspectives. The spiritual insight of our Sages is one path to knowledge; science is another. The paths converge in our understanding of what "is."

B'reishit
Rabbi Louis Rieser, 2015

The story of Creation seemingly invites us to speculate on the grand scheme of the universe, but an alternative approach might follow Deut. 10:12, which asks, "And now, O Israel, what does the Eternal your God demand of you?" Instead of looking to grasp the grand expanse of the Creation, shift your focus to what you see through your own eyes.

Rav Kook writes, "If you wish, *ben adam*, look at the light of the *Shechinah* that is in all creation, look at the paradise of heavenly life, how it expands into every nook and cranny of spiritual and material life that is before your body and your soul" (*Orot HaKodesh* 1:83). Creation surrounds you at every instant. In daily life, we categorize it, making it mundane and masking its splendor, but Rav Kook urges us to "know the beautiful magnificence within which you live."

Appreciation is not the sole goal. Rav Kook continues: "Elevate the love that is within you to the root of its strength and to the gentleness of its beauty; spread it through its branches." Love, a product of this recognition, draws the Divine Presence into our very being. "You have wings of spirit, wings as strong as eagles. Don't let them be denied to you."

B'reishit—from the beginning, the Divine Presence that surrounds you imbues you with love. Think how it might change the world if you could see every person and every creature that surrounds you as filled, in every nook and cranny, with the Divine Presence.

Bereishit
Rabbi Louis Rieser, 2016

We were taught that the expression *tohu vavohu* (Gen. 1:2) is a hendiadys, two words expressing one thought. What if Torah's intent is to convey that prior to creation of the physical world as we understand and experience it, there were elementary particles that could be combined and recombined to create the matter that constitutes the world we know, but all derived from one source? It is even tempting to identify *tohu vavohu* metaphorically with the Higgs boson, discovered in 2012 at CERN, which makes it possible for massless particles to have mass; the Higgs boson makes matter a reality.

Perhaps the meaning of *tohu vavohu* is that viewing the universe as composed of disparate particles is not the best way (religiously).

Kabbalah teaches that above *Binah*, where the physical universe comes into being, there are *Keter* and *Chochmah*. Could there be a parallel between *Keter*-and-*Chochmah* and *tohu-vavohu*—everything in the universe is connected to us and to everything else? Nothing is entirely "separate" or "alien" from us because everything derives from the same Source of *tohu vavohu*. This means that dividing the world into good and bad, righteous and evil, reflects our ideas, but not underlying reality.

Once we internalize the unity of all, the way we see the world and other people will change. Rebbe Nachman of Bratzlav said that even within those whom we identify as evil, there is a spark of the Divine; focus on that spark and perhaps you can bring them around.

B'reishit
Rabbi Ruth Adar, 2017

We read the Torah again from the beginning, starting with the two famous Creation stories. Neither is long, but their presence at the beginning of the scroll is puzzling: Why two Creation stories, in particular accounts that contradict one another?

The early Rabbis, for whom contradictions in Torah were both distressing and intriguing, attempted to harmonize them. They believed that contradictions point us toward deeper meaning via more diligent study. These more complex levels of study, *remez*, *d'rash*, and *sod* (allegorical, midrashic, and mystical meanings) enrich the *p'shat*, the literal meaning of the text.

What if those two conflicting stories are meant to be neither a puzzle nor a goad to dig deeper, but instead a clue for reading the books that follow? What if we understand them as a rubric telling us, "Some of the stories that follow will not hold up to a literal reading. Instead, ask questions, confer, contrast, consider ideas you have never considered before!" In the twenty-first century, these are the very stories that produce unbearable anxiety for fundamentalists. They insist on using them as a litmus test to discern "saints" from "sinners."

Perhaps in a way these stories are a test: Who can bear the ambiguity built into Torah? Who cannot?

B'reishit
Rabbi Amy Scheinerman, 2018

When Rav Kahana was caught hiding under his master's bed, he defended his indiscretion with these iconic words: "This, too, is Torah and I must learn it!" (*Babylonian Talmud B'rachot* 62a). The Torah he was "citing" was not Written Torah, but rather the Torah of *derech eretz*, behavioral norms learned from scholars immersed in Torah and its values that became Oral Torah. The S'fat Emet says something similar in his commentary on *Parashat B'reishit*.

The S'fat Emet cites the familiar question of why Torah began with an account of Creation rather than the first formal mitzvah in Exod. 12:2. He says, "Indeed, Torah was revealed primarily for the mitzvot. That is the Written Torah. But God also wanted to make it clear that all of Creation, including the world itself, had come about by the power of Torah. . . . All the sections that tell of the Patriarchs are there to show how Torah was made out of their actions. . . . The task of humans is to . . . show how every deed takes place through the life-energy of God. A person who acts in accordance with this Torah-power, fulfilling the Creator's will, renews the light that lies hidden within the natural world."

Written Torah explicates the formal mitzvot, but righteous actions create Oral Torah when others see them and accept them as appropriate social and ethical norms. For the S'fat Emet, deeds of righteousness done in response to God's will are part of the ongoing process of Creation, the continuing revelation of Oral Torah.

נח *Noach*
(Genesis 6:9–11:32)

Noach
Rabbi Joshua Minkin, DMin, 2010

Noach ish tzaddik . . . b'dorotav, "Noah was a righteous person . . . in his generation" (Gen. 6:9).

We are all familiar with the Rashi on this verse. The word *b'dorotav* can be viewed either positively or negatively. First, positively: despite his generation, Noah was righteous—as if there was a righteousness meter and Noah reached the level that any generation would call a *tzaddik*. Alternatively, Noah could only be considered righteous in his own generation, the generation of the Flood.

Too often we take this dichotomy into our own spiritual lives. How do we know how much we need to do in order to be good? Is there a level of study, *tzedakah*, or hospital visits we should be doing? Where do these levels come from? Yet, we are also told that we need to spend time with our families, go on vacations, network with colleagues, and even have a social life. The most limited resource for any rabbi is time. Are we doomed to a guilt-ridden life of "If only I had done more?" (I already hear—"Nu, what do you expect, we're Jews!") Whether we use subjective or objective measures, will that voice in our heads (mother? superego? conscience?) ever let us be content?

We, as much as our congregants, need to remember Reb Zusya's lesson: "In the world-to-come, they will not ask me, 'Why were you not Moses?' They will ask me, 'Why were you not Zusya?'" Whether Noah was righteous only in his generation or in any generation is less important than whether Noah was the best Noah he could be. So too for us. As we reflect on each day and each year, let us not forget the wonderful contributions we have made to the lives of so many. Let us remember our own limits and the importance of practicing self-care. To truly do our best is difficult enough. We are so used to saying, *Hineini!*—Here I am!; let us not forget our tradition also includes, *Lo alecha ham'lachah ligmor*, "You are not required to complete the task" (*Mishnah Pirkei Avot* 2:21).

Noach
Rabbi Amy Scheinerman, 2011

The story of the Tower is strangely nestled in between the genealogies of Japheth, Ham, and Shem, as if Torah is encouraging us to find a connection between the story of the Flood and the story of the Tower. A few disconnected observations:

First, the genealogy of Japheth seems to begin atop Mount Ararat. The genealogy of Shem ends in the valley of Haran. From solitary existence atop a mountain, the people move to community and civilization in the valley. But what kind of civilization? The people of the valley of Shinar, who build the Tower, are scuttled in their efforts. The Tower, mirroring the ziggurats of Babylon, earns the Torah's disdain.

Second, the Flood is a story of all-out destruction and massacre. God indiscriminately wipes out virtually every life on earth, preserving only enough to facilitate reproduction. The Tower story, however, is one of far greater moderation on God's part. God merely diversifies the language spoken by the Tower builders. No one dies. They are merely scuttled in their wasteful and errant pursuit.

Third, language appears not to be important in the ark. Not a word said is reported. We have the sense that even Dr. Dolittle's talents are not needed. Once outside the ark, still only God speaks; the people remain silent until Noah curses his son Ham for his disrespect toward Noah himself and blesses his sons Shem and Japheth (Gen. 9:25–27). Yet soon after, we find an interesting contradiction concerning language: Gen. 10:5, which precedes the Tower story, tells us that the descendants of Japheth spoke many languages, yet Gen. 11:1 reports, "Everyone on earth had the same language and the same words." What is Torah telling us about language and communication, especially in a world with an increasingly number of avenues for communication?

Noach
Rabbi Rabbi Bill S. Tepper, 2012

Parashat Noach offers one of the first and most powerful illustrations of the role played by water in our tradition. Though a source of life, it is also—as natural disasters have demonstrated—a cause of destruction.

With water, God destroys nearly all of Creation, while simultaneously cleansing the earth in order that Creation—humanity in particular—may begin anew. With water, Abraham generously bathes the feet of God's messengers. It is near a well that Abraham's servant encounters Rebekah and that Jacob first sees Rachel. Both are pivotal meetings that ensure the perpetuation of our people. At the Sea of Reeds and at the Jordan River, our ancestors cross through water and undergo their transformation toward nationhood. In our own day, water remains associated with transformation and cleansing. Water is essential for *tahorah*, *tashlich*, and *mikveh*—traditionally understood as purification of body, spirit, and relationship.

The magnificent rivers, lakes, and oceans that define so much of our natural landscape and are sources of indescribable beauty can also bring about suffering, either through human misstep or act of nature. Niagara Falls is breathtaking to observe, but images of Hurricane Katrina conjure up horror and despair.

Only a slender thread separates delight and pain. May we today not retreat to our own arks as we continue to both cherish and fear the water that is fundamental to our lives.

Noach
Rabbi Janice Garfunkel, *z"l*, 2013

The rainbow represents God's promise to never again destroy all of humankind. But does that mean that humankind will never be destroyed?

My ten-year-old fears black holes. I can't seem to convince her that black holes pose no danger to us. She also worries about the eventual death of our sun.

What are the ramifications, philosophically, of recognizing that humanity might end some day? If we gain immortality through the good deeds we do, what if no one is left to remember or benefit from those deeds?

How do we live our lives in the face of eventual, possible oblivion?

Or does the rainbow promise mean we will never be utterly wiped out?

Noach
Rabbi Joshua Minkin, DMin, 2014

"The days of Terach were 205 years and Terach died in Haran" (Gen. 11:32).

Explaining why Torah records Terach's death while he is yet alive, and 145 years old at most, Rashi alludes to *B'reishit Rabbah* 39:7, "Even during their lifetime the wicked are called dead." The clear implication is that Terach is a wicked man. Rashi also says that aggadic midrash says that Terach even brings Avram to Nimrod's court for punishment.

Yet, the Sages interpret "You shall go to your fathers in peace" (Gen. 15:15) to mean that Abraham joins Terach in *ha-olam haba* ("the world-to-come"). How could Terach, an evil idolater, reach *olam haba*? Rashi suggests he is wicked but sincerely repents late in life.

I would like to suggest another possibility.

With regard to Terach reaching paradise, Nachmanides refers to the *Babylonian Talmud Sanhedrin* 104a, "A son can exonerate the father, but the father cannot *exonerate* the son," and suggests: "Terach has a portion of the *olam haba* by virtue of his son"—that is, not by anything that Terach does himself.

Yet there are good reasons Terach merits *ha-olam haba*. Although he worships idols (as all in his generation do), Terach creates the environment that permits Avram to become the person he is to become. Terach does not stifle Avram's curiosity. Rather, he raises Avram to be independent, to trust his own judgment, and to question authority. These are qualities we seek to instill in our own children, qualities that allow Avram to become the founder of our faith.

Noach
Rabbi Ruth Adar, 2015

Midrash Tanchuma offers details on the Noach narrative that lift it out of the mold of the familiar children's tale.

The word usually translated as "ark" in the biblical text is *teivah*, an Egyptian loanword meaning "box." This particular box kept danger (the Flood) out, but nonetheless it was a box of misery. The midrash tells us that Noach and his sons did not sleep for a year because all the animals needed feeding around the clock. Some of the animals were dangerous; a lion bit Noach so badly that he carried the scars for the rest of his life. Noach's family was trapped for forty days and forty nights with ravenous, miserable animals. Quoting Ps. 142:8, "Bring my soul out of prison, that I may give thanks," the Rabbis tell us that these words refer to Noach's prayer to be released from the prison the ark had become, because life inside his box had become nothing but misery. The Rabbis pitied Noach, but they also judged him harshly because he accepted God's orders without asking any questions. In comparison with Abraham, who advocated for his fellow human beings, the Rabbis found Noach wanting.

The Rabbis urge us to compare Noach, who only saved his own, to Avraham, who cared for people he did not know. Had Noach the courage to confront God on behalf of others, might he have saved himself and his family a nightmare? Might he have convinced God to rethink the Flood? What "boxes" do we construct in the name of comfort or safety that ultimately turn out to be prisons?

Noach
Rabbi Ruth Adar, 2016

At the end of the story of Noach and the Flood, God sets a rainbow in the sky. Most of us learned when we were little that the rainbow is a sign of a covenant that the world will never again be destroyed by flood.

Now we live in another age when the waters of the sea are rising, not from a rainstorm but from climate change. The global average sea level has gone up approximately eight inches since 1880. The Pacific Island nation of Kiribati recently became the first country to declare that climate change is rendering its land uninhabitable. The melting Arctic ice caps have set off a geopolitical contest as many nations compete for control of new Arctic waterways and mineral resources. Most scientists tell us that these changes in climate are caused by human activity.

After the Flood, Noach tills the earth and plants a vineyard, but when the grapes ripen, he makes wine and drinks far too much. His drunkenness causes trouble in his family, and his son Ham carries a curse ever after.

In the twenty-first century, we face hard decisions. Will we be drunkards like Noach and doom our children to the curses arising from global warming? Or will we keep our covenant with God, the covenant in which it is promised that the world will not again be destroyed by flood? It's up to us.

Noach
Rabbi Amy Scheinerman, 2017

Finding the world awash in the chaos of evil and corruption, God reverses the order of Creation, releasing the waters held back by the firmament and land. The world is engulfed with water, returning it to watery *tohu vavohu*. The people, who at first seemed pristine and perfect, showed their true colors while still in the Garden of Eden: imperfect human beings. So God wipes away humanity and begins anew with a new "first family"— Noah's family.

Jonathan Sacks points out in *Essays on Ethics* that in the ideal garden, the so-far perfect people needed to know they were created *b'tzelem Elohim* (Gen. 1:27), but after the Flood, when the extent of the capacity for human evil is evident, people need to know that *others* are created in God's image as well (Gen. 9:6). There is a world of difference between focusing on the divine image in one's self and recognizing it in others. As Sacks points out, the former affirms that all in Creation is good, but the latter emphasizes the necessity of covenant, which introduces moral law into the world: prescriptions to restore "good." He writes, "So, according to the Torah, a new era began, centered not on the idea of natural goodness, but on the concept of covenant—that is, moral law" (p. 12)—from "I am *tzelem Elohim*" to "you are *tzelem Elohim*."

That lesson, that the other is also *tzelem Elohim*, remains the lynchpin for morality and the hardest lesson to teach. It must become the litmus test for policies in our local communities, for our national political endeavors, and throughout the world.

Noach
Rabbi Ruth Adar, 2018

The story of Noach concludes with sadness, but I want to suggest another way to read its ending. Noach cultivates a vineyard, drinks the wine, and passes out drunk while unclothed. His son Ham looks at his nakedness and tells his brothers, Shem and Japeth, who cover Noach without looking at him. Upon awaking, Noach curses Canaan, a son of Ham, to be "a servant of servants."

The traditional interpretation draws from midrash to fill in the blanks, teaching that the sin of Ham/Canaan, the bad son, is treating Noach with contempt and disrespect. Shem and Japeth, the good sons, care for their incapacitated father with respect and compassion.

Have we correctly identified who is the good child? For an adult child of an alcoholic in the twenty-first century, the story seems both uncomfortably familiar and frustratingly unfair, a common tale of addiction and codependency that could be viewed this way: The parent, Noach, gets drunk. One child gets in trouble for reporting honestly what he saw. The other children, enablers who protect the parent from the consequences of drunkenness, are rewarded as "good children." And as far as we know, Noach went right on drinking himself into oblivion.

An updated interpretation of a story traditionally interpreted as a tale of filial respect can teach us much. Noach's body may have needed a cover-up, but his soul needed baring the truth. May we all be able to give appropriate support when we encounter families who suffer the scourge of addiction.

לֶךְ-לְךָ *Lech L'cha*
(Genesis 12:1–17:27)

Lech L'cha
Rabbi Louis Rieser, 2010

Abram has received unhappy news. In stark contrast to the women of the nine preceding generations, Sarai cannot bear children. The steady march of human growth stops. The sudden break suggests that something new is about to occur.

God calls on Abram to leave his known world and "go to the land that I will show you" (Gen. 12:1). Does Abram know where that land is? Does God? It seems absurd. As *Midrash Tanchuma, Lech L'cha* 3 notes, "Does anyone set out on a journey without knowing where he is going?" Nonetheless Abram and Sarai accept the challenge. Abram's path differs from that of Cain, who was a *na vanad baaretz* (Gen. 4:12), a "ceaseless wanderer" (new JPS). Abram traveled toward a goal. But what goal?

God promises Abram blessings, a great name, and land (Gen. 12:2–3). But is that the grand goal toward which he is traveling? Since the days of Babel people have been working to create a name for themselves (Gen. 11:4), without noticeable success. The genealogical list starting at Gen. 11:10 opens with the words *eileh tol'dot shem*, which can be mistranslated to read, "these are the generations of name," obscuring the futility of the enterprise of making a name for oneself.

The journey that begins in *Lech L'cha* ends with the *Akeidah*. The command to "get yourself up and go," *lech l'cha*, is repeated in Gen. 22:2.

Initially (Gen. 12:1) Abram had not known where he was going, but as he heads toward the *Akeidah* he sees from afar *HaMakom*, "The Place." What Abraham completes in the last trial was implicit in the first. The goal is not a name, but a place, The Place. Human destiny, the text suggests, lies not in making a name for ourselves, but in joining our name to The Place, God.

Lech L'cha
Rabbi Joshua Minkin, DMin, 2011

Seventy-five years old and still living at home—might Abraham have wondered whether he would be successful in life? Then *"Lech l'cha. . . ."*

Being a second-career rabbi, I felt I had my *lech l'cha* moment when I left my career to serve in the rabbinate, plunging into an unknown future. Now, having recently passed a significant birthday, I wonder:"Am I making a difference? What legacy am I passing on? Have I been a success?"

Surely Abraham had doubts. During the famine, did he wonder, "Why did I ever leave Aram?" Did he rue his deception when Pharaoh brought Sarai into his harem? Did he doubt God's promise during those painful years of infertility? What went through his mind when Hagar fled with his child in her womb? Surely there were times when he had doubts.

Recently, a colleague helped me realize that success need not be measured by the size of a congregation or salary or even recognition. We create our successes individual by individual. Each time we are with a person who is vulnerable and broken and help them move toward wholeness, we touch another's life and create our legacy.

Lech l'cha is not just the big changes in our lives. It is also facing each day anew. Plunging into an unknown future. Being open to its possibilities. Finding new opportunities for small successes and becoming God's promise to Abraham: "And you shall be a blessing."

Lech L'cha
Rabbi Norman Hirsh, 2012

Thomas Mann opened his magisterial novel *Joseph and His Brothers* with these words: "Very deep is the well of the past. Should we not call it bottomless?"

Where is our human beginning? We do not know. Perhaps human past recedes beyond our discovering. Yet we need some point of origin, a place to stand on. So as Mann wisely remarked, each people picks a time and says: Here we begin.

Abram is our point of origin. Here our story begins; yet from the first two words, *lech l'cha*, the place of origin is a place of leaving. And even beyond those two crucial words, the first nine verses of the Jewish story make it very clear: we begin by leaving. Abram, even if he doesn't fully know where he is going, never stops setting out. The journey is the key: leaving, arriving, leaving, Abram on the move. He departs Haran, comes to Canaan, moves south to Shechem where we might expect him to stay—yet Abram goes on to the mountains near Beth El, and then, by stages, toward the Negev. A man seeking to fulfill his purpose.

Abram's life is a paradigm for our lives; many of us seek a passage to meaning. A journey means adapting, thinking, redefining who we are. It means becoming—not stopping too long with what is and who we are. Becoming is our secret. We are commanded by God, who, insofar as God can, inspires the journey that is in us. Leaving, arriving, leaving, Abram on the move.

Lech L'cha
Rabbi Louis Rieser, 2013

"And you shall be a blessing" (Gen. 12:2). Blessings are serious business. We bestow blessings constantly, but what do we actually transmit to those we bless?

According to *Tanchuma, Lech L'cha* 4, God grants Abraham the power of blessing, but when he realizes that Isaac will sire both Jacob and Esau—one who will be righteous and one who will not—Abraham balks. Why? Apparently the midrash believes that blessings are substantive and can be misplaced or misused. When do you feel that a blessing is warranted, and when not?

The *Zohar* 78a cites Rabbi Shimon's teaching that blessing begins on the right side with *Chesed*, moves to the left side adding *G'vurah*, and becomes a blessing as it merges into the middle with *Tiferet*. Blessing, then, represents the balance point of compassion and strength in appropriate measures. How do we achieve that balance in ourselves? How can we transmit it?

The *Zohar* 79a suggests that blessings create a bond between the giver and the receiver of the blessing: "For whoever leads another to virtue is credited with that virtue, which never departs from him." In what way do our actions—words or touch or embrace or recognition—move the person we bless? How do our actions lead another toward virtue?

The *Zohar* 86a reminds us that "arousal above depends on arousal below." Recall the most powerful blessing you have received. In what way did that blessing below stir powers above? You bear the power and the responsibility to bless others. May you always stir the powers above and below toward shalom.

Lech L'cha
Rabbi Joshua Minkin, DMin, 2014

I imagine Avram in 2014: He is forty years old, a bit of a geek, still living (along with his wife Sarai) in his parents' basement. Recently, he lost his job. His employers claim it was because he mishandled merchandise, but he insists he was not the one holding the hammer. So he works at the local Sheep and Shear and spends much of his time lying around listening to his iDol 4s and thinking.

Life is like an iDol 4s, he thinks. Each activity we do is like an app. There is an app for cooking and an app for driving. Whatever action he thinks of, he realizes, "There's an app for that." For a while he is delighted by his cleverness. But then, he begins to think, "If life is made up of apps, what makes up apps?" Apps are just sets of instructions that tell the iDol what to do. We have norms, values, and customs in our society that tell us what we should do.

But he is puzzled; if apps are sets of instructions written by programmers, whence norms and values? What chooses the rules by which we live our lives? The more he thinks, the more he comes to realize that life needs a CTO . . . no, more, an ultimate system engineer, the one who created the operating system that governs how everything else works.

"AHA," he cries, "There must be a G.O.D. (Generator of Organizational Design) who is the ultimate architect." And thus Avram's name is changed to AvrAHAm.

Lech L'cha
Rabbi David Novak, 2015

Some years ago I was speaking with a woman who knew she was dying and felt great fear. She asked if there were words of comfort I might offer. After reflecting on her question, I turned to *Lech L'cha* and shared with her that Abraham was leaving for a place he did not know and was doing it after living a full life, grounded in family and place. She found this text comforting, for it was a concrete way of expressing the unknown from a place of familiarity and knowing.

Lech L'cha affords us the opportunity to draw inspiration from Abraham's reaction to God's call to leave all that Abraham knows without knowing the "why." It is a leap into the unknown, a radical leaving of all that is familiar.

Long before our final leave-taking, each time we encounter *Lech L'cha* we might ask ourselves: What leap do I need to take? We can use Abraham's example to disturb ourselves from becoming complacent in our work, in our relationships, and in situations that cause us anxiety. We can hold out Abraham's model as a powerful pastoral tool for those who are fearful of what their futures may hold. There can be comfort in knowing that it is okay not to know, as there was for the woman with whom I was speaking.

Lech L'cha
Rabbi David Novak, 2016

A recent visit to the city of my birth, where I spent the first part of my life, reminded me how indelibly etched this place will always be on my being. In almost every direction waits a memory—some of people who still live there, others of those who are gone, either from moving away or dying. Leaving this birthplace four decades ago was a radical leaving, one that was not of my choosing.

Many of us find ourselves remembering foundational experiences in places we had to leave behind. Some of these leavings we initiate; others are imposed on us. Imagine what it was like for Avram at the age of seventy-five to leave all he had known, with no knowledge of his destination. Torah's terseness allows us to speculate on why

Avram left, leaving us hanging in our unease of God's ask and Avram's response.

Our general discomfort with leaving is reflected beautifully in a prayer in *Mishkan T'filah*, p. 231: "Once or twice in a lifetime, a man or woman may choose a radical leaving, having heard *Lech l'cha: Go forth*. God disturbs us toward our destiny by hard events and by freedom's now urgent voice which explodes and confirms who we are. We don't like leaving, but God loves becoming."

In our *lech l'cha* moments, let us listen to ourselves and be unafraid to leap into the unknown, despite our unease, to discover and embrace what will be.

Lech L'cha
Rabbi Stephen Wylen, 2017

"The nation that your descendants serve I shall also judge" (Gen. 15:14).

Saadyah Gaon wrote: "If upon the promise of just these two words God performed so many miracles and wonders, including the Ten Plagues upon Egypt, then one can only imagine how great will be the signs and wonders that accompany the ultimate redemption, about which the prophets spoke so many words."

Saadyah, living in a time when the Jewish people was far from redemption, offered the Jews two consolations: meaning and hope. The sufferings of the Jews were endurable because they served a purpose of bringing about the redemption and because they were mitigated by hope in a glorious future when all of our sufferings will be more than recompensed.

The condition of the Jews is better in today's world, but the human condition is just as uncertain as ever. Judaism must continue to offer its two eternal gifts: meaning and hope. Our lives are not random; the choices we make have cosmic significance. If we make the right choices, our future will be glorious. Judaism is a blueprint for a meaningful life and a pointer to future hope.

Lech L'cha
Rabbi Amy Scheinerman, 2018

Avram and Sarai's faith in God (Gen. 12:4) is exemplary. Yet a few verses later, to escape famine, they leave the Land of Israel for Egypt, where

Avram compels Sarai to lie and risk far worse. Could God not have protected them?

Not long after, Sarai sends Hagar to Avram, and no sooner is Hagar pregnant than Sarai perceives disrespect and treats her cruelly. Where is their faith in God?

Unlike many commentators, Nachmanides does not defend Avram and Sarai. He comments on the disconcerting juxtaposition of Avram and Sarai's initial glorious faith with subsequent acts of faithlessness (coupled with ethically questionable behavior): "Know that Abraham our father unintentionally committed a great sin by bringing his righteous wife to a stumbling block of sin on account of his fear for his life. He should have trusted that God would save him and his wife. . . . It was because of this deed that exile in Egypt at the hand of Pharaoh was decreed for his children" (commentary to Gen. 12:10); "[Sarah] transgressed by this cruelty [to Hagar], as did Abraham by allowing her to do so. Therefore, God . . . gave [Hagar] a son who would be a 'wild ass of a man' to afflict the seed of Abraham and Sarah" (commentary to Gen. 16:6).

For Nachmanides, Jewish suffering past and present is explained by the behaviors of our ancestors—*midah k'neged midah*. Are we to read this as the sins of the parents visited on the children? Or as a warning that all historical events are causative and intertwined?

ויראVayeira
(Genesis 18:1–22:24)

Vayeira
Rabbi Amy Scheinerman, 2010

Is there a culture in which hospitality is not viewed as the foundation of civilization? *Vayeira* cycles through two rounds of hospitality and inhospitality. The *parashah* begins in the tents of Avraham, paradigm of *hachnasat orchim*. The three strangers who appear out of the desert are treated to the best Avraham has to offer: food, comfort, conversation, and above all, a full and sincere welcoming. The strangers bear the message that Sarah will conceive and bear a child, the successor to God's covenant, and the fruit of Avraham and Sarah's kindness to strangers.

The scene shifts to S'dom, the paradigm of inhospitality. As if the Torah's description is not sufficiently graphic, the Rabbis catalogued at length the emotional and physical cruelties of the Sodomites: corruption of justice, and violations of property and possession that characterized the people of S'dom (*Babylonian Talmud Sanhedrin* 109ab). The outcome is pain and death; even Lot's family does not survive intact.

The scene shifts back to the tents of Avraham, where Sarah has become pregnant and the promise of a child is fulfilled in Yitzchak. There is laughter, joy, and a great feast to which many are welcomed.

The story should end here, but it does not. The hospitality that marked Avraham's tents becomes constricted by Sarah's jealousy of

Hagar and Ishmael. They are exiled to the desert, where Ishmael nearly dies.

Vayeira reminds us that the quality of hospitality extends beyond our synagogues and institutions, homes and neighborhoods: it is present in our interactions with others hour by hour, day by day—or it is lacking. The consequences can be momentous, both for us and for others.

Vayeira
Rabbi Joshua Minkin, DMin, 2011

We tend to think of Torah as sexist, reflecting its milieu, but we can find bits and pieces where the women seem very strong.

I notice that while patriarchs dominate our early history, women choose which male will lead. The women are the kingmakers.

Ishmael was Abraham's firstborn, but Isaac was Sarah's firstborn, and the Torah makes clear that the second generation of the covenant is not merely Abraham's son, and not necessarily his firstborn, but rather the one who is the firstborn of the first matriarch, because it is she who determines who will be the next link in the chain of generations: "Whatever Sarah tells you, do as she says, for it is through Isaac that offspring shall be continued for you" (Gen. 21:12).

Isaac preferred Esau, but Rebekah determined that Jacob would inherit the covenant and wear the mantle of leadership. Interestingly, Rebekah passes the scepter to the more "feminine" of her twin sons, the dweller in tents, the "mama's boy."

The most surprising is the third generation. Jacob has twelve sons, two wives, and two concubines. Yet it is clear that Rachel is the matriarch in this generation: the greatest attention is paid to Jacob's eleventh son, Joseph, who is neither the patriarch's firstborn nor his youngest, but is Rachel's firstborn.

Much is made of "overthrowing" primogeniture in Genesis, but it must be noted that Isaac is Sarah's firstborn; Jacob is a twin, but his mother's favorite; and Joseph is Rachel's firstborn. Perhaps primogeniture isn't the point after all. Perhaps it is about the subtle power of women to determine which males lead.

Vayeira
Rabbi Amy Scheinerman, 2012

The Rabbis make the stunning claim that God never intended for Abraham to offer Isaac as a sacrifice. God intended for Abraham to exalt his son in love.

B'reishit Rabbah 56:8, playing on the root עלה (*ayin-lamed-hei*) says:

> "Take your son, your favored son, Isaac, whom you love, and go to the land of Moriah and offer him up [והעלהו / *v'haaleihu*] there" (Gen. 22:2).
>
> They [the Rabbis] recited a *mashal* [parable]: It is like a king who said to his admirer, "Offer up [העלה *haaleih*] your son on my table." The admirer, a knife in his hand, brought his son. The king said, "Did I tell you to offer him so as to eat him? I said, 'Raise him up [exalt him] in love!'"
>
> *Nimshal* [lesson]: This is what is written: "It never occurred to Me לא עלה עלי / *lo alah alai*]" (Jer. 19:5)—this verse refers to Isaac.

Consider this in light of Rabbi Joseph B. Soloveitchik's view in *The Lonely Man of Faith*: "The man of faith . . . is able to reach a point at which not only his logic of the mind but even his logic of the heart and of the will, everything—even his own 'I' awareness—has to give in to an 'absurd' commitment. The man of faith is 'insanely' committed to and 'madly' in love with God" (pp. 60–61).

Soloveitchik's viewpoint seems to support a mind-set that can lead to dangerous and even violent fanaticism. *B'reishit Rabbah*, in contrast, counsels restraint: we might have misinterpreted what we heard or read.

Vayeira
Rabbi Michael Boyden, 2013

The idealization of Jewish family life sets standards that are sometimes difficult to achieve. It is, therefore, perhaps comforting to read of the trials and tribulations of Abraham and Sarah. It is also good to know that, unlike in certain other religious traditions, our founding ancestors don't have to be perfect.

As if it were not difficult enough for the two of them to be childless after God had promised Abraham that he and his seed would possess the land of Canaan, they then must come to terms with Hagar giving birth to Abram's first child.

We are told that "Abram was eighty-six years old when Hagar bore Ishmael to Abram" (Gen. 16:16). Sarah is not mentioned, and Ishmael will live as part of the family for no less than fourteen long years before Isaac is born.

And then there is the expulsion of Hagar and Ishmael at Sarah's behest. Abraham is silent. All we are told is that "the matter distressed Abraham greatly" (Gen. 21:11). Did he share his pain with his wife of so many years, or did he keep it to himself?

Perhaps Sarah suspected that her husband was really in love with Hagar. After all, when Sarah dies, we are told that Abraham took Keturah as his wife, whom *B'reishit Rabbah* 61:4 tells us was none other than Hagar!

And then there is the *Akeidah*. How can Abraham take Sarah's only child to offer him up as a sacrifice on Mount Moriah without even sharing his moral and religious predicament with his wife? He leaves without even saying goodbye, and she will never see him or Isaac again.

There are so many unanswered questions about a dysfunctional family at the very outset of the history of our people.

Vayeira
Rabbi Ruth Adar, 2014

How are we to behave toward visitors? *Parashat Vayeira* offers a lesson on the mitzvah of hospitality. Abraham, our role model, runs to greet his guests, even though they are unexpected, even though he is old and recovering from circumcision. The text is generous with details: he washes their feet, calls upon Sarah to bake, and orders a calf slaughtered and dressed. Abraham himself waits upon the table.

The contrast is stark between this story and the next. The angels proceed to the city of Sodom. Lot greets them at the gate, hurrying them to his house. Lot is afraid for good reason: a mob surrounds the house and demands that the strangers be given to them—they intend to rape them. The prophet Ezekiel clarified, lest we think that the sin was purely sexual: "See, this was the sin of your sister, Sodom: pride, gluttony, and carelessness were in her and her daughters, nor did she strengthen the hand of the poor and needy" (Ezek. 16:49). The *Babylonian Talmud Sanhedrin* 109a–b, expands on the story, explaining that the men of Sodom systematically abused all strangers and the poor in their city, enshrining that abuse in law. This sin merited their utter destruction.

Vayeira
Rabbi Amy Scheinerman, 2015

B'reishit Rabbah 56:8 has a fascinating take on the *Akeidah*:

> "Take your son, your favored son, Isaac, whom you love, and go to the land of Moriah and offer him up [והעלהו *v'haaleihu*] there" (Gen. 22:2).
>
> They [the Rabbis] recited a *mashal* [parable]: It is like a king who said to his admirer, "Offer up [העלה / *haaleih*] your son on my table." The admirer, a knife in his hand, brought his son. The king said, "Did I tell you to offer him so as to eat him? I said, 'Raise him up in love!'"
>
> *Nimshal* [lesson]: This is what is written: "It never occurred to Me [לא עלה עלי / *lo alah alai*]" (Jer. 19:5)—this verse refers to Isaac.

The midrash is an apology for God. If God is king, Abraham the admirer, and Isaac the son, it appears that the Rabbis are responding to deeply troubling questions: How could God command Abraham to sacrifice his son? Is this God sadistic? How could Abraham believe God would require him to kill his own son?

The midrash resolves these questions by positing that it was all one big misunderstanding. But their solution begets more troubling questions. If God never intended for Abraham to sacrifice his son, but rather to exalt Isaac, then Abraham utterly misunderstood the command. Why didn't God foresee that Abraham—who had acceded to commandments few of us would—would interpret the command as he did? Why didn't God, who used words to create the universe, communicate clearly? And this, in turn, raises more questions . . .

Vayeira
Rabbi Amy Scheinerman, 2015

I have had the experience of being a guest at someone's home and feeling like I was doing them a favor by visiting. So, too, I have had the experience of feeling that I was an unwanted imposition. *Vayeira* offers two models of hospitality: one is successful, the other dangerous and disastrous.

Abraham is the host you want to have: In a flurry of activity and efficiency, Abraham sees to the needs of his guests and sends his household running to prepare a sumptuous feast for them. Then he sits down with them. The outcome is a significant exchange with God's messengers, followed by an encounter with God that is life-changing.

The angels who arrive in Sodom find Lot sitting at the gates of the city. Like Abraham, he rises, bows, and invites them home, where he spreads a feast before them. The evening itself unfolds rather differently due to the egregiously unwelcoming culture of Sodom. What begins with gracious welcoming deteriorates rapidly.

I have visited synagogues that believe they are Abraham's tent but, while they certainly don't descend to the depths of Sodom, the superficial friendliness quickly gives way to . . . being ignored. Many people have told me that they have had the same experience: someone greeted them with a smile, asked their name, showed them around, and then left them alone. Among the fascinating findings in Robert Putnam and David Campbell's *American Grace* is a clear message about what it means to be a welcoming community: going beyond the first superficial steps to truly befriend people and bring them into the community.

Vayeira
Rabbi Amy Scheinerman, 2016

Norma Rosen (*Biblical Women Unbound*) envisions Sarah trekking after Avraham and Yitzchak, having overheard God speaking to her husband. Along the way, God attempts to waylay her with conversation. God asks Sarah why she is attempting to save Yitzchak, given that she expelled Avraham's first son, Ishamel. Sarah finally arrives at this response: "We gave Hagar all the freedom there was, yet the slave within was too great. She'd lost ambition, and would have stayed in her position forever. A push through the door was what she needed. To enter her real destiny, I mean. Like Your demanding that Abraham set out into the world when you told him to go. . . . So Hagar and Ishmael went out into the world and their names grew great" (p. 55). Blaming the victim is a classic defense. Blame the poor for lacking ambition; blame refugees for failing to protect their communities; blame girls and women who are raped for being there, or drinking, or seducing their attacker.

Recent research in social psychology has compared proponents of "individualizing values" (unconditionally prohibiting harm) to proponents of "binding values" (promoting purity, obedience, and loyalty). While the two sets of values are not mutually exclusive and one individual can endorse a combination, in general the more people identified with "binding values," the more they saw victims as "contaminated" and attributed blame and responsibility to the victim.

We need to be ever vigilant against blaming the victim, lest we fall into the trap.

Vayeira
Rabbi Charles Middleburgh, PhD, 2017

The haftarah for *Shabbat Vayeira*, taken from II Kings 4, tells the story of the unnamed Shunammite woman, a person of dignity and standing, who offers the roaming prophet Elisha a rooftop bedchamber in her home. Touched by her hospitality, he promises her that she will have a son. His words are realized, but tragically, the child gets a sunstroke and dies. His mother rides off to Elisha and, upon reaching him, rounds on him for the grief he has put her through. Elisha promptly travels home with her and, in a mysterious rite, brings the son back to life. This rich story of hospitality and its rewards mirrors that of Abraham and his visitation by three "men" who promise Sarah a son.

At the outset, the Shunammite woman, a great lady in her district, talks to Elisha via an intermediary, not even entering the space the prophet occupies. When disaster strikes, however, all constraint is lost: she falls at his feet and grabs him in despair and supplication. And when her son is revived, she prostrates herself in self-abnegation to express her deep, wordless gratitude.

Consider the range of powerful emotions the Shunammite woman experiences within a story told in thirty-seven verses—the very same range of emotions with which our congregants approach us. Some we will sadly disappoint, and they may be lost to us forever—but those we help, however high or mighty, may not fall at our feet, but will remember our words and deeds forever.

Vayeira
Rabbi Stephen Wylen, 2018

Abraham looks and sees three "men" coming toward his tent. These are the angels who have come to announce the birth of Isaac. Later two of the angels go on to Sodom to warn Lot of the impending destruction. The Torah says that Lot saw the angels coming to his home.

This is the crucial difference between Abraham and Lot: Three beings of the highest order came to visit him, but Abraham only saw "men"—people in need of hospitality. Lot, on the other hand, immediately noted the high status of his visitors, and he responded accordingly. Both Abraham and Lot showed hospitality, but Abraham is completely unaware of the status of his visitors. To Lot, this is important. Lot is righteous, but Abraham is saintly.

Whatever kindness we are prepared to show to our fellow men and women, we should be ready to show it regardless of their status. We feed the hungry, defend the oppressed, and comfort the afflicted because they are our fellow human beings. Our concern should be to serve God by doing a mitzvah and to serve our brothers and sisters in humanity. Considerations of how our own social standing is affected by whom we serve ought to be secondary.

Congregants have periodically asked me, "Rabbi, do you show extra consideration to people who give a lot of money to the temple?" I respond, "Try me!"

חיי שרה   *Chayei Sarah*
(Genesis 23:1–25:18)

Chayei Sarah
Rabbi David Novak, 2010

It is ironic that a *parashah* that primarily deals with Avraham's grief and the purchase of the Cave of Machpelah as a burial place for his beloved wife is called "Life of Sarah." Ironic because it is called "Life of Sarah," and she has none—life, that is.

Sarah's death is not dealt with relating to the life she lived, but only through the eyes of Avraham, her husband, who is not recorded as speaking to Sarah after the *Akeidah* in the previous *parashah, Vayeira.* Very strange indeed.

Sarah's life was incredibly complex: from pretending to be Avraham's sister (twice) to helping welcome the guests, to giving Avraham permission to cohabitate with Hagar, to banishing Hagar and Ishmael from the premises after she has Yitzchak. It is in this last episode that we can see how this wondrous matriarch can be cruel not only to Hagar and Ishmael, but to her own husband: through the use of language that echoes language used in the *Akeidah,* Sarah banishes Ishmael.

Much speculation has ensued about Sarah's motives for acting so harshly and being so lacking in empathy. What we are left with in *Chayei Sarah* is a memory of our matriarch, an astonishing woman who is portrayed as both extraordinary and profoundly human.

Chayei Sarah
Rabbi Amy Scheinerman, 2012

Rebekah is referred to as a *naar* ("young man") five times (Gen. 24:14, 24:16, 24:28, 24:55, 24:57) in *Chayei Sarah*. In each instance, Torah notes it as a *k'rei uk'tiv*: the text is written *naar* but is pronounced *naarah* ("young woman") when read aloud.

Rachel Brodie, in *Torah Queeries*, suggests that the use of the masculine *naar* five times in connection with Rebekah reflects Rebekah's decidedly "masculine" traits: Rebekah is strong, direct, self-confident, decisive, and adventurous; and she is an independent thinker.

Rebekah is remarkably strong. She draws water for Eliezer's ten camels. Could you do that? She makes her own decisions and speaks for herself. Rebekah invites Eliezer home; compare that with Jethro's daughters, who didn't bring Moses home until their father instructed them to (Exod. 2:16–20)! Rebekah decides to go with Eliezer and marry Isaac; her father and brother recognize that she makes her own decisions. Rebekah is a headstrong, adventurous, independent woman.

If Brodie is correct, we might ask: Is Torah subtly suggesting that gender barriers are meant to be broken? Isaac is a man who needs a woman to hold and protect his emotions. He seems to have few of Rebekah's supposedly masculine traits.

Rebekah has the "masculine" traits, and Isaac has the "feminine" traits. They will conceive two boys: one a classic "manly man" and the other a classic "mama's boy." Yet it is the latter who will inherit the covenant and grow into many of the traits needed for leadership.

I would like to think that the subtle message of Torah's inversion of supposedly masculine traits and supposedly feminine traits is that in an ideal world, gender is not a barrier to anyone being who they truly are.

Chayei Sarah
Rabbi Joshua Minkin, DMin, 2013

"Adonai had blessed Abraham in all things" (Gen. 24:1).

On its face, this verse has two possible interpretations: either Abraham was blessed with all the things he wanted, or all his endeavors were blessed with success. Yet both seem impossible. The difficulty is the word "all." Rabbi Bradley Shavit Artson, in his book *The Everyday Torah*, suggests the blessing is not in what Abraham did or owned, but rather that at the end of his life he could look back over *all* of his life and feel blessed.

Certainly, Abraham was not blessed with an easy life. His life was filled with challenges, losses, and heartrending decisions. We know that every life includes moments of joy and triumph, and times of despair and failure. A blessed life is not one of unalloyed joy without a hint of pain or loss. It entails the ability to accept what has happened and move on, treating our setbacks as learning experiences and opportunities for growth.

Like Abraham, we must not allow our negative experiences to paralyze us. To live fully, we must risk failure. To love, we must risk loss. Like Abraham, we must accept our humanness, including the pain and loss that come with it.

Artson writes, "Only by embracing the totality of life's experiences can we truly live. By allowing ourselves to dwell in the suffering and the ecstasy, to embrace the disappointment and the hurt along with the delight, we can experience the joy of being alive, the holiness of being itself" (pp. 34–35).

Chayei Sarah
Rabbi Louis Rieser, 2014

"I will make of you a great nation" (Gen. 12:2). This promise, given at the beginning of Abraham's journey, is fulfilled by the issuance of a coin featuring Abraham and Sarah as an old man and an old woman on one side, a young man and a young woman on the other (*B'reishit Rabbah* 39:11; *Babylonian Talmud Bava Kama* 97b). I side with those who believe the one side portrays them in their youth, while the other image reflects their old age. Symbolically it reminds us that the days and years of our life are our only true currency.

Tal Ben-Shahar, best known for teaching the course on happiness at Harvard writes, "For a human being the ultimate currency is not money, nor is it any external measure, such as fame, fortune, or power. The ultimate currency for a human being is happiness," which Ben-Shahar defines as "the overall experience of pleasure and meaning" (*Happier: Learn the Secrets to Daily Joy and Lasting Fulfillment*, pp. 33, 53). Our ultimate *cheshbon nefesh* reflects our values more than our bank account or career.

I believe the Torah concurs with Dr. Ben-Shahar. The odd way in which Sarah's age is recorded—one hundred and twenty and seven years old—suggests that something of those stages of life remained throughout her life. In contrast to the classic reading, I believe it reflects the values of our ultimate currency: the dignity one hopes accompanies old age, the curiosity of one setting out into the world, and the playfulness of a child discovering her independence. It is a challenge to maintain our values with consistency throughout our lives. The path of Torah can help us stay the course.

This week we might ask ourselves: When did I last personally welcome a stranger to my table? Or have I reserved my personal hospitality for those best known to me and those from whom I might profit? Am I following the example of Abraham, or of Sodom?

Chayei Sarah
Rabbi Amy Scheinerman, 2015

Tucked away at the end of this *parashah* is material for a good Jewish trivia question: How many wives did Avraham have? The answer is unclear.

Genesis 25:1–4 tells us that after Isaac married Rebekah, his father married Ketura. The Sages disagree about her identity. Some claim she is Hagar, arguing that *vayosef* (another) should be understood through Isa. 8:5, "Again God spoke to me"—that is, Avraham married Hagar "again" and gave her a second name to reflect her fine qualities: she was perfumed (*mekuteret*) with mitzvot and good deeds and had refrained from sexual intimacy throughout all the years she was separated from Avraham (*B'reishit Rabbah* 61:4; *Pirkei D'Rabbi Eliezer* 29; *Midrash Tanchuma, Chayei Sarah* 8). Rashi agrees.

Others accept the text at face value: in his old age, Avraham remarried and had six children by Ketura. Rashbam, Radak, and Ibn Ezra follow the *p'shat*.

Bible scholars hold that the names of the descendants of Ketura seem to be a tribal confederation that interacted with early Israelites, possibly as trading partners, and were at some later point in history enemies, in much the same way that other genealogies of Genesis record tribal groupings, mixings, enmities, and mergers.

We can, however, view this as a story of reconciliation: After Sarah dies, Isaac brings Hagar back to his father because he knows Abraham still loves her and she will provide comfort in his old age (*B'reishit Rabbah* on Gen. 24:62). Perhaps this explains (emotionally, not physically) how Abraham, who miraculously fathered Isaac at 100, now effortlessly fathers six more children at 140. The reconciliation is completed only after Abraham dies, when Ishmael reunites with Isaac: "[Avraham's] sons Isaac and Ishmael buried him in the Cave of Machpelah" (Gen. 25:9).

Chayei Sarah
Rabbi David Novak, 2016

What makes Sarah a memorable mother? Is it that she gives birth to a promised child, well beyond her childbearing years? Is it that her only biological son would fulfill God's promise to be progenitor of a people too numerous to count? Is it that she orders her husband to expel Hagar and Ishmael, Avraham's firstborn?

Now, in a *parashah* dedicated to her life, there is only silence. We have heard nothing about her since Hagar and Ishmael's expulsion, even in light of her beloved son's near-death experience at the hand of his father. Sarah reenters Torah's narrative after her death, some twenty to thirty years after we last heard her voice. Given Torah's earlier portrayal of this strong woman who, unquestioningly, left Haran with her husband, one wonders how such a vivid and protective personage could vanish so completely from her family relationships, only to be powerfully mourned in death. Her beloved son is comforted in her tent; her widower overpays for her grave.

In its lack of reflection on the entirety of Sarah's life, *Chayei Sarah* leaves us with great difficulty in understanding her complexity. The textual lacunae may remind us of the fact that whenever we work with those for whom we care, they usually tell us only what they want us to know about their lives and relationships. It is our challenge to listen carefully and discreetly probe what is being asked of us. In so doing, we are reminded of the gaps in Sarah's story, a powerful life story left partially untold.

Chayei Sarah
Rabbi Amy Scheinerman, 2017

"Avraham was now old, advanced in years, and Adonai had blessed Avraham in everything" (Gen. 24:1).

Remember the bumper sticker: "You can't have everything—where would you put it?" Our consumer-driven culture has had enormous social, political, and ecological ramifications and skewed our values away from who we are and what we do to what we possess.

The *Babylonian Talmud Shabbat* 127a, conveys a teaching of Rabbi Yochanan (similar to *Mishnah Pei-ah* 1:1) that for most mitzvot, the reward comes in *ha-olam haba*, "the world-to-come." Gemara asks: Is this the case, that the benefits of honoring parents, *chesed* ("grace"), peacemaking, and *talmud torah* ("Torah study") are experienced in this world? The Slonimer Rebbe, Sholom Noah Berezovsky (1911–2000), draws on the Rambam's commentary to *Mishnah Pei-ah* 1:1—even when the reward accrues in the world-to-come, the mitzvah benefits others in this world, doing it inspires others to do good, and benefits redound to the person who performed the mitzvah.

The Slonimer Rebbe teaches in *N'tivot Shalom* that the "everything" with which Avraham was blessed was not wealth and possessions, but rather *chesed*. There are two types of *chesed*: the *B'reishit* variety, which is to obey the mitzvot, and the *D'varim* variety, to "do what is right and good in the sight of Adonai" (Deut. 6:18).

Burying Sarah was *chesed shel emet* ("the grace that is in truth") and also *hidur mitzvah* ("a beautification of a mitzvah"). Berezovsky writes: "A *B'reishit* variety leads to discovering the complete structure of halachic life. This was the experience of the *Avot* [Patriarchs]. A *D'varim* variety leads their descendants to find new and otherwise unlegislated opportunities to fulfill what we sense is God's will."

Chayei Sarah
Rabbi Charles Middleburgh, PhD, 2018

Grief manifests itself in many ways, and no two individuals' mourning is alike. We assume that grief subsides in time, but this process is also not universal. There are losses that color the rest of our lives. Such, I believe, is the case with Isaac.

Isaac's trauma over the *Akeidah*, combined with the impact of his mother's death, lay heavily upon him for the rest of his days. We meet him toward the end of *Chayei Sarah*, a sadly diminished figure taken to walking around aimlessly in the early evening talking to himself. An aura of misery surrounds him. When Rebekah, arriving from Haran to be his wife, learns that this *nebbishdik* man will be her husband, she falls from her camel in shock. For Isaac, Rebekah's arrival is wonderful. He brings her to the tent that was his mother's, where they formalize their union; then we are told he loves her and is comforted for the death of his mother. Yet even Rebekah does not dispel the pervading gloom that surrounds him. Isaac is someone who does very little, but to whom much is done. He is manipulated by his father and his brother, traumatized and abused. The one relationship he needs—with his mother—is denied to him. Rebekah, the text implies, is a substitute mother, yet even she conspires with their son to deceive him.

Only a heart of stone could fail to feel pity for Isaac.

תולדות *Tol'dot*
(Genesis 25:19–28:9)

Tol'dot
Rabbi David Novak, 2010

"Isaac pleaded with the Eternal on behalf of his wife, because she was barren; and the Eternal responded to his plea, and his wife Rebekah conceived. But the children struggled in her womb, and she said, 'If so, why do I exist?' She went to inquire [*lidrosh*] of the Eternal" (Gen. 25:21–22).

This inquiry set into motion this most Jewish way of interpreting our textual tradition, the digging deeper, beyond the surface meaning, to give the text room to breathe.

Rebekah, our second matriarch, is given credit for inquiring of the Eternal. She received her response directly from God. We inquire and learn from each other: rabbis, educators, informed laypeople. There are many instances in our textual tradition that call out *darsheini*, "explain me." Rebekah finds out that there are twins in her womb and that the younger will rule the elder. As our textual tradition is built on Torah, Mishnah, Talmud, midrash, medieval philosophers, Chasidim, and modern Jewish thinkers, we are privileged to enter into Rebekah's world, by answering the call *darsheini*, "explain me." In so doing we segue from what the text says into meanings not so easily revealed. These meanings aid in elucidating the text, deriving evolved meanings, and making

Torah and the subsequent tradition as relevant today as when they were first introduced.

Tol'dot
Rabbi David Novak, 2011

It is an enduring mystery: Is Rebekah manipulating her husband because she has foresight that will change the course of the lives of the patriarch? Or is she doing it because she truly believes it is the right thing to do, no matter whether she is (to use a modern expression) trading on insider information? Jacob is portrayed as (reluctantly) going along with his mother. The complexity of the intergenerational relationships of our patriarchs and matriarchs allows us, these many years later, to continue to discuss their motivations and the story's outcome.

This is the challenge of the Torah for us today: to grapple with multiple understandings of its stories, and to try to wrest meaning from them as we consider our own family situations. We rabbis also live in complicated families, with loving and manipulative, stronger and weaker people.

In *Tol'dot*, we see one such complicated family and its challenging dynamics between a blind father, a hunter/gatherer son, a stay-at-home son, and Rebekah, the *materfamilias*. All families make choices. When we work with families in our congregations and institutions, we seek to help them make choices that strengthen the family system and all its members. That Jacob ended up running away from Esau for twenty years, fearing him all that time, should give us pause when we approach a complicated family dynamic, understanding that what we say could have lasting effects.

Tol'dot
Rabbi Janice Garfunkel, z"l, 2012

What a wonderful opportunity *Tol'dot* provides us to explore masculinity in Judaism! Rivkah gives birth to twins, one of whom is stereotypically masculine, the other stereotypically feminine. Surprisingly, the more *feminine* son wins the birthright and becomes a patriarch, a father of the Jewish people. The more *masculine* of the two is actually somewhat demonized by later Jewish commentators.

This preference for the more feminine male seems to continue to typify or at least speak to some aspects of Jewish culture through the ages. It is amazing to me that a characteristic first mentioned at the very beginning of Judaism continues all the way to the Woody Allen, *nebbish* stereotype of a certain kind of Jewish man today. What a long lineage (*eileh tol'dot Yitzchak* [Gen. 25:19])! We Jews seem to have distinguished ourselves from our neighbors through time and in many different countries by encouraging strong women like Rivkah and intellectual, nonviolent men like Yaakov (and, like in Keillor's *Lake Wobegon*, all our children are above average).

Why is this feature of Judaism so different from so many of the cultures among whom we have lived? How do we feel about it? Embarrassed or proud? There was a time in modern Israel's history when the effete (emasculated?) Diaspora Jew was rejected in favor of a more Esau-like warrior image. Where does modern Israel stand today on the Esau/Jacob divide? Do we Diaspora Jews still embrace the Jacob type of masculinity? What does Jewish feminism say about this?

Have fun pondering Judaism's images of masculinity and femininity and how they apply to us today.

Tol'dot
Rabbi Stephen Wylen, 2013

"When Isaac grew old his eyes darkened so that he could no longer see, and he called to his older son Esau and said to him, 'My son,' and he replied, 'Here I am'" (Gen. 27:1).

What follows, as we know, is that Jacob steals the blessing from Esau, and the household is broken up in the aftermath.

The Mei HaShiloach (Rabbi Mordechai Yosef Leiner of Izbica) notes that the life experience of Isaac is exactly opposite to that of Moses. Isaac, alone among the Patriarchs, lives his entire life, birth to death, in the Promised Land of Israel. Yet, "his eyes became dim and the power of sight was taken from him" (Gen. 27:10). Moshe Rabbeinu was not permitted to enter the Land of Israel, but of him it was said, "See with your eyes that you will not cross this Jordan" (Deut. 3:27). Where Isaac's eyes grow dim, Moses's eyes remain "undimmed" to the very end (Deut. 34:7), and God allows Moses to view the Promised Land from afar. Perhaps this is why Isaac bungles the transfer of the covenant to the next generation, while Moses, in contrast, never enters the Land but leads the Israelites to the border and ensures that they will enter and settle it.

Isaac and Moses are two types. The strife between Jacob and Esau prevents Isaac from living at peace in the land of the covenant. Isaac lives the dream but cannot appreciate it due to the turmoil in his personal life. Moses lives with hardship because he always strives toward the Land, never quite reaching it. The tragedy of Moses is not that he dies—we are all mortal—but that he dies without ever reaching the Promised Land. Although Moses in his solitary life never experiences what Isaac experiences every day of his life, Moses's life is filled with direction and purpose, and every day brings him one day closer to the Land.

If you had to choose, would you rather be an Isaac or a Moses?

Tol'dot
Rabbi Michael Boyden, 2014

The prime focus of our *parashah* is the rivalry between Jacob and Esau, who represent two different kinds of personalities. At first sight, Esau is the "good provider," who goes out in search of food for his family, while Jacob is the "mama's boy," who stays at home.

Jacob is the one who, according to the midrash, goes to study Torah with Eber, while Esau receives condemnation. The Noda Biyhudah (Rabbi Yechezkel Landau) comments that only Nimrod and Esau were hunters. Jews don't do that kind of thing!

In order to make Jacob and his descendants the preferred offspring, Esau and his children are characterized as the epitome of evil. Chizkuni explains that you cannot hunt unless you are sly and deceitful. Esau does not have a chance because, ironically, it is precisely Jacob who exhibits those negative characteristics in wresting the birthright from his brother and stealing Isaac's blessing.

But our tradition has no time for hunters and those who are cruel to animals. The philosopher Rabbi Joseph Albo explains that killing animals requires one to be cruel. Eating meat leads to insensitivity, and the Torah teaches us not to "draw abomination upon oneself."

There could not be a clearer example of the consequence of being insensitive to the suffering of animals than in a passage from the *Babylonian Talmud Bava M'tzia* 85b. There we learn that Judah the Prince suffered greatly. This, we are told, was as a consequence of his reaction to seeing a calf being led to slaughter. When the calf cried before the rabbi about his bitter fate, he responded, "Move on. That's what you were created for!" Then they said in heaven, "Since he showed no compassion for the calf, he too will suffer."

Tol'dot
Rabbi Joshua Minkin, DMin, 2015

"Isaac dug anew the wells that had been dug in the days of his father Abraham and . . . he gave them the same names his father had given them" (Gen. 26:18).

Family therapists have tracked behavior from one generation to the next. Alcoholism, child or spousal abuse, and depression all occur with greater frequency if one's parents exhibited the same behaviors. This should not surprise us. Our parent(s) teach us what is *normal* behavior by example: How parents treat one another informs how their children come to understand marriage. How parents treat their children is their children's primary model for parenting.

Isaac emulates Abraham in many important ways. During a famine, he schnorrs off the same king his father did, executing the same ruse. He favors one child over another. Does he think these are normal behaviors? He is so tied to his father's example that in our verse, he reopens the wells his father had used and even calls them by the same names.

However, our pedigree does not foreordain our own behavior.

While examining our upbringing may cause "Contention" and "Enmity" (the names of Isaac's first two wells; Gen. 26:20–21) in our families, this need not be the result. Through further exploration, a third well is found that Isaac calls "Room" (Gen. 26:33), suggesting that despite rejecting our parents' behavior, there is room enough to not reject our parents.

Understanding the origins of their behavior may allow us to break the cycle and let go of some of the enmity we feel, so that no longer will "the iniquity of the father be visited upon their children unto the third or fourth generation" (Exod. 20:5).

Tol'dot
Rabbi Charles Middleburgh, PhD, 2016

Be of the disciples of Jacob? Or Esau? Forget Aaron—we need to make an earlier choice about whom we follow.

Jacob: serial deceiver and thief, a spineless man of poor judgment. For Jacob, life is a series of bargains that have to mean something to him and gain something for him. He loves only one woman, because his love is always metered, and one son, though he has eleven others. He remembers everything and forgets nothing. And once he knows he has the upper hand, he becomes icy, haughty, and ungiving. Jacob is unable to accept forgiveness.

Esau: happy-go-lucky, plugged into nature and his family. Esau has a simple philosophy: as long as his needs are satisfied, he is happy. He loves the land he lives in and the creatures who live in it. He is devoted to his old dad. But in his very simplicity there is an abundance of warmth, love, and an expectation that others will be to him as he is to them. Esau truly loves, and his love makes him a bigger person. Esau is happy to forgive and forget.

Twin babies, struggling in the womb; two boys who grew into two very different men. For the Sages only one could be paramount, and that was Jacob, our third patriarch, all of whose sins could be forgiven. So Esau, the mensch of the two, is trashed.

Yet in a choice between them, Esau is my man.

Tol'dot
Rabbi Charles Middleburgh, PhD, 2017

Jacob and Esau, Israel and Edom, Jerusalem and Rome, Judaism and Christianity . . . so near and yet so far!

From twins fighting in the womb, to estranged countries, to at-odds global cities, and back to divided sibling faith traditions. How easy it is to polarize, and once you start, you never stop. When we look at the politics of the United Kingdom, the United States, France, Israel, and many other countries, we see a growing tribalism and polarization, almost to the extent that one side can find nothing good in the other, so that systems of governance, and thus the stability of the nation, are put at risk.

The rivalry and enmity between Jacob and his wronged brother Esau, commencing in *Tol'dot*, has terrible consequences—not immediate but postponed. As the vicious diatribe that is the Book of Obadiah details, when the Babylonians sacked Jerusalem in 586 BCE, the Edomites, Judah's kin, delighted in the calamity that had befallen their neighbor, egged on the plunderers and helped themselves, and betrayed the whereabouts of escapees to their Babylonian enemy.

Yet another betrayal, yet another grudge for generations yet unborn to bear, yet more hate. How recently we read these texts and associated them simply with past enmities; how unwise we were to do so. The challenges facing humanity now from internecine "religious" warfare demand of us that we show unity of higher purpose against some chilling existential threats, particularly against climate change. The story of Jacob and Esau, and the outcome of their rift, is all too stark a warning for us.

Tol'dot
Rabbi Ruth Adar, 2018

Tol'dot begins with the travails of Rivkah, a childless woman. Five women in *Tanach* are referred to as *akarot*: Sarah, Rivkah, Rachel, Samson's unnamed mother, and Hannah. The stories follow a pattern: a woman has difficulty conceiving, and God answers her prayer with a child. The moral of the story seems simple: fertility depends on God, who listens to prayer.

The familiar pattern engenders a twenty-first-century challenge. To the specialists who treat modern couples, infertility is a medical problem. While modern-day women may identify with Rivkah, her solution (prayer) is not their solution. Taken literally, her story may seem to mock the childless couple, suggesting that were they to pray properly, all would be well. Does the story of Rivkah offer anything to a twenty-first-century couple?

"If this is so, why am I?" says Rivkah, at a difficult moment in her pregnancy. Twenty years of empty arms are distilled into that anguished cry.

For Jews who have imagined themselves as links in a chain between past and future, an embodiment of *shalshelet hamasoret* ("the chain of transmission"), reproductive problems can engender a profound spiritual crisis. Doctors and technology may heal the physical aspects of infertility, but the spiritual wounds of infertility require spiritual healing. Prayer and a patient spiritual companion may be invaluable to a couple as they travel this difficult road to, we hope, a happy conclusion as envisioned in Ps. 113:9: "[God] sets the *akarah* among her household as a happy mother of children—Hallelujah."

ויצא *Vayeitzei*
(Genesis 28:10–32:3)

Vayeitzei
Rabbi Amy Scheinerman, 2010

For the Rabbis, Leah's prayers are powerfully efficacious. *B'reishit Rabbah* 70:16, commenting on *v'einei Leah rakot* (Gen. 29:17), tells us Leah's eyes were weakened from weeping as she prayed she would not have to marry evil Esau, as destiny had decreed. Rav Huna comments, "Great is prayer because it annuls the decree [*batlah et hag'zeirah*], and not only that, but she even preceded her sister."

In the *Babylonian Talmud B'rachot* 60a, we find a discussion of *t'filah l'vatalah* (futile prayer). The example from the mishnah is a man who prays that his pregnant wife will give birth to a son. Rav cites Leah as a counterexample, explaining that Leah, pregnant for the seventh time with a boy, calculated that Yaakov was destined to have twelve sons and since Leah had already given birth to six, and Bilhah and Zilpah two each, if Leah's seventh child were another boy, Rachel would have at most one son and not be equal in childbearing status to even the handmaids. This calculation is understood as a prayer, and "forthwith the child was transformed into a girl."

Few of us view God as a cosmic vending machine: insert prayers, out come blessings. The purpose and efficacy of prayer are not new questions, but rather perennial issues with which we, and those we serve and teach, struggle. New modes of prayer, as well interpretations of classical prayers, help make the experience of prayer relevant and meaningful, rather than a rote and empty recitation.

Vayeitzei
Rabbi Michael Boyden, 2011

In Jacob's dream, he envisions a ladder "whose top reaches heaven" (Gen. 28:12). The words remind us of the efforts of the inhabitants of Babel, who try to build a tower "whose top would be in heaven" (Gen. 11:4).

However, whereas the laborers in Babel believe that they are god, Jacob's dream, by contrast, describes his encounter with God and reinforces the idea that human beings are just that and no more.

To date, Jacob has little to recommend him. He has wrested the birthright from his famished brother; he has deceived his father into thinking he is Esau, and he has stolen the blessing.

Later, his uncle Laban will treat him in similar fashion. Jacob will be given Leah rather than Rachel and be forced to work an additional seven years for the wife he really wanted—and this in spite of Laban having told him, "You are my bone and flesh" (Gen. 29:14).

However, the deceit and the thievery do not end here. Later, Laban will angrily accuse Jacob of having cheated him, taken his daughters captive, and stolen his household gods.

Life is fully of treachery, and families are not necessarily immune from it. Not surprisingly, at the end of the *parashah*, after Jacob has built a mound as a sign of the pact between him and Laban, the latter comments, "May Adonai watch between you and me when we are out of sight of one another" (Gen. 31:49). God can be trusted; human beings less so.

Vayeitzei
Rabbi Joshua Minkin, DMin, 2012

In the beginning of *Vayeitzei*, Jacob experiences God in a dream. Upon waking, Jacob is awestruck by the experience. He vows, in essence, "If *YHVH* protects me and brings me safely home, then *YHVH* will be my God" (Gen. 28:20–21).

Jacob's vow to accept *YHVH* is conditional. It appears Jacob is unable to accept that his experience is genuine. He seems to be bargaining with God, to be saying, "If you want me to believe in You, You better take good care of me." What chutzpah! Does he think he can force God's hand? Attempting to make God/nature do what we want is blatant idolatry.

In the *sulam* ("ladder") dream, God explicitly promises Jacob protection and a safe return to this land (Gen. 28:15). Then God promises to keep the promise.

Despite Jacob's shock and awe, he does not seem ready to rely solely on God's protection. Jacob is skeptical. He cannot blindly accept that his dream is true. Was it really a divine communication? He needed to put the dream's promises to a test. This is exactly what his vow proposes. Is this a bad thing?

People believing that God spoke to them did not end with the Bible. Today we see people willing to do anything because they believe it came from God. Truth and decency can become casualties of this fanaticism.

May those who believe they are on a mission from God learn a bit of skepticism from our patriarch Jacob.

Vayeitzei
Rabbi Amy Scheinerman, 2013

Jacob has been grasping, snatching, and seizing from the moment he emerged from Rebekah's womb holding the heel of his brother. His orientation is toward acquisition: What can he procure for himself? The birthright? The blessing? Rachel? Laban's herds and flocks?

Jacob is demanding: "Sell me your birthright" (Gen. 25:31). "Sit up and eat my game so you can give me your innermost blessing" (27:19). "Give me my wife" (29:21). "Give me my wives and my children . . . that I may go" (30:26). In our modern context, we might well say that Jacob has a massive entitlement complex.

Set against Jacob's way of being in the world is that of his wives, Rachel and Leah, particularly as the Sages viewed them. Torah paints a relationship of rivalry, so palpable that we can feel Rachel's agony when her wedding to her beloved is transformed by Laban's deception into Leah's. For the Rabbis, however, Rachel was not the passive victim, but rather the hero who, as *Derech Eretz Zuta* puts it, sets aside her heart's desire for the sake of another. The *Babylonian Talmud* (*M'gilah* 13b; *Bava Batra* 123a) tells us that Rachel, knowing her father's proclivity for deception, conspires with Leah to ensure that the marriage to Leah is consummated so that Leah is not humiliated—despite the searing pain of seeing her sister marry her beloved. *Eichah Rabbah* (proem 24) goes so far as to claim that Rachel's ability to privilege her relationship with Leah above acute jealousy stirs God to end the First Exile.

Jacob and Rachel offer us two models for being in the world. One focuses on acquisition and entitlement; the other on loyalty and relationship.

Vayeitzei
Rabbi Stephen Wylen, 2014

Jacob protests to Lavan, "These twenty years I have spent in your service, your ewes and she-goats never miscarried, nor did I feast on rams from your flock. . . . Often, scorching heat ravaged me by day and frost by night; and sleep fled from my eyes" (Gen. 31:38–40). Moses lived 120 years; for 40 of those years he was a shepherd for Yitro. King David lived 120 years; for 40 of those years he was a shepherd in the service of his father. Rabbi Akiva lived 120 years; for 40 years he was a shepherd in the service of Kalba Savua.

We may romanticize the life of the shepherd. We may think of it as an idyll for an intellectual, who dreamily follows the sheep while thinking his thoughts and concocting his philosophy of life. In truth, the work of a shepherd was brutal and exhausting, as Jacob reminds us in his protest to Lavan.

One who would wish to be a leader in the school of Moses, David, and Akiva must remember this lesson. It is not sufficient to cultivate one's mind, to be a person of intellect and culture. One who would lead must be ready for long hours, exhausting labor, and little appreciation—like Jacob in the service of Lavan. One who cheerfully accepts these demands is ready to lead.

Vayeitzei
Rabbi Louis Rieser, 2015

Degel Machane Ephraim (Rabbi Moshe Chaim Ephraim of Sudikov, 1748–1800) views Jacob's ladder as a symbol of our spiritual life upon which we ascend and descend at various times throughout our life. He insists that it is impossible for a person to remain steadily on any one level or to constantly ascend in holiness. "One ascends and descends, and the descent is necessary for the ascent." The ability to rise higher on the ladder depends on the times we fall.

It is, perhaps, a daunting and scary thought, but it makes sense. It is when we are in a state of contraction or smallness (*katnut*) that "one focuses one's heart, with a knowing recognition that one is in this low, small place, and prays to God." Then one will, like Jacob, *vayifga bamakom*, "come upon *HaMakom*, the Holy One" (Gen. 28:11)—Moshe Chaim understands Jacob to have encountered God that night. From the openness created by descent, one is likely to "search from there . . . and find God" (Deut. 4:29). The descent sends us to the ground; in being grounded, we can once again ascend.

We know this story: Illness leads one to discover that every day of life is precious. People enter 12-step programs when they hit bottom; in recovery they can hoist others up. If one is attuned, there is much to be learned in the descent, and we rabbis have the privilege of helping people grasp the opportunity to learn in the midst of trouble and sorrow. If we are capable, we can lead those in the greatest need to higher holiness.

Vayeitzei
Rabbi Ruth Adar, 2016

Toward the end of *Parashat Vayeitzei*, after the drama between Jacob and Laban has played itself out, we find the account of a treaty between the two men.

They don't like one another. Each believes himself to have been cheated by the other. Finally, Jacob sneaks away with his wives, his household, and his flocks, and Laban follows in hot pursuit. He gripes that Jacob crept away secretly, denying him the opportunity to say goodbye to his daughters, and even robbing him of his household gods.

Jacob roars back at Laban, and the twenty years of resentment pours out of him. And then, just at the moment we expect the two men to come to blows, Laban points out that, like it or not, they are family: Laban's daughters are Jacob's wives. They have more in common than their grudges. "Come, let us make a pact, you and I, that there may be a witness between you and me" (Gen. 31:44). Jacob sets up a pillar, they erect a pile of stones, and they share a meal. In a telling detail, they offer the place two different names—Laban calls it Yegar-sahaduta in Aramaic, and Jacob names it Gal-eid in Hebrew—names that mean essentially the same thing: "the mound of witness." As alike as they are in many ways, ultimately they do not understand one another at all.

Sometimes, when families or individuals cannot get along and do not understand one another, peace looks like a boundary line, respected by both.

Vayeitzei
Rabbi Amy Scheinerman, 2017

"Standing beside [Jacob] was Adonai, who said, "I am Adonai, the God of your father Abraham and the God of Isaac: the ground on which you are lying I will assign to you and to your offspring" (Gen. 28:13).

How does a trickster and deceiver come to be elevated to the model human being, as "beautiful as Adam" (*Babylonian Talmud Bava Batra* 58a) and the paragon of virtue?

The S'fat Emet points out that Jacob, the figurative "Mitochondrial Eve" of the Jewish people, encompassed the entirety of the people Israel, *Eretz Yisrael*, and the holiness of Shabbat: Jacob's image was engraved beneath the Throne of Glory (*B'reishit Rabbah* 78:3). Rabbi Yitzchak explained the verse above as follows: "This teaches us that the Holy Blessed One rolled up the whole Land of Israel and put it under our father, Jacob [to convey] that it would be very easily conquered by his descendants" (*Babylonian Talmud Chulin* 91b). Rabbi Yochanan taught in Rabbi Yosei's name, "One who celebrates Shabbat will be given an inheritance without, indeed beyond, limit" (*Babylonian Talmud Shabbat* 118a). The S'fat Emet connects the inheritance to Jacob by Isa. 58:14.

Arthur Green notes that "Jacob is the perfect human being, the parallel within humanity to the Sabbath in time and the Holy Land in space . . . 'as beautiful as Adam' . . . inscribed on God's throne. . . . Perhaps there is a message of hope in this . . . : Jacob, even Jacob, was capable of becoming Israel, the one who prevailed over God and man. You too, O ordinary mortal" (*The Language of Truth*, p. 44).

Vayeitzei
Rabbi Joshua Minkin, DMin, 2018

"Rachel said to Jacob, 'Give me children, or I shall die.' Jacob was incensed at Rachel, and said, 'Can I take the place of God, who has denied you fruit of the womb?'" (Gen. 30:1–2).

Infertility can indeed feel like death—if not of oneself, then of one's hopes, dreams, and identity.

Coming from a tribal tradition that emphasizes lineage, to be denied progeny is truly an ending.

The seed from which we have come will propagate no further. Genetic immortality dies. For many, infertility is a "death" that must be grieved. Unable to be fruitful and multiply, one cannot help but be open to feelings of failure and frustration.

Rachel, unable to contain her feelings anymore, lashes out against her husband, Jacob. His response is essentially, "Don't blame me, it's not my fault. I've already shown that I can produce children. Take it up with God." Surely, this only compounds Rachel's bitterness.

All too often, in attempting to avoid facing painful realities, people play the "blame game." Rachel blames Jacob, who angrily throws it back in her face and suggests she blame God. Avoiding "blame" becomes the goal, rather than solving the problem. We are not privy to the conversation that follows. At some point Rachel and Jacob move beyond recriminations and are able to find an alternative solution.

So, too, do we hope to move beyond—or better yet, avoid entirely—the "blame game" and face painful situations with compassion.

וישלח   *Vayishlach*
(Genesis 32:4–36:43)

Vayishlach
Rabbi Stephen Wylen, 2010

"Thus Rachel died. She was buried on the road to Efrat—now Bethlehem. Over her grave Jacob set up a pillar; it is the pillar at Rachel's grave to this day" (Gen.35:19–20).

Despite a commitment to direct prayer, Jews have also prayed intercessory prayers. We often invoke the merits of the *Avot v'Imahot* ("Patriarchs and Matriarchs") when praying for others. As reported in *Eichah Rabbah*, the tears of Rachel are especially noted by God, even when the gates of heaven are closed to other pleas.

Thirteen and a half years ago, a woman in my congregation asked me to pray for her and her husband, because they were trying to have a child after many years of waiting. I promised that I would pray for them. A few weeks later I was standing at Kever Rachel (Rachel's Tomb) just north of Bethlehem. This is where Jews go to pray for fertility. I prayed. Two weeks and nine months later, a child was born to that couple. Thirteen years later, this past May, that child became bat mitzvah.

Reform Judaism is the religion of reason. We do not believe in miracles. But sometimes they happen whether we believe in them or not.

Vayishlach
Rabbi Louis Rieser, 2011

We see the corrosive power of violence at work in the story of Dinah, Jacob's daughter.

Simon and Levi believe they are acting justly by avenging the honor of their sister, but Jacob berates them, "You have brought trouble on me, making me odious among the inhabitants of the land" (Gen. 34:30). Jacob will never forgive his sons. At the end of his life, he says about them, "Simon and Levi are a pair. . . . Let not my person be included in their council. . . . Cursed be their anger so fierce. . . . I will divide them in Jacob, scatter them in Israel" (Gen. 49:5–7). The Torah's judgment emerges more subtly. It is in the longer term that we see their fate. Simon has disappeared from the list of tribes (Deuteronomy 33). Levi inherits the priesthood, only to spend his days with blood-soaked hands. His descendants expend their time and energy on sanctified killing, over which they have no choice and from which they have no escape. They spend their days watching the life force depart from every animal led to the altar.

Within our congregations and communities, we know people who have been stained by violence. Veterans of war have stories they tell only to other veterans; who else would understand? Victims of abuse carry the imprint of that violence with them for life. In what ways might we learn to offer support to those who carry this legacy within their souls? Can we embrace those who suffer from PTSD with *rachmanut* (compassion)? Can we guide those in need through a process of *t'shuvah* (repentance)? Can we point out a path of redemption that can counteract the corrosive power of violence?

Vayishlach
Rabbi David Novak, 2012

"Now Dinah, the daughter whom Leah had borne to Jacob, went out to see the women of the land" (Gen. 34:1).

Dinah, whose very name means "justice," should be one of the heroes of the Torah. As the only daughter of both Jacob and Leah, Dinah goes out one day to see the local women. She does not seek anyone's permission. *Acting independently*, Dinah sets out from a family and society dominated by male actors to specifically see the women of the land. She is curious and perhaps wishes to learn more about women in societies different from her own. What might she expect to find? The text is silent; leaving it to our imagination to ponder what might have happened had the story not taken its tragic turn, focusing as it does on the local men who encountered Dinah.

Would she have found other women like herself, with whom she could relate and share stories, and from whom she could learn and grow? Dinah does not get that opportunity, and we are left with a story that establishes her as a victim rather than a hero, like many others of the strong women in our sacred texts—Tamar, Rebekah, Sarah, Ruth, and Esther.

Let us pause when reading the first verses of Genesis 34 to think for a while about Dinah. In the very act of exploring her curiosity about the women of societies not her own, we are reestablishing some of her dignity and heroism.

Vayishlach
Rabbi Amy Scheinerman, 2013

"Jacob was left alone. And a man [*ish*] wrestled with him until the break of dawn" (Genesis 32:25).

Who is that masked man? Is he a manifestation of evil intended to weaken or frighten Jacob? *B'reishit Rabbah* 77:3 suggests he is Esau's guardian angel. Rashbam sees him as God's messenger sent to prevent Jacob from fleeing from what he must do. Many have suggested he is Jacob's conscience, supported by the Torah's unequivocal claim that Jacob was alone that night. The wound the *ish* inflicts is that which afflicts those of conscience.

In the *Babylonian Talmud Chulin* 91a, amidst an attempt to prove that the injured thigh was on the right side, we find an attempt to identify the *ish*:

> Rabbi Sh'muel bar Nachmani said: "He appeared to [Jacob] as an idolater, and the Master has said (*Babylonian Talmud Avodah Zarah* 25b): 'If an Israelite is joined by an idolater on the way, he should let him walk on his right.'" Rav Sh'muel bar Acha said in the name of Rava bar Ulla in the

presence of Rav Papa: "He appeared to [Jacob] as a disciple of the Sages, and the Master has said: "'Whoever walks at the right side of his teacher is uncultured'" (*Babylonian Talmud Yoma* 37a).

Both *Amoraim* agree that Jacob was wounded on the right side, but for very different reasons. One walks with an idolater on one's right so that if attacked, one can respond more quickly and effectively. One walks on his teacher's left as a sign of deference and respect. If Jacob is alone, perhaps the idolater and disciple represent two sides of Jacob himself. Jacob has acted in ways unworthy of Torah too numerous to count, from childhood onward. He is a consummate deceiver. But now, as he stands on the threshold of reuniting with Esau, he is a disciple of the Sages, risking much to make amends and establish peace. Jacob splintered his family, but he now repairs the breach. We all have two sides, and we, like Jacob, wrestle with both.

Vayishlach
Rabbi Amy Scheinerman, 2014

"Jacob was left alone. And a man [*ish*] wrestled with him.... He wrenched Jacob's hip at its socket, so that the socket of his hip was strained as he wrestled with him" (Gen. 32:25–26).

Who is that masked man? Discussing the prohibition against eating *gid hanaseh* ("sciatic nerve") of an animal, the only provision of kashrut that is linked to an event in Torah, the *Bavli* (*Babylonian Talmud Chulin* 91a) offers us three opinions:

> Rabbi Y'hoshua ben Levi said: "Scripture says: "When he struggled with him" (Gen. 32:25)—like a person who embraces his fellow, his hand reaching to the right-hand thigh-hollow of his fellow. Rabbi Sh'muel bar Nachmani said: "He appeared to him in the guise of an idolater." . . . Rav Sh'muel bar Acha [said] before Rav Papa in the name of Raba bar Ulla: "He appeared to him in the form of a disciple of the Sages."

An average fellow (someone like me), an idolater, and a *talmid chacham* ("Jewish scholar") cover a remarkably wide spectrum of personages evoked by the *ish* who wrestles with Jacob. Yet it is just one *ish* who challenges him that night. Perhaps the *ish* is a mirror: Jacob is wrestling with a wide range of his own familiar (fellow) feelings, proclivities, and potential choices, coming to recognize both his inner demons (the idolater) and his better angels (the *talmid chacham*). In the end, Jacob's better angels lead the way, and he effects if not reconciliation, at least a truce with Esau.

The ability to distinguish between our better angels and our inner demons and to identify and evaluate our comfort zone will stand us all in good stead.

Vayishlach
Rabbi Michael Boyden, 2015

Our *parashah* deals primarily with Jacob's life: how his name is changed to Israel, and his reconciliation with his brother Esau. It concludes with a list of their progeny. However, there is one child missing—Leah's daughter, Dinah.

Whereas the Torah provides interpretations for the names of each of Leah's children, when it comes to Dinah, all we are told is that "afterward [Leah] bore a daughter and called her Dinah" (Gen. 30:21).

And then Dinah is raped by Shechem. But no one cares about Dinah. All that concerns her family is the shame the rape has brought upon them.

Dinah has no independent identity. She is "Leah's daughter" (Gen. 34:1); she is "Jacob's daughter" (34:3); she is her brothers' "sister" (34:13). Even Shechem refers to her as "a girl" (34:12) or "a child" (34:4).

Dinah only finally appears in her own right in the list of Jacob's descendants who go down to Egypt (Gen. 46:15). This gives the midrash *Pirkei D'Rabbi Eliezer* (37) grounds to suggest that Potiphar's wife raised Dinah's daughter, whom Joseph would later marry. That may be poetic justice on the part of the midrash, but it fails to excuse the behavior of a society unwilling or unable to respond to the needs of a rape victim.

Vayishlach
Rabbi Amy Scheinerman, 2016

Who is Jacob's mystery man?

The master of deceit, trickery, and manipulation has burned one too many bridges. He left *Eretz Yisrael*, fleeing from his brother Esau. He left Paddan-Aram when he had nothing more to gain from Laban, though not until he had fleeced him of his flocks. In returning to *Eretz Yisrael*, Jacob must face Esau, and even more fundamentally, he must face himself. In eight verses, Torah describes the complete transformation of Jacob from audacious and hubristic bully to vulnerable, injured, and humble human. Who is the *ish* whose face Jacob identifies as the face of God? Is this an angel? Is this his conscience?

Dara Horn suggests that Jacob does, indeed, encounter an *ish*: It is Jacob's brother, Esau, and the wrestling match is "a physical re-enactment of Jacob's first moments when . . . Jacob and Esau wrestled with each other in their mother Rebecca's womb. Now Esau has his opportunity to finish that first wrestling match, knowing all that Jacob has done to wrong him, but also knowing how time and life can change what matters most to us." (Dara Horn, "Jacob: Some Notes on Character Development and Repentance," in *Reading Genesis: Beginnings*, pp. 175–176. Jacob sees the face of God because he faces the one he has most wronged: Esau. And in facing Esau, he faces himself and he changes. As Jacob says to Esau when they meet the following day, "To see your face is like seeing the face of God, and you have received me favorably" (Gen. 33:10).

What matters most to you? What will you need to change in yourself to reach that goal? Jacob shows us the path and inspires us to walk it.

Vayishlach
Rabbi Joshua Minkin, DMin, 2017

"Jacob's sons answered Shechem and his father Hamor—speaking with guile" (Gen. 34:13).

Although Genesis 34 tells the story of the abduction of Dinah, we never hear her voice— she is silent. Does she fall in love with Shechem, as suggested by Anita Diamant in *The Red Tent*, or is she held against her will and ashamed, as traditional commentaries imply? Her brothers act in her name, contracting a sham marriage, but then slaughtering and plundering the town while *rescuing* her. On his deathbed, Jacob makes his view of his sons' actions clear: "Let not my person be included in their council, let not my being be counted in their assembly" (Gen. 49:6).

Currently, world Jewry is reacting to the Israeli government's decision to abrogate the agreement creating a pluralistic prayer space at the Kotel. This agreement, three years in the making, was viewed as an answer to the bitter struggle for egalitarian worship at the holiest site in Judaism. The Israeli government had long dragged its feet in fulfilling its commitments, often acting only when forced by the Supreme Court. One wonders if there was ever any intention of fulfilling the agreement, or was it just a ploy to allow the emotional fires of the moment to die down, hoping the problem would fade away?

The duplicity of Dinah's brothers is being reenacted in modern times. This time around, Dinah's voice must not be silenced. Women's voices, and religious needs, must be clearly heard and addressed in Israel.

Vayishlach
Rabbi Louis Rieser, 2018

Kalonymus Kalman Shapira, the Piaseczner Rebbe, wrote about faith under duress during the Holocaust. He described the war's assault on the faith of Jews in the Warsaw Ghetto. In his *Derech HaMelech*, he focuses on Jacob's prayer the night before his reunion with Esau: *Katonti mikol hachasadim*, "I am unworthy of all the proofs of mercy" (Gen. 32:11). For the Piaseczner Rebbe, the words of prayer are not enough to make prayer meaningful. Passion is required.

Citing *Mishnah Pirkei Avot* 4:4—"Rabbi Levitas of Yavneh taught: Be exceedingly humble, for a mortal's only prospect is the grave"—Shapira notes that the trials and tribulations of life can inspire in us a need that we can transform into passion. "And this is the essence of matters of worship: to strengthen his passion and his power, and this always depends on internal strength. And this strength is greater than all the [physical] powers of the body [to overcome] all the obstacles and trials [of life], because this desire is the inner passion that God's holiness spreads over him."

Jacob has passion, but it is his alone, and that is not enough. If one says, "I've got this passion and it's all mine," then they really have nothing. As essential as passion is for worship, to be powerful and transformative it must form a conduit to God, a connection with the Divine. Passion should go both ways: you to God, and God to you. Shapira is saying, in essence: Make your prayer with God, not merely to God. That is what Jacob comes to realize. He connects with God: *katonti mikol hachasadim* bespeaks the channel Jacob has opened with God.

We are not Jacob and therefore might doubt the quality and depth of our efforts and passion. Therefore, Shapira assures us, "It is much easier to devote many years to diligent learning and even to engage in maximum self-denial than it is to devote one day of your life to serve God honestly, sincerely, and properly even according to your own understanding. . . . Still, this is no cause for despair or even to be lax. On the contrary: this best service that we can do for today, this is our unique life work. And the effort we put in, together with our yearning for higher, is the aim of our life work. Let us devote these to our Creator" (*To Heal the Soul: The Spiritual Journal of a Chasidic Rebbe*, p. 89.)

וישב *Vayeishev*
(Genesis 37:1–40:23)

Vayeishev
Rabbi Janice Garfunkel, z"l, 2010

It is easy to point a finger at Jacob for favoring Joseph over the others. But favoritism is endemic to our society and worthy of some serious thought.

I was a guest at an Orthodox shul, and a friend who is a member complained to me that the rabbi has never invited him for a Shabbat meal. I thought his criticism was unfair, but then, I was not in a position to judge him inasmuch as I was going to that rabbi's home for lunch! I was the one with the *k'tonet pasim* (coat of many colors) that day.

Wherever there is a winner, there are losers. Whenever we honor someone with an award, a dinner, an accolade in the newsletter, we are putting a *k'tonet pasim* on one person and not on everyone else. Our world is filled with Jews who have failed, those who have no great accomplishments, and those whose accomplishments are of the everyday variety and go unnoticed and who never receive awards or recognition.

The teachers at my children's Montessori school have a gift for being able to see the magnificence of each child. I am in the process of reading a book called *You Are Oprah: Igniting the Fires of Greatness*, by Howard Glasser, in which he argues for seeing the greatness in oneself and all others.

On the one hand, *if everyone is great, no one is*. On the other hand, it seems such a blessing to see the greatness in each and every individual and acknowledge it. Can we award *k'tonot pasim* to some and not others without thereby making the same mistake Jacob made?

Vayeishev
Rabbi Amy Scheinerman, 2011

The idea of *hashgachah* (divine providence) emerges in commentaries on *Parashat Vayeishev*, just as it issues forth from the mouths of many conservative politicians these days.

At his father's behest, Joseph goes to search for his brothers in Shechem. His initial response to his father's request had been *"Hineini"* (Here I am), signaling that his journey has covenantal significance (Gen. 37:12–17).

We are not told that Joseph brought food, money, or a message. What is the purpose of his trip? Joseph does not describe his brothers to the man (*ish*) he meets in Gen. 37:15. Does the man not need a description? Ibn Ezra and Rashbam lean on *p'shat* to tell us the *ish* is a wayfarer and the encounter proves Joseph's fine character in diligently carrying out his father's request.

Rambam and Ramban, however, ascribe supernatural significance to the encounter. Rambam identifies the *ish* as an angel. Ramban and others claim the encounter is evidence of God's *hashgachah*, the divine plan for Israel to go down to Egypt: "God prepared for [Joseph] a guide who, without him being aware of it, brought him into [his brothers'] hands. And this is what *Hazal* meant when they said that these people were angels, for the story . . . teaches us that God's will is fulfilled." Abarbanel claims that because God is directing the shots, Joseph's brothers do not bear responsibility for their behavior—after all, they behave according to God's will! At the same time, don't they all have free will? The events could have unfolded in another sequence.

We may reject *hashgachah* on the macro level, but what about the level of our personal lives? Many liberal Jews express the belief that events *happen for a purpose* and God is directing their lives. How is this consistent with free will, moral responsibility, and science?

Vayeishev
Rabbi Amy Scheinerman, 2012

The opposite of human dignity is humiliation. The Rabbis promoted human dignity, in large part, by assailing public humiliation. One of the most powerful Rabbinic discussions on the subject is found in the Babylonian Talmud *Bava M'tzia* 58b–59a, where a *Amora* draws a moral equation between public shaming and murder.

Rabbah ben Bar Chanah said in Rabbi Yochanan's name, "It is better for a man to cohabit with a doubtful married woman rather than to publicly shame his neighbor." David serves as the example of one who appeals to God that when others humiliate him in public, it is worse than his relationship with Batsheva.

What Mar Zutra bar Toviyah says in Rav's name ramps it up even beyond these: "Better that a man throw himself into a fiery furnace than publicly shame a neighbor. Whence do we know this? From Tamar, for it is written, 'When she was brought forward, she sent to her father-in-law . . .' (Gen. 38:25)."

Tamar's willingness to suffer the consequences of having played the harlot rather than reveal Judah's complacency is, for the Rabbis, an exceptionally righteous act.

Tamar reveals the seal, cord, and staff only in private, where Judah could condemn and kill her. Judah says, "She is more in the right than I" (Gen. 38:26) in recognition that his failure to marry his son Selah to her is worse than her playing the harlot.

It is the Rabbis who point out what Judah does not realize: Tamar has taken the ultimate risk to prevent his public humiliation. Public humiliation is all too common these days. It bears more discussion.

Vayeishev
Rabbi Amy Scheinerman, 2013

When we read the account of the birth of Perez and Zerah to Tamar (Gen. 38:27–30), we cannot help but think of the birth of Jacob and Esau to Rebekah (Gen. 25:19–26).

The similarities are striking: Both stories tell us, *V'hineih t'omim b'vitnah*, "Behold there were twins in her womb!" Zerah emerges with a crimson thread tied onto his hand by the midwife, and Esau emerges red all over. Esau becomes the progenitor of the Edomites, with whom the clan of Zerah is associated (Gen. 36:17; I Chron. 1:37). Jacob, born second, receives and transmits the covenant; Perez, who should have been born second, but pushed his way out first, is the direct ancestor of David. God explains to Rebekah the significance of her pregnancy and travail, but what about Tamar?

B'reishit Rabbah 38:17 understands Tamar's scheme and its outcome to have come about by God's intervention in the form of an angel that ensured Judah would notice Tamar and engage her as a prostitute in order to produce—ultimately—not just David, but the Messiah.

Throughout Genesis, the role of women in determining who will receive and transmit the covenant and lead the next generation remains intact with Tamar. Sarah employs coercion, insisting upon Isaac over Ishmael; Rebekah chooses Jacob over Esau as the fulfillment of God's message to her and, accordingly, deceives Isaac; Tamar tricks Judah into fathering the line that will give rise to David. Aside from textual questions around the history of these stories, this engenders philosophical questions, such as means versus ends, and social leadership questions, such as how we can recognize those who have insight and intuition we should follow.

Vayeishev
Rabbi Michael Boyden, 2014

At first glance, our *parashah* seems to begin in a good place. Jacob is settled in the land of Canaan (Gen. 37:1). What could be better than that? However, Rabbi Yochanan observed that wherever the term *vayeishev* is used, it is always associated with anguish (*Babylonian Talmud Sanhedrin* 106a).

On the one hand, being settled creates a sense of security, but it can easily be accompanied by self-satisfaction and haughtiness.

In the very next verse we read: "And Joseph brought bad reports [about his brothers] to their father" (Gen. 37:2). Jacob's love for Joseph blinds him to the complicated relationship Joseph has with his brothers. One might have hoped that having himself endured years of struggling with Esau, he would have learned much and been more sensitive to what was happening with his own children. To wit: Jacob's mother had dressed her favorite son in Esau's clothes (Gen. 27:15) in order to deceive Isaac, and now, a generation later, Jacob will make his beloved son a coat of many colors. Clothes can hide and complicate matters. Not by chance is the Hebrew word *beged* ("clothing") from the same root as *b'gidah* ("treachery"). The theme of clothing will enter the life of a more mature Joseph when Potiphar's wife will molest him and he will flee, leaving his clothes in her possession (Gen. 39:12).

Having started his life by bringing bad reports about his brothers to their father, Joseph will later bring his family to Egypt and save them from famine. In both cases the term *vayavei* is used. In the first instance, Joseph is self-centered and casts aspersions about his brothers. However, the second use of the word is not egocentric but rather shows how Joseph has matured and reflects his desire to help his family by bringing them to Egypt thereby saving them from the famine. Joseph has become a better person, but Jacob's lot has not improved. Having settled in Canaan, he will end his days as a displaced person in Egypt. In that sense Rabbi Yochanan was right.

Vayeishev
Rabbi Stephen Wylen, 2015

"Joseph was a *naar* with the sons of Bilah and the sons of Zilpah" (Gen. 37:2). Rashi interprets *naar* as the foolish vanity of youth. Joseph spent four hours a day in front of a mirror, curling his hair and putting mascara on his eyes.

The Chidushei HaRYM (grandfather of the S'fat Emet) does not like the literal sense of Rashi's explanation. He interprets the word *naar* metaphorically. Joseph was a *naar*, but also a tzaddik. The true fool is a person who tries to improve himself by working on his faults, trying to strengthen his weaknesses. The tzaddik ignores his own faults and works on his strengths, doing what he does best for the benefit of self and others. Joseph was aware of his vanity, but he did not fight against it. He let it be. Joseph focused on fulfilling his mission in life, which ultimately was to save the life of his family and all the people of Egypt in a time of famine.

Professional reviews focus on weaknesses. Synagogues, which tend to adopt the worst aspects of every management fad, tell the rabbi to work on what the rabbi is worst at. But the central Jewish pedagogic principle, often repeated in Chasidic teachings especially, is to focus on your strong points, not your weak points. If the rabbi is a good preacher but an uncomfortable hospital chaplain, work at being a great preacher. If the rabbi is not a good preacher but is a warm pastor, work at being a great pastoral presence. Build on your strengths, and be like Yosef HaTzaddik, who was a *naar*—but so what?

Vayeishev
Rabbi Amy Scheinerman, 2016

"This, then, is the line of Jacob: At seventeen years of age, Joseph tended the flocks of his brothers as a helper to the sons of his father's wives, Bilhah and Zilpah. And Joseph brought bad reports of them to their father" (Gen. 37:2).

The S'fat Emet points out that Torah tells us that Joseph's brothers hate him because he is Jacob's favorite, not due to his talebearing, of which they were seemingly unaware. Why then does Torah tell us of Joseph's bad reports? The bad reports were the reason that God decided to have Joseph be sold into slavery in Egypt, for had he remained with his family in *Eretz Yisrael* and continued to bring such reports to Jacob, the tribes would have been sidelined in favor of Joseph alone. It would seem, then, that the brothers' action in selling Joseph was necessary and therefore not to be condemned as reprehensible. To this suggestion, the S'fat Emet responds that had the brothers behaved righteously in the first place, Joseph would have had no negative reports to bring to his father and consequently he never would have been sold into Egypt. Hence, the brothers bear the moral responsibility for Israel's descent into Egypt. Following this logic, one could point out that had Joseph not endured the trials of Egypt, he would not have grown into the towering figure he became. What is more, had Israel not descended into Egypt, they could not have experienced redemption and revelation as they did, and Torah would be seriously depleted and diminished.

There is a danger to intertwining causality with teleology. There is no end to the convoluted circles of "logic" and "consequence" in a worldview that ascribes teleological value to events by working backward. We run the danger of justifying immoral behavior because the outcome is deemed desirable or necessary.

Vayeishev
Rabbi Charles Middleburgh, PhD, 2017

Although most commentaries on *Vayeishev* fixate on Joseph, there are other characters of great interest, none more so than the anonymous, unnamed "wife of Potiphar." However, beyond her brazen, and nearly successful, efforts to seduce Joseph, we rarely consider her further.

Medieval Islamic tradition and the post-medieval *Sefer HaYashar* identify her as Zuleika, an Arabic name meaning "beautiful." In his monumental and unsurpassed classic *Joseph and His Brothers*, Thomas Mann portrays Zuleika not as a lascivious wanton, but as a woman trapped in a ceremonial marriage to a palace eunuch. Her emotional and physical needs unfulfilled, she develops feelings for Joseph.

In a glorious scene, the lovesick but discreet Zuleika invites her girlfriends to supper, placing an orange with a sharp knife in front of each one when the dessert course is served, and timing things so that Joseph walks into the room at just the moment the guests are peeling their fruit. All heads turn to look at him, and each then stabs herself in the hand with her fruit knife. It is a beautiful and wordless way of explaining to her friends why she aches and who she aches for.

Since reading Mann's book for the first time forty years ago, I have always had a special place in my heart for Zuleika, reminded that those who rush to an easy negative judgment need to consider more carefully before they condemn.

As Y'hoshua ben P'rachyah and Nitai HaArbeili taught: *Vehevei dan et kol haadam l'chaf z'chut*, "Judge everyone favorably" (*Mishnah Pirkei Avot* 1:6).

Vayeishev
Rabbi Michael Boyden, 2018

Sometimes we Reform Jews are accused of discarding the mitzvot. We have every reason to question the propriety and morality of some of the mitzvot that others continue to confirm. There could be no better example than those pertaining to *yibum* ("levirate marriage") and *chalitzah*, ("process to avoid levirate marriage") which have their origin in this week's *parashah*, in which Onan spills his seed rather than fulfill the mitzvah of *yibum* because he knows that any offspring would not be considered his.

It should be noted that, at first sight, *yibum* is contrary to the Levitical injunction against "uncovering the nakedness of your brother's wife; it is the nakedness of your brother" (Lev. 18:16).

However, it would appear that *yibum* was considered an exception. When a brother-in-law refused to fulfill his familial duty, the belittling ceremony of *chalitzah* was invoked to release him, but in so doing, disgrace him. Indeed, *Mishnah B'chorot* 1:7 states that marrying one's widowed sister-in-law is preferable to *chalitzah*, a view shared by Maimonides and others.

The *Babylonian Talmud Y'vamot* 39b, however, claims that *yibum* was, in its time, no longer practiced, and accordingly, *chalitzah* was encouraged. To this day, segments of the Orthodox world continue this antiquated practice, which has even been used to extort money and other assets from recently widowed women.

Our Reform forebears had the courage to declare at the Philadelphia Conference of 1869 that "the precept of levirate marriage and of *chalitzah* has lost to us all meaning, import, and binding force." One wonders how those who defend these practices can possibly justify them.

מקץ *Mikeitz*
(Genesis 41:1–44:17)

Mikeitz
Rabbi Rabbi Bill S. Tepper, 2012

Parashat Mikeitz is about the struggles of Joseph: to rise above his lowly status as a prisoner in Egypt, correctly interpret the dreams of Pharaoh that predict the approaching famine, assert himself as vice-ruler of his new country, and above all, undergo the emotional reunion with his brothers.

Joseph's struggles are reflected in the names he chooses for his Egyptian-born sons. "Manasseh" derives from the expression "cause to forget," whereas "Ephraim" may be interpreted as "becoming fruitful." What does Joseph wish to forget? The horrors of imprisonment? His Hebrew upbringing? Aviva Gottlieb Zornberg writes, "Not only the evils of the past but its loves, its beauty and its sweetness—all have become perilous to one whose business is sheer survival" (*The Beginning of Desire: Reflections on Genesis*, p. 286).

Joseph's face-to-face encounter with his brothers reveals that he has hardly succeeded in forgetting the anguish they caused him. The ordeals he forces his brothers to endure may be Joseph's way of putting off the decision of whether to punish or reconcile. But can Joseph ever forget the despair that was his lot? Should he, as the name "Ephraim" implies, seek to bear fruit from this reunion with his brothers?

Shabbat Mikeitz coincides with Chanukah, a time of rededication. As the narrative of Joseph and his brothers suggests, it may also be a time to rededicate what binds, rather than distances, us as Jews and as human beings. Just as Joseph chooses to embrace his brothers, so can we, at Chanukah and throughout the year, welcome opportunities for love and conciliation whenever they present themselves.

Mikeitz
Rabbi David Novak, 2013

Interpreting dreams is not for the faint of heart. This is especially true when it leads to complex human interactions, such as those between Joseph and his brothers, and between Joseph and Pharaoh. That Joseph is raised from the dungeon to interpret Pharaoh's dream reinforces Joseph's pattern: his brothers cast him into a pit and then raised him out to sell him. He was cast down into the dank dungeon and is now being raised up to find himself in the most unlikely scenario: face-to-face with the most powerful ruler in his world and providing him counsel.

Dreaming is an important neurological function. Contemporary neurologists tell us that our minds are at work while we sleep, making sense of what we experienced during our waking hours. We all dream. Sometimes we remember our dreams vividly, and other times we regain our conscious state without remembering anything.

The ability of the human to dream is also a powerful narrative tool to advance a story. The ability to interpret dreams—a skill once used perversely—now brings salvation: the one who taunted his brothers on the basis of his interpretations of his own dreams now ensures his family's very survival, as well as the survival of all Egypt.

Mikeitz
Rabbi Amy Scheinerman, 2015

Joseph's dreams impress us with their arrogance and cockiness. His family's sheaves of wheat bow before him; they are the moon and stars that orbit his sun. He antagonizes those around him and eventually finds himself sold into slavery in Egypt, where he finds himself utterly powerless. So long as Joseph exalts himself, his fortunes slide downward.

We begin to see a change when Joseph protests to Potiphar's wife that he cannot sin against God (Gen. 39:9). In the dungeon, a place of doom for most of its inhabitants, Joseph's arrogance evaporates even more. He interprets the cupbearer's dream and then begs him to commend him to Pharaoh (Gen. 40:14). Two years hence, when Joseph is brought out to interpret Pharaoh's dreams, he does not claim this power, but rather only the ability to convey God's meaning (Gen. 40:8, 41:15–16, 41:25, 41:28, 41:32). Humility has supplanted hubris; Joseph sees himself as God's instrument.

Perhaps it is because of Joseph's humble demeanor that Pharaoh trusts this slave fresh from the dungeon to serve as his prime minister, with power over the entire country. This Joseph is not a self-aggrandizing narcissist. He understands his limitations and distinguishes between innate power and possessing the gift to be guarded and respected.

It is Joseph's newfound humility that enables him to welcome, forgive, and embrace his brothers. His claim in Gen. 45:7, that he is merely a cog in the wheel of God's larger plan, is a statement of consummate humility that leads to reunion and reconciliation.

Mikeitz
Rabbi Amy Scheinerman, 2016

"Now Joseph was the vizier of the land; it was he who dispensed rations to all the people of the land. And Joseph's brothers came and bowed low to him, with their faces to the ground. When Joseph saw his brothers, he recognized them [*vayakireim*]; but he acted like a stranger [*vayitnakeir*] toward them and spoke harshly to them" (Gen. 42:6–7).

In a clever wordplay, Torah tells us that although Joseph recognized his brothers, he ensured that they would not recognize him. We are inclined to think, along with *Etz Hayim*, that Joseph conceals his identity at this moment because "Joseph schemes against the former schemers" (p. 259). Biding his time, his defeat will be complete, and with it will come the reward of schadenfreude.

Levi Yitzchak of Berditchev offers us an antithetical interpretation. In *K'dushat Levi*, he suggests that this incident reflects Joseph's righteousness. Recalling his adolescent dreams that foreshadowed this day, Joseph does not gloat. Rather, he acts with compassion: "It is only natural that when a person triumphs over his fellow, and the latter realizes that the other has beaten him, he feels great sadness and pain. But when one triumphs, and the other does not know by whom he has been beaten, the loss is not as painful."

By playing the stranger before his brothers, Joseph saved them the additional pain and humiliation of knowing that it was before Joseph that they humbled themselves and pled for food. Joseph recognized not only his brothers, but also the pain they would endure were they to know he was Egypt's vizier. It is far more inspiring to see Joseph as an example of compassion than as one who traffics in schadenfreude.

Mikeitz
Rabbi Michael Boyden, 2017

Parashat Mikeitz addresses some of the cardinal challenges that people face when they become successful and accumulate power.

Joseph could so easily have forsaken his family, adopted a new identity, and controlled Egypt. After all, Pharaoh had told his people, "Go to Joseph; whatever he tells you, you shall do" (Gen. 41:55). Such power could go to one's head! Joseph had every reason to bury his troubled past and open a new chapter. Nothing could signify that more than Pharaoh's calling him Tzofnat-Paneach and giving him Osnat, daughter of the priest of On, as his wife. Joseph is powerful, is assigned an Egyptian name according to the Rashbam, and is given the daughter of a pagan priest to be his wife. Could there be a more tempting, archetypal example of assimilation?

But Joseph does not follow that path. The name that Pharaoh gives him appears nowhere else in the Bible. Joseph does not claim to be Egypt's savior. On the contrary, he says, "It's not me. God will see to Pharaoh's welfare" (Gen. 41:16). He gives his children Hebrew names, signifying his sense of estrangement in the land of Egypt, and although he had every reason to despise them, he saves his family from famine.

Joseph's last words to his descendants are to "take up my bones from here" (Gen. 50:25) and bring them to the land God had promised to his ancestors. He does not even mention the word "Egypt." Joseph may have been eminently successful, but he was "a stranger in a strange land."

Mikeitz
Rabbi Amy Scheinerman, 2018

Outside *tzitzit* (Num. 15:37–41), *shaatneiz* (Deut. 22:11), and God's presumed disgust at cross-dressing (Deut. 22:5), the Bible says little about Jewish requirements for dressing (with the obvious exception of the priests). Yet clothing figures prominently in several stories in Genesis: when Jacob dresses in Esau's clothes and Tamar dons the attire and veil of a harlot, clothing serves to disguise and deceive.

In the Joseph cycle, clothing serves alternately to convey rank and to deceive: Joseph's father distinguishes him from his brothers with a fine coat; his brothers bring the same goat-blood-stained coat to their father to deceive Jacob into believing Joseph is dead; Pharaoh dresses him in regal robes and his own signet ring to convey his rank and authority; and finally, it is likely that Joseph's regalia is a major reason that his brothers cannot recognize him.

In only one story in Genesis is clothing intended as protection: God provides garments to Adam and Eve when they are expelled from the garden. Here, the coverage of clothing is God's gift, not the reflection of perceived status or deriving from a human's intent to disguise and deceive. Perhaps this first clothing mentioned in the Bible can be taken as an ideal and a model of modesty and simplicity—not a bad message to hear these days.

ויגש *Vayigash*
(Genesis 44:18–47:27)

Vayigash
Rabbi Louis Rieser, 2010

Judah approaches the vizier of Egypt, not recognizing him as his brother Joseph. At that moment he is the archetypal supplicant approaching the power broker, a classic example of an unequal balance of power. Though Joseph appears as powerful as Pharaoh (Rashi), Judah finds a way to prevail: Or HaChayim states that although Joseph is surrounded by advisors and translators, Judah bypasses them by speaking directly to Joseph. His goal is to remove the external and internal translators, those forces that maintain Joseph's official persona, in order to change Joseph's heart. Judah pleads (*B'reishit Rabbah* 93:6), "Let my words enter your ears," urging Joseph to listen to his heart because, as Rabbi Isaiah Horowitz in *Shaar HaOtiyot* teaches, "every word that goes out from the heart enters the heart." Judah wagers that through his direct appeal the sweetness of his words will prevail.

Dov Ber (cited in *K'dushat Levi*) teaches that "just as there is light and dark in the world, so is there light and dark in every individual." Judah addresses the light within Joseph in order to humanize Joseph. If he can remove the filters, then the two brothers can meet on common ground.

Judah's success is apparent when Joseph "could no longer control himself before all his attendants" (Gen. 45:1). Joseph is transformed from the vizier of Egypt into the son of Jacob. He dismisses the Egyptian officials and dines with his brothers.

In what ways have you used Judah's approach when faced with an unequal balance of power, and what have the results been? Are there times when you would advise against Judah's strategy?

Vayigash
Rabbi Amy Scheinerman, 2011

"*Vayigash eilav y'hudah* . . . Then Judah approached [Joseph] and said, 'Please my lord, let your servant appeal to my lord, and do not be impatient with your servant'" (Gen. 44:18).

The Rokeiach (Eleazar of Worms, ca.1176–1238) writes that *vayigash* occurs three times in the *Tanach* in connection with prayer—Abraham approaches God (Gen. 18:23), as does Elijah (I Kings 18:36)—giving rise to the custom of taking three steps forward before saying the *sh'moneh esreih*.

First impressions are powerful and lasting, but not insurmountable. Each time we approach someone, we present ourselves anew. Judah has presented himself unfavorably on three occasions: collecting booty after the slaughter of the Shechemites (Genesis 34), recommending selling Joseph to a caravan of traders (Genesis 37), and through his maltreatment of Tamar (Genesis 38). In addition to that, he did not distinguish himself in his first encounter with Joseph in Egypt. Now, however, Judah steps into a role of integrity, exhibiting compassion and remorse: "Now, if I come to your servant my father and the boy is not with us—since his own life is so bound up with his—when he sees that the boy is not with us, he will die, and your servants will send the white head of your servant our father down to Sheol in grief" (Gen. 44:30).

How often do we judge people on the first encounter? How often are our judgments terribly wrong!

When we approach God, we can think of the three steps as a reminder that we, who are always changing and becoming, are not the same person who presented ourselves before God previously. God doesn't rely on first impressions.

Vayigash
Rabbi Louis Rieser, 2012

We feel Judah's pain. He is entrapped by forces beyond his control. The life of his brother Benjamin and perhaps that of his father are at stake.

How would you advise Judah to act at this moment? What is the attitude he should project toward Joseph?

B'reishit Rabbah 43:6 suggests three possible characterizations:

- Rabbi Y'hudah suggests that he came prepared for battle. Angry, jerked about by this aloof bureaucrat, Judah has had enough. He comes out swinging.
- Rabbi Nehemiah counters that he approaches Joseph in a spirit of conciliation. Aware of his tenuous position, he opts to find the path to yes, no matter the cost.
- The Sages understand "approach" as a synonym for prayer. When the situation is truly out of your control, turn your life over to a Higher Power.

The Chasidic authors offer other options that speak more to Judah's inner motivation:

- The Mei HaShiloach (Mordechai Yosef Leiner, the Ishbitzer Rebbe, 1801–54) suggests that Judah overcame despair, which allowed him to touch the depths of Joseph's heart, moving him to reveal himself. Sometimes the most disarming approach is to be completely vulnerable.
- The S'fat Emet (Y'hudah Aryeh Leib Alter, 1847–1905) identifies Judah with the root *hodaah*—"thankfulness." Jews, *y'hudim*, are named after Judah because they offer thanksgiving for everything, large and small, knowing that all things come from God. Even in the darkest hour, then, Judah relies on God, sets aside his own fear, and speaks up before Joseph.

Each of us will face dark and uncertain times—disease, shaky relationships, the unreliable economy—and will need to decide our own approach. Understanding Judah's options may help clarify our own choices.

Vayigash
Rabbi Amy Scheinerman, 2013

The reunion of Jacob and Joseph is tender and poignant.

"Joseph hitched his chariot and went to Goshen to meet his father Israel; he presented himself to him and, embracing him around the neck, he wept on his neck a good while" (Gen. 46:29).

Levi Yitzchak of Berditchev comments in *K'dushat Levi*: "Why does Torah bother to tell us that Joseph hitched his chariot? Would it not have sufficed to say that he went up to greet his father? We find here advice to keep an open eye on all our deeds. We are not meant to be mere animals, but to weigh our actions, deriving from them wise hints about how to serve God."

Joseph is not the animal who pulls the chariot. He is the person who drives it with mindfulness and intentionality, a reminder of how we should live our lives. But who can live in a perpetual state of spiritual awareness? Even Levi Yitzchak acknowledges, "You sometimes get so tired that your own corporeal self begins to fade. Then a spirit flowing forth from God comes upon you. The light that you encounter is like seeing God's own face."

When we are most exhausted—emotionally and spiritually—if we can hitch our chariot and remind ourselves that everything we do and say has the potential to create *k'dushah* ("holiness") and make a meaningful difference, that in itself will energize us. Note that no sooner does Joseph hitch his chariot than he goes up and sees Jacob. For Jacob, this makes all the difference in the world: "Then Israel said to Joseph, 'Now I can die, having seen for myself that you are still alive'" (Gen. 46:30).

Vayigash
Rabbi Joshua Minkin, DMin, 2014

"Therefore, please let your servant remain as a slave to my lord instead of the boy" (Gen. 44:33).

The character of Judah is disputed in Rabbinic literature, much of it focusing on his motivation to sell Joseph to the Ishmaelites, rather than kill him. What was Judah's motivation? Was it to save Joseph? Or was

Judah content to leave Joseph to die in the pit and changed his mind only to make a quick profit on his sale?

I prefer the latter viewpoint because it can lead to a great lesson on *t'shuvah*. Judah is oblivious to his sinful behavior, sitting down to eat after leaving Joseph to die. Just as he and his brothers deceived his father, so does Tamar deceive Judah. Through her actions, he becomes aware of his need to change.

Then, when Joseph, in disguise, threatens to enslave Benjamin, Judah steps forward and accepts joint responsibility, offering all the brothers as slaves as well. Finally, Judah takes full personal responsibility, explaining that he, alone, is responsible for Benjamin's safety and he, alone, should be enslaved in place of Benjamin.

How similar this is to many cases of *t'shuvah*. At first, we are unaware that what we are doing is wrong. Sometime later, through the example of another, it becomes clear to us. Later still, we are willing to accept limited responsibility, but only with excuses or as part of a group ("Everyone does it"). Finally, we accept that we must take complete responsibility for our own actions and truly change.

Vayigash
Rabbi Ruth Adar, 2015

When Joseph interprets Pharaoh's dream, he predicts a famine and proposes a program for surviving it (Gen. 41:33–36). It sounds painless: appoint an administrator to gather grain during the years of plenty as a reserve against the years of famine.

Now, in Genesis 47, we see what this program actually requires. Once there is no bread "in all the world" (Gen. 47:13), people buy grain from Pharaoh. As a result, all the gold and silver in Egypt comes into the king's treasury. The following year people have no money, so they trade their livestock to Pharaoh for food. A year later, they trade their land for grain. In that year, Joseph orders massive resettlement of the population. Radak teaches that Joseph does this so the Egyptians will understand that the new homes are a gift from Pharaoh. Rashbam, however, compares his policy to that of the evil Sennacherib in II Kings 18.

In the final year of famine, the Egyptians become bondsmen to Pharaoh in exchange for food and seed for the coming year. By the end of the famine, Joseph has preserved the lives of the Egyptians, but every commoner among them is a penniless bondsman living on land granted by Pharaoh, grateful to pay a heavy tax.

Harold Kushner points out in *Etz Hayim* that a generation later, the Egyptians will take revenge on Joseph by enslaving the Hebrews. Economic policy in the ancient world, as in ours, has both short-term and long-term consequences.

Vayigash
Rabbi Mark Levin, 2016

Having callously cooperated in deceiving his father about Joseph's death, a ruse that caused Jacob persistent grief for twenty years, Judah loses two sons. His grief generates empathy for his father's unnecessary suffering. Tamar, whom Judah fails to recognize by the roadside, courageously plots to deceive Judah in order to achieve justice for his deceased sons and for herself (Genesis 37–38). With this history of recognition, failure, anguish, and moral coercion in his craw, Judah volunteers himself to Egypt's confrontational viceroy as Benjamin's protector in the return trip to Egypt to procure food.

In *B'reishit Rabbah* 93:6, the Rabbis list three methods for dealing with an enemy: war, conciliation, and prayer. The very name of our *parashah* demonstrates Judah's militant approach to Egypt's second-in-command, although his words superficially indicate conciliation. In the *p'shat*, Judah holds the subservient position, and thus it appears arrogant for him to speak first. However, the midrash treats Judah, also, as vice-regent of his people and thus Joseph's equivalent (*B'reishit Rabbah* 93:8). Avivah Zornberg demonstrates how in the midrash Judah confronts Joseph, escalating the clash and even threatening him in order to gain Benjamin's and Simon's freedom, as well as food for their family, and how Joseph retreats for the sake of peace (*Genesis: The Beginning of Desire, Va-yigash*).

Judah has confessed his attempt to avoid responsibility to his sons and to Tamar, saying, "She is more in the right than I" (Gen. 38:26). Now willing to assume responsibility for protecting Benjamin's and thereby Jacob's life, Judah assumes leadership of the tribes. Leadership requires honesty, insight, courage, cunning, and sacrifice, to protect the Jewish people.

Vayigash
Rabbi David Novak, 2017

The word "Judaism" derives from Judah: the territory, tribe, and the person. Looking at the character of Jacob's son Judah we see why. While he initiated the revenge scheme against his brother Joseph, selling him to traders and deceptively informing his father that he was killed by beasts, Judah is also the person who is deceived by his daughter-in-law Tamar, whom he impregnates. When she identifies him as the father, he admits his guilt. The child born of deception and confession is the progenitor of the Davidic line.

Now in *Vayigash* we see Judah pleading with his own brother. In Joseph's attempt to seize Benjamin, Judah steps forward and offers himself to Joseph. In this moment, Judah's character transformation qualifies him as the co-hero of the narrative. He is able to show the "Pharaoh" (to whom he believes he is speaking) a level of sibling compassion heretofore unknown in the person of Judah. Judah's act inspires Joseph to reveal himself and forgive his brothers. As Jonathan Sacks (*Not in God's Name: Confronting Religious Violence*) notes, this is the first time we see forgiveness granted in Torah.

Judah reminds us of the complexity intrinsic to our own characters and inherent in our interactions with others, both when we respond without thinking and when we plan, scheme, and strategize. Here, we see the value of listening to others with compassion and responding thoughtfully to avoid being hurtful. In so doing, we promote healthier relationships for ourselves and others around us, modeling behavior that we hope others will emulate.

Vayigash
Rabbi Charles Middleburgh, PhD, 2018

We celebrate the way in which Judah steps up to the Egyptian vizier when the latter threatens the imprisonment of his youngest brother, Benjamin. However, we often fail to appreciate why Judah steps up.

When the brothers threw Joseph into a pit, Judah was weak, and although he counseled against killing Joseph, he did not try to stop his siblings' malice, suggesting instead that they sell him—all this only after Jacob's firstborn, Reuben, had already forbidden the brothers to kill Joseph.

What has changed? The answer lies in the story of Tamar in *Parashat Vayeishev* (Genesis 38), which showed Judah as a man manipulated by others rather than one who calls the shots. He seemed unable to make decisions, preferring to collude with circumstance rather than change it. But then he is duped by his widowed daughter-in-law, Tamar, who can prove that he is the father of her child. This situation affords him the opportunity to confess, assume full responsibility for his actions, and at last grow up.

All of us go through a process of maturing. It may take us many years, as it did Judah, to reach a point where our sense of self is strong enough to afford us the courage and integrity to stand up and do what is right, no matter how challenging the circumstances. In *Vayigash* that moment arrives for Judah, and thanks to Tamar, he steps forward to speak truth to power.

ויחי *Va-y'chi*
(Genesis 47:28–50:26)

Va-y'chi
Rabbi David Novak, 2010

Jacob gave Joseph a blessing. He said, "The God before whom my ancestors Abraham and Isaac walked is the God who has been my Shepherd from as far back as I can remember until this day, sending a *malach* to deliver me from all evil. May the Eternal bless the lads and let them carry my name, along with the names of my fathers, Abraham and Isaac. May they increase in the land like fish" (Gen. 48:15–16).

Jacob's protector is a *malach* from God. Often translated as "angel," the word untranslated allows us more latitude to imagine what and who these *malachim* are. Instead of being limited to medieval visions of angels adorned in white and sporting expansive wingspreads, our imagination has free rein to conceive these *malachim* as part of God's retinue. The verb *shin-reish-tzadi* means "to spawn." What does it mean to spawn in the land like fish? Jacob's blessing is for Ephraim and Menasheh to have great fecundity, that their offspring should be as numerous as the fish in the sea.

Va-y'chi
Rabbi Amy Scheinerman, 2011

Jacob dies, Joseph buries him in Goren HaAtad, and mourns him seven days. Shivah over, his brothers begin to worry in earnest. "When

Joseph's brothers saw that their father was dead, they said, 'What if Joseph still bears a grudge against us and pays us back for all the wrong that we did him?'" (Gen. 50:15).

The brothers entreat Joseph to forgive them. Joseph reassures them that he neither plans nor seeks revenge. Torah next tells us: "Thus he comforted them [*va-y'nacheim*] and spoke to their heart [*va-y'dabeir al libam*]" (Genesis 50:21).

Why this unusual phrase? Isn't *va-y'nacheim* sufficient? What does *va-y'dabeir al libam* add? Perhaps *va-y'nacheim* bespeaks the words Joseph offered his brothers (Gen. 50:19–21) and *va-y'dabeir al libam* is telling us that Joseph had empathy for his brothers. He understood their fear and shame.

Daniel Goleman, author of *Emotional Intelligence*, identifies empathy as an important component of emotional intelligence. He tells us there are three kinds of empathy: cognitive empathy, emotional empathy, and empathic concern. When Joseph assures his brothers that they were not responsible for what happened because it was part of God's plan, he shows he understands their perspective; he exhibits cognitive empathy. When he speaks to their heart, he shows that he feels what they feel; he exhibits emotional empathy. When he promises to sustain them and their children, he demonstrates that he wants to help them; he exhibits empathic concern. Joseph embodies all three.

Empathy is important in every realm of life: work, family, and love relationships; effectiveness in the world of social justice, where we need to understand other perspectives; and politics and diplomacy.

Va-y'chi
Rabbi Stephen Wylen, 2012

Jacob blessed Joseph's sons with these words: "May the angel who preserved me from all evil bless these children. May they be known by my name and the names of my ancestors, Abraham and Isaac, and may they multiply [*v'yidgu*] and be a multitude across the face of the land" (Gen. 48:16).

The Chatam Sofer said, "May they multiply [*v'yidgu*] like a fish [*dag*] out of water. The continuing existence of the Jews is contrary to the natural order. Across the face of the land—like a fish on the land—so is the Jew." (The Chatam Sofer may also have meant that the Jew is not like any other person—a perspective with which I would not concur.)

He assures us that the existence of the Jews is ensured by divine providence, not by the natural order of things.

The Chatam Sofer's teaching reminds me of the words of Rabbi Arnold Jacob Wolf, who used to say, "The preservation of the Jewish people is not our task. That is God's task. Our task is to live as Jews. If we do our part, God will take care of the rest." I would add to the pun of the Chatam Sofer—*v'yidgu* and not *v'yid'agu*, "Spend less time worrying and more time being a Jew."

Va-y'chi
Fred Davidow, 2013

Va-y'chi describes the deathbed scene of Jacob. He calls his sons and gives each a final blessing. Afterward, Jacob charges his sons to bury him with Abraham and Isaac in the Cave of Machpelah. Then Jacob "expired and was gathered to his people" (Gen. 49:33). The Torah uses the very same wording to describe the death of Abraham (Gen. 25:8) and Isaac (Gen. 35:29).

The haftarah connected to this *parashah* describes the deathbed scene of David. He summons Solomon and gives him some final instructions. Then David dies, but another idiom similar to the idea of being gathered to one's people is used: "Then David slept with his fathers" (I Kings 2:10).

The idioms "to be gathered to one's people" and "to sleep with one's fathers" emphasize the importance of continuity: our life as a people is to go on from generation to generation. Of course every individual will "go the way of all the earth" (I Kings 2:2), but the bitterness of a death is diluted by believing that burial with one's relatives is a way of returning to the people to whom we belong. Whenever I walk through the Jewish cemetery of my hometown, I feel in my bones what it means to be gathered to one's people, for there lie the graves of forty-two kinfolk. Instead of the earlier pangs of grief, there is now sweet joy in the memories of lives well lived and in the prospect of lives still to come.

Va-y'chi
Rabbi Ruth Adar, 2014

Va-y'chi offers us two end-of-life accounts: the accounts of the deaths of Jacob and Joseph leave a legacy for their immediate descendants and also *Am Yisrael*.

Both Jacob and Joseph are models for making clear their end-of-life wishes. Jacob specifies his wishes to Joseph: "Bury me with my ancestors, not in Egypt." Joseph takes an oath to carry out that wish (Gen. 47:29–31). Later, when he knows that he is dying, Jacob calls all his sons together. After blessing them, he informs them of his wish to be buried in the Cave of Machpelah, with his ancestors "in the cave in the field of Machpelah, facing Mamre, in the land of Canaan" (Gen. 49:30). He lists kin buried in Machpelah, giving voice to the mitzvah of burial in a family plot (*Shulchan Aruch, Yoreh Dei-ah* 363). After his death, Joseph directs that Jacob's body be embalmed in the Egyptian fashion for transport to Canaan. He and his brothers travel together to the Cave of Machpelah.

Later, when he is dying, Joseph follows his father's example, gathering his family and blessing them with a reminder of the covenants God made with Abraham, Isaac, and Jacob. Joseph then makes his own request: "Bring my bones up from this place" (Gen. 50:25).

In our own days of advanced medical technology, there are many more things about which we should be specific with family. It is important to have the proper documents prepared: advanced health care directives, valid wills, and instructions for executors; it is also important to talk about these matters with our loved ones in such a way as to minimize conflict and confusion at a difficult time. Our ancestors Jacob and Joseph teach us the value of these conversations, a value that has only grown over time.

Va-y'chi
Rabbi Michael Boyden, 2015

At the age of thirty, and after thirteen years as a slave in Egypt, Joseph the Hebrew becomes governor of the strongest nation in the region. It is a classic Jewish Diaspora success story.

Pharaoh gives him a new name, Tzofnat-Paneach, symbolizing not only his ability to interpret dreams but also the fact that he had chosen Egypt as his home. Joseph has made it! Sound familiar?

It is, therefore, hardly surprising that Joseph takes Osnat, the daughter of Poti-Phera, priest of Ohn, as his wife. The marriage cements and symbolizes Joseph's integration into Egyptian society.

That could have been the end of the story, but it isn't. The gentile Osnat bears Joseph two sons, Ephraim and Manasseh, whose names we mention to this day when we bless our children. Why them of all people? Rabbi Joseph Soloveitchik suggested that this derives from the fact that, unlike Jacob's other grandchildren, in spite of the fact that they grew up in a country of idol worshipers, they manage to preserve their Hebrew identity and thereby merit being included among the twelve tribes of Israel.

On his deathbed, Joseph makes his children swear that his remains will be buried in the Land of Israel. Success had not caused him to forget who he is and where he comes from.

When the actor Michael Douglas, born to a non-Jewish mother, recently received the Genesis Prize in Jerusalem, he began his acceptance speech with the words "It is good to be home." Three thousand years after Joseph, the same challenges of Jewish identity continue to accompany us.

Va-y'chi
Rabbi Joshua Minkin, DMin, 2016

Just before he dies, Jacob implores Joseph, "When I lie down with my fathers . . . bury me in their burial-place" (Gen. 47:30). And after he died, "Jacob was gathered to his people" (Gen. 49:33).

Nahum Sarna maintains that Torah knows of an afterlife. He equates the phrases "lie down with my fathers" and "gathered to his people," noting they are "distinguished from death itself because the action follows the demise." "Gathered to his people," he asserts, "does not mean burial in an ancestral grave, because [the same phrase] is employed of Abraham, Aaron and Moses, none of whom was buried with his forefathers." Both idioms, therefore, testify "to a belief that, despite this mortality and perishability, man possesses an immortal element that survives the loss of life . . . an afterlife where one is united with one's ancestors" (*The JPS Torah Commentary: Genesis*, p. 174).

This interpretation contradicts the view of Neil Gillman (*The Death of Death*) and others that such a notion is unknown in Israel until later times.

Is Sarna suggesting an afterlife that affords interaction with our deceased relatives? Or incorporeal spiritual immortality? Many mourners hold the belief that they will someday see their deceased loved ones again. I struggle with what to say because my personal beliefs do not comport with theirs. Knowing that they find comfort and solace from the belief in reunification or from "visits" from deceased relatives helps me set aside my personal theology in order to be with mourners in their grief. If they want to know what our tradition says about the afterlife, I offer a variety of understandings and emphasize that there is no requirement for any specific belief.

Va-y'chi
Rabbi Louis Rieser, 2017

Parashat Va-y'chi emphasizes the importance of a place of burial.

Jacob implores Joseph to swear to bury him with his ancestors in the Land of Israel: "Please do not bury me in Egypt . . . bury me in [my ancestors'] burial-place" (Genesis 47:29–30, 49:29–32). Accordingly, Joseph goes up to bury his father, and with him go up all the officials of Pharaoh, the senior members of his court, and all of Egypt's dignitaries, together with all of Joseph's household, his brothers, and his father's household (Gen. 50:7–8). Joseph then returns to Egypt and adjures his brothers to bury him, too, in *Eretz Yisrael* (Gen. 50:25).

Where once it may have been presumed that we would be buried where our parents and grandparents rest, today we have more options. For many years, my wife and I have considered whether to be buried where I worked, where our children live, where other family members are buried, or where we live now in Florida. Even after I was diagnosed with brain cancer and underwent surgery, we were still unable to make the decision. The second surgery, however, pushed us to decide.

The choice of where to be buried considers our values and feelings about self, family, and community. Do you find the choices frightening to make and therefore delay doing so? Why? *Va-y'chi* calls us to do our own work and guide those whom we serve to face the preparations that need to be made. In order to guide our congregants through these challenging conversations, we, as rabbis, must do our own work first.

Va-y'chi
Rabbi Charles Middleburgh, PhD, 2018

Deathbed farewells dominate the conclusion of Genesis. For Joseph and his brothers, Jacob's protracted final speech is fashioned as a "blessing." It gets rehearsed when Jacob blesses his grandsons Ephraim and Manasseh. The the old rogue demonstrates his enduring ability to surprise.

Gathering his twelve sons around him, Jacob fires his final verbal fusillade. The man for whom obfuscation and deceit are second nature reveals that even on his deathbed he remains essentially unchanged by all that life has brought his way; the brother who stole his twin's blessing and birthright remains unchanged and unrepentant within his aged frame. To the majority of his sons, Jacob fires a bitter, reproachful, and even damning broadside, demonstrating that age has neither softened him nor dented his memory for filial malfeasance. Only to Judah does he give an uplifting and fortifying message, and only with Joseph does he become lyrical, demonstrating that it is only Rachel's firstborn who can inspire him to rise above himself. To his very end Jacob is a man hard to love, who leaves most of his sons with a verbal legacy of bitterness and resentment.

If nothing else, this sorry moment should inspire us to hold the right and loving conversations before we are dying, giving those we love something precious to sustain them. The reality of normal life is that most of us die having failed to consider the legacy we leave those we cherish. My mantra: remember how you wish to be remembered. But really, why wait for your deathbed?

Exodus

Exodus

שמות *Sh'mot*
(Exodus 1:1–6:1)

Sh'mot
Rabbi David Novak, 2010

"A certain man of the house of Levi went and married a Levite woman. The woman conceived and bore a son; and when she saw how beautiful he was, she hid him for three months" (Exod. 2:1–2).

The Hebrew words translated as "how beautiful he was" are *ki tov hu*. This unnamed woman saw that her son, also nameless, was *ki tov*. Where else do we find this same exact language? In *B'reishit*, chapter 1. In our first Creation narrative, God created the world day by day and pronounces it to be *ki tov*. Each day—except for the second—is given the refrain "And God saw that it was good."

What could this echo of the Creation story have in common with the birth of Moses? The first iterations of *ki tov hu* refer to the creation of the universe, everything within it, leading to the creation of the human being. This last iteration is Moses's mother observing that her son is good. God expresses pleasure in creating; here Moses's mother expresses similar pleasure in the creation of this child, whom God will choose to lead the Israelites to redemption.

Sh'mot
Rabbi Louis Rieser, 2011

When Moses seeks permission from his father-in-law to return to Egypt, Jethro responds, *Leich l'shalom*, "Go to peace" (Exod. 4:18). The

Sages (*Babylonian Talmud B'rachot* 64a) teach that this was the perfect response because it points to his future success. They contrast it with the phrase *Leich b'shalom*, "Go in peace," which should be addressed only to the deceased. What is the difference? What does that "*l'*" signify?

Tz'ror Hamor, Rabbi Abraham Sabba (Castile, 1440–1510), teaches that we who are living have not yet reached our completeness, our true *shalom*. It is a goal that lies ahead of us and to which we aspire. When someone is taking their leave from us, we offer a blessing that their travels lead them to greater wholeness.

Where will we find that *shalom*? The M'or Einayim (Rabbi Menachem Nachum Twersky of Chernobyl, 1730–97), commenting on Moses being nursed by Yocheved, offers an analogy. As long as a child nurses, she is tightly connected and draws all her vitality from her mother. Even after weaning, the mother-child bond is uniquely powerful. By comparison, Torah is our mother (Prov. 6:20), and we should be satisfied by her nourishment at all times (Prov. 5:19), wherever we travel. At Sinai, we were as tightly connected to Torah as a child to his mother. But as we journey on in life, the challenge is greater because the details and enticements of the world draw us in many directions. The blessing *Leich l'shalom* urges us to remain connected to the Source that nourishes us and gives us vitality even while we journey in the world.

Sh'mot
Rabbi Janice Garfunkel, z"l, 2012

Growing up in Pharaoh's palace, did Moses know he was adopted? The animated movie *Prince of Egypt* has a dramatic scene in which Moses, a young man, suddenly realizes his true identity (which the script writers connect to "and Moses went out and saw the suffering of his people" [Exod. 2:11]). But this scene is certainly anachronistic. Deceiving adopted children was mostly a short-lived experiment of the twentieth century, and not at all relevant to the Moses story. For most of history, adopted children knew, as most of them do today, of their adoptions.

Modern technology, however, has produced a new generation of people who once again do not know their biological origins: children of donor sperm and eggs. The majority of married couples who use donor gametes or embryos do not tell the children (though single parents and same-sex couples do, for obvious reasons).

Judaism generally eschews deception, and we learned from that twentieth-century experiment in adoption deception, and from current insights in psychological practice, that it is neither wise nor ethical for parents to mislead their children in this regard. Some reproductive endocrinologists actually encourage married couples to keep this important information secret, while many, if not most, simply make it an ethically neutral decision of the parents.

What leadership role should the Reform Movement play in encouraging and helping parents to be open and honest with their children about their origins?

Sh'mot
Rabbi Amy Scheinerman, 2013

Torah paints Pharaoh as a dangerous ruler because his worldview is us-versus-them: "Look, the Israelite people are much too numerous for us. Let us deal shrewdly with them, so that they may not increase; otherwise in the event of war they may join our enemies in fighting against us and rise from the ground" (Exod. 1:9–10). He has no trouble swallowing the absurd argument of the midwives that Hebrew women are biologically different from Egyptian women, because it confirms his worldview: "The Hebrew women are not like the Egyptian women: they are vigorous. Before the midwife can come to them, they have given birth" (Exod. 1:19).

While we may not see others as biologically different, or as potential enemies, it seems to me that there is sometimes undue and unbecoming competition within the Jewish community that does not further Torah. I hear rabbis of all stripes speak about how their congregation is thriving while others nearby are dying; they are not mourning the loss, but rather celebrating what feels to them to be a victory. I have seen instances of congregations so territorial that despite the fact that none can mount a decent adult education program or religious school, they refuse to join together to offer Torah learning, because exposure to another synagogue might cost them members.

I am keenly aware of the need for members for a synagogue to survive and thrive. I have experienced the problem firsthand. But I hope we can look beyond our immediate need and see that when we view others as a part of us and not as competition, we will grow and thrive all the more because what we offer will be more exciting, dynamic, and meaningful.

Sh'mot
Rabbi Ruth Adar, 2014

"These are the names of the sons of Israel" (Exod. 1:1).

We find not a single woman's name in the list that opens *Sh'mot*. But here's the irony: after the list of men's names, the portion is filled with the daring actions of women, actions without which there would have been no Judaism.

In chapter 1, we meet the midwives Shifrah and Puah, who refuse to murder Hebrew babies. They blatantly defy the most powerful man in the world. Realizing they aren't cooperating but unable to catch them at it, Pharaoh pursues another plan. Yet the fact remains: children survive because two women defy the king of the world to his face.

In chapter 2, another woman defies Pharaoh! A Levite woman hides her son for three months from the king's minions. When she can hide him no longer, she puts the infant in a basket and sets it afloat in the Nile, a dangerous and desperate act of resistance.

Miriam follows along on the riverbank, watching over the baby boy. Midrash tells us that Moses's sister has the gift of prophecy; she knows her little brother is no ordinary child. Nevertheless, imagine the nerve it takes to watch the basket while avoiding crocodiles, snakes, and Pharaoh's soldiers; yet young Miriam never abandons her brother.

In chapter 4, the young wife of Moses, Tziporah, witnesses her husband's near-fatal encounter with God. She thinks quickly, grabs a knife, and circumcises their son. The story is very mysterious, but one thing is certain: "Tziporah" may mean "little bird," but she herself is no shrinking violet.

So yes, Exodus may begin with the names of men, but it is the deeds of women that set this great saga in motion.

Sh'mot
Rabbi Amy Scheinerman, 2015

Rabbi Menachem Nachum Twersky of Chernobyl writes in *M'or Einayim*, "We all know the secret meaning of our exile in Egypt: *daat* [mindfulness/knowing] itself was in exile." Exile, he is telling us, is not a historical event. It's a metaphysical reality: being detached from God in one's life. The entire story of the Exodus is an allegory for our spiritual being: either we are mindful of God (the source of blessings and meaning) or we are unaware of, and separated from, God.

He explains that the primordial Torah of *B'reishit Rabbah* 1:1 was cut off from the world by the wickedness of *dor hamabul* ("the generation of the Flood"). That is why God brought the Flood. "Where was Torah cast down at that time? It fell into the shell of Egypt. That is mindfulness/knowing in exile, for the Torah represents mindfulness/knowing. And this is why Israel had to go down into Egypt, to raise up fallen Torah." It turns out that it is Torah that is in exile.

"Once we came out of Egypt, we brought mindfulness forth from exile. Even though we are indeed still in exile, mindfulness is not, except for those so totally lost that they deny reality." Exile, for us, is not a geographical reality; it is a state of mind.

If exile is a state of mind, then our geographical location and physical condition need not prevent us from mindfulness of God. How does a Jew in exile achieve mindfulness? By focusing on the *middot* (personal attributes) that bring us close to God. "For most people only the personal attributes [that express that mindfulness] remain in exile, for example *ahavah* [love], *yirah* [fear], *tiferet* [splendor], and the rest."

Sh'mot
Rabbi Stephen Wylen, 2016

"These are the names of the Israelites who went down to Egypt" (Exod. 1:1). These are the names of the Israelites who came up from Egypt. Reuven, Shimon, Levi, Y'hudah . . .

According to *Sh'mot Rabbah*, the Jews merited redemption from slavery in Egypt because even though the Torah had not yet been given, they observed four mitzvot, which all fall under one umbrella: retention of Jewish identity. The first and maybe most important of these four mitzvot was that they did not change their names. If you have a Jewish name, the world knows that you are a Jew, and you know that you are a Jew.

Jews who immigrated to America changed their names. In time, there came to be a sacred equivalents list: If you were Moshe, you became Morris. If you were Shimon, you became Seymour. So prevalent was this custom that historically Anglo-Saxon names are perceived by Jews as typical Jewish names. We know from a midrash that Jews in the Roman Empire had a similar sacred equivalents list: Reuven because Rufus. Y'hudah became Julius. Many American Jews think that this list was received *min hashamayim*, "straight from heaven." "Rabbi, his name was Christopher Robin. What would be the Jewish equivalent for that?" Hebrew names are used solely for sacred occasion.

Our names represent who we are—secretly Jewish on the inside, members of society at large on the outside. *Y'hudi b'veitecha u'vein adam b'tzeitecha* ("a Jew in your home and a human being outside of it"), as Y. L. Gordon put it.

One way to maintain our Jewish identity is to perform the mitzvah of giving our children Jewish names.

Sh'mot
Rabbi Stephen Wylen, 2017

How divine can a human be?

The Torah describes the birth of Moses: "A man from the house of Levi came and married a Levite daughter" (Exod. 2:1). Why does Torah not tell us the names of his parents, Amram and Yocheved? The commentator K'hilat Yitzchak (in *Iturei Torah* 3:16) says the purpose is to emphasize that Moses, the "man of God" who went up on Mount Sinai, was a flesh-and-blood human being. His father was a *ben* and his mother was a *bat*. Moses was born by natural means. Torah wishes to prevent Jews from committing the most enticing error of deifying a human being by claiming that Moses was divine. Not for the Jews the myth of a Christ, or a deified king, or a demigod such as the Greeks and Romans had.

According to the myth developed by some Jewish sect in the Second Temple era, the human being Enoch, seventh generation from Adam, was transported into heaven at the end of his earthly term and became Metatron or Sandalfon, the "Angel of the Presence," God's personal valet, the highest of all the angels. This myth was adopted into the *heichalot* mystical literature (see Ginzberg's *Legends of the Jews*) but subsequently faded and played virtually no role in later Jewish midrashim and mysticism. How high can a human being rise? As high as the most elevated angel, but no further. God remains God, and humans are not divine.

Sh'mot
Rabbi Louis Rieser, 2018

Everyone knows the famous midrash that lists the three reasons Israel merited redemption from slavery in Egypt: "Because of three things our ancestors merited to be redeemed from Egypt: they did not change their names, their language, or their dress." Since *Midrash Rabbah* first articulated this argument for cultural particularity, repeated by Rashi and others, rabbis have worked assiduously to ensure that Jews would remain Jewish, choose to identify as Jews, live as Jews, and transmit our traditions and identity to future generations. We applaud those who give their children biblical and Israeli names, sprinkle our language with Hebrew and Yiddish (or perhaps raise bilingual children at home), and have made *kippot* and tallitot stylish.

Today, in the second decade of the twenty-first century, what stands at the core of our Judaism? What do you do that paves a distinctively Jewish future for Jews and Judaism? The question is as important now as it was when first formulated.

You might be interested to know that the midrash I quoted above does not actually exist, famous as it is. The three elements—names, language, and dress—never appear together on one list. Rather, various versions list three or four items from this list to avoid or aspire to: names, language, *lashon hara* (gossip, slander), immorality, kosher food, dress, kindness, circumcision, not learning Egyptian, and not revealing our secrets (see kotzkblog.blogspot.com/2017/02/113-famous-midrash-which-doesnt-exist.html). The charm of these multiple lists is their flexibility and creativity.

What are your prime considerations for preserving your Jewish identity, and why and how do you keep your eyes on the prize?

ואראָ *Va-eira*
(Exodus 6:2–9:35)

Va-eira
Rabbi Stephen Wylen, 2010

God said: "I have heard the groans of the Israelites, as the Egyptians have enslaved them, and I have remembered My covenant" (Exod. 6:5).

For two thousand years Jews have found redemptive meaning in Jewish suffering. Henry Slonimsky ("The Philosophy Implicit in the Midrash") categorized the theology of Jewish suffering from persecution in a renowned article: Jews saw the suffering servant of Isaiah as none other than themselves. When the Jewish people's cup of suffering was filled to capacity, the Messiah would come. Lurianic kabbalists tried to hasten this moment with ascetic practices. Jewish poets and chroniclers exaggerated Jewish suffering as if to say to God: "Look, we have fulfilled our role. Now redeem us!" Orthodox Judaism in our time validates itself, in part, by claiming an eternal enmity between the Jewish and gentile worlds.

Salo Baron, the great Columbia University historian, warned long ago against promoting what he called the "lachrymose view of Jewish history" ("Ghetto and Emancipation: Shall We Revise the Traditional View?) In truth, most Jews remained Jewish through the centuries because it was beneficial for them, not because Jews are uniquely stubborn in the face of persecution. We should not take a historical fact as a theological position.

While it is controversial to say so, I would claim that our Holocaust education gives children a reason to choose not to be Jewish, not a reason to be Jewish. We need to focus our education more on the joys of Jewish living.

Va-eira
Rabbi Joshua Minkin, DMin, 2013

"It is the same Aaron and Moses to whom the Lord said . . ." (Exod. 6:26). Why does Aaron precede Moses here and elsewhere? While Moses and Aaron, brothers, work closely together under trying circumstances, we are much more accustomed to reading Moses's name first.

Traditional commentators explain that mentioning Aaron before Moses reminds us that both are equally great. Rabbi Moshe Feinstein suggests that occasionally Aaron is named first to demonstrate that both achieved their maximum potential. "In God's scales, achievement is measured by how well one fulfills one's personal mission" (*Stone Chumash*, p. 323).

We became rabbis to help and to make a difference. But how do we measure our success? By the size of the institutions over which we preside? By the fame, status, prestige we have accrued, and the salary we command? By the influence and connections we have amassed?

We all bring gifts to our work. We are challenged by different situations. Our text teaches us that the only metric of success that is meaningful is whether we continually give our all to whatever we do, allow ourselves to be challenged, and never rest on our laurels. We must continue to expand our skills and knowledge.

If, each day, we truthfully have done all we could, then we, like Moses and Aaron, will have maximized our potential.

Va-eira
Rabbi Janice Garfunkel, z"l, 2013

Did the events of the Exodus really happen? I tend not to wonder much about this question because the importance of the story is in the fact that it is so foundational to how we perceive ourselves as a people: we were slaves, and God redeemed us. I am impressed by the fact that our people invented for itself a history of slavery. Usually, if a history is to be invented, it is more likely to reflect superiority.

However, whether or not the Exodus happened is much less important to me than what it means to us to have this story at the very core of our tradition. What is the impact of this story on us? What do we make of a story that tells us that we were slaves and God redeemed us, particularly in the modern context, when many of us do not believe in a God who acts in history? Is a story of slavery and redemption meaningful at all?

As it happens, my parents are Holocaust survivors. This story is not one of the ancient past: my father was quite literally a slave, and he was redeemed.

Many are still enslaved today, not merely figuratively, but in reality: we suffer from human trafficking and economic conditions that are enslaving; and many women live in social contexts that deny them freedom. Who will redeem them?

As Reform Jews, we know we are partners with God in *tikkun olam*. That means it is up to us to be active participants in the acts of redemption, redeeming ourselves, and now that many of us are in fortunate positions, redeeming others.

Do we do enough to redeem the enslaved? In what way does God, today, redeem the enslaved?

Va-eira
Rabbi Michael Boyden, 2013

Most of this week's *parashah* is devoted to preparing Moses and Aaron for their encounter with Pharaoh. But why did God choose Moses?

The Torah refers to only three events in Moses's life prior to God turning to him at the ripe old age of eighty(!).

The first time Moses is mentioned in the Torah, it is described that when he saw an Egyptian taskmaster beating Israelite slaves, he "struck down the Egyptian and hid him in the sand" (Exod. 2:12). The second episode transmitted to us tells us that he saw two Israelites fighting and asked them, "Why do you strike your fellow?" (Exod. 2:13). The third incident narrated is his encounter with a group of shepherds: the shepherds chased away the daughters of the priest of

Midian from the well, and "Moses rose to their defense, and watered their flock" (Exod. 2:17).

Achad HaAm in his essay, "Moses," (p.315) tells us that all three events have one aspect in common: "the prophet's clash with life in the name of justice."

The Israelites were enslaved in Egypt for hundreds of years, and yet we do not hear a single example of any attempt to rescue them. Thousands of years later, the residents of the German suburb of Dachau went about their daily lives while at the same time more than two hundred thousand prisoners passed through its Nazi internment camp, where more than thirty thousand of them would lose their lives. It takes immense courage to stand up to a regime. Even Moses protested, "I have a speech impediment. How will Pharaoh listen to me?"

When one believes in the righteousness of one's cause, one must not give up. As Dr. Martin Luther King Jr. put it (Martin Luther King, Jr., 27 January 1965), "The ultimate test of a man is not where he stands in moments of comfort and moments of convenience, but where he stands in moments of challenge."

Va-eira
Rabbi Amy Scheinerman, 2014

The story of the Exodus is one of nested hierarchies of power—and reversals. God stands on the top rung. Pharaoh stands above the Israelites and Moses; he believes himself to stand at the top, but learns otherwise. Moses believes he stands beneath Pharaoh, until God reverses the power dynamic by means of the plagues (the first seven plagues are enumerated in *Va-eira*). The Israelites are organized in a hierarchical system (the heads of the clans are enumerated in *Va-eira*). The story turns on coercion, control, threat, and punishment.

God and Pharaoh employ and respond to control, threat, and punishment. Moses is far less self-assured (in *Va-eira*, he tells God that his speech impediment is a disqualification for authority and power). He is far more inclined, at times, toward empathy and compassion.

In *The Moral Molecule*, Paul J. Zak, the "vampire economist" and professor of psychology, reports his studies on the effect of the pro-social hormone oxytocin on human behavior. Zak argues that oxytocin is the molecule behind love, loyalty, virtue—and ultimately, prosperity. "Testosterone specifically interferes with the uptake of oxytocin, producing a damping effect on being caring and feeling," which makes hunters and warriors "less squeamish about crushing skulls in order to feed and protect the family," far more likely to take risks, and far more likely to coerce, punish, and extract revenge. Zak draws lines from molecules to families to societies.

Zak's work can inspire us to ask: What makes a great leader—the qualities of oxytocin, testosterone, or a combination? Based on extensive experiments, Zak concludes that "the benefit to the group in having at least some of its members wired to punishing is that it reinforces morality by increasing the cost—as well as the likelihood of having to pay the cost—for anti-social behaviors." We might well explore how his work informs our models of leadership.

Va-eira
Rabbi David Novak, 2015

It is no wonder that so many Jews in modernity have difficulty relating to a God who is portrayed not only anthropomorphically, but also anthropopathically. The God of Israel is essentially indescribable, yet Torah speaks of God's actions and emotions in language that reflects human senses (sight, hearing, touch, taste, smell) and feelings. Our worship language, addressing God as "You" and "Sovereign" compounds the difficulty for modern Jews.

In *Va-eira*, we are presented with a God who appears to Moses, hears, and speaks. God also promises redemption: "I will free you . . . and deliver you. . . . I will redeem you. . . . I will take you. . . . I will bring you into the land" (Exod. 6:6–8). It leads many to wonder, rightfully, where the God of Israel who acted so forcefully long ago to redeem the Israelites from slavery is today? This is particularly a conundrum in our post-Shoah world, where so many people—Jews and non-Jews—are in desperate need of redemption.

There is no easy answer to this question, but we can offer at least an attempt: the God of Israel's redemption models the attributes of godliness that we are to emulate. It is in our hands, arising out of our humanity, to enact these attributes to heal the world. As Jews, the suffering of the "widow, orphan, and stranger in our midst"—all who are vulnerable—should spur us to respond. This is how we can make this powerful narrative live in our lives, and this is how we can continue God's redeeming power in the world.

Va-eira
Rabbi David Novak, 2016

Remaining in covenantal consciousness with the God of Israel is challenging for contemporary Jews. Given that humans perceive with the five human senses, it is difficult to be in relationship with One who does not communicate in any way humans experience as familiar. In *Va-eira*, God introduces God's self and the covenant to Moses saying: "I appeared to Abraham, Isaac, and Jacob as *El Shaddai*, but I did not make Myself known to them by My name *YHVH*. I also established My covenant with them, to give them the land of Canaan" (Exod. 6:3–4). With this introduction, God extends the covenant to an inchoate people.

To some extent, our understanding of the covenant remains inchoate. Inviting Jews to think about covenant is part of what it means to be Jewish. Given the inherent disconnect of sensing a God that is not anthropomorphic, many Jews choose to ignore the covenant or any sense of relationship with God and the Jewish people. When Jews take time to embrace their textual tradition, they may look through the unique lens applied by the rabbis to the experience of God.

Making covenantal consciousness real in the lives of our people means reminding them that human perfection is not the goal. The goal is to wrestle with our varied understandings of God. We should encourage people to explore and evolve their thinking. The God of Israel does not need us to be sure of God's exact nature, but rather to be in relationship with God. Through a covenant relationship with God—however we conceive God—we have the means to make choices to live with or without God's continuous presence in our lives.

Va-eira
Rabbi Michael Boyden, 2017

The Israeli poet Zelda wrote:

> Each of us has a name
> given by God
> and given by our parents.

A Hebrew name is often used in literature to signify one's personality and one's aspirations or recalls a significant event in one's life. Our name gives expression to our essence. How people address us tells us about the nature of our relationship with them.

Although Judaism attaches so much significance to the unity of the Divine, God has many names. For example, our *parashah* informs us that God was only revealed to Moses's ancestors as *El Shaddai* and not as *YHVH* (Exod. 6:3). When Moses is confronted by God at the Burning Bush, he naturally wants to know who it is that is sending him to Pharaoh to call for the release of the Israelites. The only answer he receives is *Ehyeh-Asher-Ehyeh* (Exod. 3:14).

As Maimonides put it, "A living human being does not have the mental ability to understand the true nature of the Creator" (*Mishneh Torah Hilchot Y'sodei HaTorah* 1:10). We humans can only, as *Sh'mot Rabbah* 3:6 reminds us, know God through God's actions. We can see God's "back," but not God's "face" (Exod. 33:23).

We cannot express God's name in its totality any more than we can know God in the full sense of the term. Only the High Priest was able to pronounce the ineffable name just once a year on Yom Kippur in the Holy of Holies. Today even the sound of that name is hidden to us.

Va-eira
Rabbi Amy Scheinerman, 2018

At the beginning of *Parashat Va-eira*, God speaks to Moses and says to him, "I am Adonai. I appeared to Abraham, Isaac, and Jacob as *El Shaddai*, but I did not make Myself known to them by My name *YHVH*" (Exod. 6:2–3).

The S'fat Emet explains the meaning of *El Shaddai* in an unexpected way that resonates in our age of truthiness and untruth: this world is "the world of lies" because it is suffused with falsehoods. However, God secreted in everything elements of divine truth. This is why God is called *el she-dai* (there is enough godliness) for one to extract truth from the falsehoods.

"I also established My covenant with them, to give them the land of Canaan, the land in which they lived as sojourners" (Exod. 6:4). The work of our ancestors who struggled to identify truth and distinguish it from lies is referred to as living as sojourners.

Moses alone encountered God face to face ("through lucid glass"). The S'fat Emet writes, "But in this world everything is garbed in nature. It is by sanctifying yourself in this-worldly matters that you attain some bit of understanding. This is called the 'unlucid glass'; it is through the hiding that you come to merit revelation."

Separating truth from lies has taken on a new dimension. May we merit a view through translucent glass.

בא *Bo*
Exodus 10:1–13:16)

Bo
Rabbi Amy Scheinerman, 2010

I am amazed at how often the sins of *lashon hara* (gossip, slander) and *r'chilut* (talebearing) are used to explain suffering. Of the last plague, Torah tells us: "There shall be a loud cry in all the land of Egypt, such as has never been or will ever be again; but not a dog shall wag its tongue at any of the Israelites, at man or beast—in order that you may know that Adonai makes a distinction between Egypt and Israel" (Exod. 11:6–7).

The detail about dogs is surprising. The detail about "wagging their tongues" seems out of place in this narrative. Moreover, if loud wailing is heard throughout the country, one would hardly expect dogs to remain silent. Rabbi Yitzchak Meir Alter (1799–1866), the first rebbe of the Ger dynasty, understood "not a dog shall wag its tongue" to say that *lashon hara* and *r'chilut* brought about the Israelites' enslavement in Egypt. Yosef brought evil reports of his brothers to Yaakov, provoking them to sell him into slavery. Datan and Aviram informed on Moshe to Pharaoh after Moshe killed the Egyptian taskmaster (*Sh'mot Rabbah* 1:31)—though that was well into the period of enslavement.

While I bridle at the theology of divine punishment (and especially group punishment!), I am keenly aware that the evils of *lashon hara* and *r'chilut* have far-reaching consequences, particularly in our high-tech world. The events this past summer surrounding Shirley Sherrod's odyssey at the USDA and, as I write these words, the suicide last week of Tyler Clementi, give more than ample proof that we need to speak and teach far more about the dangers of *lashon hara* and *r'chilut* and how our use of technology facilitates and enhances their reach and effect.

Bo
Rabbi Michael Boyden, 2012

It is not fortuitous that the *parashah* that describes the last of the plagues also includes the statement "This month shall be the first month [of the year] for you" (Exod. 12:2). From here on, the Israelites will be able to plan their own time.

When the Deuteronomic version of the Ten Commandments commands us, "Observe the Sabbath day . . . and do no work . . . because you were a slave in the land of Egypt" (Deut. 5:12–15), the association is clear. Only a free person is master of his time, whereas a slave depends upon a timetable set by others.

But freedom has limits. The wicked son has no time for the seder meal, because he mistakenly confuses *cheirut* (freedom) with *chofesh*—the right to do whatever one chooses. He asks, *Mah haavodah hazot?* – "What does this service mean to you?" Having escaped the burden of slavery in Egypt, he views any other kind of service (*avodah*) as being equally intolerable. In the *Jerusalem Talmud P'sachim* 10:4, this question is interpreted to mean: "What is this burden that you impose upon us every year? All you have done is to replace one kind of service with another kind." He seeks the freedom to do what he wishes, without restriction, without a time framework.

Whereas that option to do whatever one wishes is attractive in a postmodern world of individualism and personal autonomy, our tradition teaches us that "the only one who is truly free is a person who engages in *talmud Torah* [Torah study]" (*Mishnah Pirkei Avot* 6:2). Judaism views commitment as an essential component of true freedom. How we spend our time says who we are.

Bo
Rabbi Janice Garfunkel, z"l, 2013

When Pharaoh says, "Yes, you may go, but not your flocks" (Exod. 10:24), Moses ups his demands. That isn't a usual negotiation technique! More commonly, both sides begin by demanding more than they expect to get and then gradually move closer to one another's position. But in this protracted negotiation between Moses and Pharaoh, Moses increases his demands, perhaps because with the passage of time and the progression of events, Moses sees that his position of power has risen quite dramatically.

As I write this *d'var Torah* in early December, President Morsi of Egypt has appropriated dictatorial powers, and Egyptians are trying to stand up to this modern-day pharaoh. How astonishing that a story thousands of years old is so strangely relevant. Same place. Similar issues?

It makes me wonder if we can learn any practical applications from this story for negotiating with dictators. I've often heard people say that fighting never accomplishes anything, but this story, and many in history, seems to prove the opposite: unfortunately, and tragically, in most instances, freedom and other good things come only after the application of force.

This seems an opportune time to delve into questions of negotiation strategies in our personal lives and in our national lives. Do we ask too little? Do we concede too early? Do we overreach? What is the right amount to ask for? Is it effective to begin by asking for less, with the intent of increasing our demands over time? What is the role of power in our negotiations?

Bo
Rabbi Amy Scheinerman, 2014

With the ninth plague of darkness, Pharaoh once again summons Moses to his palace. Pharaoh refuses to allow the Israelites to take their cattle with them: "Go, worship Adonai! Only your flocks and your livestock [*tzonchem uv'karchem*] shall be left behind" (Exod. 10:24). Nonetheless, Moses demands, "Our livestock [*mikneinu*], too, shall go along with us—not a hoof [*parsah*] shall remain behind: for we must select from it for the worship of our God Adonai, and we shall not know with what we are to worship *Adonai* until we arrive there" (Exod. 10:26).

When the Israelites actually depart, they bring with them an *eirev rav* (mixed multitude), and their livestock, flocks and herds, were abundant (*v'tzon uvakar mikneh kaveid m'od*) (Exod. 12:38).

Rabbi Abraham Chayim of Zloczow (1750–1816), in his *Orach L'Chayim*, connects the mention of livestock and herds with the *eirev rav*:

> This is what Moses meant when he said, "Our livestock too"—this refers to the *eirev rav*, those we have acquired and brought near to ourselves—"will go along with us; not a portion [*parsah*/hoof] of them will remain behind." The word *parsah* [hoof] can [also] mean "portion," so that these are "the portion of the letter *hei*," referring to the *Shechinah*, that latter *hei* of Y-H-V-H. It is known from the *Zohar* and other books that proselytes are rooted in that place, and no spark of them was to be left behind in Egypt.

Even in servitude, the Israelites shared their insights into the Divine, their sacred community, and their identity with those who would be drawn to them. So, too, did Hillel welcome proselytes warmly (*Babylonian Talmud Shabbat* 30b–31a), concerning which three proselytes are inspired to comment, "Hillel's kindness brought us under the wings of the Shechinah."

Bo
Rabbi Michael Boyden, 2014

We tend to focus on the release of the Israelites from slavery, but of no lesser interest is the collapse of Egyptian society. It is the tale of a mighty empire, its leaders, its people and their beliefs, and of the path that led to their destruction.

Certainly the Children of Israel have to adjust to the notion of freedom. But those who enslaved them also had to come to terms with the fact that the game was over. That is why the saga of the plagues includes the statement "And the Egyptians shall know that I am Adonai" (Exod. 7:5).

Ultimately, it is the tale of a stubborn dictator over a corrupt society struggling to hold onto power. As the Book of Proverbs puts it, "A stone is heavy and sand is a burden, but the anger of a fool weighs more than both of them" (Prov. 27:3). Living after the Holocaust, one cannot help but draw comparisons with another tyrant who fought until the bitter end at the expense of his people. The Germans, like the Egyptians, were complicit in their leader's genocidal goals. The Egyptians did not care about the Israelites' suffering, but only about the threat that they posed to the status quo. As they put it, "How long will they be a snare to us?" (Exod. 10:7).

Egypt's empire could not survive without addressing the evil in its midst. As Martin Luther King Jr. wrote from a Birmingham jail, "We are caught in an inescapable network of mutuality, tied in a single garment of destiny" (https://www.africa.upenn.edu/Articles_Gen/Letter_Birmingham.html). And so our *parashah* teaches us: "One law shall you have for the native born and for the stranger who resides among you" (Exod. 12:49).

Bo
Rabbi Ruth Adar, 2015

Parashat Bo begins on a curious note. *Bo el Paroh* is generally translated "Go to Pharaoh," but the usual translation of *bo* is "come." "Come to Pharaoh" suggests that God is with the ruler of Egypt, and the next phrase seems to confirm it: "because I have hardened his heart." So here we have a layering of paradoxes: a "come" that means "go," and a God who is somehow with Pharaoh, the embodiment of evil.

The *Zohar* solves the puzzle by reading the Torah as a metaphor: God calls to Moses from Pharaoh's throne room, summoning him into the cavern of a fearful serpent, the evil heart of Egypt's soul. The Kotzker Rebbe takes a different tack: he suggests that God is telling Moses, "Don't be afraid because I will be with you in the throne room!"

The process of Exodus is like the journey from youth to maturity. Sooner or later, those who wish to become truly mature must confront the darkest parts of their personality. "Come," our *yetzer hara* (evil inclination) calls to us, and we enter its chamber, filled with dread, because we know it to be powerful like Pharaoh. "Enjoy yourself," it murmurs, but our task is to take a sober look and see it for what it is.

This can be terrifying, precisely because the ugly thing is deep within us. It is then, the Kotzker Rebbe reminds us, that despite the terrors of this place, God is with us every step of the way.

Bo
Rabbi David Novak, 2016

What is right in front of you that you are incapable of seeing? The despotic Pharaoh's obstinacy prevents him from realizing that he is presiding over his society's demise. Pharaoh's own magicians explicitly say that they are unable to replicate the plague of the lice, unlike the first two plagues, and exclaim in dismay, "This is the finger of God!" (Exod. 8:15). Pharaoh's highest advisors counsel and warn, "How long shall this one be a snare to us? . . . Are you not yet aware that Egypt is lost?" (Exod. 10:7). The magicians and counselors closest to Pharaoh see the magnitude of the unprecedented challenge to Pharaoh.

Still, Pharaoh continues to harm his people through his obsessive disregard of the destruction happening around him—to the land, to the people, and ultimately, to his own being.

Would that personalities like Pharaoh were but distant memories. Alas, there remain too many political leaders whose goal is to amass and preserve personal power, irrespective of how destructive they are to their own people. Instead of bettering their people's lot, these "leaders" commit immoral, corrupt, and destructive acts to further their personal agenda and longevity.

Each time we study *Sh'mot*, each time we celebrate Pesach, we reexperience our freedom narrative. By observing Pharaoh, we are reminded that we should pursue justice in the world. We have been given our marching orders: remember the stranger, pursue justice, love your neighbor. We imitate God just as Rabbi Abraham Joshua Heschel did when he marched in Selma, saying that he "prayed with his feet." Let us embrace this legacy to those of us alive in this moment.

Bo
Rabbi Amy Scheinerman, 2017

Do problematic assumptions about God matter if the conclusions drawn are good?

In *K'dushat HaLevi*, Levi Yitzchak of Berditchev notes two aspects of the opening of *Bo* that constitute nuanced shifts in the narrative: first, God's instruction to Moses, "Come to Pharaoh because I have hardened his heart," using "come" rather than "Go [*lech*] to Pharaoh" as is found elsewhere; and second, ascribing the hardening of Pharaoh's heart by God.

In explaining both, the Berditchever Rebbe delves into two theological pools that some of us would find discomfiting. The first is a distinction drawn between miracles performed to punish Israel's persecutors and miracles wrought to foment a complete change of heart among Israel's oppressors. The second theological claim is *midah k'neged midah*, as expressed in *Sh'mot Rabbah* 9:12 and the *Babylonian Talmud Sotah* 10b–11a: God repays sinners in a manner corresponding to their sin and rewards the righteous in a manner that matches (or exceeds) their goodness.

"Come," Levi Yitzchak says, implies not confrontation but rather an invitation to *t'shuvah*. The latter phrase is supplied so that Pharaoh, upon repenting, can redeem himself and God will say, "For I, Myself, have made the first move in bringing Pharaoh's heart closer to Me." As intriguing as the image of Pharaoh repenting is, for Levi Yitzchak, it is prelude to a discussion of Rabbi Y'hudah's three oaths (*Babylonian Talmud K'tubot* 111a) and the eminently arguable assertion that "the nations" have complied with God's requirement that they not "oppress Israel overmuch."

While initially it seemed that problematic theology might get us to a good place nonetheless, it appears that it (inevitably?) cycles back to problematic theology and troubling conclusions.

Bo
Rabbi David Novak, 2018

God hardening Pharaoh's heart remains puzzling. Rashi comments that the plural *moftai* ("marvels") in "So that My marvels may be multiplied" (Exod. 11:9) refers "not to one wonder alone [i.e., the slaying of the firstborn], but to the slaying of the firstborn, the division of the Reed Sea, and the overthrowing of the Egyptians in it." For Rashi and for us, the *moftai* reflect our understanding of God's miraculous redemptive powers. For the Egyptians, however, they are the result of Pharaoh's rapacious leadership that brings the loss of life and the destruction of society. Two of the marvels—the horrific death of the firstborn sons of Egyptians and their non-Israelite slaves, and the destruction of the nation's elite military officers—created a national crisis for Egypt.

Apparently not an issue for the biblical writer, this is a struggle for us. Egypt loses its free labor, top brass, and military equipment. Pharaoh's unprincipled leadership in trying to compete with the God of Israel leads to his nation's unraveling.

Torah's silence on Egypt's fate is intentional. Its leader and his minions no longer drive the narrative. God's marvels bring redemption to Israel and devastating defeat to Pharaoh. God's marvels are in response to God's hearing the groans of our ancestors. Today, as we pray for God to hear our prayer, we also affirm, "Pray as if everything depended on God, and act as if everything depended on us." This reflects our understanding to remain vigilant to those pharaohs who would abuse the people, leaving destruction in their wake.

בשלח B'shalach
(Exodus 13:17–17:16)

B'shalach
Rabbi Louis Rieser, 2010

"This manna that our ancestors ate wandering in the desert—what is its meaning?" Torah warns that God provides the manna as a test "to see whether they will follow My instructions or not" (Exod. 16:4), or as Rabbi Simon bar Yochai explains, "Torah is given only to those who eat manna" (*M'chilta B'Shalach* 1). Wherein lies the test?

One hint comes in the instructions: "Gather as much as each of you requires to eat, an omer per person" (Exod. 16:16). It seems contradictory to say, "Take as much as you want, as long as it is no more or less than an omer." The manna provides a sufficient portion, not an endless feast. The lesson is that a meal has boundaries.

The lesson extends beyond food. "Who is rich? The one who is satisfied with his portion; as Ps. 128:2 says, 'You enjoy the fruit of your labor; be happy and prosper'" (*Mishnah Pirkei Avot* 4:1). Maimonides comments that one who is not satisfied with his lot will not know when to say: enough. After all, *Kohelet Rabbah* 13:1 teaches that nobody departs the world with even half his desires fulfilled. K'li Yakar (seventeenth century, Poland) argues that the people needed to walk in the desert, a barren place, in order to acquire the quality of *histapkut*, translated as "satisfaction" or "simplicity." The manna tests our ability to say *dayeinu*, "enough."

The test remains valid today. Faced with abundance in food and consumer goods, have we learned *histapkut*, to be satisfied with our portion?

B'shalach
Rabbi Louis Rieser, 2011

Safe on the far side of the Reed Sea, the people sing songs of thanksgiving. These songs, prayers of the most elemental kind, are led by Moses and Miriam. The people do not require a book, form, or template to follow; their prayer bursts from their hearts. In contrast to the spontaneous, emotional prayer at the Reed Sea, most prayers in the synagogue follow a prescribed order. Perhaps that is why synagogue prayer often fails to move us.

Prayer can give voice to the deepest parts of our soul, but it often does not. I once heard a sermon in which the service was compared to a symphony, each movement finely crafted to elicit certain emotions. How many of us sit down to design such a service? Do we consider how a *nigun* can lift a soul, as it once helped heal King Saul from his melancholy (I Sam. 16:16)? Maimonides (*Mishneh Torah, Hilchot Y'sodei HaTorah* 7:4) teaches that the disciples of prophets outfitted themselves with musical instruments to help induce their visions. Do we craft our services to help others touch the holy? How would we react if our congregants spontaneously began dancing around the room, like the women who accompany Miriam with their timbrels? Rav Kook (*Sh'moneh K'vatzim* 1:165) suggests that when we embed the prosaic parts of our life within the song of the soul, we can touch the very depths of our being. Is that our goal?

If we accept that we are the conductor of a grand, prayerful symphony, we must weigh every word and movement to ensure that the symphony moves our congregants in the desired direction. We can lead our people in prayer that opens the soul and evokes the Holy. Perhaps we can even stir echoes of our ancient dance on the shore of the Sea.

B'shalach
Rabbi Rabbi Bill S. Tepper, 2012

The tag "slow learner" was, for a long time, associated with those who experienced difficulty acquiring the most basic concepts. In our day, pedagogic professionals prefer the gentler labels "cognitively challenged" and "special needs." Nevertheless, *Parashat B'shalach* may be read as a case study in slow learning—not so much on a cognitive, but much more on an emotional, or even theological, level.

Despite evidence to the contrary, the Egyptian pharaoh is convinced that the Israelites must knuckle under. Despite the plagues that have decimated his land, the pharaoh—in a tragic miscalculation—orders his troops to pursue and destroy the departed Israelites.

The Israelites, too, take their time in seeing the light. They struggle to embrace the extraordinary act of redemption that is their due. Notwithstanding the inspired—and inspiring—leadership of Moses, and despite their emergence from centuries of servitude, the Israelites remain doubters. Massed on the shore of the Sea of Reeds, they are unconvinced of God's great plan for them. Such skepticism endures even after they cross the seabed and commence the journey into the wilderness.

For the Jewish people, hope is our legacy. Perseverance in the face of despairing obstacles is emblematic of our faith. Far from throwing in the towel or succumbing to doubt, we draw strength from our remarkable stories and traditions. The emotionally slow learners are still among us; but so are the quick studies. Anguish and skepticism continue to raise their unsightly heads. May our belief in ongoing redemption, for us and for all humanity, be unswerving.

B'shalach
Rabbi Joshua Minkin, DMin, 2013

In *Parashat B'shalach,* Israel is freed from Egypt—*Mitzrayim,* "the narrow place." We, too, are entrapped in our own narrow places. Trapped in the comfort of the familiar and the fear of change, we remain enslaved by behaviors we know are wrong but fear acknowledging. Then, from somewhere within, we encounter a Moses and realize change is possible.

Our journey to change, like the journey from Egypt to *Eretz Yisrael,* is convoluted. At the beginning, our pillar of fire leads us forward. But challenges await us. How easy it is to become overwhelmed and retreat back to the familiar. Three times in *B'shalach,* the Israelites verge on rebellion, recalling the "comfortable familiarity" of slavery with fondness.

The way forward to the Promised Land is fraught with steps backward. There may be times when old ways return. This does not mean failure. Rather, it shows how difficult the struggle to escape Egypt is. However, this does not pardon our abandoning the struggle. Each of us bears wounds and limitations that make it difficult to leave slavery behind. But difficulty does not grant permission to give up.

Leaving Egypt is the only way we can reach Sinai, the only way we can reach our potential as moral beings and as Jews. Every small step forward is a step toward righteousness.

B'shalach
Rabbi Louis Rieser, 2014

The Piaseczner Rebbe, Kalonymus Kalmish Shapira (1889–1943, also known as the Warsaw Ghetto Rebbe), finds in the opening verse of the Song of the Sea the idea of divine *sod*, "secret." His explication of the notion offers a humbling reminder that all learning depends on the heart.

A *sod*, a secret, is personal, something we hide from others for our own reasons; that we reveal only to those who have earned the privilege of hearing it. These secrets belong to us and are of our "essence and significance."

God also has secrets, like Kabbalah, revealed only to those who have earned the privilege. This is where it gets interesting. We can each learn the particulars of Kabbalah according to our own level, but intelligence is not sufficient. In order to penetrate the depths of that divine secret, one "needs to draw close to God, blessed be, unite with the Holy One, and then God reveals the *sod* that is God's essence to them, according to the extent of the person's closeness" (Kalonymus Kalmish Shapira, *Derech HaMelech B'Shalach*). Secrets are intimate, and we learn to hear them by opening our heart, accepting the risk, and entering that intimate realm.

Shapira's extended exploration teaches that gaining such intimacy requires introspection and meditation in addition to love. There is much to be learned from Shapira's detailed description, but the takeaway is simpler. The Torah of the mind is partial at best. If we wish our teaching—regardless of topic—to sink into the hearts and souls of *amcha*, "our people," we need to pursue the difficult and intimate journey into our own soul first. In discovering our own depths, we may touch the Divine.

Shabbat Shirah
Rabbi Gila Ruskin, 2014

Ask anyone to name a biblical miracle and 90 percent will say: parting the Reed Sea. *Shirat HaYam* (*Song at the Sea*) abounds in superlatives about God's sovereignty, reflecting the awe of *B'nei Yisrael* ("the Children of Israel") at the supernatural special effects. *Ki ga-oh gaah . . . nora t'hilot, oseih feleh*, "For [God] has triumphed gloriously . . . awesome in splendor, working wonders" (Exod. 15:1, 15:11). But this awe soon succumbs to fear, hunger, and thirst.

Note the "oohs" and "aahs" at a fireworks display. The pyrotechnic bursts of color against a dark sky excite us to great exclamations of wonder. And yet, how many "oohs" and "aahs" do we emit when the starter ignites in our cars as we drive home? Both are lit miraculously by sparks, but only the resplendent one in the sky inspires us to shout. We try to recapture the amazement of our ancestors at the sea by reciting *Mi Chamochah* and *Adonai Yimloch* twice every day, but I yearn for liturgical mention of my favorite miracle: the manna, the five-day-per-week predictability of one portion provided for each person; the one-day predictability of a double portion; and the Shabbat predictability of no manna to be gathered so that we can delight in God's munificence and cherish our freedom from the numbing shackles of everyday slavery.

Instead of the majesty of *Mi Chamochah*, for the parting of seas that was so easily forgotten when hunger and thirst and fear took over, I find my sense of miracles captured in the *v'al nisecha sheb'chol yom imanu, v'al nifl'otecha v'tovotecha sheb'chol eit, erev vavoker v'tzohorayim* ("for Your miracles that we experience every day and for Your wondrous deeds and favors at every time of day: evening, morning, and noon") of the *Amidah*. That is my *shirat haman*.

B'shalach
Rabbi Joshua Minkin, DMin, 2015

God is worried—"The people may have a change of heart when they see war, and return to Egypt" (Exod. 13:17)—and therefore sends them on a circuitous route to avoid the Philistines. But Moses has a plan to rally their courage: he gathers the bones (*atzamot*) of Joseph (Exod. 13:19).

Israel's self-perception is mired by centuries of slavery. They see themselves as weak and like children; they demand that Moses fix every problem and fulfill every need. Bones connote strength and firmness. In English, to "have backbone" is to possess courage, tenacity, grit—qualities Israel needs. Pharaoh had once referred to them as *rav v'atzum*, "great and mighty" (Exod. 1:9); this is the *etzem* Israel needs to reclaim.

But *etzem* does not only mean "bone." It also means "essence" or "substance." *Etzem* is one's very essence—the essence of one's character. What the Israelites require is a complete transformation.

Indeed, one can make the case that this is exactly what happened to Joseph. He remarkably transformed from the obedient servant in Potiphar's household into the grand vizier of Egypt. The bones of Joseph represent the potential inherent in Israel to transform herself from an enfeebled people into a proud and powerful nation—*am rav v'atzum*—a transformation they must undergo in order to survive in the Land of Israel.

There is yet another play on the word *etzem*. *Atzam* means "to close one's eyes." Israel must close their eyes to their current self-understanding in order to see and realize their full potential. Sometimes, we must as well.

B'shalach
Rabbi Ruth Adar, 2016

This week we read about our ancestors, a ragtag band whom God rescued from the mightiest army on earth, yet who revolted against God only six weeks into freedom. According to Ramban, the Israelites had been living on leftover matzah for six weeks. Imagine six weeks of stale matzah. Revolting.

The people turned against Moses and Aaron, as they had done before and would do again. God responded with a promise that the following morning food would rain down from the sky.

Manna came with instructions: The Israelites were permitted to gather precisely one measure per person each day and a double portion on the sixth day. They were forbidden from gathering manna on the seventh day; they were to eat the extra portion from the previous day.

When they sought manna on Shabbat nonetheless, they found none. They learned to gather an extra measure on the sixth day and save it for Shabbat.

That is how our people learned to keep Shabbat. Our people were sustained in the wilderness by a miracle food that appeared six days a week. On the seventh day, they learned to rest.

Nowadays Jews live in an entirely different kind of wilderness. With jobs to do, bills to pay, appointments to keep, groceries to purchase, and an endless stream of time-consuming annoyances—the car that needs service, the doctor's appointment, carpooling, sitting in traffic—we are starved for time, not food.

As manna was the remedy in the wilderness, Shabbat is the remedy for overscheduled lives.

B'shalach
Rabbi Amy Scheinerman, 2017

Traditionally, *Shirat HaYam* (*Song at the Sea*) is recited in the morning liturgy at the end of *P'sukei D'zimrah*. It is followed by *Nishmat* on Shabbat and festivals and by *Yishtabach* on weekdays. Therefore, *Shirat HaYam* constructs a bridge from *P'sukei D'zimrah* to *Shacharit*, or, viewed another way, sets the frame for the morning prayers to come. Our morning prayer are all about redemption past, present, and future. Our past experience of redemption is offered as a lens through which to view our redemptive experiences of the present and our hopes, dreams, and aspirations for the future.

Sadly, *Shirat HaYam* is not found in its traditional location in any of our Reform siddurim. (Given the wonderful tunes that enable people to learn its words and sing along, this is all the more a loss.) Some will say that the *shirah*'s triumphalist tone and the image of God as a "man of war" discomfit them. Yet these are images and themes that permeate Torah and Jewish liturgy. Why is this one especially egregious? The key to meaning is interpretation, and *Shirat HaYam* offers us a rich opportunity to delve into the experience of redemption, God's role in redemption, the human responsibility to bring redemption, the God-human partnership, and the risks one must take to bring about meaningful change. All these and more are implicit in Torah's account of our ancestors' crossing of the Reed Sea and our Sages' reflections on that account; the echoes of their voices are heard in *Shirat HaYam*.

B'shalach
Rabbi Mark Levin, 2018

In dangerous moments, how do masterful leaders advance their cause?

At Moses's call to his mission, God guarantees Israel will follow him: *V'shamu l'kolecha*, "They will listen to you" (Exod. 3:18). When Moses doubts God's hopeful promise, God sends signs authenticating Moses's appointment and dispatches needed help, Aaron. Moses receives what he needs: divine assurance, authority, and the necessary tool for success.

While Moses convinces the people (*vayaaminu*, "they had faith" [Exod. 14:31]), perilous moments sow doubt and fear, causing them to question their leaders' judgment. When Pharaoh pursues Israel and the Sea of Reeds lies before them, Torah says, "Greatly frightened, the Israelites cried out [*vayitzaku*] to Adonai" (Exod. 14:10). *Targum Onkelos* translates literally: "they cried out."

Although Torah does not claim that Moses cries out to God, it presents God's response as though Moses had implored the Divine—"Why do you cry out [*titzak*] to Me?" (Exod. 14:15)—employing the same verb.

Targum Onkelos and *Targum Yonatan* understand the people's response as a cry, but Moses's response as a prayer. Rashi follows suit: the people *shrei gevalt*, "raise their voices," but their leader trustingly turns to God. How is this sleight-of-hand interpretation accomplished?

In the *Babylonian Talmud Sotah* 37a, the Rabbis speak of the divine-human partnership in which God lays the foundations for human action: God famously chastises Moses for his long prayer while the people's lives are threatened. Nachshon ben Aminadab takes action; he dives into the water, spurring Moses to raise his arm and effect the redemption for which God has already established the conditions that make the splitting of the sea possible.

יתרו *Yitro*
(Exodus 18:1–20:23)

Yitro
Rabbi Jeffrey Ballon, z"l, 2010

Parashat Yitro usually inspires me to draw the attention of the congregation to the drama at Mount Sinai.

However, more recently I was reminded of the midrash that tells us the world was silent at the moment of revelation, suggesting two different ways to participate in the world: one is to be involved in the drama, and the other to be quiet in the mode of *lishmoa* ("listening").

I recently attended a Jewish men's retreat. I heard the retreat master say *shamati* ("I have heard you") as each participant finished speaking. Understanding the use of the verb *lishmoa* became an easier task. *Lishmoa*: listening, learning, and understanding all in one place.

At the opening of this *sidra* named after Jethro, these qualities of *lishmoa* are attributed to the man who is called by many names and who performs a multitude of functions. Jethro is variously described as court magician to Pharaoh, advisor to Moses, and father. When Moses flees to Midian where Jethro's daughters are watering the flock, Jethro, upon learning of the protective manner in which Moses engaged, offers Zipporah as a bride. Surely the influence of Jethro as a father-in-law changes the manner in which the Israelites are governed. In this opening verse Jethro, as a new member of Moses's family, adroitly *listens* before he gives advice.

As we read Torah again for the first time, let us attune our ears to the nuance of success.

Yitro
Rabbi Janice Garfunkel, z"l, 2011

God commands us to feel certain feelings. In *Parashat Yitro* we are commanded not to covet. Elsewhere, we are commanded to love God, to love our fellow, and not to hate or bear a grudge, among other things.

How can we be commanded to have certain feelings and not to have others? We learn in pastoral counseling and in society at large that feelings just are; they are neither right nor wrong, good nor bad. It is what we do that matters, not what we feel. Further, our society teaches that feelings just happen to us. Hence, we speak of "falling in love" and say that "love is blind." We can control what we do, but can we control what we feel?

Torah teaches that we can. We are commanded to love, and we are commanded not to covet. Torah teaches us that we do have some control over our feelings. This is good. We do not want to be buffeted about ruthlessly by forces beyond our control. Indeed, were our feelings completely independent of our will, how would any of us ever remain married? How could we be relied upon to love and care for our own children more than everyone else's?

Yitro
Rabbi Joshua Minkin, DMin, 2012

When Moses first encounters Jethro, Jethro is identified as *kohein Midyan*, "the priest of Midian" (Exod. 2:16). Following the redemption from Egypt, Moses encounters Jethro again (Exod. 18:1), and again we are told he is *kohein Midyan*. Jethro is the priest of another religion and the leader of another people, someone whose culture, religion, and ideas—and, perhaps to some extent, his values and priorities—are different from those of Moses. Yet he is Moses's father-in-law.

For the sake of the welfare of the nation, Moses is able to put these very great differences aside and evaluate Jethro's advice concerning the delegation of judgment on its own merits. Jethro's advice is sound and results in the administration of greater justice in Israel. One of the things that makes Moses a great leader is his ability to separate ideas from ideologies.

In this political season, there will be a wide spectrum of views concerning the direction our nation, states, and local communities should pursue. Let us acknowledge that many of us have strong partisan sympathies. While some are committed to always voting for a particular political party or never voting for a particular political party (*chas v'chalilah*, "God forbid"), let us not be deaf to every idea that is raised.

Let us evaluate the political ideas put forward on their own merits and, like Moses, accept good ideas regardless of their source.

Yitro
Rabbi Louis Rieser, 2013

Before meeting God at Mount Sinai, Moses meets Jethro as he approaches the Israelite camp. It is no coincidence that Moses leaves the camp in order to greet Jethro (Exod. 18:7). The *Y'rushalmi* (*Jerusalem Talmud Eiruvin* 8a) teaches that one who welcomes another person is greeting the *Shechinah*. When Moses and the elders welcome his father-in-law, the *Shechinah* accompanies them (*M'chilta Amalek* 3). The people's generous greeting of Jethro prepares the way for God to greet them at Mount Sinai.

Abraham knows the power of an open greeting. He keeps his tent open on all sides to greet any strangers who pass by. He learns this from the example of the Holy One, who "gives to everyone his wants and to everybody according to his needs. And not to good people alone, but also to wicked people and even to people who are worshiping idols" (*M'chilta Amalek* 3).

At a gathering for the eighteenth *yahrzeit* of Rabbi Shlomo Carlebach, I heard a variety of stories from the eclectic group in attendance. A moving aspect of the evening was that every person who spoke about Rabbi Carlebach told us how good it felt to be greeted by the rabbi as "Holy Brother" or "Holy Sister," regardless of whether one was Jewish or not, *frum* or not. Every individual's holy presence was acknowledged. Every story I heard was about how elevated and valued people felt when their holiness—their fundamental value—was acknowledged.

Every person who ventures into our synagogues, every person we meet, counsel, comfort, teach, and encounter, deserves a greeting that acknowledges their innate holiness. When we sincerely greet each person we meet by acknowledging their inner holiness, we merit, as did our ancestors, to stand at Mount Sinai.

Yitro
Rabbi Amy Scheinerman, 2014

We might wonder in what way "I am the Eternal your God" (Exod. 20:2) is a commandment. It seems more a statement of belief. But of course our beliefs beget behaviors.

Midrash Yalkut Shimoni tells us that God appeared to the Israelites in numerous guises, each befitting their need and their situation:

> "I am the Eternal your God." Because the Holy One appeared to [the Israelites] at the Reed Sea as a mighty man waging war (Exod. 15:3), at Sinai as a pedagogue teaching Torah, in the days of Solomon as a young man, and in the days of Daniel as an aged man full of mercy. The Holy One said: Because you see Me in many guises do not imagine that there are many gods, for I am the One who was with you at the Reed Sea, I am the One who is with you at Sinai, and I am the same everywhere. I am the Eternal your God. (*Yalkut Shimoni Yitro* 286)

This early Rabbinic invitation to revel in the images with which we think about and experience God is worth returning to now and again. It serves to remind us that we do not have a lock on God.

Even more importantly, however passionately we hold to our current understanding of or beliefs about God, they are only our current understandings and beliefs. As we grow and change, so will God in our minds and imaginations.

Yitro
Rabbi Amy Scheinerman, 2014

The long-running debate concerning precisely what was revealed at Sinai—the entire Torah? *Sefer D'varim* ("the Book of Deuteronomy")? *Aseret HaDib'rot* (the Ten Commandments)? just the first two commandments? only the first word, *anochi* ("I")?—culminates in the Chasidic teaching of Menachem Mendel of Rimanov that the Israelites heard only the silent *alef* of *anochi*. Revelation, Menachem Mendel teaches us, was an encounter with the Divine more than the conveyance of particular legal requirements.

P'sikta D'Rav Kahana (12:24) suggests several acronyms for *anochi* (Exod. 20:2). Rav interprets: "I Myself wrote it and gave it." Rabbi Berechiah offers: "I am your light, your crown, your grace," adding, "When you accept the Ten Commandments, I will be Adonai your God." Rav seems focused on the content of the revelation, while Rabbi Berechiah emphasizes the relationship between God and Israel that gives rise to revelation.

These two viewpoints can be seen as defining the endpoints on a spectrum of views about revelation and mitzvot. On one end are those who understand the content of Torah as divine fiat, the direct, unmediated communication of the *M'tzaveh* ("the One who gives commandments"), to whom Israel responded, *Naaseh v'nishma*, "We will do and obey." On the other end are those who understand mitzvot as the actualization of the covenantal relationship between God and Israel, arising from Israel's experience of the Divine Presence in this world.

In both cases, the mitzvot carry communal consciousness that defines us as a people in partnership with God, and a value system that sets boundaries and establishes aspirations for behavior we understand to be godly. The ongoing conversation between Israel, God, and Torah—conducted through study and interpretation—continuously reinforces our connection with God and one another.

Yitro
Rabbi Michael Boyden, 2015

There are three *parashiyot* in the Torah named after non-Jews: *Noach*, *Balak*, and *Yitro*. Interestingly, the very portion that deals with the revelation at Mount Sinai is named after a pagan Midianite priest!

Nachmanides tells us that Jethro was like Joseph's father-in-law, Poti-Phera, who used to "fatten calves for idol worship" (*Babylonian Talmud Sanhedrin* 82b). *That having been said*, Jethro proclaims, "I have found no god like the God of Israel" (*Midrash Tanchuma, Yitro*). He is thereby acknowledged as having converted, and Jewish tradition accords him special recognition.

The *M'chilta* tells us that Jethro was called by seven different names: "Yeter, Yitro, Chever, Chovav, Re'uel, Putiel, and Keni. *Yeter* because he caused an additional *parashah* to be added to the Torah. *Yitro* because he abounded in good deeds. *Chever* because he associated himself with God. *Chovav* because he was beloved of God. *Re'uel* because he was a friend of God. *Putiel* because he freed himself from idolatry, and *Keni* because he acquired the Torah for himself."

Now all of that is quite an achievement for a reformed idol worshiper! But then our tradition grants a special place to those who join our people, from Jethro the priest to Ruth the Moabite and the wives of both Joseph and Moses.

While rabbis may argue today about who should have the right to convert people to Judaism, some of our non-rabbinic ancestors in the Bible appear to have been able to manage pretty well without their services!

Yitro
Rabbi Charles Middleburgh, PhD, 2016

Yitro is a relatively short *parashah* dominated by the man after whom it is named, with the Ten Commandments at its heart. What else could there possibly be?

We know that Moses went down to Egypt at the age of eighty, and the conflict with Pharaoh and the exigencies of the Exodus must have exhausted energies already depleted by age. When he climbed Mount Sinai to receive the two tablets of stone from God, the physical effort required would have been enormous; yet we do not usually think about him as an old man climbing a mountain that, if Jebel Musa, is 2,228 meters high or, if Mount Catherine, is 2,629 meters high.

One additional unasked question looms large: How did he find his way to the right place? Climbing unfamiliar terrain without a map and the right gear can be a hazardous business at any age. An octogenarian climbing to the summit of a vast and lofty peak wearing sandals looks like a disaster waiting to happen.

We don't know how Moses found his way to the right place, only that he did so not once, but twice. Much is made of Moses's feats—dueling with Pharaoh, controlling a rebellious people, receiving the commandments—but little is written of his great feat in climbing Sinai in the first place! It mirrors our own lives where public acts attract attention and publicity, but the less obvious gain little or none. All too often the small and unnoticed acts that make the public ones succeed are forgotten in our fixation on outcomes; yet the carefully chosen path is just as important as the destination.

Yitro
Rabbi David Novak, 2017

Yitro, a Midianite priest, is a laudatory biblical character. As both Moses's father-in-law and the first non-Hebrew to sacrifice to Israel's God, he is portrayed kindly in giving Moses fatherly advice. Similarly, there are other notable biblical characters married to non-Israelites that our tradition reflects upon favorably. What we know about Judaism's long-held proscription of intermarriage developed much later when the Israelites returned from their Diaspora to build the Second Temple. Finding many intermarried to the local population, Ezra prescribed divorce.

Modernity is still debating Ezra's idea; who marries whom remains a sensitive issue. While the research is mixed, in "Under the *Chuppah*" (tinyurl.com/jrrqhw7), a new study from Brandeis, a majority (85 percent) of intermarried respondents who had a sole Jewish officiant at their wedding indicated that they were raising their children in the Jewish religion. The study holds the view that intermarriage may not be a net negative for Jewish life if a rabbi or cantor presides.

What then is our response to people who come to us when only one partner is Jewish? This research suggests that sole Jewish officiation, especially by Reform rabbis who accept patrilineal descent, may promote future Jewish involvement, including children being raised as Jews. Still, even with these findings, endogamy remains, as it should, the Jewish standard.

Intermarriage will always challenge traditional understandings. An aspect of leading in modernity is our ability to challenge and encourage those whom we serve to remain an active part of the Jewish community, no matter whom they marry.

Yitro
Rabbi Amy Scheinerman, 2018

"Next day, Moses sat as magistrate among the people, while the people stood about Moses from morning until evening. But when Moses's father-in-law saw how much he had to do for the people, he said, 'What is this thing that you are doing to the people? Why do you act alone, while all the people stand about you from morning until evening?'" (Exod. 18:13–14).

Much has been said about Yitro's contribution to Israelite judicial organization and efficiency.

Levi Yitzchak of Berditchev, however, focuses on the spiritual message. In *K'dushat Levi*, he notices that Moses sits while the people stand. For him, Yitro's question can be paraphrased: "Why do you make the people stand subservient before you while you sit imperiously before them?" For Levi Yitzchak, Moses is the model of a tzaddik who ought to encourage, facilitate, and nurture the spiritual growth of others. "By referring to Moses 'sitting' and the people 'standing,' Yitro points out that the present arrangement interferes with the people being able to progress through this tiresome arrangement in a spiritual way."

Moses explains that he had not initiated the arrangement. Rather, the people had come begging him to adjudicate their cases. He was doing the best he could.

The scene described in Exodus 18 coupled with Levi Yitzchak's commentary reminds us how body language, posture, and position—seemingly trivial and certainly unintentional—can convey unwanted messages, but also how, with skill and expertise, they can be marshaled to foster spiritual growth.

משפטים *Mishpatim*
(Exodus 21:1–24:18)

Mishpatim
Rabbi Janice Garfunkel, z"l, 2010

What is the role of today's Reform pulpit rabbi? In 1988, I attended a workshop at a Women's Rabbinic Network convention led by a Christian woman experienced in working with Christian pastors. Both she and we were surprised to learn that the profile of women rabbis in the room was quite different from that of the pastors with whom she was familiar. A great many pastors were adult children of alcoholics or had similar motivations to enter ministry, primarily in order to be nurturers. By contrast, our group of rabbis was motivated by their love of Judaism, learning, and Torah. Our personalities were more similar to those of academics or organizational leaders than to those of caregivers.

Parashat Mishpatim is a reminder of the traditional role of rabbis as *poskim*—halachic decision-makers. However, that seems not to be a central aspect of the Reform rabbinate today. Is the Reform rabbinate moving toward a role more similar to the role of a Christian pastor? Is it our task to nurture and provide care and concern to the individuals in our flock?

Or perhaps our roles are different still.

What do you think is the primary role of the Reform pulpit rabbi? Perhaps our role is both to inspire and facilitate greater Jewish knowledge and practice? To infuse more of our congregants' lives with Jewish values? Do our congregants agree as to what the role of the rabbi is?

Mishpatim
Rabbi Joshua Minkin, DMin, 2011

"You shall neither deceive a stranger nor oppress him, for you were strangers in the land of Egypt" (Exod. 22:20).

The *p'shat* of this text is a universal call for justice and social action. However, I suggest a *remez*: the stranger is within you, the very part of yourself you avoid or deny. For some of us it is (or was) aspects of our character we are ashamed of like alcoholism, drug addiction, or criminal behavior—some part we try not to acknowledge because it conflicts with or threatens key elements of the values we wish to embody.

We tend to project only on others this "stranger" we prefer not to see in ourselves. By distancing ourselves from these "bad" people, we avoid having to admit what we share. By segregating these traits to a repressed "negative" side (sometimes called "shadow"), we protect that part of our identity that is threatened (e.g., homophobia).

When we reject these parts of us, we reject ourselves. This can lead to depression and self-loathing. Projection can lead to bigotry and hatred.

As I read our verse, it calls us to meet the stranger within, to approach the "shadow" not out of fear and loathing, but through an understanding that we all were strangers at one point. Understood this way, Torah calls on us to stop the deception and accept who we are and, as we strive for goodness, understand that goodness comes in many forms.

Mishpatim
Rabbi Amy Scheinerman, 2012

Parashat Yitro ends, "And if you make for Me an altar of stones, do not build it of hewn stones; for wielding your tool upon them you have profaned them. Do not ascend My altar by steps, that your nakedness may not be exposed upon it" (Exod. 20:22).

Parashat Mishpatim opens, "These are the rules that you shall set before them" (Exod. 21:1), and proceeds to enumerate a lengthy compendium of laws on a wide-ranging array of topics: civil and criminal matters, cultic requirements, and moral instructions.

Midrash Yalkut Shimoni (1:271) observed that the laws of *Mishpatim* follow directly after the instruction concerning the altar: "In time to come when there will no longer be an altar, building a just society will be equivalent to bringing sacrifices."

We are accustomed to seeing Torah as a guide to building a society whose central pillar is compassionately administered justice. Do the laws of *Mishpatim* and mitzvot found elsewhere in Torah support this notion? Ramban explains that all the laws found in *Parashat Mishpatim* are extensions or amplifications of the tenth commandment, *lo tachmod* ("do not covet"). Our Rabbis debated whether *tachmod* refers to a state of mind or an actual act. Rashi resolved the dispute in his time by claiming it means stealing property. But Rambam, in basic agreement with Ramban, explained it as behavior that results from coveting. When we abide by the boundaries between what is ours and what is not, we act justly.

Yitro emphasizes two things in connection with the altar: hewn stones and nakedness. Hewn stones ensure care and deliberation—so too should justice be administered without rushing to judgment. The requirement that the priests ascend the steps dressed modestly reminds us that, above all, humility is required to exercise true justice.

Mishpatim
Rabbi Bill S. Tepper, 2013

Years ago, my family and I accompanied a social services van that drove during the night through the city delivering soup, sandwiches, and warm clothes to homeless people. Hours passed and the temperature dropped. How could anyone live outdoors and survive such deprivation? What would happen to these people without the assistance they received?

The Torah tells us, "For there will never cease to be needy ones in your land, which is why I command you: open your hand to the poor and needy kin in your land" (Deut. 15:11). *Parashat Mishpatim* adjures us, "You shall not wrong nor oppress a stranger, for you were strangers in the land of Egypt" (Exod. 22:20). In our day and age, the homeless are "strangers" to us. The *parashah* tells us ways to fulfill this mitzvah: "If you lend money to My people, to the poor among you, do not act toward them as a creditor; exact no interest from them" (Exod. 22:24). The same compassion that fuels *tzedakah* requires consideration for the poor in other situations as well: "If you take your neighbor's garment in pledge, you must return it to him before the sun sets; it is the only available clothing—it is what covers the skin. In what else shall [your neighbor] sleep?" (Exod. 22:25–26).

Consider this: "You shall not subvert the rights of your needy in their disputes" (Exod. 23:6). Note that the Torah says *evyoncha* ("your needy"). Yes, they are ours—our responsibility. One way we can fulfill the Torah's mandate is by providing space to sleep in our synagogues, preparing meals, and sharing our resources with the homeless. *Mishna Pirkei Avot* 1:5 adjures, "Let your house be open wide; let the poor be members of your household."

This year, *Mishpatim* falls on Shabbat Sh'kalim. The *maftir* (Exod. 30:11–16) details the Torah's command to contribute a half-shekel toward the maintenance of the Tabernacle. Why such a paltry sum? To teach that everyone must be involved; everyone must participate in the life of the community, in the lives of others.

Mishpatim
Rabbi Amy Scheinerman, 2014

Mishpatim opens with the disturbing reality of slavery in the ancient world: "If you acquire a Hebrew slave, he shall serve six years; in the seventh year he shall go free, without payment" (Exod. 21:2).

The Chasidic teacher Asher Tzvi of Ostrog (d. 1817), in *Ma'ayan HaChochmah*, interprets this verse about concrete physical reality in purely spiritual terms. He recalls a teaching of his master, Dov Ber, the Magid of Mezeritch, stating that *shaah* ("hour") in Gen. 4:5 may also be understood as "turning": God does not "turn" to Cain and his sacrifice. Combining the two meanings, "hour" and "turning," Asher Tzvi teaches us that there are those who succeed in turning their lives around in only an hour, such as the executioner of Rabbi Chananiah ben Teradion in the *Babylonian Talmud Avodah Zarah* 10b. But he also reminds us that the Sages actually relativized the statement: the executioner acquires "his world," not "the world." The Rabbis knew that one cannot jump the spiritual ladder, skipping all six rungs and landing on the top on the seventh rung all at once. If you do pursue the express method—without investing the time and work to study and improve yourself—you will have gone free, but *yeitzei l'chofshi chinam*—you will go out to a freedom worth nothing. On a spiritual level, Exodus 21:2 teaches us that true spiritual ascent takes time and effort.

In a society promising quick fixes, Asher Tzvi reminds us that there is no shortcut to religious enlightenment and moral development. These take time, effort, patience, and diligence.

Our beloved colleague, Rabbi Rabbi Janice Garfunkel, z"l would have approved this message. In her life, she exemplified one who did not take shortcuts, but rather invested heavily of her time and effort to grow as a Jew, as a human being, as a mother, and as a rabbi. *Zeicher tzaddeket livrachah.*

Mishpatim: Shabbat Sh'kalim
Rabbi Stephen Wylen, 2015

The Torah says, "You must not eat flesh torn by beasts in the field; you shall cast it to the dogs" (Exod. 22:30). This curious sentence about *t'reif* meat thrown to dogs opens the door to a wider discussion about how we think about and improve our own behavior.

M'chilta D'Rabbi Yishmael on Exodus 11:7 teaches that dogs receive this treat as a reward because they did not bark at the Israelites as we departed from slavery in Egypt. The dogs overcame their natural inclination.

The Sages expressed a concern. They worried that obsessively working on overcoming our evil inclinations was, in a sense, in itself a natural inclination to be overcome. The sage Samuel, who deprecated self-mortification, termed excessive fasting a sin. Resh Lakish agrees: "The pious do good to their souls rather than punish their bodies" (*Babylonian Talmud Taanit* 11ab).

Rabbi Meir Yechiel of Ostrovcha teaches us that it is foolish to even attempt to entirely overcome our evil desires. We as humans are perfectly capable of doing good. We possess a pure soul and many good inclinations, and we need to strive to keep our soul pure and focus on the good within us, instead of meditating overmuch on the bad.

This theme recurs in other Chasidic teachings. We should not dwell on the bad that we could do, but on the good of which we are capable. The quickest way to improvement is to focus on what we do best, and do it. If one is always trying to overcome one's worst capabilities, then one will spend all of one's time in frustration and depression. Leave what you cannot do well to others, and focus on your strengths!

Mishpatim
Rabbi Michael Boyden, 2016

The thunder and lightning of Mount Sinai as portrayed in the previous *parashah* (*Yitro*) may be the stuff of which Hollywood movies are made, but we cannot live our lives with that much drama. And so we move on to *V'eileh hamishpatim*, "And these are the rules" (Exod. 21:1), with the *vav* reminding us, as Rashi put it, that although our *parashah* may lack the fireworks of the previous one, it is nevertheless still part of the same revelation.

Parashat Mishpatim is full of mitzvot, ranging from the call to release Hebrew slaves in the seventh year to the demand that we provide compensation in the event of our having burned somebody else's crops. Now that may not sound like the stuff of which holiness is made, but, as Jonathan Sacks put it, quoting the architect Mies van der Rohe, "God is in the details."

Perhaps one of the key features of Judaism as a religion is the fact that holiness is not evoked primarily through spiritual experiences, but rather through practical deeds in this world. Hence *naaseh* ("we will do") takes precedence over *v'nishma* ("we will understand") (Exod. 24:7).

More than two thousand years before Abraham Lincoln, our *parashah* was already asserting that slaves had rights. Deuteronomy goes even further and insists that those released should be given of their master's flock, threshing floor, and vat (Deut. 15:14).

Ultimately the object of all of these mitzvot is expressed in the words "You shall be holy to Me" (Exod. 22:30). It doesn't say "You are holy," but rather "You shall be holy." Holiness is an aspiration that we may not always live up to, but that doesn't mean that we should ever cease trying.

Mishpatim
Rabbi Ruth Adar, 2017

"If you lend money to My people, to the poor among you, do not act toward them as a creditor; exact no interest from them" (Exod. 22:24).

This verse establishes the top of the Rambam's famous ladder of giving: it begins with *im talveh* (if you lend), not with *im titein* (if you give). Why is lending the preferred form of assisting the needy?

The clue is in the word *k'nosheh* (like a creditor). A creditor is in a position of advantage over a debtor. And yet are we not all equal before our Creator?

Rabbi David Kasher points out in his *d'rash* "A Lender Be" that Rabbeinu Bachya affirms Rambam, saying, "The loan is greater than the gift because it strengthens the recipient and he need not be ashamed of it." He then quotes *Sh'mot Rabbah* 31:15:

> "When you lend money to my people, to the poor among you . . ." All the creations of the Holy borrow from one another. The day borrows [time] from the night, and the night borrows [time] from the day. . . . The moon borrows [light] from the stars, and the stars borrow [light] from the moon. . . . Wisdom borrows from Understanding, and Understanding borrows from Wisdom. . . . The Heavens borrow from the Earth, and the Earth borrows from the Heavens.

Borrowing and lending is the nature of creation: manure lends its nutrients to the soil, the crop borrows moisture and nitrogen from the soil, the cow eats the crop and leaves its manure on the ground. All creations of the Holy borrow and lend from one another, and we are no different, borrowing and lending equally before God.

Mishpatim: Shabbat Sh'kalim
Rabbi Amy Scheinerman, 2018

Torah is light on law until we come to *Parashat Mishpatim*, which deluges us with *mitzvot chukim u'mishpatim*, including the ever-confounding *lex talionis*: "Eye for eye, tooth for tooth, hand for hand, foot for foot, burn for burn, wound for wound, bruise for bruise" (Exod. 21:24–25). While we are accustomed to explaining that since ancient times Jewish courts have rejected a literal interpretation in favor of monetary restitution, a question remains: Whose eye, tooth, hand, or foot?

The Talmud calculates the restitution payment through valuation of the victim as if a slave: the difference between the victim's value prior to the injury and after determines what the offender owes the victim. There is, however, an interesting dissenting opinion expressed in a baraita in the *Babylonian Talmud Bava Kama* 84a:

> Rabbi Eliezer said: "'Eye for eye' should be interpreted literally." Could it enter your mind [that Torah intends] an actual eye? Doesn't Rabbi Eliezer [agree with] the *Tannaim*? Rav Ashi assures us that Rabbi Eliezer concurs regarding monetary compensation, but holds that the offender does not pay the value of the victim's eye; rather, he pays a ransom based on the value of his own eye.

What is at stake in the difference? As the two stories that follow in the Gemara illustrate, valuation based on slavery is demeaning. We might add, as well, that the offender will likely value his own limbs more highly than those of others—whether or not a slave trader or buyer would—and therefore more readily appreciate the need for compensation.

Mishpatim
Rabbi Joshua Minkin, DMin, 2018

"You shall not oppress a *ger*, for you know the feelings of the *ger*, for you were *gerim* in the land of Egypt" (Exod. 23:9). *Gerim* in the Bible are sojourners, temporary residents, non-citizens. They are undocumented aliens, as my grandparents were. Over and over again we are commanded not to mistreat the *ger*, even to love them (Lev. 19:34). They are considered to be among the powerless, which includes widows and orphans (Exod. 22:21–24), whom we must look after.

Yet we hear: "They're bringing drugs," "They're bringing crime," "They're rapists"—all uttered without a shred of evidence. Words of hate spew across our screens as videos show people held in cages and children crying as they are separated from their parents.

Rabbi Jonathan Sacks writes in "Loving the Stranger" that once we are no longer vulnerable ourselves, we risk forgetting:

> It is terrifying in retrospect to grasp how seriously the Torah took the phenomenon of xenophobia, hatred of the stranger. It is as if the Torah were saying with the utmost clarity: reason is insufficient. Sympathy is inadequate. Only the force of history and memory is strong enough to form a counterweight to hate. . . . You know the heart of the stranger because you were once a stranger in the land of Egypt. If you are human,

so is he. If he is less than human, so are you. You must fight the hatred in your heart as I once fought the greatest ruler and the strongest empire in the ancient world on your behalf. I made you into the world's archetypal strangers so that you would fight for the rights of strangers. (The Office of Rabbi Sacks, February 2, 2008, http://rabbisacks.org/covenant-conversation-5768-mishpatim-loving-the-stranger/)

תרומה *T'rumah*
(Exodus 25:1–27:19)

T'rumah
Rabbi Amy Scheinerman, 2010

Parashat T'rumah's details, like the *Aron* (Ark) itself, contain treasure. Here are two nuggets of gold:

"Overlay [the Ark] with pure gold—overlay it inside and out—make upon it a gold molding round about" (Exod. 25:11). Why cover the inside of the Ark with gold? No one will ever see it, because the ark is sealed and never opened. The *Babylonian Talmud Yoma* 72b, comments, "Any Torah scholar whose interior is not like his exterior is no Torah scholar." Slick facade lacking substance or façade covering a lack of integrity—we have all seen it in people who assume positions of leadership. Talmud reminds us to make sure it does not describe us.

"Make for it [the Ark of acacia wood] a rim of gold round about" (Exod. 25:24). The *Babylonian Talmud Yoma* 72b, comments, "Rabbi Yochanan said: There were three crowns: of the Altar, of the Ark, and of the Table. The one of the Altar [representing the priesthood], Aaron deserved and received. The one of the Table [representing royalty], David deserved and received. The one of the Ark [representing Torah] is still available, and whoever wants it may come and receive it." We can continually receive Torah as we continually increase our learning. As Hillel taught (*Mishnah Pirkei Avot* 2:5), "Fix a time for study."

Thus the Gemara continues, "Rabbi Yochanan pointed out a contradiction. It is written *zar*, yet we read it *zir* [crown or wreath]: if he deserves it, it becomes a wreath for him; if not, it remains alien to him."

T'rumah
Rabbi Amy Scheinerman, 2011

"Take for Me offerings from every person whose heart is so moved" (Exod. 25:2).

Does intention matter in the performance of rituals? Is it sufficient to do as prescribed, or must our hearts and minds be aligned with the rite observed? The Rabbis vacillate on this issue, sometimes leaning toward validation through proper performance, and at other times emphasizing intention.

Midrash Tanchuma comments:

> They fashioned with [the surplus offerings] the hammered gold overlay for the Holy of Holies. You find that the Holy One of Blessing chose two offerings [*t'rumot*]: the offering for the building of the *Mishkan* and the priestly offering. The priestly offering [was given to them] so they would become students of Torah. Rabbi Yannai said, "Any priest who is not a student of Torah, it is permitted to eat it on his grave."

Rabbi Yannai's disdain for an unlearned priest is palpable: Without Torah learning, he likely does not collect the offering properly and does not know it must be eaten in a state of *tahorah* (purity); hence it is not truly *t'rumah*, and therefore others may eat it in a cemetery—on his very grave! Without Torah learning, the priest cannot be trusted to take the offering for God ("for Me"). Knowledge is needed for intentionality, and intentionality is needed for *t'rumah* to be consumed properly.

The Ishbitzer Rebbe, in *Mei HaShiloach*, goes further, commenting that "the *t'rumah* never had any *k'dushah* [holiness] as far as [the unlearned *kohein*] was concerned . . . that is, the entire greatness of the *k'dushah* of *t'rumah* is if it is separated for the sake of heaven." Holiness requires intentionality.

T'rumah
Rabbi Stephen Wylen, 2012

"You shall make for Me a sanctuary, and I shall dwell within it" (Exod. 25:8).

When the Reformers came to Rabbi Samuel Mohilever seeking his support for the use of an organ in the synagogue, he replied: Let me tell you something that I saw recently in Bialystok. A fire burned down the house of one of the wealthiest men in the city. All that he had was lost. The family was devastated. Now this man had a brother who was a great musician, but lacking in common sense. He came to console the family, saying, "You have lovely voices. If you would weep in rhythm, and each of you would harmonize with the others, you could sound really nice." Concluded the Mohilever: The Jewish people are pouring out their hearts to God, and you want them to harmonize with an organ? (*Iturei Torah* 3:210).

As a rabbinical student, I attended Lincoln Square and other synagogues to master Modern Orthodox worship. Then one Shabbat I went to a neighborhood Hungarian *landsmanschaft* shul. I realized that the Modern Orthodox had become "Reform," organizing their worship in pleasing unity. I am told that in German, *grosse Synagoge* used to be a term for any chaotic and leaderless project.

Rabbi Mohilever's words reflect an underlying philosophical difference between the aesthetically pleasing worship of Jewish modernists and the *balagan* of old-school daveners, who view prayer as a personal petition to a God who responds to individual pleas. We post-Enlightenment Rationalists join Maimonides in viewing prayer as praise, introspection, and self-exhortation. This meaningful distinction leads to stylistic differences.

T'rumah
Rabbi Stephen Wylen, 2013

"You shall make the planks for the Tabernacle of acacia wood, upright" (Exod. 26:15).

> And where, indeed, would the Israelites have found the wood to make planks when they were in the middle of the desert? The Torah says, "the planks," not just "planks." This refers to the planks that Father Jacob made long ago. He said to himself, "Someday my children will build a Tabernacle for the service of God, and they will need wooden planks for that service. I will make them the planks, and they will be available when needed." The planks made by Father Jacob were preserved by the Israelites in Egypt. They brought them out with them in the Exodus. When the planks were needed, they were ready. (*Sefer HaAggadah*, based on *Tanchuma T'rumah*).

Like Father Jacob, we also want future generations to carry on with Judaism. Father Jacob needed acacia wood to make his planks. Those who follow us will need our help: They will need to find the materials for the continuation of Judaism ready at hand for them to use as needed. What "planks" are you making so that the future generations will have what they need Jewishly? What resources are you applying to the foundations of Judaism?

T'rumah
Rabbi Michael Boyden, 2014

The building of the *Mishkan* in the wilderness did not come about as a result of one major naming gift, but is rather a joint effort. As the Torah puts it, "You shall accept gifts for Me from everyone whose heart is so moved" (Exod. 25:2).

Why was there a need to build a *Mishkan* in the first place? Did the Children of Israel also suffer from an edifice complex? Perhaps the answer lies in what happened at Mount Sinai: Moses was slow in coming down from the mountain, and so the people in their insecurity turned to Aaron in search of "a god who will go before us" (Exod. 32:1). Once the *Mishkan* is built, "the cloud of Adonai would rest over the Tabernacle by day, and fire would appear in it by night, in the sight of all of the House of Israel throughout their journeys" (Exod. 40:38). The *Mishkan* is the Israelites' travel insurance!

The problem with any religious building is the fact that some people mistakenly believe that God is to be found specifically there. Perhaps that is why some stick *kvitelach* ("notes") in the crannies of the Western Wall. However, ours is a religion that generally sanctifies time rather than space. We take twenty-five hours and turn them into Shabbat. We praise God for our having reached "this time"—not "this place."

On occasion, we need to be reminded of the words of Isaiah: "Heaven is My throne. . . . What kind of a house could you build Me?" (Isa. 66:1). As Samson Raphael Hirsch wrote, paraphrasing Exod. 25:8, "Let them make their lives a sanctuary and I shall then dwell within them."

T'rumah
Rabbi David Novak, 2015

One might ask: Why does Torah include an abundance of exquisite detail in *Parashat T'rumah*? Why such vivid descriptions for every measurement, decoration, color, fabric, and material? To my mind, this richness of detail allows us to imagine the magnificent place for God to dwell among the people.

Detail is especially important today, as so many people have a difficult time accessing God's reality. *T'rumah* allows us to concretize God's presence among the Israelites and, hopefully, in our lives.

To what might this be compared? Think of places you have never been, yet which are familiar to you. For example, the set of *The Honeymooners*, *I Love Lucy*, *The Brady Bunch*, or *Seinfeld*. Many of us remember the kitchen, the living room, the door where the characters entered and exited; yet none of us has ever physically stood in any of these spaces. How many of us can draw a blueprint of *The Addams Family* home from the sets we saw on TV?

These quondam sets remain vivid in our memory because we were able to see them and experience them, time and again. That is how Torah helps us in *Parashat T'rumah*. Setting the stage for God's dwelling place among the wandering people, we can read about this richness of detail as the exquisite decoration for God's presence not only in the lives of our ancestors, but in our lives as well.

T'rumah
Rabbi Louis Rieser, 2016

The Torah commands us to build a *Mishkan* within which God will dwell. After the Temple was destroyed, we needed to define this commandment in a new way. Many commentators state that Torah's command to make a *Mishkan* should be understood metaphorically: instead of referring to a building, *Mishkan* refers to a person. According to Rabbi Chaim of Volozhin, there is no truer Temple than the God-given soul of the individual (*Nefesh HaChayim* 4:1). In what way is our soul God-given?

Assuming that the souls of most adults are familiar with sin, and therefore defiled to a certain extent, the Talmud teaches, "The world endures only for the sake of the breath of schoolchildren, for their Torah is learned in purity, undefiled by sin" (*Babylonian Talmud Shabbat* 119b). How can we as grown-ups safeguard the purity of childhood in order to preserve the *Mishkan* within us? Rabbi Abraham Isaac Kook, in a commentary on *Chayei Sarah*, warns that society coarsens us, "by the spirit-numbing reality of the factory floor and the cynical manipulations of greedy corporations" (*Sapphire from the Land of Israel*, pp. 230–31). Our task, particularly as rabbis, is to nurture the childhood qualities of purity and innocence within us.

Rabbi Joseph Soloveitchik teaches that "God created the world to reside in it rather than reside in transcendence" (*Chumash Mesoras Harav—Chumash with Commentary Based on the Teachings of Rabbi Joseph B. Soloveitchik*, p. 226). Reminding ourselves of God's presence in the world allows us to connect to our childhood spiritual gifts.

T'rumah
Rabbi Stephen Wylen, 2017

Progressive Jews divide the Bible into the "interesting" parts and the "boring" parts, unlike a teaching I recall: "Whoever spends a whole day meditating on 'These are the five kings who ruled in Moab before Israel entered the Land' (Gen. 36:31) is deserving of great praise."

This week's portion, *T'rumah*, represents the great shift into the "boring" stuff. From *B'reishit* to *Mishpatim* we have read almost all of our foundational stories and great laws of social justice importance. From *T'rumah* until the Book of Numbers, the Torah deals with the Sanctuary, the sacrifices, the priesthood, and laws of holiness and purity.

It would seem that our ancestors who edited the Torah were not aware that this could be "boring." Why not?

Despite the contemporary tendency to turn the Torah into "the story of us," the central theme of the Torah is neither us nor God, but the relationship between us and God. The *b'rit* (covenant) is the central figure of the Torah. With this in mind, *Parashat T'rumah* represents an exciting transition. The Jewish people are preparing to build a home for God's presence on earth, in our midst. This seals the *b'rit*.

How seriously do we take the *b'rit* in our own Jewish lives? What can we do to make a home for the *Shechinah*, not only just in our spiritual life but also in our society?

T'rumah
Rabbi Michael Boyden, 2018

It's no easy thing to raise money!

This point is emphasized by the opening words of our *parashah*: "Tell the Israelites to take donations. You shall take donations for Me from everyone whose heart so moves him" (Exod. 25:2). The word "take" appears twice. People don't generally give unless they are pressured to do so. Abarbanel idealistically explains, "The fund raiser should not ask for a specific donation, but should take what the donor offers."

There is a discernible difference between how the Israelites behaved when they built the Golden Calf and their attitude when it came to erecting the Sanctuary in the wilderness. In the former case we are told, "And all of the people took off the gold rings that were in their ears and brought them to Aaron" (Exod. 32:3). However, when it came to the *Mishkan*, the donations had to be taken! In his commentary on Exod. 35:5, Karo says that Moses was angry with the people and told them they should be just as eager to fulfill a mitzvah as they had been to transgress. In the end, Moses manages to raise sufficient money to build the *Mishkan*—or almost as much.

Rabbi Yosei tells us that "an ark of fire, a table of fire, and a menorah of fire descended from heaven" (*Babylonian Talmud M'nachot* 29a). Rabbi Yosei reminds us of another important aspect of communal giving: although the Israelites raised enough money to construct the building, they needed God's help (and ours) to reach completion.

תצוה *T'tzaveh*
(Exodus 27:20–30:10)

T'tzaveh: Shabbat Zachor
Rabbi Stephen Wylen, 2010

"Oil of olives, crushed for lighting" (Exod. 27:20). Rashi says, "Crushed for light, and not for depression," *katit lamaor, v'lo katit lam'nachot* (literally, "for the menorah, and not for the meal offering").

Rashi's comment is often taken out of context and presented as a saying of popular psychology. This makes only sense when we recall that the olive, whenever mentioned in the *Tanach*, is a symbol for the Jewish people. We have suffered much in our history, but in response to suffering we became a light to the nations.

How do you respond when life has crushed you? Torah teaches us that first we must acknowledge, not deny: "Yes, I am crushed." Then we must be determined to respond positively: "I know that I am crushed, but I am determined to make some good of this."

Our response to life's disappointments is in our hands. We do not believe that our crushing is desired by God, nor determined by the will of God. However, we can turn it into the service of God.

Whenever, in my life and my rabbinate, I have been crushed, I meditate on this verse and its Rashi, and I let that determine my course of action.

T'tzaveh
Rabbi Amy Scheinerman, 2012

T'tzaveh opens, "You shall bring forward your brother Aaron, with his sons, from among the Israelites, to serve Me as priests" (Exod. 28:1).

Sh'mot Rabbah 37:3 comments that this may be compared to a king who summons his friend into lifelong service to protect him. The friend-protector is not permitted to leave the palace and eats what the king leaves over. So Aaron, from among the people, was designated as the lifelong protector, and Lev. 21:12 and 2:3 confirm that he remains in the Sanctuary and eats what is left of the meal offering.

Aaron is entrusted with the core rites that ensure the well-being of the nation, just as our elected leaders are entrusted with the core rights of Americans. As long as our elected leaders serve in office, they are, just like Aaron, bound to seek the well-being of their constituents and the nation. We need committed public servants, not seasoned politicians who, the moment they are elected, begin campaigning for the next election. As we enter another presidential election season, we are reminded that Aaron was designated to serve and ensure the well-being of the people.

Exodus 29:20 describes the investiture of the priests. Blood of the sacrifices was applied to their right ears, thumbs, and big toes. The right side implies conscience and morality. Nahum Sarna notes, "The singling out of the ear, hand, and foot may well symbolize the idea that the priest is to attune himself to the divine word and be responsive to it in deed and direction in life" (*The JPS Torah Commentary: Exodus*, p. 189). How easily that can be translated to the modern political realm and the responsibility of our elected officials.

T'tzaveh
Rabbi David Novak, 2013

On Shabbat Zachor, the Sabbath of Memory immediately preceding Purim, we read, "Blot out Amalek's memory but remember him: do not forget" (Deut. 25:19). We recall how Amalek preyed on the weakest people in the back of the multitude of Israelites moving slowly from Egypt to the Promised Land, how they took advantage of the elderly, the weak, and the slow. Often the Torah is read as history; yet we know that historicity, as we understand it today, was not necessarily the agenda of the biblical author(s). They meant the texts to be read with historical lenses, irrespective of whether there is or was historical proof that an event actually happened. This raises an important question for us: do these accounts that we read time and again need to be historically factual to be meaningful, or is it more important that their repeated tellings allow us to glean from them the wisdom to shape our actions?

The Exodus is a case in point. We are told to remember what it was like to be slaves in Egypt; that we have in our very DNA the experience of oppression. This intimate knowledge is expected to guide us to treat fairly the widow, the orphan, and the stranger. So, too, with Amalek. Being commanded to remember the mortal enemy of the Jewish people—immediately before Purim—reminds us that evil always lurks close by; it is part of the human condition. We cannot let it paralyze us. We must be moved and we must move.

T'tzaveh
Rabbi Amy Scheinerman, 2014

The *Kohein Gadol* wears an elaborate uniform, from head to foot. Each piece is described in detail in Torah, and many of the pieces have symbolic meaning or a ritual function. Taken all together, the *Kohein Gadol* must have been a spectacular sight garbed in full regalia, the sun glinting off the jeweled breastplate, ephod, headpiece frontlet, and golden bells that adorned the hem of his garment.

When I was at Hebrew Union College–Jewish Institute of Religion, I witnessed a discussion concerning whether rabbis should wear something distinctive, as Catholic and Episcopal priests do, to identify them as rabbis. Of course, rabbis are not Levitical priests and do not function in any way our tradition recognizes as priestly. But are we clergy members "priests" in a more generic way? As I recall the conversations, the reasoning in favor of a "uniform" or identifying garment for rabbis involved recognition and status. In an age when *k'vod harav* is as much the exception as the rule, I understood why this discussion was taking place.

The *Babylonian Talmud* (*Shabbat* 31a) recounts that once a gentile was so awed by the *Kohein Gadol*'s attire that he came to Hillel prepared to convert so that he could be made *Kohein Gadol* and don the vestments. Contemplating the *Kohein Gadol*'s elaborate and stunning garb, I wonder what we can do to elevate rabbis as teachers of Torah in the eyes of the community, in order to inspire our people to learn Torah.

T'tzaveh
Rabbi Amy Scheinerman, 2015

"These are the vestments they are to make [for the High Priest]: a breastpiece, an ephod, a robe, a fringed tunic, a headdress, and a sash. They shall make those sacral vestments for your brother Aaron and his sons, for priestly service to Me" (Exod. 28:4).

In a world of obsessive attention to fashion and wardrobe malfunctions, we must admit that clothing conveys messages concerning position, status, self-image, or a combination of all of the above. Polonius said, "For the apparel oft proclaims the man" (*Hamlet*, act 1, scene 3).

Our Rabbis had a different view. Based on Torah's juxtaposition of sections on sacrifices and priestly vestments, the Sages (*Babylonian Talmud Z'vachim* 88b) explain each element as a means for atonement: the *k'tonet* ("coat"), recalling Joseph's *k'tonet pasim*, atones for bloodshed; the *michnasayim* ("breeches") atone for lewdness; the *mitznefet* ("headdress") atones for arrogance; the *avneit* ("sash") atones for impure thoughts; the *choshen mishpat* ("breastpiece") atones for neglect of justice; the ephod atones for idolatry; the *m'il* ("robe") atones for *lashon hara*; and the *tzitz* ("headplate") atones for brazenness. Imagine if we ascribed meaning to each garment we donned, permitting it to remind us of a value we cherish!

Similarly, we find (*Babylonian Talmud Shabbat* 10a) that Rava bar Rav Huna donned fine shoes to pray. In contrast, Rava removed his cloak and prayed like a servant before his master. Which is correct: to dress up, or to dress down? Dressing up can remind us of the infinite potential of the human soul for growth. Dressing down can elevate our souls through humility. Clearly, apparel can shape the soul.

T'tzaveh
Rabbi Amy Scheinerman, 2016

The most prominent myths of cultures around the world and throughout time evolved around the acquisition of fire and its usage to punish, reward, purify, and destroy. Many worship rituals—involving sacrifice, dance, storytelling, and much more—are centered on fire. In fact, it is surprising that our Creation stories do not entail fire.

> You shall further instruct the Israelites to bring you clear oil of beaten olives for lighting for kindling lamps regularly. Aaron and his sons shall set them up in the *Ohel Mo-eid* [Tent of Meeting] outside the *parochet* [curtain] that is over the *Eidut* [(the Ark of) the Pact], [to burn] evening to morning before Adonai (*Exod.* 27:20–21).

The *ner tamid* (eternal light) hanging before every synagogue ark is understood to symbolize the lamps in the *Mishkan* ("Tabernacle"), signifying that every *beit k'neset* ("synagogue") is a *mikdash m'at* ("small sanctuary"). Rav Sheishet cites a baraita (*Babylonian Talmud Shabbat* 22b) that teaches that the light was an *eidut*, ("a testimony,") to all humanity that the *Shechinah* dwelled with Israel. How so? Rav explained:

> Every evening a priest would measure equal amounts of oil into each cup to keep it burning all night, yet the *ner maaravi* [there is a debate concerning precisely which of the seven lamps this is] burned continuously, and its flame was used to relight the others the following evening.

The *Babylonian Talmud Yoma* 39a, reports that this miracle ended forty years before the destruction of the Second Temple. (The Arch of Titus symbolizes the defeat of Jerusalem by depicting the menorah being carried away to Rome.)

Fire is not only a biblical avatar of God and a means by which Israel serves God, but also the barometer of Israel's relationship with God.

T'tzaveh: Shabbat Zachor
Rabbi Joshua Minkin, DMin, 2017

Coming off an election campaign that seemed to have more surprises than any Purim celebration, many feel that we now have a leader reminiscent of Haman. For them, our portion may offer a glimmer of hope.

In a biblical version of "clothes make the man," *T'tzaveh* spends much time discussing the dress of the High Priest. "Make holy garments for Aaron and his sons so they may minister to Me" (Exod. 28:4). In the context of an inherited priesthood, the quality of the person seemed to matter little. It was the role that defined him, not he who elevated the role, and that role could not be performed without the trappings of office—the *bigdei kodesh*. These were so important that Josephus explains that the Romans kept control of the priestly garments in order to keep the Jews compliant. The priestly garments seemed to convey sanctity to those who wore them, rendering them fit to serve Adonai.

We no longer have leaders attired in *bigdei kodesh*. Let the president's oath of office stand in their place and let us hope that it gives the new president the temperament, wisdom, and counsel to lead the country responsibly and with righteousness and integrity, despite his vile rhetoric during the campaign.

In discussing the ritual of anointing the right earlobe, thumb, and big toe, *Etz Hayim* refers to a midrash on Exod. 29:20 "that a *kohen* must listen to the people, act on their behalf, and go forth among them" (p. 513). If the new president begins in this way, it would augur well for the country.

T'tzaveh
Rabbi Stephen Wylen, 2018

The Torah says, "This is the daily offering, forever, at the entrance to the Tent of Meeting, before God" (Exod. 29:42). A Chasid was pouring out his troubles before Rabbi Abraham Joshua Heschel of Apt. At the end of their conversation the rebbe said to the Chasid, "You should know that an even greater tragedy than all that has befallen you occurred today; the daily sacrifice was not offered because our Temple lies in ruins."

Superficially this *meise* ("story") may indicate a lack of compassion on the part of the rebbe. However, if we listen to the response from the standpoint of the two characters in the story, we discover that the rebbe spoke words of comfort. In Kabbalah, the suffering of the individual Jew is a reflection of the suffering of the Jewish people, which in turn is a reflection of the suffering of God, who is exiled from the *Shechinah*. The cosmic dimension of individual suffering lends it meaning.

How good can we expect things to be when Israel is in exile from our land and the *Shechinah* is in exile from the Godhead? Our sufferings, when we respond rightly, help to bring closer the messianic age of redemption.

Kabbalah helps us see the connecting threads that bind the individual, the social, and the cosmic levels of being. Our responses to suffering today often focus on the individual. The Apter Rebbe teaches us a path to consolation by reaching beyond ourselves.

כי תשא   *Ki Tisa*
(Exodus 30:11–34:35)

Ki Tisa
Rabbi Amy Scheinerman, 2010

"This is what everyone who is entered into the records shall pay: a half-shekel by the sanctuary weight—twenty *gerah*s to the shekel—a half-shekel as an offering to Adonai. . . . The rich shall not pay more and the poor shall not pay less than half a shekel when giving Adonai's offering as expiation for your persons" (Exod. 30:13, 30:15). The half-shekel is a nominal amount, but all matters related to money have the potential to be either divisive or unifying. We have all seen this in families, in synagogues, and in civic society.

At a time of economic uncertainty, this is doubly true. Thus, Rabbi Elimelech of Lizensk (1717–86) taught, "Money is fire. Like fire it can destroy and annihilate, or illuminate and warm, depending on how it is used."

Menachem Mendel, the Kotzker Rebbe (1787–1859) explained: Moses could not understand how a mere coin could serve a person as "a ransom for his soul to God." God answered him by showing him a "coin of fire." God was saying that when people perform even a modest act of charity with the fire of passion and enthusiasm, they are indeed giving a piece of their soul. As we learn to live on less, we must learn to appreciate each act of generosity—a good idea at all times, but a necessity now.

Midrash HaGadol says that the essence of the half-shekel mitzvah is that each person should contribute half the value of the dominant coin at the time, be it a *takal,* a *selah,* or a *darkon.* A Chasidic master asked, "Why not a complete coin? To teach that no person is complete unto oneself." Only by joining with another can a person become a whole being.

In the case of the half-shekel, two half-shekels combined are not sufficient either. The contributions of the entire community are needed: the creativity, strength, enthusiasm, participation, and caring of everyone is needed for the Tabernacle to function properly. So, too, for our institutions and communities. Our task is to encourage everyone to see that their half-shekel is worth intrinsically more than its nominal monetary value.

Ki Tisa
Rabbi Louis Rieser, 2012

Sh'mot Rabbah 42 teaches us to advocate for those at risk, as Moses advocated for the Jews in the story of the Golden Calf. Safely in heaven, Moses sees "the angels prepared to destroy all Israel" and concludes, "If I leave Israel to their fate and descend, they will never survive." Moses recognizes that he can achieve more by not stirring "from here before I have sought mercy for them." His position in heaven offers him a more effective platform than he would have standing alongside the people.

Moses is no apologist. He does not attempt to justify the Golden Calf nor excuse the weakness of the people. Rather Moses speaks to their strength: "Remember to their credit the acceptance of Torah, how they welcomed me as Your messenger," and more. An ally does no favors by deriding those with whom he or she wishes to stand. Moses stands proudly by the Jews in order to sway God in their favor.

Moses persists. God presents a list of particulars against the Jewish people, but Moses is not persuaded. Aware of their fallibility, Moses will not rest until he succeeds.

Even more, Moses risks his own standing. God goes so far as to excommunicate Moses (*Sh'mot Rabbah* 42:3). An ally is easily tarnished or dismissed as a fellow traveler. It takes courage to remain steadfast.

Finally, Moses does not allow himself to be seduced by favors. Recall that God is willing to begin anew with Moses, but Moses is not willing to be bought. Moses stands on principle. As a result, God shifts from the throne of justice to the throne of mercy.

For the sake of peace in the world, may we, like Moses, be steadfast allies to those at risk.

Ki Tisa
Rabbi Michael Boyden, 2013

Ki Tisa is about leadership and the question of how we deal with disappointment.

Moses is on Mount Sinai to receive the two tablets, "stone tablets inscribed with the finger of God" (Exod. 31:18). This should have been the pinnacle of his career. However, sometimes, just when we think things are going well, everything gets turned on its head.

While Moses is "out of town," the people turn to Aaron and plead for "a god who shall go before us, for that man Moses, who brought us from the land of Egypt—we do not know what has happened to him" (Exod. 32:1).

Only twelve chapters after the revelation at Mount Sinai where "the people saw the thunder and the lightning, the blare of the shofar and the mountain smoking" (Exod. 20:15), all is forgotten. They can't even maintain their faith in their leader for forty days!

Moses responds by breaking the stone tablets. Why did he do that? Was he angry? Or perhaps we should adopt the Rashbam's explanation that "when [Moses] saw the [Golden] Calf, he became weak and no longer had the strength [to hold the tablets]."

How does Moses cope with disappointment? While he may lose his temper, he does not distance himself from his people, but rather sides with them and pleads to God on their behalf: "If I have gained Your favor, Adonai, let Adonai accompany us, even though this is a stiff-necked people. Pardon our iniquity and our sin, and take us for Your own!" (Exod. 34:9).

Ki Tisa
Rabbi David Novak, 2014

"When the One who speaks finished speaking with [Moses] on Mount Sinai, the One who writes gave Moses the two tablets of the Pact, stone tablets inscribed with the finger of God" (Exod. 31:18).

"Eternal" or "Lord" is the usual translation for God's holy name in this verse. Here God's name is translated metaphorically. Through these metaphors, we can more readily understand God's actions in this verse: God speaks and writes. God who speaks utters *Aseret HaDib'rot* ("the Ten Commandments"). God who writes inscribes them in stone. Moses brings God's written words down Mount Sinai in a language the human beings, here the Israelites, can understand.

We who encounter this text today have to take a leap that our God is one who speaks and can be understood and who writes in a language we can comprehend. God is multivalent, discernible beyond words; yet we humans use language to create knowledge through the pathways we use for perception: our senses. For our sakes, God must have pathos, feelings. For us, God must have eyes, ears, hands, fingers, form—because we humans use our senses to communicate with other people and the world around us.

Whether or not God speaks in a discernible language or writes with a finger, what is important for us is that our human senses allow us to experience God. Rather than reject these words as "supernatural" or "unsophisticated," we should embrace them as a sacred human path to experiencing the One.

Ki Tisa
Rabbi Ruth Adar, 2015

"Adonai, Adonai, God, merciful and gracious, long-suffering, and abundant in goodness and truth; showing mercy unto the thousandth generation, forgiving iniquity and transgression and sin, and pardoning" (Exod. 34:6–7). The liturgical formula we recite on the *Yamim Noraim* (Days of Awe) is known as the thirteen attributes of mercy. The Rabbis tell that God demonstrated to Moses how to recite this verse before a congregation and assured him that any time Israel sins, *yaasu l'fanai k'seder hazeh*, "let them perform before Me this procedure [i.e., these attributes]" *vaani mocheil lahem*, "and I will forgive them" (*Babylonian Talmud Rosh HaShanah* 17b). Is this to say that the recitation of the thirteen attributes is a "magical formula"? The notion that we can manipulate God by reciting a charm is surely a troubling notion to a modern Reform mind.

Rabbi Isaiah Horowitz (seventeenth century) explains in *Sh'nei Luchot HaB'rit* that we should not merely recite the thirteen attributes as they have come down to us. We should rather act with compassion, mercy, and forgiveness; God will then treat us in kind (Singer and Lauterbach, "Middot Shelosh-'Esre," *Jewish Encyclopedia*).

When we emulate the attribute of mercy, our deeds bring God's mercy into the world; there is no magic formula that can only be spoken. Therefore, it is up to us to strive daily to be "merciful and gracious, long-suffering, abundant in goodness and truth, showing mercy, forgiving iniquity and transgression and sin, pardoning." This is a tall order indeed, but as human beings who view ourselves as the pinnacle of Creation, created in the image of God, and who strive to live in covenant with God, it is how we can bring forgiveness into the world for others and for ourselves.

Ki Tisa
Rabbi Stephen Wylen, 2016

In his opening comments to *B'reishit*, Abraham ibn Ezra says that God as Creator is not all that important an issue, and if you wish to know what is important, look at *Ki Tisa*. He is apparently referring to Exod. 34:6–7, the passage that the Sages refer to as "the thirteen attributes of God's compassion."

It doesn't matter whether there is a God. It only matters that we can relate to God. And that only matters, in turn, if we can count on divine forgiveness for our sins, our failings, and our weaknesses. Yet consider these verses: "Extending kindness to a thousand generations . . . but visiting the iniquity of parents, children and grandchildren to the third and fourth generation" (Deut. 5:9–10). One phrase contradicts the other.

Ibn Ezra resolves the contradiction by suggesting that the Torah is conveying the ratio of God's forgiveness to God's punishment: God is 250 times more forgiving than punitive, precisely what is needed, it seems, for Israel to continue to follow and worship God after the sin of the Golden Calf. The relationship can only continue if God is willing to forgive and move on.

Imitatio dei. Every important relationship in our life—spouse, parent-child, sibling, friend, rabbi-congregation—depends upon acceptance of the human limitations of the other and a willingness to forgive and move on. If we insist on perfection, the relationship will come to a speedy and uncomfortable end. We must, like God, endure insult and rejection and forgive. We must insist, as did Israel, upon being forgiven as the price of our ongoing devotion. Do you forgive me, really forgive me? No wonder this is the only *parashah* recited numerous times during the year. This is what matters most.

Ki Tisa
Rabbi Amy Scheinerman, 2017

The second set of tablets securely in hand, Moses descends from the mountain to return to the people.

"Thereupon Moses turned and went down from the mountain bearing the two tablets of the Pact, tablets inscribed on both their surfaces: they were inscribed on the one side and on the other. The tablets were God's work, and the writing was God's writing, incised upon the tablets" (Exod. 32:15–16).

This was the last moment in history that the entire people of Israel agreed on the meaning of the inscribed words: they had neither seen nor heard them yet. When a text is deemed all-important, it is inevitable that arguments concerning its meaning and application will ensue. Perhaps that is why the disputes between Beit Hillel and Beit Shammai are iconic and the words *eilu v'eilu divrei elohim chayim*, "These and these are the words of the living God" (*Babylonian Talmud Eiruvin* 13b) are, if not our touchstone, our deepest aspiration.

The Chasidic teacher Rabbi Uziel Meisels (1744–85), referring to the fact that the tablets were inscribed on both sides, writes in *Tiferet Uziel*:

> This means that words of Torah are indeed "like a hammer splits the rock" (Jer. 23:29). There are reasons to say "Pure!" and reasons to say "Impure!" and similar cases. This is the writing on both sides. One [per-

son's opinion] may differ from another's as widely as possible, but "both are the words of the living God."

Nice to have this affirmation from yet another source. Even nicer to inculcate the belief in our communities for matters beyond interpretation of Torah.

Ki Tisa
Rabbi Joshua Minkin, DMin, 2018

Over and over again the Torah warns to beware of adopting the practices of the Canaanites among whom we will settle, and even to destroy their cultic sites (e.g., Exod. 34:12–14).

We live in a society where truth is under attack. Information that undermines people's beliefs and opinions is rapidly dubbed false facts. Conspiracies abound. In this era of Photoshop, even photographs can be rejected as fake. To avoid accusations of bias, politically motivated fabrications are presented as legitimate alternatives to science.

Why are the idols we are told not to worship often described as molten? What goes into the molten mix is unknown. Could it symbolize that fundamentally, they may not be how they appear? Similarly, the false solutions being presented: They are pretty. They promise to resolve problems, if only we believe them. They seem to be based on a kernel of truth. But ultimately, they are meant to deceive.

Ki Tisa warns that Canaanite ideas may be a snare leading us to believe a false truth. Hearing a refrain over and over again, people tend to give it increasing credence whether it comes from Canaanite neighbors or Facebook friends.

When we are forced to choose, it is much easier to make up an excuse or try to ignore the dilemma. For example, in our *parashah*, Aaron is complicit in making the Golden Calf. The pre-twentieth-century commentators either try to find a way to let Aaron of the hook or ignore the incident completely.

We don't have that luxury.

ויקהל/פקודי   *Vayak'heil/P'kudei*
(Exodus 35:1–38:20 and Exodus 38:21–40:38)

Vayak'heil/P'kudei
Rabbi Louis Rieser, 2010

The closing portions of Exodus concern the construction of the *Mishkan*: details of weighing, measuring, and counting. Where can holiness be found amidst these mundane acts of construction?

The Chasidic master Levi Yitzchak of Berditchev (*K'dushat Levi* on *P'kudei*) raises a similar question when citing *P'sikta D'Rav Kahana* (6:10): "God's blessing is not bestowed upon that which is measured, weighed, or counted." If so, then how can the work described in this portion bring blessing? One might say that blessing lies in our *kavanah*, motivation. Our motivation, so to speak, blesses the act. Levi Yitzchak, however, offers a contrasting approach. He teaches that when a person sees the holy power that enlivens an object, and then connects that object to its root, he or she draws down blessing from the Source to the particular object. Levi Yitzchak focuses on the inherent holiness out there, not on our inner attitude.

If only we could remember that every object comes from the Creator. Recall the tale of the scientist who challenges God saying, "I can create life in my laboratory." God accepts the challenge. When the scientist starts by saying, "I take a bit of soil," God objects and says, "Create your own soil."

Levi Yitzchak teaches that when we connect an object to its holy root, we bring blessing, and warns that when we disconnect them, curse follows. How might our own life change if we saw holiness in every object that surrounds us?

Vayak'heil/P'kudei
Rabbi Michael Boyden, 2012

Our *parashah*, like the three that precede it and the one that follows, deals with the building of the *Mishkan*, or Tabernacle, in the wilderness.

Building a *Mishkan* in the middle of the desert represents, in effect, the concentration of holiness in a place that is, on the face of it, both spiritually barren and empty. Why was that necessary?

Three chapters back, the root of *Vayak'heil*—*kuf-hei-lamed*—is employed when the Children of Israel gathered and called upon Aaron to make them a god (Exod. 32:1). Their appeal to Aaron raises the question: how does one sustain one's belief in a God without a continuous, direct, and personal experience?

The menorah, which was overlaid with gold, represents the divine response to the Golden Calf. Human beings may donate of their wealth to the building of the Sanctuary—or of a synagogue—but they should not confuse their creation with the Divine.

The construction of the *Mishkan* is very different from that of the Golden Calf. Whereas the latter represented the spontaneous, uncontrolled passions of the Children of Israel and the epitome of evil, the construction of the menorah resulted from the channeling of those same forces in a planned manner into the design of a religious symbol that was placed at the very heart of the Sanctuary.

The *Mishkan* is constructed to meet human needs, not God's needs. That is why God said, "Build Me a sanctuary that I may dwell within them" (Exod. 25:8)—within them, not within it.

Vayak'heil/P'kudei
Rabbi Amy Scheinerman, 2013

Vayak'heil opens with an invitation to the people to bring gifts to build the wilderness Tabernacle, and *P'kudei* closes with God's presence settling into its new domicile. Is the *Mishkan* a crude precursor to the glorious *Mikdash* in Jerusalem? Or perhaps the *Mikdash* is modeled on the pristine *Mishkan*?

The *Mikdash* symbolized and facilitated the centralization of Jewish power and authority in Jerusalem, and particularly in the Davidic dynasty. It was a fixed, "permanent" structure conveying the permanent anointment of the Davidic dynasty and the fixed, eternal connection of *Am Yisrael* to *Eretz Yisrael*. Nearly two millennia after its destruction, it comes to represent our eternal connection to the Land and our hope for the messianic future (though many of us would vote with Rambam on the issue of sacrifices. Moses Maimonides (1135–1204) wrote in his law code, the *Mishneh Torah* (*Laws Concerning Kings and Wars* 11:1), that when the Messiah comes, the Temple will be rebuilt and the sacrificial services restored, suggesting that God intends them to be eternal. However, in his philosophical treatise, *Moreh Nevuchim* (*Guide for the Perplexed* 3:32), Rambam explained that God commanded the institution of sacrifices to draw Israel away from the idolatrous practices, suggesting that the sacrifices commanded in the Torah were not meant to constitute Jewish practice forever.).

The *Mishkan* in some sense is the opposite: it is purposefully migratory, attached to no particular tract of land, and certainly no monarchical dynasty. Rather, it is the nexus of heaven and earth, the place where God and Israel meet. The *Mishkan* is our assurance that wherever we are, when we gather as a community, God is among us.

Living at a time when Jews have a sovereign nation in the Land, yet live scattered among nations across the globe, both *Mikdash* and *Mishkan* take on special meaning. We juggle and balance our various commitments and outlooks on the State of Israel, the Land of Israel, where to find God, how to be a community, how to relate to one another—all of which are implicit in the tension between *Mishkan* and *Mikdash*.

Vayak'heil
Rabbi Joshua Minkin, DMin, 2014

J. P. Morgan said, "I can do a year's work in nine months, but not in twelve."

"Six days you shall work, and on the seventh day you shall observe a Sabbath of rest, holy to the Eternal; whoever does any work on it shall be put to death" (Exod. 35:2).

Here and elsewhere, Torah combines the obligation to work with the obligation to rest. God expects us to contribute productively to the building of the world and also to cease from work and rest one day in seven to recharge our physical, emotional, and spiritual batteries. But if I forgo Shabbat, can't I get more work done?

Wellness expert Elizabeth Scott writes about the importance of taking a break from work (*How to Take a Break From Work (and Why You Need It)*, https://www.verywellmind.com/why-you-should-take-a-break-3144576):

> The body is designed to respond to short bursts of stress, but when stress is prolonged and the stress response is triggered repeatedly and on a regular basis . . . the situation turns into one . . . where the real health problems set in. Those who experience chronic stress are more susceptible to conditions ranging from more frequent headaches and gastrointestinal issues to more serious conditions like high blood pressure, which brings an increased risk of heart disease and stroke. . . . At this point . . . we're not able to respond from a place of strength and wisdom, but rather from a place of anxiety, or we work on auto-pilot.

Without periodic rest, strength and wisdom wane, and work quality declines significantly. Denying ourselves a Shabbat does not mean we get more done. Both quality and quantity of our work decline because we cannot work to our potential. Even more, as Torah warns, we threaten our health and hasten our death.

P'kudei
Rabbi Michael Boyden, 2014

The opening words of our *parashah*, which deal with the construction of the Sanctuary in the wilderness, state, "These are the records of the Tabernacle" (Exod. 38:21).

Rashi tells us that "all the weights of the donations in silver, gold, and brass that the Children of Israel contributed for the *Mishkan* were recorded."

Why was that necessary, particularly since the chairman of the building fund committee was none other than Moses, of whom God declared, "He is trusted in all My household" (Num. 12:7)?

Perhaps it was in order to establish norms of public behavior in the administration of community funds.

Sh'mot Rabbah 51 states, "At least two people should be appointed when handling community funds. You might argue that Moses administered the funds alone.... However, although Moses was the sole treasurer, he called on others to audit the accounts."

The same midrash also tells us that when a person went to the Temple to make a donation, he did not do so behind a screen, so that no one could accuse him of taking money from the Temple should he become wealthy.

No one is entirely above being corrupted. The Torah tells us that the Ark of the Covenant was overlaid within and without with pure gold. Alluding to this, Raba commented, "Any sage whose inner person is different from his persona is no sage" (*Babylonian Talmud Yoma* 72b).

Vayak'heil/P'kudei: Shabbat Parah
Rabbi Amy Scheinerman, 2015

Vayak'heil and *P'kudei* include a recapitulation of instructions and a detailed accounting of all the materials used to fashion the Tabernacle and its furnishings. The road is paved for *Vayikra*'s intense attention to issues of purity. On this Shabbat Parah we study the law of the red heifer, which purifies from the gravest source of impurity—death. It thereby signals the formal kickoff of Pesach preparations.

In *P'sikta Rabbati* (14:1) we are told that Rabbi Eliezer dissented from the Sages by teaching that a red heifer may not be purchased from a gentile. Rabbi Pinchas ben Chama recounts an attempt by the priests to purchase a red heifer from an unscrupulous gentile who hiked the price to more than 250 times its market value and then, in an effort to make the Jews look foolish, put a yoke on her the night before they came to get her. The priests recognized the signs she had been yoked, and the gentile lost the lucrative sale.

Y'rushalmi (*Jerusalem Talmud Pei-ah* 5b–6a) and *Bavli* (*Babylonian Talmud Kiddushin* 61b) tell virtually the inverse of this story in the context of illustrating honoring one's parents: The Rabbis visit Dama ben Netina to purchase a replacement jasper for the *choshen mishpat* (breastplate), but he refuses to sell it to them because his father is asleep on the chest containing the jewel. Dama ben Netina refuses to disturb his father. Even when they twice offer him a far larger sum of money, he declines. When his father awakens, he sells the jewel at the first agreed-upon price, refusing to accept the latter exorbitant sums offered. God rewards Dama ben Netina with a pure red heifer born to his herd.

A second story in *P'sikta Rabbati* (14:2) recounts the story of a gentile purchasing a plowing heifer from a Jew. The heifer refused to plow on Shabbat, inspiring the gentile to observe Shabbat himself. "If an animal without speech and understanding acknowledges the Creator, so should he!"—and he converted.

Consider the different perspectives and attitudes to non-Jews reflected in these stories.

Vayak'heil: Shabbat Sh'kalim
Rabbi Joshua Minkin, DMin, 2016

"The Israelites brought a freewill offering to Adonai; every man and woman, whose heart made them willing" (Exod. 35:29).

Our *parashah* contains a lexical anomaly. The phrase *ish v'ishah* (man and woman) occurs only three times in the entire Torah, two of them in this *parashah*. There is also another unique phrase, *haanashim al hanashim*, which is extremely close, but in the plural. Why does the Torah use gender-specific language?

For the first time, the Israelites are given the opportunity to express the depth of their gratitude to God, and they do so generously. Women are not relegated to the side. The Torah is quick to point out their contribution, much of which is the work of their hands. How appropriate that the term *avodah* can mean both "worship" and "work."

Today, some streams of Judaism continue to actively prevent women from taking part in worship. While women are not obligated to wear a tallit and don *t'fillin*, they are also not prohibited from doing so.

There is no better example for this kind of religious discrimination than ultra-Orthodox reaction to the Women of the Wall. For active worship, in tallit and *t'fillin*, they have been subjected to extreme harassment and even arrest. In order to be a *kahal* (community), everyone must be included.

P'kudei
Rabbi Ruth Adar, 2016

Many people start out to read the Torah and find that the first book, Genesis, is one interesting story after another: Adam and Eve, Cain and Abel, the Flood, the Tower of Babel, and then the patriarchal narratives. Exodus, the second book, begins with panache: a Pharaoh arises who does not know Joseph, and more exciting stories follow.

Toward the end of the Book of Exodus, the going gets heavier, and by this week's *parashah*, we are reading the final report of a construction project. Everything is "spelled out," so that we learn not only about the exact amounts of gold, silver, and copper, but also about the minute details of embroidery on the priests' robes. The whole thing is about as exciting as a corporation's annual report. Our eyelids droop; we space out.

We want to be entertained; we want to think about heroic stories and glorious epiphanies, but attention to detail is precisely what Torah requires of us. We can intend to feed the hungry, but for it to happen someone must gather the funds, buy the ingredients, cook the food, distribute the meals, and yes, at the end of the project, provide an accounting to the donors of where their contributions went. Similarly, we can have the best of intentions to comfort mourners, but unless someone disseminates the information concerning when and where shivah will take place, the mourners will feel abandoned.

Torah calls us to honor life's details.

Vayak'heil/P'kudei
Rabbi Amy Scheinerman, 2017

Mordechai Yosef Leiner, the Ishbitzer Rebbe, notes in *Mei HaShiloach* that when Moses gathers the people to work on the *Mishkan*, he first reminds them of the mitzvah of Shabbat (Exod. 35:2–3).

It says that "with the building of the *Mishkan*, all the hearts of Israel were united without anyone feeing superior to another. . . . When they saw how all the disparate elements fit perfectly together, every curtain and board, and every element perfectly suited every other one as if it was the work of one person," they recognized God's hand. "How could one feel superior to another when all that was done was only with the help of the blessed God?"

The Ishbitzer draws a parallel to Talmud's account of the writing of the seventy Greek translations of the *Tanach*, the *Septuagint* (*Babylonian Talmud M'gilah* 9a): every translation was identical to every other, thanks to God's influence.

The essence of Shabbat, the Ishbitzer says, is the intention that what one does is for the sake of heaven. That is why Moses mentions it prior to the commencement of work on the *Mishkan*, and that is why the people worked together without competition or rancor.

In our lives, Shabbat precedes our entry into the week and all it entails. May we live our lives "for the sake of heaven."

Vayak'heil
Rabbi Michael Boyden, 2018

Most of us are challenged by the need to raise money, whether for capital projects or for programs. Our success, it would appear, is primarily dependent upon the commitment of our donors.

I wish we all were in the position of Bezalel and Oholiab, who, when building the Tent of Meeting in the wilderness, couldn't stop the donations coming in(!). They protested, "The people have raised too much money for the work involved" (Exod. 36:5).

Of course, they should not have been surprised. The Israelite community had already demonstrated its generosity when it came to the Golden Calf. There we read, "And all the people took off the gold rings that were in their ears and brought them to Aaron" (Exod. 32:3).

In view of the overabundance of donations for the Tent of Meeting, Moses puts out the word for every *ish v'ishah*, "man and woman," to desist from donating (Exod. 36:6). Referring to the fact that women are explicitly mentioned here, Rabbi Samson Raphael Hirsch points out that "this serves to guarantee sexual equality." He notes that both words, *ish v'ishah*, come from the same Hebrew root, thereby implying equal status.

I wish that were the case today. Just look how women are treated at the Kotel!

It is worth noting that whereas women were fully involved in efforts to build the Tent of Meeting, *Midrash Tanchuma* (*Pinchas* 7) observes that they did not participate in building the Golden Calf. Apparently, women demonstrated greater discernment than men concerning the question of where to invest their money!

P'kudei
Rabbi Amy Scheinerman, 2018

Parashat P'kudei invites us to consider the construction of the *Mishkan* as an adumbration of Creation. Torah recounts that having finished the work of Creation, God blessed it (Gen. 3:1–3). "When Moses saw that [Israel] had performed all the work—as Adonai had commanded, so they had done—Moses blessed them" (Exod. 39:43). As God created the universe from the blueprint of Torah, so Israel created the *Mishkan* from the blueprint of Torah. The *Mishkan* therefore completes God's Creation by supplying a nexus between heaven and earth—the Holy of Holies—and a means of engagement—the altar. No wonder the *Mishkan* is erected on the first day of the first month (Exod. 40:2).

"Thus was completed all the work of the *Mishkan* in the *Ohel Mo-eid* [Tent of Meeting]. The Israelites did so; just as Adonai had commanded Moses, so they did" (Exod. 39:32). Noting that the term for "work" in both the account of Creation and here is *m'lachah*, the S'fat Emet comments, "The *Mishkan* redeemed doing itself . . . the labor of the *Mishkan* redeemed every deed that exists in the world. . . . By means of the *Mishkan*, Israel separated out the goodness within doing; the *Mishkan* was made of it. . . . Now all doing could follow the command of God."

Sensitive to Torah's suggestion that Creation and the *Mishkan* are opposite sides of the same creative coin, the Rabbis identify "work" as the tasks that contributed to the *Mishkan*. How might we define "work" today to honor the created universe, our aspiration to engage with God, and our own sense of godly endeavor—and incorporate this in our celebration of Shabbat?

Leviticus

ויקרא   *Vayikra*
(Leviticus 1:1–5:26)

Vayikra
Rabbi Janice Garfunkel, z"l, 2011

Many Reform Jews wince when the week's *parashah* is about sacrifice. Why? The sacrificial cult seems irrelevant to us, but more than that, it seems primitive, barbaric, and embarrassing.

Some reassurance: Christianity is built around a human sacrifice, the ultimate offering, that of the "lamb of God." Islam today still has a holy day where every family is supposed to slaughter and eat a sheep. Many of us romanticize the Native Americans who, when they killed a deer, sanctified the event. Buddhists place plates of food in front of statues. Maybe reading about the sacrifices our ancestors gave over two thousand years ago is not so embarrassing after all.

Is factory farming really so much more palatable to us? Buying our meat in individual servings, wrapped in cellophane at the grocery store, enables us to divorce our eating of animal flesh from any thoughts concerning the spilling of animal blood and the question of whether or not this is acceptable to the Holy One. But is it truly less barbaric, primitive, and embarrassing?

Davar Acheir: What would we be willing to sacrifice for God? Eating meat altogether? Significant gifts of money or time? Do we give anything to God because it is a gift to God or only because we expect the gift to benefit us in return ("I pray because it gives my life meaning," "I stopped eating meat because it is healthier and saves the planet")? Do we do anything that is purely for God, and not really for ourselves?

Vayikra
Rabbi Stephen Wylen, 2012

"Calling out to Moses, God spoke to him from the Tent of Meeting, saying . . ." (Lev. 1:1). Rabbi Assi said, "Why do we start the little students with the Book of Leviticus and not the Book of Genesis? Little children are pure and the sacrifices are pure. Let the pure ones come and study purity" (*Vayikra Rabbah* 7:3).

For two thousand years, Jewish children began their education learning Leviticus. Rabbi Assi's rationale for this is after-the-fact. Most likely, children were initiated in *Vayikra* so that they would look at Torah as a collection of laws, mitzvot. This matches the lesson that the first verse taught to children was *Torah tzivah lanu moshe* ("Moses charged us with the teaching," Deut. 33:4) and only afterward *Sh'ma Yisrael*. Revealed rules precede and lead to faith.

This is Rabbinic Judaism.

Contrast this with the American Reform Jewish curriculum, rooted in the Sunday school of Rebecca Gratz. Patterned after Protestantism, American Jews begin with Bible stories. The most universal educational experience for non-Orthodox Jewish students is the story of Abraham smashing his father's idols.

Often, students in America spend their pre–bar/bat mitzvah year learning about the Holocaust. What is our purpose? American Jewish curriculum needs to be based on a vision of the Jew we are trying to create. I believe that in our free society the aim of a Jewish curriculum should be the joy of Jewish living.

Vayikra
Rabbi Joshua Minkin, DMin, 2013

Vayikra begins with a lengthy discussion of sacrifices that are central to Israel's relationship to God. The first of these is the *olah* (burnt) offering (Lev. 1:3). Given that each of us contains within us a spark of the Divine, can *Vayikra* teach us something about our relationships with one another and our relationship with our own selves?

The Torah: A Women's Torah Commentary (ed. Tamara Cohn Eskenazi and Andrea L. Weiss) notes that "the burnt offering usually appears first in a series of sacrifices [which] suggests that its purpose may be to open up communication with the Divine; if so, then that goal would be accomplished by manifesting generosity—giving part of one's wealth to God" (p. 572).

Certainly communication is key in any relationship. This insight into the *olah* suggests that opening communication begins with generosity. It is not our wealth, but our self, which is the *olah*, the offering. We sacrifice our most precious possession: our ego. We lower the boundaries that protect who we truly are from exposure and gradually reveal our vulnerabilities. This requires us to trust another. In being generous, we suspend judgment of another, sacrificing our preconceived notions and expectations. *Mishna Pirkei Avot* 1:6 reminds us, "Judge everyone favorably."

Can we learn to communicate openly and honestly with our own divine spark? Each year we take a *cheshbon nefesh*, our personal accounting of who we truly are. We open ourselves up to the parts of us we try to hide even from ourselves. How much more vulnerable can we be? We should not forget to be generous to ourselves as well. We need to shed the preconceived notions we have carried from childhood and trust our ability to not just see ourselves for who we are, but to accept ourselves with love and gentleness, as well.

Vayikra
Rabbi Louis Rieser, 2014

The Book of Leviticus is concerned about the ways we approach the altar, presenting ourselves to the Holy One of Creation. According to Rav Kook, the very first word of the book bespeaks that concern.

Noting that *vayikra* is written with a small *alef*, Rav Kook reminds us that the Torah consists of black letters written over dynamic white space. The black letters embody and convey the intellectual content, the data needed in order to do Torah. The white space corresponds to the realm of contemplation. Five blank lines mark the boundary between the books of the Torah; this extended white space affords time for Moses (and us) to reflect upon and absorb the previous lessons.

How do we prepare ourselves to stand before the Holy One, whether at the altar in days of old or in prayer and action today? It was, it seems to me, an act of chutzpah to present God's own creation—oil, grain, and animals—on the altar and to expect a response, except that those goods were not the essential offering. Our heart and presence were what mattered, then and now. Standing before the Great and Mighty One of the Universe requires attention and intention. The risks, as Nadav and Avihu will soon remind us, are high. So, Rav Kook suggests, before entering into the Book of *Vayikra*, we are given a slightly longer time to contemplate than might be afforded by the standard five lines of white space separating the books. The *alef* is reduced to grant us more time for contemplation, that we might hear the still, small voice before we respond to the call.

Vayikra
Rabbi Michael Boyden, 2015

Vayikra is a strange name for a book! After all, the title did not have to be taken from the very first word. Perhaps that is why the Vulgate, based upon the Septuagint, preferred the word "Leviticus." Indeed, *Midrash Sifra* employs the term *Torat HaKohanim* ("The Pristly Code"), which more accurately describes the book's contents.

God does not simply address Moses. The text tells us that "Adonai called to Moses and spoke to him" (Lev. 1:1). Surely it would have been sufficient to have stated, "Adonai spoke to Moses." However, when we call a person over before addressing her, rather than shouting across the room, we give her a chance to prepare herself. That is the way of *derech eretz*, "the way of the world."

It is interesting to note the different ways in which our *parashah* deals with sin. On the one hand it says, "If the whole community of Israel has erred" (Lev. 4:13), but later on it states, "When a chieftain sins" (Lev. 4:22). Why the different choice of words? When it comes to leaders, sin comes with the territory. Rabbeinu Bachya wrote, "A prince's heart is very vulgar; and pride, which is the cause of sin, is a function of his rule."

When we teach Bible to children in religious school, we tend to start with the fables at the beginning of Genesis (the Creation, Noah, the Tower of Babel). Perhaps we ought to begin in Leviticus with laws such as loving one's neighbor as oneself. The midrash asks, "When we begin teaching little children Torah, why do we commence from the Book of Leviticus rather than Genesis? The Holy One, blessed be God, said, 'Since sacrifices are pure and little children are pure, let those who are pure occupy themselves with things that are pure'" (*P'sikta D'Rav Kahana* 6).

Vayikra: Shabbat Zachor
Rabbi Charles Middleburgh, PhD, 2016

Jews are called to remember many things: stories from holy texts, the rationales of the *chagim* (festivals), events in our history (some brighter than the sun, others blacker than the darkest night), and great women and men (some among the finest in human history). Yet on Shabbat Zachor we are commanded to remember not only our redemption, but more specifically our enemy whom we are charged with obliterating. This is remembering of a very different type; this is remembering an act of evil in the hope of repaying it in kind one day.

Two decades into the twenty-first century the world is awash in hatreds, violence, and inhumanity, much of it promulgated in the name of God. Possessors of a progressive Jewish mind-set find it hard to conceive how ancient feuds and unrighted wrongs continue to plague modernity, casting a shadow on an age bursting with potential that could transform the lives of so many. Yet we need look no further than Shabbat Zachor and the demonization of Amalek to realize that the fault lies not in our stars but in ourselves—and also in our tradition.

Our challenge today, when there are forces at large we could easily label as Amalek, is to raise ourselves above the temptation to resort to atavism. Instead, we need to fight to make others see that the only value in remembering the past is to rise above it, and not to repeat the errors that marked the lives of all those who came before us—our Jewish ancestors as well as all humanity.

Vayikra
Rabbi Amy Scheinerman, 2017

Leviticus opens with God's call to Moses. "*Adonai* called to Moses and spoke to him from the Tent of Meeting" (Lev. 1:1). God's call seems more of a summons to acknowledge God's authority and is followed by a speech whose content is God's requirements for Israel.

The S'fat Emet addresses a theme that appears many times in our texts and commentaries. Citing Ps. 103:20, which suggests that the angels obey God and only subsequently hear God's word, S'fat Emet tells us that this accords with the order prescribed by the Sages: first *Sh'ma* (acknowledging the "yoke") and only after that "It shall be if you truly listen" (Deut. 11:13ff.). Doing comes first; hearing the sounds of God's word, or truly listening, comes second. How are we to understand an order that seems illogical, if not downright impossible?

> This means that the sound of God's speech is present in each commandment. Our sages taught that each limb calls out to the person, "Fulfill the commandment that depends on me!" Each fulfillment is an acceptance of divine rule, and afterwards one comes to hear more. Thus we should "do God's word" in order "to hear" more.

How often in life must we do in order to comprehend? Living in a society that privileges skepticism, this approach can keep many far from Jewish practices. Practices must be experienced to be understood and appreciated.

Vayikra: Shabbat HaChodesh
Rabbi Ruth Adar, 2018

The phrase *vayikra Moshe* appears twice in the Torah, and each time it is an invitation to receive instruction for living. In the first occurrence, following his ascent up the mountain, God calls to Moses from the midst of God's Glory, the cloud covering Sinai (Exod. 24:16). With these words, God invites Moses to enter the cloud and receive instruction.

Here, at the beginning of the Book of Leviticus, God calls to Moses, inviting him to enter the Tabernacle to receive the instructions for the Tabernacle cult. Just as the story at the beginning of Genesis describes the creation of a world, the instructions in Leviticus create a new world: the world of the Tabernacle cult.

Millennia after the physical Temple was reduced to rubble by the Romans, the Temple cult remains intact, enshrined in the words of Leviticus—and thereby available to us. In our own era and without the physical Temple, we cannot carry out the *korbanot* (sacrifices). Many of us in the Reform Movement understand that as progress. As Maimonides asserted, we have outgrown the need for animal sacrifices, substituting *korbanot* with prayer. Every *Amidah* evokes the spiritual altar of Leviticus.

Intertwined with the ritual commandments regarding the sacrifices, Leviticus conveys ethical mitzvot directing us to live according to specific values.

This week God invites us in, as long ago Moses was invited into the cloud, God's presence, and into God's home, the Tabernacle. What instruction will we hear as we receive the world of Leviticus anew?

צו *Tzav*
(Leviticus 6:1–8:36)

Tzav: Shabbat HaGadol
Rabbi Stephen Wylen, 2010

"Command Aaron and his sons thus . . .
the fire on the altar shall be kept burning continually" (Lev. 6:1–2).

> In my heart a sanctuary I shall build,
> To the splendor of God's honor.
> And in the sanctuary an altar I shall place,
> To the rays of God's glory.
> And for an Eternal Flame I shall take me
> The fire of the *Akeidah;*
> And for a sacrifice I shall offer to God my soul,
> My one and only soul.

"The fire on the altar must be paralleled by a fire in the heart of the officiating priest, whose enthusiasm for the sacred nature of the work must never be lost. The congregation, for its part, must recognize its responsibility to see that the enthusiasm and dedication of the clergy is never extinguished" (Harold Kushner, in *Etz Hayim*, p. 613). And the *Baal Shem Tov* said, "This is the Torah of the *olah*—which Torah teaching is it that rises upward? That which is burning upon the altar—the Torah teaching that is taught with *hitlahavut,* inner passion."

How does one maintain this passion in the face of the often deflating realities of congregational life? When I decided to become a rabbi, I interviewed many rabbis. Their message varied but for one thing: all said, "You must know yourself." A leader cannot afford to listen too much to the praises, nor to the criticisms. We must be responsive, but we must know who we are and what we stand for. If you take the praises seriously, then how will you defend your spirit from unjust criticism? We must stay on task. "For lack of vision the people perish" (Prov. 29:18).

Congregational lay leaders, for their part, must do a better job of being supportive. They must cease to see their task as detectives, uncovering and revealing every fault of the clergy team to the eyes of the public, and instead see themselves as advocates for their mission, of which the rabbi is the chief representative.

Tzav
Rabbi Amy Scheinerman, 2012

Parashat Vayikra details sacrifices brought by an individual Israelite—all but one. *Parashat Tzav* describes in detail the *olah* (burnt) offering—made only by the *kohanim* (priests)—in great detail. We are then told about the only other offering an individual may make: the *todah*, the thanksgiving offering (Lev. 7:12). Why is the *todah* not listed in *Vayikra* with the others?

Rashi tells us that the personal sacrifices delineated in *Parashat Vayikra* are brought by "one who experienced a personal miracle." He provides four examples: surviving ocean or desert travel, being jailed and released, and recovery from illness. For each of these, people still *bensch Gomeil* to this day, although travel and many illnesses are no longer life-threatening. Nonetheless, when something potentially risky happens and we are not hurt, we are grateful.

Why is the *todah* offering listed separately? Perhaps this is to awaken our consciousness to the silent, unnoticed miracles we experience every day, the ones that the *Nisim B'chol Yom* bring to consciousness: we didn't wake up ill, blind, or unable to walk; we have sufficient food for our needs; our loved ones are healthy; we have a job; we made it to work without incident or accident—whichever of these pertain to our lives.

These comprise a different sort of miracle, yet no less important, and no less worthy of our gratitude.

It is Shabbat HaGadol, and Pesach is around the corner. We will recount the greatest redemptive miracles of our tradition, which serve as proof and prelude to the redemption to come. That redemption will be built with the bricks of the larger, recognizable miracles, but also the many silent, unnoticed miracles.

Tzav
Rabbi Amy Scheinerman, 2013

There are eight animal sacrifices falling into three categories: those eaten by the person who brings it; those eaten by the priests; and the *olah*, which is entirely burned on the altar. Rambam and Abarbanel tell us that animal sacrifices are no longer needed. Rashi says it was Israel who wanted them, not God. If God doesn't need it, isn't it a waste of nourishment?

Perhaps the meaning and value of the *olah* is that it is a total sacrifice, an act of altruism that trains the Israelites to be altruistic.

Psychologists debate whether humans ever exhibit genuine altruism. Could we not say that knowing you have done a good thing is a form of reward? But biologists and neurologists believe we are evolved and programmed for it.

Charles Darwin argues in *The Expression of Emotion in Man and Animals* that all mammals suffer, experience empathy, and express empathy through touch. In previous books, he posited that communities populated by empathetic members could more successfully raise offspring to the age of reproduction, a pillar of evolutionary theory. Neurologists concur. We have what they call "mirror neurons," the biological source of human empathy.

The Jerusalem Talmud recounts two stories of altruism in *Taanit* 1:4 about a donkey driver and a brothel owner, whose prayers bring rain during drought because of one altruistic act each performed.

As the *olah* ascends to heaven, an altruistic act ascends as well, which is to say that it is sacred and repairs the world. The *olah* helps train people to act according to the better side of their nature. Rather than worrying with psychologists and philosophers whether we are truly capable of altruism, perhaps we can take comfort from biologists and neurologists in knowing we are evolved and wired for it—and then take that knowledge and run with it.

Tzav / Shabbat Zachor
Rabbi Joshua Minkin, DMin, 2014

"Remember what Amalek did to you. . . . Blot out the memory of Amalek" (Deut. 25:17–19).

Taken at face value, this command is abhorrent. As Rabbi David Golinkin points out, "Despite the biblical commandment to blot out the memory of Amalek . . . a number of Rabbinic sources express clear discomfort with this commandment" (*Schechter on Judaism*). We should not be surprised, then, to find allegorical interpretations, including one of Amalek representing the *yetzer hara* ("evil inclination"). But complete dissolution of the *yetzer hara*, as suggested in the verses above, can lead to problems. "[Without the *yetzer hara*] one would not build a house, marry, beget children, or engage in business" (*B'reishit Rabbah* 9:7). The world's generativity comes from that which also inspires cruelty. Therefore, we are told to *master* the evil inclination.

Can we truly accept what is inherent in human nature when we consider it to be evil?

Often, our evil inclinations are inner, hidden desires, and fulfilling these desires is quite pleasurable!

Once we realize that we harbor immoral desires, shame may arise. Often we blame others for engendering our strong desires of lust, anger, or hate. The "Other" becomes "evil Amalek," preying on our weaknesses. Responsibility has been outsourced.

If we truly accept the *yetzer hara* as part of who we are (as our tradition suggests), we need not feel shame for having immoral desires. They are part of our humanness. Only through acceptance can we truly erase Amalek.

Tzav
Rabbi Michael Boyden, 2016

Parashat Tzav is all about sacrifices. While Orthodox Jews continue to pray for the building of the Third Temple and the re-institution of the sacrificial cult, most of us feel a disconnect from this goal.

The *parashah* details eight kinds of animal sacrifices that fall into three categories: those that were eaten by their presenters; those that were eaten by the priests; and the *olah*, which was burned in its entirety. Interestingly, whereas the English word "sacrifice" is derived from the Latin words *sacra* and *facere* indicating a holy act, or in modern parlance "giving up," the biblical word *korban* simply expresses the notion of "drawing near." On the one hand, the sacrifice was being drawn near to God; but no less significantly, the very offering of the sacrifice brings its presenter closer to God. Frequently the very act of giving serves the needs of the giver no less than that of the receiver.

In his *Guide for the Perplexed*, Maimonides provides two rationales for what lay behind the sacrificial cult. First, it permitted that which others forbade. He specifically refers to the sacrifice of cattle in the Temple in contradistinction, for instance, with the status of the cow in Hinduism and other pagan cultures. More well-known is his assertion that the purpose of the sacrificial cult was to wean early monotheists from idol worship.

At a time when Jews and Muslims argue about who has the right to the Temple Mount, we as Reform Jews can be proud of preferring the message of Isaiah entreating us to "pursue justice and champion the oppressed; give the orphan his rights and plead the widow's cause" (Isa. 1:17).

Tzav: Shabbat HaGadol
Rabbi David Novak, 2017

Tzav sets out the blueprint for the priesthood's facilitation of the sacrificial cult, both in the wilderness and, ultimately, in a centralized location in the Promised Land. Immediately after Torah's promulgation of these rules, two of Aaron's sons, Nadav and Avihu, are immolated by God for offering "strange/alien fire" (Lev. 10:1). Aaron is silent; Torah's proscriptions for sacrifice are not to be trifled with.

The priestly line continues to Shiloh (I Sam. 1:3) where the priest Eli's two sons, Hophni and Phinehas, are described as "wicked and corrupt." They pervert the holiness of the sacrificial system through gluttony and sexual avarice: they appropriate edible sacrificial offerings (including the prohibited fat) for themselves to fulfill their desires, and they abuse vulnerable women seeking God's guidance. Their self-absorbed behaviors subvert the idea of the sacrificial site as a place to reach God, to touch the Holy.

Unlike Nadav and Avihu, Eli's two sons will both die in battle at the hands of the Philistines when the Ark of the Covenant is captured. Upon hearing the news, Eli dies, as does Phinehas's pregnant wife. The family line has ended. A transition from priesthood to prophecy is under way. The prophet Samuel will anoint Saul king of Israel.

In this *parashah*, the blueprint for the sacrificial cult is given, but it is violated by corruptible human beings.

It was something to guard against then, as now.

Tzav
Rabbi Stephen Wylen, 2018

The absolutely final word of prophecy is that God will bring Elijah the prophet "to reconcile parents with children and children with parents" in anticipation of the Day of God (Mal. 3:24).

When I was younger I thought, "What, that's it? Why won't Elijah come to bring world peace or to end poverty? Why just to reconcile parents and children?"

From many years of officiating at funerals I have learned what a huge and important job has been assigned to Elijah. When parents die while there is unfinished business between the generations—unresolved anger and arguments—the younger generation becomes stuck in life, unable to move forward and to live life to the fullest. It is truly the reconciliation between the generations that enables human life on earth to progress.

Until Elijah comes, it is the sacred task of the officiating rabbi to give the surviving children some inner peace upon the death of a father or mother. The graveside is in many ways the final opportunity to make peace. Until the burial, the departed are dead and yet they are still with us. The children have a last chance to apologize or to forgive. It is too important a moment for us not to allow every opportunity.

שמיני *Sh'mini*
(Leviticus 9:1–11:47)

Sh'mini
Rabbi Louis Rieser, 2010

No Torah story requires the reader's participation more than the brief account of the death of Nadav and Avihu (Lev. 10:1–7). The text offers no commentary on the events. The interpretation of what happened depends entirely on the reader's evaluation of the character of the two men.

A brief catalog of classic responses illustrates the point:

- *Sifra Sh'mini* 22 suggests that they intended to serve God and that God dealt with them kindly.
- *Babylonian Talmud Z'vachim* 115b approves their deeds: "'Through them that are near me I will be sanctified' (Lev. 10:3). . . . When Aaron understood that his sons were *yodei makom*, knowledgeable of God, he was silent and rewarded."
- *Sifra Sh'mini* 32 credits them with adding love upon love, but with misunderstanding the process and bringing fire from a private stove.
- *Sifra Sh'mini* 21 ascribes to them a desire to usurp power and position from Moses and Aaron.
- *Jerusalem Talmud Gittin* 5b agrees that they arrogantly taught halachah before Moses.

- *Vayikra Rabbah* 20:9 suggests that they were drunk, they entered the *Mishkan* naked, they entered without the preparatory steps of washing their hands and feet, and they refused to sire the next generation.

So many contradictory possibilities. Once we judge the character of Nadav and Avihu, we can weigh the import of their actions. Judgment demands participation.

Sh'mini
Rabbi Israel Zoberman, DMin, 2013

Parashat Sh'mini alerts us to the unexpected, both in the human condition and the divine response. In the midst of the Tabernacle's zenith of joyful dedication, two of the four sons of Aaron the High Priest, who just a short while ago were consecrated as *kohanim* (priests), are tragically consumed by fire. We are told and taught—though ponder we must—that the victims' attendance to holy duties went awry.

The text reads, *vayidom aharon*, "And Aaron turned silent" (Lev. 10:3). He had no words. Perhaps he could find no words given the shock's magnitude of a double loss of his dearest of the dear. *Vayidom aharon*, yet conceivably Aaron chose not to speak that he may not utter, out of the depths of pain, blasphemous words offensive to God and mocking his own calling. Thus, choosing to remain silent but not necessarily speechless was Aaron's best possible option under terrifying circumstances that challenged him personally as well as professionally and threatened to undo his very being.

At the risk of lifting a verse out of context, the following verse of *Sh'mini* resonates with overwhelming relevance to Yom HaShoah: "And your brethren the entire household of Israel will bemoan the *s'reifah* [the burning fire]" (Lev. 10:6).

Sh'mini
Rabbi David Novak, 2014

Sinai, the mountain, is a fixed place geographically. Our Torah tradition needed to find a method to reassure the Israelites (and us) that God's presence would be with them no matter where they found themselves.

That is the genius in *Parashat Sh'mini*: with a consecrated priesthood, the people are able to bring offerings to the *Mishkan* for various kinds of sacrifices and know that God is with them. Leviticus 9:23–24 recounts a magnificent moment: "When [Moses and Aaron] came out [from the Tent of Meeting] they blessed the people, and the Presence of YHVH appeared to all the people. Fire came forth from before YHVH and consumed the burnt offering and the fat parts on the altar. And all the people saw, and shouted and fell on their faces."

The importance of this theophany, Jacob Milgrom (*Leviticus: A Book of Ritual and Ethics*) writes, "cannot be exaggerated." It renders the experience of revelation ongoing, independent of a particular place, and an "assurance of the permanent presence of the Deity in Israel's midst."

This concept becomes even more essential and profound to those of us serving Jewish communities in the Diaspora. Our obligation remains to make it known to people that God remains right before our eyes. By creating strong emotional connections to God's presence in our lives and in the lives of the people we serve, we truly foster spiritual development.

Sh'mini
Rabbi Michael Boyden, 2015

The first ten chapters of Leviticus are devoted to the holiness of the *Mishkan*, its formal dedication, and the instruction of the *kohanim* (priests). In the last chapter of *Parashat Sh'mini*, however, the focus shifts from the sanctuary to the laws of permitted and forbidden foods for all Israel. This is not the first time we have come across a categorization of animals and discussion of permitted and forbidden food: at the time of the Flood, God gave Noah precise instructions concerning the number of pure and impure animals to be taken into the ark (Gen. 7:2).

Commentators differ as to the purpose of these classifications. While Maimonides (*Guide for the Perplexed* 3:48) argues that kashrut contributes to a healthy diet, Torah itself is very specific as to the intention of these regulations: "You shall not draw abomination upon yourselves. . . . You shall sanctify yourselves and be holy, for I am holy" (Lev. 11:43–44).

But what is holiness? Nachmanides, in his commentary to Lev. 19:2, tells us that holiness is a matter of boundaries and separations. We use the term *kadosh* when we set something or someone aside for a specific, predefined purpose or role. We may set aside the Sabbath as a day of rest (*shabbat kodesh*), our partner in marriage (*kiddushin*), or the Jews as a holy nation (*goy kadosh*).

The French gastronomist Anthelme Brillat-Savarin famously said, "Tell me what you eat and I'll tell you what you are." What is the case with people in general is especially true of the Jews. In an age of assimilation, we need to remind ourselves that a culture that wants to survive cannot just be "like everybody else." Kashrut provides the distinctiveness that reminds us of our holy purpose and potential.

Sh'mini
Rabbi Amy Scheinerman, 2016

The Torah has three midpoints. The *Babylonian Talmud Kiddushin* 30a, explains that the early Sages were called *sofrim* ("counters") because they would count all the letters of the Torah. Doing so, they identified the *vav* in *gachon* (Lev. 11:42) as the central letter of Torah, *darosh* in Lev. 10:16 as the central word of Torah—both are found in *Parashat Sh'mini*—and Lev. 13:33 in *Parashat Tazria* as the central verse of Torah. Verse, word, letter. What are we to make of these three centers?

Gachon is any creature that crawls on its belly; it is a *sheretz* ("abomination") and may not be eaten. The belly crawler that comes readily to mind is the snake, often associated with the *yetzer hara* ("evil inclination"). The *vav*, according to one interpretation, symbolically cuts the belly-crawler—the *yetzer hara*—in two, blocking its negative power and reminding us of the importance of living a moral life.

Darosh concerns Moses's inquiry into the goat for the purification offering, which Aaron's sons had neglected to eat. The term itself connotes questioning and inquiry, the foundation of learning, reminding us of the importance of having a life of the mind.

The central verse concerns the quarantine of the *m'tzora* until the person has recovered and the role of the priest doing the examination. It comes as a reminder of the importance of community in our lives. What do we bring to the community? How should the community care for and support the individual?

The very notion of a midpoint suggests balance.

Taken together, the three midpoints remind us of the balance Jewish living encourages and calls us to maintain: focus on morality, intellectual curiosity and inquiry, and meaningful communal connection.

Sh'mini
Rabbi Amy Scheinerman, 2017

Sh'mini famously delineates the biblical laws of kashrut: "You shall not draw abomination upon yourselves [*nafshoteichem*] through anything that swarms; you shall not make yourselves unclean therewith and thus become unclean" (Lev. 11:43).

Why does Torah phrase the prohibition this way? Rashi, noting the use of *nefesh*, tells us that eating *sheketz* ("anything that swarms") has a spiritual dimension: "If you make yourselves unclean with them here on earth, you shall become unclean, from My perspective, also in the world-to-come and the heavenly academy."

For Sforno, however, the spiritual lessons and repercussions already had taken place. He tells us that God had intended to live directly among Israel without the medium of a *Mishkan*. Following the sin of the Golden Calf, however, Israel "removed their spiritual crowns, which they had attained at the time of the giving of the Torah, and through which they were deemed worthy that the Divine Presence dwell in their midst without any intermediary," and God refused to dwell among them (Exod. 33:3). Moses built the *Mishkan* in order to lure God back into the life of the people.

God acceded but sought "to remedy [Israel's] temperament, in order that [the people] be predisposed to be illuminated with the light of everlasting life." To inculcate a spiritual temperament, God provided extensive rules and regulations pertaining to kashrut and *nidah* ("ritual purity"). The foods prohibited by Torah, Sforno tells us, defile our moral character and mental power.

The Kaplanian model suggests that communal history and identity are sufficient reasons for Jews to live observant Jewish lives. Sforno says we need spiritual motivation and meaning to inspire Jewish practice. Food for thought.

Sh'mini
Rabbi Charles Middleburgh, PhD, 2018

We obsess on kashrut when *Sh'mini* comes around, and in so doing miss something even more special. *Sh'mini* is the single greatest repository of natural history in the *Tanach*. There are references to birds and animals in other biblical texts (Zephaniah and Job, for example), but none compares in terms of detailed nomenclature with Leviticus 11, where we encounter nineteen species of birds and eight other animal species—yet we fail to take account of what this represents! We hold up our Jewish environmental credentials when we read *bal tashchit* (do not destroy) in Deuteronomy 20, but fail to appreciate the implications of the detail in *Sh'mini*.

What does this extraordinary list tell us? It demonstrates the levels not just of observation of the natural world in very ancient times but an awareness of different species and an initial attempt to classify them. It demonstrates that our earliest ancestors were immersed in the world in which they lived, appreciated and cared for it, and saw in it a paean of praise for the Creator of all things.

As a conservationist and environmentalist, I am moved and inspired by how much our forebears knew and understood about the world in which they lived and the animals with which they shared it. I am also encouraged by the thought that however hard their lives may have been, they lifted their gaze to what surrounded them and recognized God in all of it.

Al achat kamah v'chamah, "even more so," should we, who know so much more about our world, treat it and its creatures with reverence and respect.

תזריע/מצרע   *Tazria/M'tzora*
(Leviticus 12:1–13:59 and Leviticus 14:1–15:33)

Tazria/M'tzora
Rabbi Stephen Wylen, 2010

(based on Gevurat Sh'lomo, as quoted in *Iturei Torah* Vol. 4, p. 69.)

This is what we learn from four contexts in which the word *adam* (human being) appears in Torah:

- "Should any *adam* contract a skin disease . . . that person should go to the priest" (Lev. 13:2).
- "When any *adam* among you brings a sacrifice to God" (Lev. 1:2)
- "Should an *adam* among you die under a roof" (Num. 19:14)
- "*Adam* or beast, God will redeem them" (Lev. 27:28)

According to the *Y'rushalmi Makkot* 2:6, 7a, these four verses correspond to four different attitudes toward forgiveness and the restoration to grace:

> A person asks: What shall be done to the sinner? Wisdom answers: Let that person suffer the consequences of sin. The prophets say: The soul that sins shall die. Torah responds: Let them bring a guilt offering as a sacrifice and they shall be forgiven. The Blessed Holy One says: Repent and it shall be forgiven you.

We learn that one who repents before God is absolved from punishment, death and sacrifice, and is restored to God's good grace. We note that as one rises to higher *k'dushah* ("holiness"), the demand for punishment and restitution diminishes, while the will to forgive increases. From where you stand on this scale, you can tell how high you have risen toward holiness.

Tazria/M'tzora
Rabbi Louis Rieser, 2013

Adonai s'fatai tiftach, "God, open my lips" (Ps. 51:17). We customarily use these words to open the *Amidah*, to pray that we might find the right words to express the yearnings of our heart. Prayer at its best is hard work, as we who try to mentor others in that skill well know. In reality, all speech is difficult.

Words, the basic building blocks of creation, are powerful. The M'or Einayim (Rabbi Menachem Nachum Twersky of Chernobyl, 1730–97), commenting on this *parashah*, notes that God creates the world through words for the sake of human beings (okay, he says "Jews," but I choose to broaden his understanding). God takes great joy in every human being, so when you or I speak words of *lashon hara* ("gossip"), even true words, we spoil God's joy. God, as it were, becomes sad, and afflictions follow.

This clarifies the teaching in *Tosefta Pei-ah* 1:2, "These are the evil things that one collects interest on in this world while the principal remains . . . and *lashon hara* is equivalent to them all." Words, the tools of creation, are similar to the tools of destruction. As the M'or Einayim says: When God is silenced because we have misused words, we can no longer know the divine will. We are left rudderless.

The M'or Einayim, based on *Sefer Y'tzirah*, identifies words with God's power and majesty. Words give us divine power, so beware. It is always a good idea to pause before you speak and to ask *Adonai s'fatai tiftach*— "God, guide me as I open my lips."

Tazria
Rabbi Amy Scheinerman, 2014

We think of the priests' duties to examine sufferers of *tzaraat* as a messy business. The S'fat Emet sees it otherwise. Like a surgeon who opens the body and sees not "blood and guts" but the wondrous miracle of

Creation inside, when the Gerer Rebbe operates on *Tazria*, he finds that we are creatures of light garbed in skins of corporeality. Introducing a wordplay on *or* ("skins" with which God fashioned garments for Adam and Eve, Gen. 3:21) and *or* (Moses's "skin" shone with "light," Exod. 34:35), the S'fat Emet tells us that originally Adam and Eve were composed entirely of *or* (light)—they were purely spiritual beings—but after they disobeyed God they became corporeal creatures needing *or* (skin coverings). And so humanity remained until *matan Torah* (giving of the Torah), when Moses's *or* (skin) shone like *or* (light). Subsequent sin, however, brought Israel back down to the physical level.

We might think that the S'fat Emet has bought into the matter/spirit dualism, which brands matter coarse and sinful, and spirit pure and good. But no, he has more to say: It is also known that the skin is porous, containing many tiny holes. These allow the light to shine through its "shells." Only sin clogs up those pores so that "darkness covers the earth" (Isa. 60:2). That is why the leprous affliction is translated (in Aramaic) *s'giru*, or "closing."

We are both *or* ("light") and *or* ("skin"). As embodied creatures, we have not lost our capacity for spiritual purity—the light always shines through. The S'fat Emet's teaching is a prescient reminder of the good and potential in all people.

M'tzora
Rabbi Stephen Wylen, 2014

Skin disease. The leprosy of houses. Oy, what is a preacher to do? Fortunately, based on the story of Miriam in Numbers 12, the laws of leprosy have traditionally been associated with the laws of *lashon hara* ("gossip").

The common excuse for speaking *lashon hara* is "Everything I am saying is the absolute truth." It is precisely the truth of a derogatory statement that makes it *lashon hara*. Were the statement false, it would be *malshinut* ("slander"). The law is that one may not speak a truth about another person that lowers the subject in the esteem of the listeners, unless the listeners have a clear and present need for this information to protect them from material or bodily harm. The excuse "People will be better off knowing what a rotten person my enemy X is" will not suffice.

B'reishit Rabbah 8:5 states that God threw the angel of truth to the ground in order to create humankind. While the midrash is based on a reading of Ps. 85:11, it points to a higher truth: human society cannot coexist with absolute truth. There is no mitzvah against lying, only against false testimony and falsely swearing oaths. We need gentle lies to keep our social relationships in good order. What we need is not more truth, but more compassion.

Tazria
Rabbi Amy Scheinerman, 2015

"If a woman conceives and bears a male child, she shall be impure seven days. . . . On the eighth day, the flesh of his foreskin shall be circumcised" (Lev. 12:2–3).

Why does Torah mention *milah* ("circumcision") in the context of *tumat hayoledet* (the ritual impurity of a woman after giving birth)? We learned about circumcision in Gen. 17:10–11, where God commands *milah* as a sign of the *b'rit* ("covenant") with Abraham. But it is clear from Gen. 17:6–9 that fertility is at the core of the covenant: God promises Abraham and all future generations the land, protection, and generativity. And, perhaps, something more.

Midrash Tanchuma (*Tazria* 5), reflecting the Hellenistic world's repulsion regarding circumcision, a rite they (like some today) considered mutilation of natural, human perfection, records a conversation between Rabbi Akiva and Turnus Rufus, who asks, "Whose deeds are better—those of God or humans?" Surprisingly, Rabbi Akiva replies that human deeds are superior and offers two examples: sheaves of wheat versus fresh-baked rolls and raw flax versus finished clothing. "These are God's works and these are human works—are those of people not better?" Rufus then contends that circumcision proves that Jews hold themselves out as superior to God. Anticipating this accusation, Rabbi Akiva explains that God gave Israel the Torah, including *milah*, as a means to refine themselves.

The mitzvah of *milah* serves as a reminder that the natural world is amoral—it is not all necessarily good—but through practice of mitzvot, one can refine oneself and combine the potential of the natural world with human creativity and morality to create a better world.

M'tzora
Rabbi Louis Rieser, 2015

Our portion opens, *Zot tih'yeh torat ham'tzora*, usually translated as "These are the instructions regarding the *m'tzora*" (Lev. 14:2). The S'fat Emet (*S'fat Emet* 3:141, in Arthur Green, *The Language of Truth*, p. 175), however, understands it as "These are the spiritual lessons learned from the case of the *m'tzora*." What are we to learn?

The *m'tzora* is quarantined outside the camp until both cured and purified. Using Isaiah's words "Shalom, shalom to the near and the far" (Isa. 57:19) to focus our attention, the S'fat Emet pivots from those with a skin disease to redefine the *m'tzora* as any of us who have wandered far from God through misguided action or thought. The S'fat Emet teaches that there are some who attain wholeness only through creating distance, by being sent out of the camp. Perhaps you know those who through lack of love or an excess of pride, or as a result of brokenness or fear, leave the community or are sent away. Their redemption, he counsels, comes from within this distancing. From afar they make the journey back. In his words, such a person "has to accept this distancing with love and learn that within it is to be found one's redemption."

It can be a challenge to welcome back those who have wandered far from our communal camp. They come carrying the baggage of their wanderings, and that can make us uncomfortable. The S'fat Emet suggests that what looks like wandering to our eyes is part of a divine intention for this person who needed to travel far to uncover their inner shalom, wholeness. We have the possibility and privilege to offer aid as they return to our "camp." May we have the wisdom and patience to help them do so.

Tazria: Shabbat HaChodesh
Rabbi David Novak, 2016

The laws of *Tazria* stipulate that a woman who has given birth is considered *t'mei'ah* ("ritually impure") because of the blood expended in the process of childbirth. Blood flow is distressing, even to contemporaries. Throughout Leviticus, one sees that the outward manifestations of certain afflictions render one *tamei* and that some combination of time, sacrifice, and ritual is required to become *tahor* (ritually pure) again. All bodily efflux rendered one *tamei*, but blood—perhaps because Torah knows it as the "lifeblood"—most of all. Hence during menses, from onset in the teen years through midlife, women who were *nidah* ("ritually impure") were considered *t'mei'ah*; and the laws of family purity, including the prohibition against a man having sexual relations with his wife when she was *nidah*, followed from the blood taboo.

Today, we do not consider blood taboo, so rather than focus on the women being *t'mei'ah*, perhaps we might sanctify this holy aspect of womanhood—the ability to conceive, nurture a fetus, and deliver a baby into life—and mark not only childbirth with blessings, but also the many months when there is a discharge of blood. Consider the liminal moment when a young girl menstruates for the first time. How might one assert a life-affirming message then and during each subsequent cycle? Similarly, when the body begins to change, and the cycles stop, we might develop a ritual to mark that life event, as well.

Our teacher and colleague Rabbi Dr. Rachel Adler suggests that instead of a well-intentioned male (me) creating a ritual for something I, as a man, have never experienced, women construct new rituals to celebrate childbirth and mark menses. In so doing, they can give voice to their own reality, sanctifying experiences that deserve ritual recognition.

M'tzora: Shabbat HaGadol
Rabbi Stephen Wylen, 2016

"I will send you Elijah the prophet before the coming of the great and terrible Day of God. He will reconcile parents with children and children with their parents, so that when I come I do not strike the whole land with utter destruction" (Mal. 3:23–24).

Reconciliation between parents and children is the task for which Elijah the prophet returns to earth. It seems like such a small thing for Elijah to do. Could he not come back to bring peace or to reveal to us the eternal truths? No, he comes to reconcile parents and children.

As we gain experience, we come to see the cosmic significance of Elijah's task. This is especially true for us as rabbis. How often have we been with a family at the time of the death of a parent where there is no consolation because there is still "unfinished business"? How often has a person who bounces from one failure to the next in life confessed to the rabbi, "You know, the root of my problem is that I never grieved when my father/mother died"?

Our atonement depends upon our reconciliation. No father and no mother is perfect. Some are far from perfect. But we have to learn to live with the ones we get. So often the rabbi is asked, "Do I have to honor this father?" If every parent were worthy, we would not need the commandment. We do not have to obey our parents nor follow in their footsteps. We do have to deal with the heritage they have granted us, may it be for good, and if not, we still have to deal. On this condition alone society may endure.

Tazria/M'tzora
Rabbi Louis Rieser, 2017

"[The *m'tzora*] shall be unclean as long as the disease is on him. Being unclean, he shall dwell apart; his dwelling shall be outside the camp" (Lev. 13:46).

Biblical doctor-priests knew *tzaraat* as a disease that afflicted not only the human body, but also clothing and houses. The Rabbis, however, understood *tzaraat* to be a moral disease brought about by negative behaviors—*motzi shem ra*—that afflicted the soul. For both, the remedy to the ritual impurity imparted by *tzaraat* is separation from the community, as Torah instructs.

An increasing number of health practitioners acknowledge that ailments have both physical and spiritual components. Just as there is no true separation of body and mind, there is no real distinction between physical and spiritual illness.

So what is the wisdom requiring the *tzaraat* to be separated from the community? If every illness includes some measure of spiritual ailment, we need to address spiritual health. For true healing to occur, the one afflicted must discover those broken places deep within. This can only be accomplished by having a time out of life's normal daily activities.

Our job as spiritual healers is to guide toward wholeness and holiness.

Tazria/M'tzora
Rabbi David Novak, 2018

To the authors of Torah's Priestly Code, visible afflictions of human skin or garments caused great concern for ritual purity. In order to reestablish purity, Torah has the priests remove the affected individual from the population center until a priest is able to declare the person "pure." This declaration of the person's recovery makes sure that the remaining Israelites be free of visual physical defects. Underlying the process is an unspoken fear of God-imposed illness for human behaviors.

The Talmudic Sages asserted that *Tazria*'s underlying cause is *lashon hara* ("gossip"), as we learn from the incident in which Miriam is afflicted with *tzaraat* after she and Aaron gossip about Moses's wife. Our Sages saw Miriam's illness as a punishment for what remains an ongoing and harmful human behavior.

To connect God-inflicted punishment with disease is problematic. When a person contracts illness, however it manifests, people often seek to spiritualize it, asking, "Why did God do this to me?" Illness of all kinds, though, happens to human beings because we are biological organisms. Even though there are connections between human behavior and ill health, we do not have any indication that ill health is God's punishment for bad behavior.

It is incumbent that when we teach *Tazria* or any text that may suggest illness as punishment from God, we should impart that the God of the Torah—the God of love—rejects malevolent action. Simultaneously, we should emphasize that the quality of our lives is incrementally improved when we use our gift of speech for good.

אחרי מות / קדושים
Acharei Mot / K'doshim
(Leviticus 16:1–18:30 and Leviticus 19:1–20:27)

Acharei Mot / K'doshim
Rabbi Jeffrey Ballon, z"l, 2010

How do we as rabbis teach our tradition? Often we teach by example, combining what is most human in us and what is most godly about being human.

After becoming a bar mitzvah, I was taken to shivah minyanim conducted by my father. I was given instructions to reinforce the dazed behaviors of the mourning family by sitting quietly. I learned that my presence in a time of sorrow was sufficient. We have all experienced events of such magnitude that we are stunned. We learned that sitting in silence can be the best response.

"Then Moses said to Aaron, 'This is what Adonai meant when God said, "Through those near to Me I show Myself holy, and gain glory before all the people."' And Aaron was silent" (Lev. 10:3).

Most of us are initially stunned by loss. After 9/11 we didn't immediately know what to do or how to do it. Sometimes these moments stay with us and stun us for the rest of our lives: 9/11 is America's Tishah B'Av. Why does Tishah B'Av stay with us despite our liberal historical and theological explanations of Temple ritual and its irrelevance? Because we are stunned anew when we relive destruction in our minds.

In the opening verses of *Acharei Mot*, Aaron enters the *Kodesh*: "Thus only shall Aaron enter the Shrine: with a bull of the herd for a purification offering and a ram for the burnt offering" (Lev. 16:3). By offering a *chatat* and an *olah*, Aaron models for the people that the response to tragedy is to bring sanctity to people's lives.

Acharei Mot / K'doshim
Rabbi Amy Scheinerman, 2012

Living in a culture that worships youth, what are we to make of Lev. 19:32, "You shall rise before the aged and show deference to the old; you shall fear your God: I am Adonai"? Some public buses in Israel post this verse.

I have taught Talmud to many age groups. While the elderly often find the technical and logical intricacies more difficult than younger learners do, they more quickly and easily see what is beneath the text, because they have accrued a life full of experience and wisdom. There is a tendency these days to value information over wisdom. That would be a tragic mistake, especially because it requires great wisdom to sort and use appropriately the tsunami of information available to us.

A proverb has it that "for the ignorant, old age is winter; for the learned, old age is the harvest." Many elderly are learned in the ways of the world, life, and relationships, and we should profit from and celebrate the harvest of their wisdom.

There are ways to capture and hold the wisdom of our elders. One is to have them share their stories. I recommend *Family Tales, Family Wisdom: How to Gather the Stories of a Lifetime and Share Them with Your Family* by Robert Akeret and Daniel Klein.

Another way is to encourage elders to write ethical wills. As with elder tales, this requires some organization and structure. It's worth the effort because the outcome is priceless. You might wish to consult *Ethical Wills: Putting Your Values on Paper* by Barry Baines.

The *Alphabet of Ben Sira* says, "Who respects the elderly is as if he respects Adonai."

Acharei Mot
Rabbi Stephen Wylen, 2013

"After the death of the two sons of Aaron, who came close to the presence of God [*lifnei adonai*] and died . . ." (Lev. 16:1)

> Rabbi Tanchuma said: This shows that Nadav and Avihu prided themselves and gazed directly upon the *Shechinah*, and as Rabbi Y'hoshua of Siknin said in the name of Rabbi Levi, Moses averted his eyes and avoided gazing directly upon the *Shechinah*, and thereby he merited that Moses's own face shone with a halo and everyone stood back from him in reverence, while Nadav and Avihu failed to benefit from the Divine Presence and they died in the presence of God when they offered strange fire.
>
> Rabbi Yonatan said: And did they die in the actual presence of God? [Literally? Can anyone actually be in the presence of God?] Rather, the Torah tells us that when the children of a tzaddik die in the lifetime of the tzaddik, God cannot turn the divine gaze away from this great sorrow. God never ceases to see this tragic turn of events. That is the presence of God (From *Midrash Tanchuma Acharei Mot* 6).

We learn from Rabbi Yonatan how to interpret and preach the Torah. God does not zap us with tragic loss as a punishment for sins that we must search out in order to validate our sorrows. Rather, when we grieve a tragic loss, God is always with us, grieving alongside of us. God is not an avenger, but a fellow mourner. God's sorrowing eye is always upon us.

Acharei Mot
Rabbi Amy Scheinerman, 2014

Midrashim tell us that Nadav and Avihu were drunk, or disrespectful to their elders, or self-important, or initiated a sacrifice that God had not commanded. Rabbi Menachem Nachum Twersky of Chernobyl, in *M'or Einayim*, has an entirely different view:

> In their intense devotion and righteousness, [Nadav and Avihu] attained fulfillment, giving themselves over to death. They became so wondrously attached to God that their souls just remained there, cleaving to the divine light, a channel of energy rising upward. Their souls departed into the One! This is the meaning of "when they approached Adonai and died" (Lev. 16:1).

Nadav and Avihu brought about their own deaths—against God's desire—by clinging inseparably to God. The Chernobler Rebbe goes on to say that the purpose of elevation to the holy sphere and achieving union with God is to draw down blessings from the upper realm into our world. Nadav and Avihu not only forfeited their lives, but the blessings they might have bestowed upon Israel.

That is why Aaron is now warned not to come at all times into the Holy (Lev. 16:2). He should indeed come into the Holy with the devotion shown by his sons. But let him not die: rather, he should add to the life-flow of blessing and holiness pouring forth upon him.

It's easy to dismiss this as a message to mystics not to go too far, but we can all take counsel here. How often do people become singularly and obsessively involved in our work or a specific goal, to the exclusion of all else and everyone else?

K'doshim
Rabbi Gila Ruskin, 2014

Hochei-ach tochi-ach, "You shall surely rebuke" (Lev. 19:17). These words rang in my ears as I listened to the laudatory eulogies of a rabbi who had harassed and intimidated countless women for half a century. For years, many of his colleagues kept silent concerning a situation that we were well aware of but chose to ignore. Why had I kept silent? Because I didn't want to get involved. Because what business was it of mine? Because what good would it do anyway? Because it was awkward and embarrassing. Because remaining silent was so much easier. Because it wasn't really "rape." Because *hochei-ach tochi-ach* is one of the most onerous and painful mitzvot to fulfill.

Why is the verb doubled in *hochei-ach tochi-ach*? Rava teaches (*Babylonian Talmud Bava M'tzia* 31a) that the double verb calls upon us to rebuke even an authority figure, acknowledging that it is doubly difficult to confront a teacher, parent, employer, colleague, or major donor.

When Elazar ben Azariah did not rebuke his neighbor for placing a Shabbat-forbidden strap on his neighbor's cow, we learn that the *aveirah* now belongs to Elazar, as well as his neighbor; hence the double verb (*Babylonian Talmud Shabbat* 54b).

When I did not rebuke this colleague, when our community did not rebuke, we doubled the *aveirah*; we now bear that guilt. There is no doubt that rebuking would have been awkward and embarrassing, but the guilt we shoulder for not having rebuked is infinitely more painful. And beyond this concern, how many incidents of harassment and abuse could have been prevented? That is, after all, why we are commanded to rebuke.

Acharei Mot / K'doshim
Rabbi David Novak, 2015

It was only ten years ago that the revised Plaut commentary changed the commentary for "You shall not lie with man as with woman, it is *to-eivah*" (Lev. 18:22; *The Torah: A Modern Commentary*, rev. ed., pp. 789–90) from the condemnatory language of the first edition. A similar revision occurred in the Conservative Movement's *Chumash, Etz Hayim* (p. 691). Previous translations for *to-eivah* as "abhorrent" or "abomination" were amplified by commentary that was hurtful to generations of gay and lesbian Jews encountering these words as they were exploring their own sexualities.

In context, *to-eivah* is about the foreign practices of Egypt and Canaan. We were to be a nation and to set ourselves apart from those whom we knew or would come to know. The term "homosexuality" did not come into parlance until the late nineteenth century; it is only in recent years that sexuality has been understood to most likely be hardwired from birth in a majority of people. Torah could never have imagined that same-sex attraction would be a biological urge rather than an idolatrous practice. It is cruel and inhumane to use this text to deny people's experience.

The changes in the commentaries, as in our society, are helping to create a more embracing environment for our gay and lesbian brothers and sisters. We, as rabbis, are obligated to interpret our sacred texts as tools of love and embrace. In so doing we are raising another sacred principle from Torah: *k'vod hab'riyot*, "honoring all of God's creation."

Acharei Mot
Rabbi Michael Boyden, 2016

Although many feel an urge to eat a juicy steak from time to time, Jewish tradition, while affirming the sacrificial cult, would appear to embrace vegetarianism.

It all begins with God's words to Adam and Eve: "See, I give you every seed-bearing plant . . . and every tree that has seed-bearing fruit; they shall be yours for food" (Gen. 1:29). We are told three verses earlier that they will rule over all living creatures, but it does not say that they will eat them!

Nachmanides points out (ad locum) that it is only in Noah's time that his family is instructed, "Every creature that lives shall be yours to eat" (Gen. 9:3). Why the difference? Perhaps because Adam was created *tov m'od* ("very good"), meaning perfect and pure, whereas Noah was just the best of his generation.

Later in Lev. 17:13, we are told that a hunter must cover the blood of his kill with earth. Why? The Rashbam suggests that the reason is to render the blood inedible. Deuteronomy 12:23 reinforces the prohibition against eating blood by declaring that the blood is the life, and you must not consume the life with the flesh.

Particularly appealing is Nachmanides's understanding of this mitzvah: "What is eaten returns to the body of the consumer, and they become one flesh. If a human being eats the life [*nefesh*] of an animal, they become linked . . . you will become vulgar . . . and resemble the nature of the animal that you have eaten."

Rav Kook concludes (David Cohen (ed.), חזון הצמחונות והשלום מבחינה תורנית, p. 14.), "If the prohibition again killing animals were to receive religious and moral affirmation . . . then the world would be a better place."

K'doshim
Rabbi Amy Scheinerman, 2016

"You shall be holy, for I, Adonai your God, am holy" (Lev. 19:2). Is this statement descriptive or prescriptive? Are we holy simply because we exist, created *b'tzelem Elohim*? Or must we make ourselves holy through covenanting with God, or specific deeds, or perhaps something else?

Dov Ber, the Magid of Mezeritch, offers one understanding of what it means to be holy. Quoting midrash, "There will be no death in your midst," he draws a connection to Ps. 118:17, "I shall not die, but live and proclaim [*asapeir*] the works of YAH," which he interprets: "For as long as I am alive, may I not be considered (God forbid) 'dead'; I will maintain pure thoughts and speak from the depths of [my] heart, and thus I *asapeir*, meaning 'to shine clearly,' and I will shine and proclaim 'the works of YAH,' which are Wisdom [*Chochmah*] and Understanding [*Binah*], from which all divine blessings flow, and from there I will shine and light up all the worlds." For the Magid, being truly alive means being a conduit for the *shefa*, the divine flow, so that blessings from the Source find their way into our world and into our lives. One becomes a conduit by cleaving to the Source through pure thought and intense devotion. Doing so brings God's light into the world. This is how one becomes holy.

The Magid adds a dimension to our thinking about holiness. Beyond notions of inherent attributes or deeds that make us holy, he introduces the notion of the attitude of purity and depth with which we may approach everything in our lives.

Acharei Mot / K'doshim
Rabbi Charles Middleburgh, PhD, 2017

The value of a good aphorism, whether it be of the divine, sublime, or ridiculous kind, is how succinctly it expresses wisdom that might otherwise take paragraphs to spell out. Its genius lies in the fact that while its principal meaning may be obvious, there is still room for inspiring and thought-provoking individual interpretations.

With this in mind, one great aphorism is the midrash on the words *Acharei Mot K'doshim* ("After death, speak holiness"), the Jewish equivalent to the Latin *De mortuis nihil nisi bonum* (effectively, "Do not speak ill of the dead"). Once people have left the stage, what point is there to castigating and denouncing? Yet for those worthy of denigration—the stage is crowded—Anthony's words over Caesar's body will have it just about right: "The evil that men do lives after them, the good is oft interred with their bones" (*Julius Caesar*, act 3, scene 2).

In our dystopian "post-truth" world (some will prefer Stephen Colbert's "truthiness"), there are doubtless many who will exult in ascribing bizarre meanings to treasured phrases from the past. Yet this week's combined *parashiyot* (*Acharei Mot/K'doshim*) end on the high note of *K'doshim*—"being holy people." There can be little wiggle room, for the meaning of this word is beyond dispute. "Holiness" means being special, though not in a glib way; it means setting yourself apart from the common herd; it means doing good with your life and for the lives of others, standing for your best even when others race for the worst in themselves. This meaning is undeniable and unalterable; it stands as a testament to Torah's divine and abiding truth.

Acharei Mot / K'doshim
Charles Middleburgh, PhD, 2018

I was six years old and in Venice with my parents on June 3, 1963, when Angelo Giuseppe Roncalli, Pope John XXIII, died. I remember walking up to a stand covered in black-edged newspaper front pages announcing his death. My father stopped, looked, and cried. When I asked why, my dad replied, "He was a truly holy man."

Years later I learned a great deal more about Papa Roncalli and agree wholeheartedly with my father that he was indeed a "holy" man. But what does "holiness" actually mean?

Leviticus 19 explicitly defines holiness by listing the key mitzvot: honor your parents; keep Shabbat; leave the gleanings of your field for the poor; don't steal, lie, or cheat; don't misuse God's name; be honest; respect others, including those with disabilities; treat everyone fairly; don't profit through another's misfortune; don't bear grudges; love and respect others as you do yourself.

Holiness can be found not just in sanctuaries where one expects to find it, but in the places where one doesn't. Holiness is not only in the extraordinary acts of exceptional people, but in the extraordinary acts of ordinary people and even the ordinary acts of ordinary people. We live most of our lives unaware of the potential for touching—and achieving—holiness. We neglect the holiness inherent in ourselves and ignore it in others, and we forget that performing specific actions in prescribed ways can raise seemingly mundane deeds into vehicles for communion with God.

אמר *Emor*
(Leviticus 21:1–24:23)

Emor
Rabbi Amy Scheinerman, 2010

The first half of *Emor* is devoted to what we often consider arcane matters of the priesthood, including the holiness of the *kohanim* (priests), sacrificial offerings made by *kohanim*, and the requirement that *kohanim* be without physical blemish.

Leviticus 21:1–4 tells us that a priest may not subject himself to ritual impurity by attending the death or burial of any save his closest blood relatives: parents, children, a brother, and an unmarried sister. Glaringly absent from this list of "close relations" is his wife.

The *Bavli* seeks to correct this startling omission. In the *Babylonian Talmud Y'vamot* 22b, the Rabbis read *sh'eiro* (Lev. 21:2) as "his wife" and thereby include the wife among those closest to the *kohein*. Rashi, quoting *Sifra*, echoes the same explanation. Rambam states explicitly, "Concerning the wife of the priest, one must become impure, even against his will. . . . They [the scribes] gave her the status of *meit mitzvah* [whom one is commanded to bury]."

This is yet another example of how the Rabbis went beyond *p'shat*, employing their moral compasses and best reasoning to interpret Torah. Similarly, the Rabbis unraveled *ben soreir u'moreh* (the wayward and defiant son; Deut. 21:18–21), capital punishment, slavery, and the Torah's prohibition against annulling foolish vows. When Rabbi Y'hoshua ben

Chananiah declared, *Lo bashamayim hi!* ("It is not in heaven!"; *Babylonian Talmud Bava M'tzia* 59b), he simultaneously stated the importance of the human element in the divine-human relationship.

But isn't the "human element"—attuned to God, Torah, and Israel—of divine origin and quality? Torah flows in two directions, continuously between heaven and earth, as we seek to live our lives in response to God.

Emor
Rabbi Joshua Minkin, DMin, 2011

"You shall take choice flour and bake of it twelve loaves. . . . Place them on a pure table before Adonai in two rows, six to a row" (Lev. 24:5–6).

Etz Hayim (ed. David L. Lieber, Rabbinical Assembly, 2001) tells us (p. 731): "The Talmud states that 'a great miracle was performed in the Tent of Meeting; the sacred loaves of bread never grew stale' (*Babylonian Talmud M'nachot* 29a). According to Hirsch, those words were not meant to be taken literally. They convey the idea that the sanctuary was immune to the process of boredom and habit that afflict many religious institutions. Rituals did not grow stale or obsolete there."

The Talmud recognizes that while repetition breeds familiarity, it also often leads to boredom and rote performance. This applies as much to our own spiritual lives as to those of our congregants. For how many of us is a week without our own Shabbat the norm? When leading the service prevents us from feeling a divine connection, even if we insist on a day of rest, do we have something in our lives that nourishes our souls? We ignore our own spiritual lives at our peril, risking depression and burnout. Retreats, classes, study, and prayer need to be part of our lives.

The *lechem panim* (bread of display) was replaced from week to week. We are not. We serve our people and our religion best when we nourish that spark of the Divine within. We owe this to our congregants, our profession, our families, and ourselves.

Emor
Rabbi Amy Scheinerman, 2012

We find several festival and holy day calendars in Torah, and Passover is mentioned in each. Exodus 23:15 and 34:18 speak of Chag HaMatzot at the outset; Deut. 16:1 begins by naming the festival Chag HaAviv. However, Lev. 23:5–6 tells us to make the *pesach* sacrifice at twilight on the fourteenth day of the first month, and to keep Chag HaMatzot on the fifteenth day: "In the first month, on the fourteenth day of the month, at twilight, there shall be a Passover offering to Adonai, and on the fifteenth day of that month Adonai's feast of unleavened bread" (Lev. 23:5–6). Numbers 28:16–17 similarly speaks of the *pesach* and the prohibition of eating leavened bread but does not name the festival at all.

The Leviticus and Numbers versions seem to preserve a memory of divergent traditions: shepherds who offered newborn lambs in the spring, and farmers who observed the feast of unleavened bread at the same time. Both celebrated the beginning of a new "harvest," a precious gift from God. Yet they celebrated in very different ways, and their differences were rolled into the festival whose name derives from the paschal sacrifice and whose main feature is abstaining from leavened bread—thus celebrating both.

Throughout our history there has been a tension between centralization and uniformity on the one hand and diversity on the other. We see the push for uniformity early on cultic sites and later concerning halachic observance. We see historical diversity in the varying traditions of Ashkenazic, Sephardic, Mizrachi, and Yemenite Jews and today in the numerous streams of Judaism. This affirmation of diversity, however subtle, is invaluable.

Emor
Rabbi Janice Garfunkel, z"l, 2013

We are outraged that disabled *kohanim* were excluded from bringing sacrifices (Leviticus 17). But before we get too high and mighty, let's look at our own attitudes toward those who are different.

Yes, we all know we need to replace steps with ramps, and we can recount moving stories of seriously disabled children celebrating bar/bat mitzvah. But do mildly disabled kids, kids with annoying behavioral problems caused by Asperger's, or ADHD, or no known reason, feel not merely tolerated and permitted to participate, but embraced? Loved? Supported? To what an extent do their parents feel judged for their children's misbehaviors? Do you really, truly, want those children in your sanctuary?

I recently was told by a mother that her difficult children had their most negative encounters in, of all places, shul.

How sad.

I think it is hardest for rabbis and Jewish community leaders to stand up for these children when we happen to be the parent of one; it hits too close to home, and we can be accused of defending our own child rather than promoting a moral principle.

At our summer camps and in our religious schools, how much time do we devote to teaching our campers, teachers, and counselors how to make sure every child feels embraced, wanted, supported? How do we react to odd or unusual behaviors? Would a parent in your community consider your shul a place to come for support for themselves and their different children, or do they need to go to non-Jewish places to find that? Has our community's emphasis on success, on young Jewish leaders, delivered the message that the only people we value are the best and the brightest, and if you are not destined for our idea of success, well, our Young Adults program isn't really for you?

Emor
Rabbi Michael Boyden, 2015

Rashi tells us in his comment on Deut. 14:1 that the Amorites engaged in certain behaviors but that we, as God's children, should behave in a more befitting manner.

As much as Torah restricts the behavior of Israelites, it restricts the behavior of the priests even more. *Parashat Emor* opens with a detailed list of restrictions to the behavior of the *kohanim*, ranging from shaving their heads to making incisions in their flesh. The Mishnah informs us that only those with unblemished and unstained hands are permitted to bless the people, so that the people can concentrate on the blessing rather than on the person giving the blessing (*Mishnah M'gilah* 4:7). Additional restrictions concern the proximity of priests to corpses and cemeteries.

What was this all about? Why were *kohanim* required to be any different from the rest of the people? The Torah's response is unambiguous: For they offer "Adonai's offerings by fire . . . and so must be holy" (Lev.

21:6). People who serve a public office thereby represent the people as a whole and are therefore required to live up to higher standards than those who appointed them. As Ibn Ezra explains in his commentary to Lev. 21:1: "Having warned the Jewish People and the priests in general terms [in *Parashat K'doshim*] about the need to be holy, the sons of Aaron are warned that they need to be careful when it comes to additional matters, because they are God's servants."

What held true for the *kohanim* in Temple times surely holds true for *k'lei kodesh* ("holy vessels") today.

Emor
Rabbi Amy Scheinerman, 2016

Emor delineates rules for the *kohanim*, beginning with the prohibition against ritually defiling themselves through contact with a corpse. Torah immediately provides an exemption so the priest can bury most close relatives. The Rabbis provided additional exemptions: *meit mitzvah* ("mitzvot on behalf of the deceased") when no one else is available, and the death of a *nasi* ("the head of the community").

Presumably, the priests need to remain in a state of ritual purity at all times in order to be available for service in the *Mishkan* (or *Mikdash*) when required. Rabbi Mordechai Yosef Leiner of Izbica, in *Mei HaShiloach*, cites a parable in *Tanchuma Emor* in which a king tells his cook that the cook's job is to ensure the king's pleasure, and therefore he may never look upon death, because that would bring the king sadness. The Ishbitzer Rebbe points out that death is the opposite of joy, and therefore the priests' prohibition is intended to ensure that they "be careful not to cause the opposite of their task, since they were chosen to bring down an effluence of joy into the world and to create a pleasing spirit before the Holy One, blessed be God, with their service."

This perspective raises many questions, among them: Would you agree that death is the opposite of joy? While the thrust of Chasidism is the pursuit of spiritual joy, what would we say is the core of Jewish spirituality today? Is there a parallel between the God-priest relationship and the congregation-Rabbi relationship; this is, is it the responsibility of a rabbi to project joy and inspire joy in others?

Emor
Rabbi Amy Scheinerman, 2017

Among the more troubling and confusing passages in Torah is the account of the blasphemer, the son of an Israelite mother and an Egyptian father, who gets into a fight and pronounces the ineffable Name (Lev. 24:10–23).

The passage is peculiar, with laws considering other matters inserted in the middle. God instructs Moses to have the community join together in stoning the blasphemer. Torah then promulgates laws concerning killing or maiming people or animals, stating that there shall be one standard for stranger and citizen alike, and then returning to the fate of the blasphemer: "Moses spoke thus to the Israelites. And they took the blasphemer outside the camp and pelted him with stones. The Israelites did as Adonai had commanded Moses" (Lev. 24:23).

Interpreting Lev. 24:23, Rashi tells us the stoning took place then and there, but Ibn Ezra says, "With regard to one who causes an injury, the Israelites began to follow this rule from that day forward," apparently referring to the laws about killing or maiming people or animals.

Nachmanides, who believes that Ibn Ezra's comment concerns the stoning of the blasphemer, says:

> Ibn Ezra is not correct . . . the verse describes what they just did: they "pelted him with stones." . . . In my opinion, the implication of our verse is that the Israelites stoned the man not because they hated this son of an Egyptian who had fought with an Israelite, but in accordance with God's command through Moses, to remove this stain from their midst.

Sforno draws the same conclusion.

There seems to be a high level of anxiety around this verse. Does it arise from the harsh sentence? The parentage of the blasphemer? The two in combination? Curiously no one justifies the stoning on moral grounds; they point out that God commanded it.

Emor
Rabbi Amy Scheinerman, 2018

"No animal from the herd or from the flock shall be slaughtered on the same day with its young" (Lev. 22:28).

God instructed Adam to "tend and till" the garden, but not to care for the animals. Torah fully acknowledges that animals may be rightfully used by people for work and food.

Yet our Sages associated this verse with prohibitions against yoking an ox with a donkey (Deut. 22:10) and muzzling an ox while plowing (25:4) as well as *shiluach hakein* ("the sending away of the mother bird before taking her eggs;" 22:6–7). They also created the much broader category of *tzaar baalei chayim*.

The most honest translation of *tzaar baalei chayim* is "not to cause an animal undue pain." Is this genuine compassion?

Why did the Sages seek to cultivate compassion toward animals?

The *Zohar* expresses it clearly: "We have learned that actions below arouse corresponding actions from above. Thus if one acts with kindness on earth, one awakens loving-kindness above. . . . It is like this also for the opposite. If one acts with cruelty in the world, cruelty is aroused on that same day and strikes him. In the same way that one deals with the world, so too is he dealt with" (*Vayikra* 92b). *Midah k'neged midah* ("measure for measure"). Compassion is not an end in itself; it is instrumental in securing our own well-being.

Few of us subscribe to the Rabbinic or Zoharic theological instrumentality of *tzaar baalei chayim*. We need a new theology of the relationship between people and animals, not merely as part of our relationship to the environment, but as the living creatures they are.

בהר/בחקתי B'har/B'chukotai
(Leviticus 25:1–26:2 and Leviticus 26:3–27:34)

B'har/B'chukotai
Rabbi Louis Rieser, 2010

What are the lessons of *Sh'mitah* (Sabbatical year) and *Yoveil* (Jubilee year) for contemporary readers? I read these sources primarily as texts about *bitachon*, "trust." If you depend on the produce of the land for your food and livelihood, it takes an enormous amount of trust to let all your lands go fallow at the same time for an entire year. Once you take the plunge and opt not to sow your seed, you are fully committed; there is no backup plan.

On a similar note, I particularly like a passage from *Everyday Holiness: The Path of Mussar* by Alan Morinis (p. 209). Morinis quotes Rabbi Yosef Yozel Hurwitz, Alter of Novarodok, as saying, "A person who tries to practice trust in God while leaving him/herself a backup plan is like a person who tries to learn how to swim but insists on keeping one foot on the ground."

The *Babylonian Talmud* (*Kiddushin* 29a) teaches that among other skills, a father must teach his son to swim. Swimming requires an existential trust: you will survive even when your feet are not solidly on the ground. The Sabbatical and Jubilee years require a similar trust: God will care for you, and you will survive. The alternative is to claim that we can be in control—a claim we know exceeds our human ability.

How do we, as Reform Jews, cultivate a sense of *bitachon*, trust in God, for our own lives or for the individuals in our communities?

B'har
Rabbi Louis Rieser, 2011

The grand aim of the Book of Leviticus is the establishment of holiness.

It begins by describing the ways we approach God in the most holy spot, the *Mishkan*, and ends by describing the ways we establish holiness of the land through *Sh'mitah* (Sabbatical year) and *Yoveil* (Jubilee year). The book opens on the vertical axis with burnt offerings and ends on the horizontal axis describing the ways in which we must aid our kinsmen when they fall into hard times. Leviticus dramatically makes the connection between those acts that are *bein adam lamakom* ("between humans and God") and those that are *bein adam lachaveiro* ("between humans"). When we read (Lev. 25:39) "If your kin under you continue in straits and must be given over to you, do not subject them to the treatment of a slave," we should understand that slavery and similar oppressions remove holiness from the world.

Yet it persists. According to www.iabolish.com ("Slavery in the United States"), "today there are 27 million people enslaved around the world," including all six inhabited continents.

Slavery can be opposed, and laws against slavery and the trafficking of human beings can be passed. Our actions to end slavery and its analogs increase holiness between human beings, between humans and God. What could be better? Name the actions you do that reach out simultaneously for God and our fellow human beings.

I think of Heschel's famous teaching, "When I marched in Selma, my feet were praying." We do not need to wait for dramatic events such as the civil rights marches; we have the opportunity to unite heaven and earth in holiness through our actions every day.

B'chukotai
Rabbi Amy Scheinerman, 2011

Winter came early to Maryland this year, bringing bitter cold temperatures and biting winds in November. Usually, bitter cold means no more than that I need to dress warmly; it has never impacted my food supply ... until this year. Late last summer we joined a CSA (Community Supported Agriculture) and purchased ten weeks of shares. The tenth share never came because the bitter cold weather destroyed the remaining crops in the field. Produce that had come reliably each week suddenly stopped coming. This experience got me thinking about how removed I am from where my food comes from and how utterly dependent on the environment I am.

The first half of *Parashat B'chukotai* is all about the Land: rain and fertility, peace and security, punishment and devastation. The theology behind Leviticus 26 is troubling. Perhaps it is not surprising that our ancestors saw rain as direct beneficence from God, and drought as a sign of God's displeasure (Lev. 26:3–5), but the notion of a micromanaging God who rewards generously but punishes severely does not even register as neutral with me; it is negative.

What I do glean from Leviticus 26 is the truth that the well-being of all humans and animals is integrally tied to the well-being and health of the land—indeed, planet Earth—and that we are responsible for this planet. The widespread presumption that earth is a basket of limitless resources at our disposal has led to massive degradation of forests and animal habitats, dangerous pollution of air and water, and global climate change. *B'chukotai* reminds us that all is intertwined.

B'har/B'chukotai
Rabbi Bill S. Tepper, 2012

As *Sefer Vayikra* draws to a close, the Israelites are—as they have been throughout the recitation of the Levitical laws—*b'har*, at Mount Sinai, receiving instructions to care for *Eretz Yisrael* and the people with whom they shall inhabit it. With its focus on the laws of *Sh'mitah*, the Sabbatical year, the text emphasizes the reverence with which the Israelites must approach the land. The S'fat Emet (Rabbi Y'hudah Leib Alter, 1847–1905) wrote, "The Torah states clearly that man must sow and harvest six years, just as it states that man must work for six days and rests on the Sabbath. This recognition infuses holiness and purpose into our work years and our workdays."

In *Parashat B'chukotai*, with which *B'har* is combined, we read of both the conditional reward and punishment for Israel's devotion to the commandments. Perhaps the most cherished reward is the promise of peace, to which we aspire no less in our own day. Rashi, commenting on Lev. 26:6 ("I will grant peace in the land, and you shall lie down untroubled by anyone; I will give the land respite from vicious beasts, and no sword shall cross your land") writes, "Here is food, here is drink, but if there is no peace there is nothing! From here we see that peace is as weighty as everything else combined." The work the Israelites do, day in and day out, year after year, with the exceptions of Shabbatot and *Sh'mitot*, can lead to peace, as can our efforts each day.

B'har/B'chukotai
Michael Boyden, 2013

"If your brother is facing difficulties and becomes dependent upon you, you shall treat him as a resident alien and let him live with you" (Lev. 25:35). Given the unstable global economy, that is an important message.

But what does "live with you" mean? To what degree are we responsible for our fellow human beings? Wikipedia claims that where someone's life is in danger, the common law of most "anglosphere" countries does not demand that we come to their rescue. Is this view compatible with "You shall love your neighbor as yourself" (Lev. 19:18)?

Indeed, the *Babylonian Talmud Sanhedrin* 73a, teaches, "If one sees one's fellow human drowning in a river, being dragged by a wild animal, or being assaulted by robbers, one has a duty to rescue the person. As Scripture teaches: Do not stand by the blood of your neighbor (Lev. 19:16)"; and it is stated in the *Babylonian Talmud Bava M'tzia* 71a, that if there is not enough money to go around, "the poor of your town take precedence."

But how far does that principle extend? The *Babylonian Talmud Bava M'tzia* 62a, tells the tale of two people who are traveling together, and only one has a canteen of water. If both drink, they will both die. However, if only one drinks, that person will make it back to safety. Ben Petura teaches that it would be better for both of them to drink and die rather than see their fellow human die. But Rabbi Akiva quotes our *para-*

shah: "Your fellow should live with you," that is, not without you. Your life takes precedence over that of your fellow human being. It seems only natural for us to care first and foremost for our own: "If I am only for myself, what am I?" (*Mishnah Pirkei Avot* 1:14).

B'har/B'chukotai
Rabbi Amy Scheinerman, 2015

Parashat B'har provides instructions concerning the Sabbatical and Jubilee years.

If the produce of the land grows in response to God's will, what good is there of letting the land lie fallow and risking hunger? Torah reports that Moses foresaw the anxiety of our ancestors and addressed it: "And should you ask, 'What are we to eat in the seventh year, if we may neither sow nor gather in our crops?" (Lev. 25:20).

The S'fat Emet (1847–1905) wonders why the Israelites would even ask the question

> "What are we to eat in the seventh year . . . ?" Did they not trust God to provide for their needs? . . . It is best that they did not assume that God would always provide, because then the existence of Israel would have depended upon a miracle, and not all generations are deserving of miracles.

The S'fat Emet then draws a seeming distinction between a miracle and a blessing,

> which is somewhat closer to nature. . . . Really, Jews should understand that miracles and nature are all one. In fact there is no miracle so great and wondrous as nature itself, the greatest wonder we can know. When this faith becomes clear to Jews, it is no longer a problem to be fed by miracles. . . . The word *neis* ("miracle") refers to uplifting; this is a way of conducting the world that is lifted out of the natural state, especially for the Children of Israel. The Maharal claimed that just as there is a natural order, there is also a miraculous order, one set aside for Israel.

This seems confusing and self-contradictory on the surface. Does the supernatural God operate through the natural world, or does God abrogate natural law? Or is the distinction between natural and supernatural only in our imaginations, in our failure to recognize the miracle of the natural world?

B'har
Rabbi Charles Middleburgh, PhD, 2016

B'har, at fifty-four verses, is one of the shortest *parashiyot*. Preceded by the richly detailed *Emor* and followed by the hard-edged execrations of *B'chukotai*, it is quite easy to pay it scant attention. Yet aspects of *B'har* are truly intriguing: it commences with the command to allow the land a Shabbat every seventh year, and it concludes with a command to observe God's weekly Shabbatot. This sandwiching is highly unusual and suggests that a painstaking editor with a true sense of literary style shaped this short section. Additionally, the word *yamuch* occurs three times in the center of the *parashah*. The root, *mem-vav-chaf*, occurs only in *parashiyot B'har* and *B'chukotai*. The root means "to be low, to become poor," and its recurrence in a section of Torah about Sabbatical and Jubilee years cannot be coincidental.

As we pillage more and more of earth's natural resources and beauty, ideas of Sabbatical and Jubilee years get shunted aside and squashed underfoot in our headlong rush to consume; yet as we become increasingly aware of the environmental impact of our irresponsibility—the depletion of rain forests, the murderous onslaught on endangered species, the disappearance of ice sheets, the instability of the weather—we must confront what we have done. Repetitions of a verb referencing poverty and deprivation sandwiched between instructions about enforced rest suggest that our behavior carries a heavy cost.

We must ask ourselves what might be the greater cost tomorrow of our behavior today.

B'chukotai
Rabbi Michael Boyden, 2016

Our *parashah* has quite a lot to say about the relationship between our deeds and meteorology! In brief:

> If you follow My laws . . . I will grant you rains in their season. . . . However, if you don't obey Me . . . I will make your skies like iron and your earth like copper. . . . Your land shall not yield its produce, nor shall the trees of the land yield their fruit. (Lev. 26:3–4, 26:14, 26:19–20)

Some commentators, like the thirteenth-century French commentator Chizkuni, took the promise and the threat quite literally: "If you do what I have entrusted you to do, the clouds, the earth and the trees that were created for you will do what they are entrusted to do." Explaining the words "rains in their season," he commented, "But when they do not come in their due season, they rot the produce." Many of us will have difficulty accepting this mechanical description of reward and punishment, even if in an ecologically sensitive world we are now more aware of the relationship between our actions and their effect on nature.

Interestingly, even the fifteenth-century rabbi Isaac Abarbanel steered away from the literal interpretation of these verses. He wrote, "The good and bad . . . come neither as a reward nor punishment for mitzvot, because our true reward and punishment is spiritual."

Abarbanel understood reward in terms of the afterlife, but each of us will interpret it in his or her own way.

B'har/B'chukotai
Rabbi Amy Scheinerman, 2017

"If you follow My laws and faithfully observe My commandments, I will grant your rains in their season" (Lev. 26:3–4).

Similar to the second paragraph of the *Sh'ma*, the opening verses of *B'chukotai* link the performance of mitzvot to the proper functioning of the physical world. Many Jewish thinkers throughout the ages have held that Torah observance ought to be a matter of faith and obedience (*naaseh v'nishma*), not insight and understanding.

Rambam vigorously disagreed. "It is appropriate that one meditate, according to their intellectual capacity, regarding the laws of the Torah to understand their deeper meaning. Those laws for which one finds no reason and knows no purpose should nevertheless not be treated lightly" (*Mishneh Torah, Hilchot M'ilah* 8:8).

Dov Ber Friedman of Mezeritch, in *Or Torah*, draws an analogy to a king whose servant must fulfill his master's wishes without asking the king's reasons for them. The king's son, however, stands in a different relationship to the king. "His love for his father persuades him to fulfill all his commands and decrees, even if he does not understand them. But it is the son's role to ask his father why he commands things. That is what the king wants as well; he desires that his son ask and come to know the reason for things." For Friedman, questioning leads to learning the king's wisdom.

Rambam, a rationalist, and Friedman, a kabbalist, share the same insight: our love for God is expressed in our search for the meaning and purpose of the mitzvot; it is also expressed in our willingness to commit to Jewish observance even before we achieve insight.

B'har/B'chukotai
Rabbi David Novak, 2018

Our movement's consternation over biblical reward and punishment is most evident in *Mishkan T'filah*'s omission of the second paragraph of the *Sh'ma*. The omitted paragraph begins *V'hayah im shamo-a*, "If you heed/obey." So, too, *im* is repeated time and again throughout the *tocheichah* ("rebuke") in *B'chukotai*. Blessings and curses are enumerated as the consequences of behavioral choices: "if you obey . . . if you violate."

Most Reform Jews give little thought to these blessings and curses; few expect that God will alter reality in response to their personal choices. How might we actualize these blessings and curses? *B'chukotai* calls on us to wrestle with its fundamental underlying claim: human behavior influences God to act. Even before we face that question, modern neuroscience gives us pause to ask: how do we act?

Heidi M. Ravven in *The Self beyond Itself* argues that the concept of human free will is a myth initiated by Augustine. Ravven argues that we humans make ethical decisions less freely than we would like to think and that our abilities to act are infinitely more complicated than the biblical idea of reward and punishment.

This is food for thought as Torah continues to reveal itself in every generation.

Numbers

במדבר   *B'midbar*
(Numbers 1:1–4:20)

B'midbar
Rabbi David Novak, 2010

How does it feel to go from being inchoate (without form or boundaries) to being a functioning community? It is messy.

That, on one foot, is *B'midbar*. Often translated as "in the desert," it really means "in the wilderness." We could understand this wilderness as physical wilderness, but perhaps it is better thought of as the emotional wilderness that the Israelites experienced on their journey from slavery (land without choices) to the Promised Land (choosing for self and community).

This *parashah* begins with a counting—a census of all the males aged twenty to fifty. The accounting of men came to 603,550; we should assume there were as many women, as well as children and the mixed-multitude that attached itself when the Israelites left Mitzrayim.

Counting does not, however, prepare people for all of the challenges that come from being part of such a large community. Prescriptions (and proscriptions) from Above do not create order. As this generation of Israelites, counted at the beginning of *B'midbar*, will soon find out, they get to start the journey to the Promised Land, but they will not complete it. Infighting, political maneuvering, war and violence, foreign lands, despotic leaders—all conspire against them. Most unfortunately, the people (knowingly and unknowingly) conspire against themselves. They moan, groan, and in general behave in a way that is unbecoming for a newly freed people who are being given the most wonderful gift of all: freedom from slavery. They will pay a price. They will not set foot in the Promised Land. They become the liminal generation.

The experience of the Promised Land will be for a future generation, born on the journey.

B'midbar
Rabbi Joshua Minkin, DMin, 2011

B'midbar evokes memories of the northern Negev. Although the area is a desert, autumn rains (*yoreh*) fall on the parched land, brown from the summer heat. The land soaks up the water like a sponge. Dark, wet patches appear, yet they dry and lighten in moments. Within days, flowers appear—green, red, orange, and yellow, where formerly there had been only brown, black, and gray—arising from seeds that had lain dormant in the earth for many months.

Our teacher Dr. Leonard Kravitz often told the midrash (*Tanchuma P'kudei*) that Jews know the entire Torah in utero. At birth, an angel knocks us on the head, causing us to forget everything. But having once learned it, we have a natural affinity for learning Torah.

The *Babylonian Talmud* (*Eiruvin* 54a) says that we should be like a desert. Torah and learning, so often compared to water in our tradition, are the rains that nourish our souls. The seeds of Torah are planted in our youth.

In part, we rabbis are Torah farmers, planting seeds in the minds of our students. However, despite our best efforts, many students disappear from the scene of Jewish education after bar/bat mitzvah or confirmation. They enter a dry season, when the Jewish education they received seems to wither.

I suggest, rather, that like the seeds of the Negev wildflowers, their knowledge lays dormant, waiting for another teacher to dip into the waters from the wells of our tradition to bring them back to life.

B'midbar
Rabbi David Novak, 2012

How does the experience of complete unfamiliarity and disorientation shape us?

That is the underlying question of the Torah in *B'midbar*, translated as "in the desert" or "in the wilderness." Metaphorically, the wilderness experience is where everything—EVERYTHING—is unfamiliar.

Disorientation affects all of our senses: sight, hearing, smell, taste, and feeling. We are knocked off balance by the lack of familiarity, the lack of order in our lives. You're driving and you take a wrong turn. You put something in your mouth and it tastes like something entirely different from what you expected or anything you know. You temporarily lose your way. It is destabilizing.

Yet over time we learn that unfamiliarity leads to knowledge and growth. For it is in the unfamiliar that we grow: the discomfort we feel from stretching ourselves from unfamiliar to familiar is also known as growing. Through the discomfort, we encounter new truths and learnings.

Let us, then, transform our wilderness experiences into growth.

B'midbar
Rabbi Tom Alpert, 2013

Parashat B'midbar reminds us how to live without daily drama. The *Etz Hayim* Torah commentary (p. 769) writes, "What must it have been like to experience the transition from the grand events of Sinai and the Sea of Reeds to the daily routine of the wilderness? The answer might lead us to the lesson that life is lived, not so much in the grand moments, as in uncelebrated ordinary time."

Shavuot commemorates the ultimate wedding between the Jewish people and God, with a great view of a mountain and plenty of dramatic weather. But before we even get there, we read *B'midbar* with its endless to-do lists, a *parashah* that sets the tone not just for the remainder of the Book of Numbers but also for the quotidian life that the Jewish people will live with God. If Shavuot is the wedding, *B'midbar* tells us what the marriage will be like.

In the haftarah, Hosea tells us that our marriage will work when we stop calling God *baali*. One meaning of that word is "my master." Perhaps Hosea is saying that the people need to lose their illusion of God as the master who can fix everything. Maybe they have to see God for who God is: an everyday partner, not an everyday sea-parter. And God too has to see us for who we are: people living in ordinary time, wandering, complaining, arguing, but doing the best we can. Then, as partners in the marriage, we will see each other without illusions, and even so, we will want to be together.

B'midbar
Rabbi Louis Rieser, 2015

Why does God command Moses to count the Israelites in the Sinai wilderness (Num. 1:2)?

Rashi (on Num. 1:3) focuses on the detail of the counting of those who fit a certain age profile and concludes that this census is preparation for the coming conflict in the land of Canaan.

Sforno, focusing on *b'mispar sheimot*, "number by name" (Num. 1:2), teaches that this first census accounts for every individual according to their particular character.

Is the importance in the individuality of those counted or in the nation as a whole?

Levi Yitzchak of Berditchev blends aspects of both. Noting that the number of Israelites equals the letters of the Torah, he comments, "The souls of Israel form the body of the Torah. . . . Each one of us constitutes one of Torah's letters." He thereby accounts for a census that numbers the whole but simultaneously honors the importance of each individual. As one letter within the body of Torah, you are immeasurably important and holy. Separated from the whole you retain your holiness, but you are incomplete. What are the Jews without the Torah; what is the Torah without the Jews?

There are so many ways to play with this teaching. Where would you find your letter in the Torah? As we worry over the latest demographic study, are we mindful of the holiness inherent in those we count? As we hold up the Torah, can we remember that it is incomplete if we discount those Jews with whom we disagree? As we distribute honors, can we be humble enough to recall that even the silent *alef* among our membership is as necessary as every other letter?

We Jews need Torah; Torah needs us Jews.

B'midbar
Rabbi Charles Middleburgh, PhD, 2017

A single image overwhelms me the Shabbat we start reading from *B'midbar*: the desert. One of my most searing memories is spending several hours flying over the Rub al-Khali (Empty Quarter) of Saudi Arabia—650,000 square miles of arid and unforgiving sand dunes. Its vastness and its emptiness are awesome, in the truest sense of that overused word; it does, and always will, define for me what a desert is.

In spite of the fact that Jews have been urbanized for millennia, the desert plays a constant part in our religious and spiritual identity. Not only is one of the Torah's books named for the desert, that terrible wilderness of Sinai, but the formative period in our mythical history took place over the course of four decades in the desert.

To survive in the desert, you need to be tough, for only the toughest survive, and you need to be resourceful. You need determination. You may also need a God who controls an environment that cannot be tamed by human hands, combined with rules and laws that are clear, unequivocal, and uncompromising. Above all, you need hope, for only armed with hope can you successfully traverse the desert and find the will to continue a journey without signposts or confirmations of your progress.

The Israelites' desert experience shaped them and continues to influence us. Despite our urbanity, we carry some of the desert with us and reconnect with it spiritually on a regular basis. It is good that we do so, for it makes us strong.

B'midbar
Rabbi Joshua Minkin, DMin, 2018

"Nadab and Abihu died before Adonai, when they offered strange fire . . . and they had no children" (Num. 3:4).

The Tiferet Yehonaton (Jonathan Eibeschitz, 1690–1764) quotes the *Babylonian Talmud Bava Batra* 116b: "David, who left a son like himself, is referred to as having lain down, while Joab, who left no son like himself, is referred to as having died." Eibeschitz comments, "Here [Num. 3:4] we are told that Nadab and Abihu died. Why doesn't the Torah state that they 'lay down'? The answer is that 'they had no children,' and therefore one cannot say they 'lay down'" (*Torah Gems*, vol. 3, p. 19).

"Lying down" is an expression for "died" that connotes "being at peace at the end of life," but those who are not parents and ache for children can never feel at peace. Having children is part of their raison d'être. One need only remember Rachel's lament to Jacob: "Give me children, else I am dead" (Gen. 30:1). Parenting the next generation lends our lives purpose.

Nonetheless there are other ways to shape our posterity. Our tradition emphasizes the ongoing legacy of learning—teachers impart Torah to the next generation. Sometimes, teachers are to be honored even above parents. When we reach out to an individual with respect, empathy, and kindness, we have a positive effect on them and those they will touch in their lives. Ours are the shoulders upon which later generations shall stand.

נשא *Naso*
(Numbers 4:21–7:89)

Naso
Rabbi Michael Boyden, 2010

Sometimes we Reform Jews can be challenged or even threatened by the apparent certainty of Orthodoxy and the seductiveness of Chabad. It takes a Torah portion like *Naso* to remind us of why their way is not ours.

The Torah was written in a male-dominated, chauvinistic society, and it reflects these values: property is primarily passed down from father to son, men take wives and divorce them, and they are commanded not to covet their neighbors' wives or other property. If there is an occasional exception where women hold center stage, such as with Ruth or Esther, it only serves to prove the rule.

There could not be a clearer example of this male bias than the story of the man who suspected his wife of infidelity. He is commanded to take her to the priest to administer the Trial of Bitter Waters. If she is guilty, "her belly shall distend and her thigh shall sag; and the woman shall become a curse among her people" (Num. 5:21).

Needless to say, there is not a parallel trial for suspected male infidelity, whereas the poor wife is required to undergo this ordeal even whenever her possibly paranoid husband has a fit of jealousy. What possible justification can there be for such injustice?

The Talmud is conscious of the problematic nature of this trial. Tractate *Sotah* (*Babylonian Talmud Sotah* 28a) tells us that it was only effective when the husband was innocent. *Mishnah Sotah* 9:9 tells us that "when there were more adulterers, the Bitter Waters ceased [to be effective] and Rabban Yochanan ben Zakkai stopped [the practice]."

In a world of "honor killings," where young women are still murdered to protect the family name, we understand that it probably made sense to hand over jurisdiction in such matters to the priest. Nevertheless, there could not be a clearer example of how Judaism has evolved and must continue to adapt to meet the needs and values of our time.

Naso
Rabbi David Novak, 2011

Parashat Naso contains perhaps the most well-known blessing in the Torah, which is also one of Torah's oldest texts:

> May the Eternal bless you and keep you.
> May the Eternal's face give light to you and show you favor.
> May the Eternal's face be lifted toward you and give you peace.
>
> (Num. 6:24–26)

In traditional synagogues, those who consider themselves to be descendants of the *kohanim* ("priests") pronounce these words. In our liberal communities, we incorporate a range of innovations. Sometimes the prayer leader blesses the community. Sometimes people in the community bless one another.

In all cases the pronouncing of these words is meant to affirm the relationship between the Holy One and us and between the Holy One and our communities.

Bless, protect, give light, show favor, lift of face, and grant peace: for all that the God of the Hebrew Bible is accused of that which is less than laudatory, this blessing, also known as *Birkat Shalom* ("Blessing of Peace"), immerses the relationship into hope and optimism. *Kein y'hi ratzon*—"may it be God's will"!

Naso
Rabbi Amy Scheinerman, 2012

The trek through the wilderness is like an extended camping trip.

The Israelites don't travel light. *Parashat Naso* describes in minute detail how the *Mishkan* is disassembled and carried along as the Israelites journey. The Levites dismantle, transport, and assemble the Tabernacle. In *Naso*, we learn that the Gershonites and Merarites (Levitical clans) are also involved: they help to dismantle and assemble the *Mishkan*, and during the journey, they guard it. In fact, here and elsewhere in *B'midbar*, we come to learn that everyone has an assignment.

I wonder if this is a model for congregations and perhaps other institutions. If we are a nation of priests, the message is that everyone has an assignment. Just as the half-shekel suggests, everyone must contribute to the financial maintenance of the *Mishkan*. *Naso* tells us that everyone should actively contribute in another way. Imagine a congregation in which every household was expected to contribute their time and effort to the congregation, or through social justice work, or by volunteering in the community. Each of these contributions builds and maintains the Tabernacles of modern Jewish life.

Of course, this is an idea—but it's a worthy ideal.

Naso
Rabbi Janice Garfunkel, z"l, 2013

At first blush, how odd that the Torah uses up so much precious space and parchment to tell us that each of the twelve tribes makes the identical donation for the dedication of the *Mishkan*.

Each and every Israelite is represented by their tribal leader at this dedication ceremony. Each person feels equally connected; no one tribe is superior or more important. Good inter-tribal politics.

Today, we still struggle with our attempts to make sure that every Jew feels equally enfranchised, involved, and part of our shuls. We have all heard the ridiculous, imagined slights: "I saw the rabbi at the grocery store, and he/she did not say 'hi' to me!" Some folks are very insecure and it doesn't take much to confirm their feelings of inferiority and not fitting in. We need to scrupulously guard against saying things that are heard as exclusionary by some congregants. Then there are the parents with a noisy baby: Do we give them the "hairy eyeball"? If not, will other congregants scold us for not managing the service well enough? If we do, will the parents leave the congregation in embarrassment, saying, "This congregation is not 'child-friendly'"?

Perhaps we can address these issues directly with our congregants (and nonmembers). In what ways do individuals and segments of our community feel undervalued and unappreciated, inferior or excluded? What can we do to help everyone feel that the shul is his or her own special community? Does this have any part to play in our much too low affiliation and participation rates?

Naso
Rabbi Ruth Adar, 2015

In *Parashat Naso*, the Torah deals with a category of wrongdoing called *maal*, "the appropriation of property" or, more broadly, "an act of treachery or faithlessness." The word is part of the priestly vocabulary, and indeed we first heard it in Leviticus 5. In Leviticus, *maal* is the defrauding of God of sacred donations, usually by accident. The sinner must make an *asham*, a guilt offering, plus pay one-fifth of the amount of the error.

Numbers 5:5–10 expands this concept. First, it states that the *maal* offense may be committed by "a man or a woman." Secondly, the text requires that the sinner confess before making restitution. It is not enough to return misappropriated goods with 20 percent interest; one must confess in order to make things right. Third, a *maal* may be committed against a human being, not only against God, although the text specifies that a *maal* against another human being is also an offense against God.

These instructions are the bare bones of what would become the process of *t'shuvah*. Jewish practice evolves over time. The *sotah* ritual, also Numbers 5, became a purely academic exercise after the loss of the Temple (if, indeed, it was ever practiced). However, long after we stopped to offer sacrifices on an altar, the seemingly minor practice of confession and restitution would ultimately bear the burden of restoring souls to health. While the word *t'shuvah* only appears four times in *Tanach* (twice in Chronicles, twice in Job), it is today a major form of Jewish religious observance, a cornerstone of the High Holy Days.

Naso
Rabbi Michael Boyden, 2017

There is a common denominator between this week's *parashah* and our Haftarah, which comes from the Book of Judges: asceticism.

Abstention is generally associated with Christianity or Buddhism, but *Parashat Naso* outlines the restrictions that the Nazirites are to impose upon themselves. This links up with the Haftarah's story of Samson.

The steps Nazirites must take to renounce their vow of abstinence are particularly interesting. The Torah details the various sacrifices that they are to bring, which include "one ewe lamb in its first year, without blemish, for a sin offering." Why must people who have lived a life of abstinence bring a sin offering?

As is sometimes the case, Nachmanides and Maimonides disagree as to what lies behind this.

Nachmanides argues that "it would have been appropriate for him to have abstained forever and lived his life as a Nazirite holy to his God. . . . And so he has to make atonement for becoming defiled once more by worldly desires."

Maimonides, however, is of an entirely different opinion. "Our Sages commanded us only to refrain from those things that the Torah specifies. Our Sages said: 'Aren't the Torah's restrictions sufficient for you that you have to impose upon yourself additional restrictions?'" (*Mishneh Torah Hilchot Dei-ot* 3:1). In Rambam's view, the sin offering was intended to atone for exaggerating.

In a world in which religious extremism and zealotry are seen by some as a virtue, Maimonides reminds us that everything should be in moderation.

Naso
Rabbi Amy Scheinerman, 2018

The novel *Arcadia* by Lauren Groff follows "Bit," the first child born in a fictional late-sixties commune that resembled an encampment, through the community's inception, growth, and ultimate demise. Despite its founders' idealism, Arcadia is place of chaos, self-indulgence, recklessness, gnawing poverty, and ever-present hunger. It dissolves before Bit is grown up. We meet him again as a grown-up, a man of compassion and commitment, integrity and ideals—values that derive from and exist because Bit continues to be anchored to Arcadia.

Rabbi Mordechai Yosef of Izbica explains in *Mei HaShiloach* that from the first mention of the building of the *Mishkan* in *T'rumah* until *Naso* there are seventeen *parashiyot*. The numerical value of *tov* ("good") is seventeen, "hinting at the primary goodness of place: *makom tov*. . . . With the completion of the *Mishkan* and camping of the Tribes around it, *k'dushah* is fixed in the center of Israel." The *Mishkan* created a good place, a *makom tov*, for the words of Torah to be fixed in the hearts of the Israelites.

Even places in our lives, far removed from being any kind of *Mishkan*, or a *makom tov*, may have helped us apprehend wisdom, engage with God, and experience holiness. Arcadia, by any measure a terrible place, nonetheless remained Bit's anchor, and the goodness he exhibited later in life he learned there. Perhaps the symbolism of the mobile *Mishkan* hints to the importance of learning and creating *k'dushah* even in a place that seems devoid of it.

בהעלתך *B'haalot'cha*
(Numbers 8:1–12:16)

B'haalot'cha
Rabbi David Novak, 2010

We've had a reputation problem for a long time. In our Yom Kippur confessions, we say that we are a stiff-necked people. Here we have our ancestors again behaving badly: "The people took to complaining bitterly before YHVH. YHVH heard and was incensed; a fire of YHVH broke out against them, ravaging the outskirts of the camp" (Num. 11:1). Why?

> The riffraff in their midst felt a gluttonous craving; and then the Israelites wept and said, "If only we had meat to eat! We remember the fish that we used to eat free in Egypt, the cucumbers, the melons, the leeks, the onions, the garlic. Now our gullets are shriveled. There is nothing at all. Nothing but this manna to look to!" (Num. 11:4–6)

Torah tells us that the manna tasted like rich cream. It is hard to square the circle that the people were complaining, given that (1) they were receiving manna from the hand of God, a supernatural miracle that sustained them on their journey; and (2) it was received in constant abundance, with a double portion falling before the Shabbat each week. Yet complain they do.

They even get their meat. There is so much meat that the people behave like gluttons. "With the meat still between their teeth, not yet chewed, the anger of YHVH blazed forth against the people and YHVH struck the people with a very severe plague" (Num. 11:33).

Food and attitude are metaphors in *B'haalot'cha*. Living in gratitude is being human witnesses of the miracle. Complaining and gluttony are the complete opposite.

B'haalot'cha
Rabbi Michael Boyden, 2011

We live in a world that expects its political leaders to exude self-confidence and charisma. The same is expected of rabbis. But what does our tradition teach us to be?

When Aaron and Miriam challenge Moses's leadership and criticize his choice of wife, the Torah's response is "The man Moses was more humble than anyone on earth" (Num. 12:3).

How did his humility express itself? Nachmanides tells us, "He never quarreled. . . . He never expected anyone to hold him in esteem and did not boast about his merits."

A midrash in the *Babylonian Talmud Chulin* 88b, tells us that Rabbi Elazar ben Yosei, who had witnessed with his own eyes how the Romans had sacked the Temple and taken the booty to Rome, remarked on how different Jewish leaders and idol worshipers were from one another:

> Even when I make you great, you belittle yourselves before Me. I made Abraham great, but he told Me, "I am but dust and ashes." When I promoted Moses and Aaron, they remarked, "Who are we?" David said, "I am a worm and not a man." But idol worshipers are different. I made Nimrod great and he responded by saying, "Let us build a city for ourselves." Pharaoh said, "'Who is God?"

It takes a person as great as Moses to have the capacity to recognize his own limitations and fallibility. Such a human being, although he met God at Sinai, would probably not pass the screen test in today's world, where self-assurance and self-esteem are prerequisites for success.

B'haalot'cha
Rabbi Janice Garfunkel, z"l, 2012

Are there Jewish personality traits?

- One theme of *B'haalot'cha* is complaining, and anyone who has led a synagogue knows that more than three thousand years later, Jews still kvetch.
- Deborah Tannen has documented a specifically Jewish conversational style: interrupting and talking over one another. In a different way, so has Woody Allen.
- Centuries of Talmud study have honed our argumentative and analytical skills.
- To be an activist, as so many Jews are, one needs first to be dissatisfied with the status quo, which brings us back to the theme of our *parashah*.

Obviously, not all Jews are more dissatisfied than the average person, and plenty of gentiles are plenty dissatisfied. There are even quiet, shy Jews (or so I've been told). If there are Jewish personality traits, they are more common among Jews, but not a universal law for all Jews.

Assuming there is such a thing as Yiddishkeit or a *yiddishe n'shamah* ("Jewish soul"): Will intermarriage and assimilation eventually eliminate these traits? Should we actively preserve our Jewish traits? Can we consciously instill Yiddishkeit in our children? Are Jewish traits learned from Jewish parents; is there a genetic component? Would a Jewish baby raised by converts who grew up Episcopalian still talk too much (with her hands, of course) and want to change the world?

Food for thought, after you pick that quail meat out from between your teeth.

B'haalot'cha
Rabbi Louis Rieser, 2013

"Speak to Aaron and say to him, 'When you mount the lamps. . . .' Aaron did so" (Num. 8:1–2). Why note Aaron's compliance with a straightforward task? Rashi (on Num. 8:3, citing *Sifrei*) states that this verse is praise for Aaron, who did as he was told without changes. It seems odd, however, to publicly praise someone for simply following directions.

The Eish Kodesh, Rabbi Kalonymus Kalmish Shapira of Piaseczno (1889–1943), in his commentary *Derech HaMelech*, suggests that Aaron deserved praise because hearing is a difficult task. Hearing, he reminds us, is not about sound stimulating the auditory nerve, but about understanding and accepting that which is heard. When we talk with someone who is distracted, troubled, or consumed by other things, they have trouble hearing us. Even when they nod in agreement, we might not feel heard; it is better to catch them when they are calm and centered.

On a deeper level, the Baal Shem Tov teaches that "only if the hearer is able to understand the soul of the speaker does he actually hear." We have to respond to that which is most alert and most alive in a particular person—their soul. Communication, at its best, links us soul to soul. That happens when we not only hear, but understand, empathize with, and bond with another person. We comprehend both what is said and what lies unsaid beneath the words. It is the gold standard of hearing.

Perhaps Rashi was right after all. Aaron deserves praise for hearing and acting upon exactly what the Holy One said. Wouldn't it be wonderful if our hearing were that acute?

B'haalot'cha
Rabbi Stephen Wylen, 2014

How long should a prayer be? The shortest prayer in the Torah is in this week's *parashah*. Moses prays for God to heal Miriam when she is struck with *tzaraat* for gossiping against Moses. Moses's prayer is a mere five syllables in length: *El na r'fa na lah* ("God, pray heal her;" Num. 12:13). The longest prayer is Moses's prayer for God to forgive Israel for the sin of the Golden Calf. Moses prays for forty days and forty nights.

Forty days and nights and the people are forgiven. Five monosyllables and Miriam is forgiven. Same result. Why does Moses pray for forty days and nights if five syllables would suffice? Some would say that the lengthy prayer fulfilled a need for Moses. Others would say that while God is poised to forgive, since God loves to hear the prayers of Israel, God withholds the grant of forgiveness until Moses exhausts his capacity to pray.

Rabbi Akiva used to pray all night long when he was praying by himself, but when he was leading the community he kept it short so as not to burden anyone (*Babylonian Talmud B'rachot* 31a).

The effectiveness of worship is not dependent upon the length of the service. The traditional Jewish three- or four-hour service is consistent with the cultural custom of Eastern Europe. Russian Orthodox Sunday worship is approximately that length. The hour-long worship of classical Reform is consistent with the culture of Central and Western Europe.

The best length for a worship service is that which best suits the needs of the worshipers.

B'haalot'cha
Rabbi Amy Scheinerman, 2015

"Miriam and Aaron spoke against Moses" (Num. 12:1), yet only Miriam is afflicted with *tzaraat* and excluded from the camp seven days. *Sifrei* (*B'midbar* 99), questioning the apparent inequity, explains that Miriam is the first to criticize Moses's marital choice. In contrast, Rabbi Akiva (*Babylonian Talmud Shabbat* 97a), referring to the strength of the plural *vayichar af adonai bam* ("the Eternal was incensed with them;" Num. 12:9), asserts that Aaron also was struck with leprosy. The general Rabbinic consensus, however, is that Miriam committed *lashon hara* and was therefore justly punished with *tzaraat*.

The story of servitude, redemption, revelation, and wandering has served up few women characters. Shifrah and Puah speak bravely and cleverly to Pharaoh and save countless lives; Pharaoh's daughter, at great risk to herself, undermines her own father to save the infant Moses. Tzipporah acts promptly and courageously, performing an apotropaic circumcision of Gershom to save her husband and son (it is unclear from Exod. 4:24 who is in danger). These women are strong, bold, and daring.

Miriam, a prophet, is by far the most prominent woman in the Exodus-Redemption-Wilderness narratives. In Egypt, a young Miriam acts bravely and cleverly to secure Moses's survival. At the Reed Sea, she leads the women in celebration. Rashi tells us that we learn from the juxtaposition of the account of Miriam's death and the ensuing water shortage, "all forty years, [the Israelites] had a well [that moved through the wilderness with them] due to the merit of Miriam."

Shifrah, Puah, the daughter of Pharaoh, Tzipporah, and Miriam all have something important in common: they are all people of action. Torah preserves no inspiring sermons or even maxims in their names, but rather an account of deeds that made all the difference. We tend to pay more attention and accord greater honor to those who speak eloquently than to those who act admirably. Perhaps we might reexamine our priorities?

B'haalot'cha
Rabbi Joshua Minkin, DMin, 2017

"Now the man Moses was very humble, more so than anyone else on the face of the earth" (Num. 12:3).

Humility is a trait highly prized in our tradition. *Musar* stresses that it should be the first soul-trait worked on, because humility entails an unvarnished and honest assessment of one's strengths and weaknesses. Our understanding of the world and ourselves is refracted through the lens of ego. Those who have an inflated view of themselves fail to recognize their faults and magnify their accomplishments.

However, humility is not humiliation. Too often we think the paradigm of humility is I. L. Peretz's Bontche Schweig, a man utterly lacking in self-esteem. Excessive humility excuses one from taking responsibility for self and others.

Ironically, arrogance and prideful behavior are often a mask for low self-esteem. Rabbi Elyakim Krumbein, in *Musar for Moderns*, says he learned from Rav Kook that "only one who is unconvinced as to his inherent worth will feel the need to find artificial compensation in approval from without" and speaks "the wallowing pre-occupation with one's past achievements, which is needed to compensate for the missing conviction of self-esteem."

Krumbein asserts that "positive pride actually assists humility." This genuine, balanced humility says, "No matter how much I have done . . . it will never be enough, because I know myself well enough to realize that I could have done much more."

Here is the rationale for Moses's humility. Despite being the great lawgiver and teacher and knowing God *panim el panim* ("face to face"), Moses restrains his pride. He takes advice, acknowledges his ignorance, and always places the prestige of Israel above his own.

B'haalot'cha
Rabbi Ruth Adar, 2018

Parashat B'haalot'cha (like much of Torah) may be seen as a study in contrasts. There are those who are ritually pure for Pesach and those who are not, who are in need for a way to observe the mitzvah. God guides the people in the form of a pillar of a cloud by day and of fire by night. Within these two manifestations resides another set of contrasts: a cloud guides, yet sometimes obscures; fire guides, but as the portion shows, it may also kill and terrorize.

Several commentators have pointed out the contrast between the black skin of the Cushite woman and the whitening of Miriam's skin with *tzaraat*, as well as the contrast between the two women's powerlessness and the power of Aaron and Moses, who pray for Miriam's healing. Indeed, there is also a contrast between silence and speech in this passage: Miriam sins with her speech, and the Cushite woman is silent.

Perhaps more than anything, this portion illustrates the inclination of the human mind to view the world in a binary fashion. Rabbi Arthur Gross-Schaefer, in a lecture on ethical decision-making at Hebrew Union College–Jewish Institute of Religion in Los Angeles, taught that it is important to look beyond reductionist binaries to a fuller spectrum of options. We tend to frame our choices as "this or that," but a good counselor will assist people in seeing many more shades of possibility. In that way, we can escape the limiting illusion of black-and-white and see our world in its true and abundant colors.

שלח-לך *Sh'lach L'cha*
(Numbers 13:1–15:41)

Sh'lach L'cha
Rabbi Micky Boyden, 2010

Our *parashah* begins with God's call to Moses: "Send men to scout the land of Canaan" (Num. 13:2). Actually, the translation misses the nuance of the Hebrew *sh'lach l'cha* to mean "If you want to. I am not commanding you." In other words, Moses sends out the spies in response to his own and the Israelites' uncertainty, not God's. Trust is a central theme throughout the entire story. Our Sages tell us that this explains why the episode of the spies appears immediately following Miriam and Aaron's challenge to Moses's leadership.

It is not easy to be in a place of authority. How quickly the Israelites are prepared to criticize even God, contending "it would be better for us to go back to Egypt" (Num. 14:3)!

In frustration, God offers to make Moses's offspring into a nation far greater and stronger than the Israelites (Num. 14:12). Most politicians would leap at the opportunity! But Moses is different. He pleads for those at whose head he stands in words that we recall from the Yom Kippur liturgy: "Pardon, I pray, the iniquity of this people according to Your great kindness" (Num. 14:19). Moses promotes his people, not himself. Such is true leadership!

The *parashah* concludes with the mitzvah to place fringes on the corners of one's garments, "that you not follow your heart and eyes in your lustful urge" (Num. 15:37–40). Had the spies trusted in God rather than followed their hearts and eyes, a whole generation would have entered the Promised Land rather than be condemned to perish in the wilderness.

Sh'lach L'cha
Rabbi Janice Garfunkel, z"l, 2011

"We were like grasshoppers in our eyes, and so we were in their eyes" (Num. 13:33).

How accurate is perception? Because ten scouts considered themselves small and insignificant, they immediately despaired and were prepared to give up.

We tend to think "objective facts" exist, but facts are always open to interpretation. Imagine if, in 1967, the leadership of Israel had pointed out the obvious "fact" of the Arab armies' combined superiority in numbers and weapons, and thrown in the towel. In our own lives, we are constantly interpreting reality, most of the time unconsciously. Family Systems Theory teaches us to notice when we experience "reactivity," when we have a knee-jerk, emotional response to a particular person or situation. That is a signal that our subconscious mind is filtering "reality" through a distorted lens, most likely from our familial past. We distort reality when we have depression or mania. Most of us are too quick to say "I could never do that" about at least one thing we probably could do if we were brave enough to try. How often do we imagine motives in someone else, never learning how completely wrong we are?

Perhaps one of the goals of life is to learn to see things more as they really are, and less through the distorting filter of our past experiences, prejudices, and inclinations.

Sh'lach L'cha
Rabbi Louis Rieser, 2012

What good is religion?

The spies are sent to scout (*v'yaturu*) the land. Moses charges them to see (*ur'item*) the land. While the two tasks sound similar, they differ. The spies see a land flowing with milk and honey (Num. 13:27) but report that the land is one that consumes its inhabitants; that they are but insignificant grasshoppers before giants (Num. 13:32–33). Their eyes and their hearts led them in different directions from Joshua and Caleb, who dissent and attempt to convince the people with rational arguments.

Neuropsychology, describing the different areas of the brain, explains the contrasting behavior we find in *Sh'lach L'cha*. The amygdala, the oldest part of our brain, is protective and governs the flight-or-flight impulse. It also generates anger, anxiety, and defensiveness. The newest part of our brain, the frontal lobes and the anterior cingulate, processes social awareness, logic, and reason, allowing us to form cooperative alliances. A strong frontal cortex allows reason to overcome fear. Could it be that the ten spies responded from their primitive, protective brain, while Joshua and Caleb relied on their higher, more rational and spiritual brain?

The daily news can overwhelm us with real and imagined threats, bolstered by shrill proclamations from various politicians and activists—echoes of the spies. These echoes speak directly to the amygdala, the older protective center of our brain. But that path leads to years of wandering in the desert. Our work is to follow the more challenging path of Joshua and Caleb. Neuroscience demonstrates that meditation, prayer, and focused spiritual activities strengthen the newest parts of our brain. Religion provides us tools to teach our communities to emulate God, who is compassionate and long suffering, slow to anger, abounding in kindness and faithfulness (Exod. 34:6).

Sh'lach L'cha
Rabbi Amy Scheinerman, 2013

The *Y'rushalmi* (*Jerusalem Talmud Taanit* 4:5) enumerates the events of Jewish history that correlate with the Ninth of Av. Among them, we are told, are the spies sent to reconnoiter the land, returning on the Ninth of Av. When they reported, "We saw the Nephilim there . . . and we looked like grasshoppers to ourselves, and so we must have looked to them" (Num. 13:33), the *Y'rushalmi* tells us that God responded, "How in the world did you know how you appeared in their view?!"

Good question! Self-schema is constructed to a large degree by the messages concerning ourselves we receive from others. Positive messages uplift, invigorate, and encourage us; negative assessments wound and discourage us. But the Y'rushalmi tells us, "In every city [the spies] entered, the most important man in the city died, so while the people were occupied burying him, the spies reconnoitered the town and came out again. No one ever knew they had been there." The spies received no messages because the Nephilim never saw them; hence God's question.

How often do we believe that others perceive us negatively when in fact there is no evidence that this is true? The spies' negative self-schema, Torah tells us, doomed the Israelites to four decades in the wilderness.

Every individual and every congregation believe it has an "image" or "reputation," and sometimes this perception makes it difficult to move the culture in a positive direction. Fighting reality is one thing; fighting a flawed or distorted image can be even tougher, because while there is no external evidence to corroborate it, neither is there external evidence to refute it.

Sh'lach L'cha
Rabbi Joshua Minkin, DMin, with Rabbi Amy Scheinerman, 2014

"We saw the Nephilim there . . . and we looked like grasshoppers to ourselves" (Num. 13:33).

I am a procrastinator. Often I put off a task thinking it is so easy that it will be a snap to get it done later. There always seems to be something more critical to do, until the task I have put off has become the critical one. I sometimes avoid projects I believe will be difficult or distasteful. When I finally get to it, it has become enormous and I am as a grasshopper in my own eyes.

Experts report that 20 percent of the population self-identify as chronic procrastinators. Psychologists often term procrastination a maladaptive "lifestyle," or a learned response to authoritarian parenting that prevents a child from learning self-regulation, or a rebellion against domineering parenting. Some procrastinators lie to themselves (e.g., "I work best under pressure").

Some focus on what others think, fearing failure or even success. The ten spies seem unaware that Moab dreads the Israelites (Num. 22:3), even though Rahab reports to the spies who penetrate Jericho, "The dread of you has fallen upon us" (Josh. 2:9). Their fear outstrips their ability to perceive reality.

The happy news is that psychologists tell us that procrastinators can change. Menachem Mendel of Kotzk envisioned God asking the ten spies, "Why are you so concerned with how the Canaanites see you, so much so that it distracts you from your sacred task?" Often I find the solution is to do what Joshua and Caleb urge the Israelites to do. Just do it. Trust that in the end, success will follow.

I write—something, anything—and the page is no longer blank. Intimidating, yes, but I am now a creator, not a grasshopper.

Sh'lach L'cha
Rabbi Joshua Minkin, DMin, 2015

"And they said to one another, 'Let us head back for Egypt.'" (Num. 14:4)

Faced with a challenge, the Children of Israel once again are ready to give up at the first sign of difficulty. As slaves in Egypt, the Hebrews lived lives in which their most basic needs were provided for. They made very few consequential decisions. They bore no responsibility for what happened to them.

In the wilderness, there is no other human being who is responsible for taking care of them. With freedom comes the necessity of making choices. And with this comes the possibility of choosing poorly. Without prior experience in decision-making, they see every situation as black or white; either they are all doomed or they will survive only to repeat their current agony at the next challenge. How much easier to give up and go back to Egypt and not have to deal with what felt like excruciating decisions of life and death.

As parents, each of us wants to shield our children not only from harm, but also from painful disappointments that arise from making poor decisions. However, it is only through the process of making mistakes that our children can learn that making a mistake isn't the end of the world and that it is okay to be wrong. If we allow them to grow up completely shielded from disappointment, they may respond like the Hebrews when faced with difficult decisions: they may become paralyzed by fear and unable to move forward into the unknown.

Sh'lach L'cha
Rabbi Louis Rieser, 2017

"Speak to the Israelite people and instruct them to make for themselves fringes on the corners of their garments throughout the ages; let them attach a cord of blue to the fringe at each corner" (Num. 15:38).

Rav Kook (http://www.ravkooktorah.org/SHLACH59.htm) described a hierarchy of soul/character/behavior, according to which Tzitzit are an expression of the character of the soul:

1. The core of the soul comes from God.
2. The soul is "clothed" with what we call our character.
3. Tzitzit are the external expression of the soul, mediated by our character traits and values: "Through its distinctive characteristics, the soul reveals itself to the outside world."

Rav Kook noted that the sky-blue *t'cheilet* connects us to the very Source of life from whom all forces flow. Rabbi Jonathan Sacks notes, "Tsitsit with their thread of blue remind us of heaven, and that is what we most need if we are consistently to act in accordance with the better angels of our nature."

Rabbi Sacks (http://rabbisacks.org/assembling-reminders-shelach-lecha-5775/), marshaling evidence from Behavioral Economics proving that people behave differently if they believe they are being watched or are reminded of the values to which they subscribe, tells us regarding the role of tzitzit, "Look at it and recall all the commandments of Adonai and observe them" (Num. 15:39).

If our tzitzit are to have a living soul, it is because we give them one by connecting our actions to our values. To do that, it might help to live "as if" we are being watched by God.

Sh'lach L'cha
Rabbi Charles Middleburgh, PhD, 2018

The phonic link between *Lech L'cha* and *Sh'lach L'cha* cannot be ignored. *Lech L'cha* may be interpreted as an inward-looking command, an instruction to Abraham to go into himself to find his inner strength and faith.

With *Sh'lach L'cha*, God appears to instruct the spies to do the opposite, to think outside of themselves and go beyond their comfort zone.

While we should always strive to avoid self-obsession, honest self-appraisal can be a very good thing, helping us to reason out our strengths and weaknesses and honestly face aspects of our character that we might improve. Honest aspiration can inspire us to reach for what we might otherwise consider impossible, to aspire to something better; but it can also lead to disappointment, bitterness, and even despair. A willingness to take risks is essential for growth; we may not be successful straight away, or at all, but every risk taken contains the kernel of achievement.

Abraham was willing to risk leaving home and country. He prevailed, though not without cost. The spies face a risk that affords an opportunity not for themselves, but for the nation. They fulfilled their mission but failed to communicate to the Israelites that they should take the risk as well.

We do well to remember the wise words of Benjamin Franklin: "Nothing ventured, nothing gained."

קרח Korach
(Numbers 16:1–18:32)

Korach
Rabbi Joshua Minkin, DMin, 2010

From time to time, a voice within each of us says, "Who am I kidding? Who am I to make such a pronouncement?" This is the voice of our internal Korach, suggesting we are mere charlatans. We fear precisely what Korach charged Moses and Aaron with: raising ourselves above the community. In our congregations and institutions, there are often people who are smarter, possessing greater expertise, superior speakers, and better teachers than we are. Although as objectively true as Korach's claim, "The entire congregation is holy," it is also irrelevant. Leadership is not only about skills. It is also about commitment, dedication, and vision.

We are the leaders who look after both the community as a whole and each individual member. It is precisely because each member of the community is holy—a divine spark—that we set aside our own egos and spend hours helping each individual reach the holiness he or she seeks. We are the ones who show up week after week, racking our brains for new ways to explain age-old traditions. The question is not "Can someone do our job better?" The job is not theirs; it is ours.

We will always have our Korachs, both internal and external, but we must not forget that we are the ones chosen to lead our flocks to the best of our abilities. That is what God demands of us, no less, but also no more. It matters less that we are not perfect than that we are the ones showing up, getting the work done, and stepping forward to give our communities spiritual direction, thereby creating blessing.

Korach
Rabbi Stephen Wylen, 2011

How did Korach show up Moses before his followers? Korach asked Moses, "Does a tallit all of blue still require blue fringes?" and "Does a room full of Torah scrolls still require a mezuzah?" (*Midrash Tanchuma*). By asking such questions, Korach demonstrated the inconsistencies that inevitably lie within any religious system, inconsistencies that lay every religion open to the accusation of hypocrisy. Korach made the Torah of Moses seem ridiculous in the eyes of his followers.

When I was growing up, we Reform Jews often ridiculed Orthodoxy by pointing to some of the absurd consequences of halachah: one cannot shave the beard but can use Nair; one cannot bathe on Shabbat lest one wring out the towel; one straps leather boxes on head and arm to fulfill literally what was obviously intended as a poetic teaching of inner devotion. Christian polemicists have historically mocked Rabbinic Judaism for debating whether an egg laid on Shabbat can be eaten.

It is easy to mock. It is more difficult to devote oneself to a religious path. The big question is not "What do I reject?" but rather "What can I affirm with integrity?"

Korach
Rabbi Stephen Wylen, 2012

B'midbar Rabbah 18:3 and *Tanchuma Korach* 2:

> Korach made tallitot all of blue, with white fringes, for his 250 followers. Moses said to him, "These tallitot are not kosher." Korach said, "A whole garment of blue is not kosher, but four little threads of blue are kosher? The Torah is not from God and Moses is not a prophet!"—In this and like manner Korach fomented his rebellion.
>
> When Pharaoh saw the success of Korach, he commented, "Had I known the power of mockery, I would not have bothered throwing the babies into the Nile to drown."

It has been noted in the modern age that while each of the major movements of American Judaism has a difficult time validating its own philosophy and practices, they are at their best in revealing what is ridiculous about the other movements. To mock is easy and, unfortunately, highly effective. To explain why you do what you do, and why you find it a valid service of the Blessed Holy One, is challenging. No form of religion is without its inconsistencies; its inherited rituals have been reinterpreted over and over, and its articles of faith may seem random to those who stand outside the system.

To mock is the way of Korach. To hold to one's integrity while accepting the right of others to a variant observance is the way of Hillel.

It is worth remembering that the fear of appearing ridiculous in the eyes of others is a major impediment to taking on a new religious practice. Don't wonder—you will always seem ridiculous to some people. Therefore all that matters is whether you are growing toward God.

Korach
Rabbi Joshua Minkin, DMin, 2013

"You shall discharge the duties of the Sanctuary and the duties of the altar" (Num. 18:5).

American corporations are notorious for taking the short-term view, maximizing profits, regardless of the consequences for society. The perennial excuse is that they are obligated to their shareholders and therefore must do whatever is possible and necessary to increase the share price, dividend, and value of the company. Our *parashah* speaks to this practice.

Sifrei suggests that Num. 18:5 is directed to the (future) Sanhedrin. Malbim explains that since verse 5 says much the same as verse 7, verse 5 must apply to someone else: the Sanhedrin is tasked with ensuring that the priests responsibly perform "the duties for the Sanctuary and the duties for the altar." In modern terms, we can view the priests as corporate executives and the Sanhedrin as the board of directors that oversees management's performance of their duties. The priests are the ones responsible for performing the duties, and the Sanhedrin is top management.

I suggest that the repetition of the word *mishmeret* ("duties") implies two separate types of duties incumbent upon corporations. One is to *hamizbei-ach*—the "altar," the place where the day in and day out sacrificial worship occurs—the business of running a business. The other *mishmeret* is to *hakodesh*—the "Sanctuary," where God's presence is made manifest. In the parlance of modern business, service to *hamizbei-ach* is the ethical running of a company and making sure it turns an honest profit. However, the Sanctuary no longer stands, but God's presence still fills the world. Service to *hakodesh*, then, looks beyond the walls of the corporation to its ethical responsibility to the broader world.

Korach
Rabbi Michael Boyden, 2014

This week's Torah portion tells us of how Korach and his band rebel against the authority of Moses and Aaron, contending that inasmuch as all of the community is holy, they have no right to set themselves above the rest. Of course, neither Moses nor Aaron has chosen their respective roles. It is God who told Moses to go to Pharaoh in spite of the former's misgivings; Aaron, in turn, was called upon to minister in the Tent of Meeting.

Perhaps it is time for a change of leadership, and Korach's act could, therefore, be viewed as a revolution rather than as a rebellion. Are Korach and his followers really so evil that they deserve to have the earth swallow them up?

Whereas the disputes between Hillel and Shammai were *l'shem shamayim* ("for the sake of heaven"), Korach is motivated by ego and self-interest, and therefore our tradition condemns him. He is accused of having asked Moses annoying questions such as whether one needs to affix a mezuzah to a house filled with holy books or whether a tallit that is entirely blue requires fringes (see Rashi on Num. 16:1). The Talmud tells us that Korach discovered one of the treasure troves hidden by Joseph (*Babylonian Talmud P'sachim* 119a) and was, therefore, very wealthy. Rich people frequently seek power.

However, perhaps Korach's greatest fault is in stating that "all of the community is holy" (Num. 16:3). Holiness is not a state of being, but rather an aspiration. *K'doshim tih'yu* (Lev. 19:2) is a call to strive to be holy. Korach thinks that he is already there. Rabbi Eliezer HaKapar taught that envy, desire, and honor drive a person from the world (*Mishnah Pirkei Avot* 4:21). Unfortunately, Korach fails to understand that.

Korach
Rabbi Ruth Adar, 2015

Mishnah Sanhedrin 10:3 offers us a list of those who have no portion in the world-to-come: the generation of the Flood, the generation of the Tower, the men of Sodom, and the ten spies who rejected the Land of Israel. Then Mishnah offers us an additional list about which there is disagreement: According to Rabbi Akiva, the generation of the wilderness, the congregation of Korach, and the Ten Tribes also have no portion in the world-to-come. But Rabbi Eliezer disagrees. For each of those in Rabbi Akiva's list, he cites a text suggesting that redemption is possible. Concerning the followers of Korach, Rabbi Eliezer cites Hannah's prayer: "Adonai kills, and makes alive; brings down to the grave, and brings up" (I Sam. 2:6).

The Torah text is unequivocal in its condemnation of Korach: all is lost, the men offering incense are consumed by fire like Nadav and Avihu were, and God commands Moses to order Eleazar to remove the fire pans and have them hammered into plating for the altar, as a warning to others. But our Sages were not willing to give up on the followers of Korach. From the time of the Mishnah, the Rabbis persist in a hope that (as Rabbi Y'hudah ben B'teira expressed it in the *Babylonian Talmud Sanhedrin* 109b) they will yet be found like a lost object that is still being sought.

Should we not follow their example and refuse to give up on our fellow Jews, even when we think they are utterly wrong about something?

Korach
Rabbi Amy Scheinerman, 2017

Are there people so evil they are beyond any possibility of redemption?
Mishnah Sanhedrin 10:3 lists among those who have no *cheilek baolam haba* ("share in the world-to-come") and his followers.

Rabbi Akiva and Rabbi Eliezer argue the "finer points" of each group's ignominious demise: Will they stand in judgment at the time of resurrection or be consigned immediately to dissolution? Are some people irredeemably evil and therefore God utterly obliterates them? Rabbi Akiva asserts that Korach and his minions will forever remain in Sheol, never to be brought up. Rabbi Eliezer (on the basis of I Sam. 2:6) disputes this: all those who entered into covenant with God have a *cheilek baolam haba*—even those who committed egregious sins.

The Gemara (*Babylonian Talmud Sanhedrin* 109b) on this Mishnah begins with a baraita:

> "[They went down alive into Sheol, with all that belonged to them;] the earth closed over them and they vanished from the midst of the congregation" (Num. 16:33). This is Rabbi Akiva's view. Rabbi Y'hudah ben B'teira said: They are a lost article, which is sought, as it says, "I have strayed like a lost sheep; search for Your servant, for I have not neglected/forgotten Your commandments" (Ps. 119:176).

Rabbi Akiva is focused on the enormity of their sin and God's retribution. Rabbi Y'hudah is concerned with God's enduring concern for all God's creatures.

When we consider the issues of crime, incarceration, and capital punishment, do we resemble Rabbi Akiva or Rabbi Y'hudah?

Korach
Rabbi Louis Rieser, 2018

Reflecting on the nature of the service of the Levites in the Tent of Meeting (Num. 18:23), Shne'ur Zalman of Lyady writes in *Maamarei Admor HaZakein*: "The service of the Levites is in song, to arouse such [emotional] qualities as love, awe, and joy. Their arousal below brings about the arousal of those above."

The Levites' songs arouse emotional responses with a keen spiritual component. Music that arouses us spiritually moves us beyond the power even of the melody. You can recite the words of a psalm of prayer, but it is only when you sing it that the full emotional power is expressed and experienced. Shne'ur Zalman explains that the music of the Levites also engendered contemplation, *chochmah* ("wisdom") "that lies beyond all these qualities" and, indeed, beyond the music itself, transporting one to the place where *ein od milvado*, which as a kabbalist he understands to mean "there is nothing else [but God]," for all is contained within God.

Silence is the next step. "Silence reaches higher than sound, which is the Levites' song." Levites achieve a certain spiritual level through song, but silence facilitates a spiritual experience beyond the body, bringing prayer to the highest level. Silence is the moment after, when you're taking it all in and feel the full impact. I experienced this in the music of Cantor Stephanie Shore and recommend to you two versions of *Hashkiveinu*, one paired with "Count My Blessings" (https://tinyurl.com/yd5kwk85) and the other with "Bridge over Troubled Water." Music can engage our minds, our hearts, and our souls—and then there's the silence that comes after the music stops, when we are transported to another plane.

חקת/בלק *Chukat/Balak*
(Numbers 19:1–22:1 and Numbers 22:2–25:9)

Chukat
Rabbi Amy Scheinerman, 2010

It is difficult to imagine a more recondite ritual than the burning of the red heifer and the use of its ashes for purification. Indeed, the Sages contended that even King Solomon admitted, "I have labored to understand God's teaching, and have understood it all except the ritual of the red heifer" (*B'midbar Rabbah* 19:3). Rabbi Yosei bar Chanina claimed that God disclosed its purpose only to Moses (*B'midbar Rabbah* 19:6).

B'midbar Rabbah 19:8 tells us that a heathen challenged Rabban Yochanan ben Zakkai:

> The things you Jews do appear to be a kind of witchcraft. A heifer is brought, burned up, pounded, and its ashes are gathered up. Then when someone is defiled by contact with a corpse, you sprinkle two or three drops of ash on him and say, "You are purified!"

Yochanan's response is disingenuous, and his disciples demand a more honest response. Yochanan replies:

> As you live, the corpse does not defile, nor does the water [containing the ashes] purify. The truth is that the rite of the red heifer is a decree of the Ruler who is the Ruler of Rulers. The Holy One said: I have set down a statute. . . . This is a statute of the Torah (Num. 19:2).

Are there things we do simply because they are tradition or because they are obligations to God? Does this diminish their value or enlarge their spirituality?

Curiously, *B'midbar Rabbah* 19:8 continues by offering a rationale: "Let the mother come and atone for the misdeed of the [Golden] Calf." They found a purpose. Do we? Do we always need to?

Balak
Rabbi Amy Scheinerman, 2010

The blessing God compels Bilaam to bestow upon Israel does not escape into the far corners of Torah. It emerges front and center in our liturgy each morning: *ma tovu ohalecha yaakov, mishk'notecha yisrael* ("How fair are your tents, O Jacob, your dwellings, O Israel," Num. 24:5). Within these spare seven words, we find a poetic redundancy: *ohalecha* and *mishk'notecha*. Both terms connote temporary dwellings. Both are associated with the people of Israel, but also with God (the *Ohel Mo-eid* encompassed the *Mishkan*).

The *chachamim* (Sages) understand *ohalecha yaakov* as referring to the women, and *mishk'notecha yisrael* as referring to the men; thus Bilaam blessed the entire Jewish people. Sforno understands *ohalecha* as houses of learning and *mishk'notecha* as synagogues; thus Bilaam blessed the two loci where Israel assembles to serve God through study and prayer.

Perhaps the two terms suggest different modes of spirituality, as well. *Ohel* connotes spreading out, tent-like, to cover or shade. It suggests change, growth, and movement. In our covenant with God and our life with the community, we seek to grow and evolve, striving for greater understanding, intensified spiritual experiences, expanding horizons. We are forever climbing Mount Sinai for a glimpse of God, a new experience of the Divine. *Mishkan* suggests sitting still, resting between travels, dwelling for a time in one place. At times, simply to sit with God and with our people, enveloped by the familiar, provides a religious experience of great depth and meaning. Perhaps the goal is to balance the two.

Chukat
Rabbi Amy Scheinerman, 2011

After Miriam dies, the well evaporates and panic ensues. The people complain to Moses, "Why did you make us leave Egypt to bring us to this wretched place, a place with no grain, figs, vines, or pomegranates? There is not even water to drink!" (Num. 20:5). True: no grain, figs, vines, or pomegranates. How quickly the Israelites discount their redemption from slavery, and the manna and quail that has sustained them for thirty-nine years! How ungrateful they seem to be for all that God, Moses, and Aaron have done for them.

How do Moses and Aaron respond? They withdraw to the *Ohel Mo-eid* ("Tent of Meeting"), but God sends them back to the people. God tells Moses to subdue their fear by bringing water from a rock. Moses meets their fear with anger rather than compassion. Addressing them as *morim* ("rebels"), he strikes the rock twice; perhaps he would rather strike the people. In a sense, Moses mirrors the people's lack of trust in God—he does not trust that the people can rise to the occasion. Even more, he allows their behavior to drag his own behavior down.

How often do we complain about our congregants and about the Jewish community in general? How often do we criticize or condemn their values and choices without understanding what fears and insecurities may be driving them? Connecting this passage with the account of the *parah adumah* (Red Heifer) that precedes it, we read in the *Babylonian Talmud Bava Kama* 28a, "Just as the ashes of the red heifer atone for sin, the death of a righteous person does the same." Hopefully, that will inspire in us self-scrutiny.

Balak
Rabbi Joshua Minkin, DMin, 2011

Many have interpreted Jacob's fight at the Jabok as a confrontation with an angel. I suggest Balaam's can be viewed as a confrontation with self.

Balaam is presented with a desirable opportunity that he knows to be wrong. At first he seems willing to live by his scruples. However, as the payoff increases, he convinces himself it is possible to reap the harvest while not disobeying God. He represses his guilt. Three times his conscience (the donkey) tries to bring this repressed knowledge to the surface, and three times Balaam is able to beat it down. Finally it explodes into consciousness with the vision of the sword-bearing angel. Like an alcoholic finally recognizing the destructiveness of his habit, Balaam realizes his existential danger. He calls a halt to his behavior and, at least with regard to Balak, is the epitome of rectitude, bestowing upon Israel the highest of blessings.

There is a clear difference between Jacob's interaction and Balaam's. Jacob wrestles with his past, subjecting it to a critical analysis and emerging transformed: from crooked Yaakov to straight Yisrael. Balaam submits, but never truly engages. His behavior is changed, but underneath he is the same person, out to make a quick buck. Like a crooked accountant, he is honest only as long as he thinks he may get caught.

The final words of Balak's haftarah are "Walk with your God" (Micah 6:8). Walk with, not run away from—engage. Let us not be afraid to look critically at ourselves and engage in the internal dialogue that leads to true change.

Chukat
Rabbi Michael Boyden, 2012

Some leaders—including both laypeople and rabbis—don't know when it's time to retire.

It's worth remembering that Moses was already eighty years old when he led the Israelites out of Egypt. He took an unruly band of slaves and turned them into a people, transmitting to them a code of conduct that we call Torah. However, Moses, whom Ahad HaAm referred to as "the foremost of prophets," was not perfect. Upon descending Mount Sinai and seeing his people worshiping the Golden Calf, he smashed the tablets of the covenant that God had just given him. Later, when the Israelites complained that they were dying of thirst, he responded angrily by saying, "Listen, you rebels, shall we get water for you out of this rock?" (Num. 20:10).

Like many, Moses became less patient with the passing years. Ahad HaAm points out that Moses was "no longer capable of standing at the head of the people and was obliged to relinquish his post to another." What did Moses do wrong at the rock? Rashi said that he erred by losing his temper. Maimonides makes the point that Moses referred to God's people as "rebels"—a response hardly worthy of a leader. Nachmanides commented that Moses implied that he would bring water out of the rock, whereas the miracle was of God's doing. Rabbi Joseph Albo says that when confronted by the people, Moses and Aaron went to the Tent of Meeting. A true leader does not run away.

Perhaps Moses should have retired earlier. Nevertheless, in its concluding words the Torah tells us that "never again did there arise in Israel a prophet like Moses" (Deut. 34:10).

Balak
Rabbi David Novak, 2012

What if Dr. Doolittle, who sang, "If I could talk to the animals . . . just imagine it," really understood the thoughts, motivations, and feelings of the creatures with which he communicated? These animals that share the natural world with us are portrayed with thoughts, understanding, and speech! Animals who can communicate their feelings!

How are we to understand Balaam's talking she-ass? Three times she protects Balaam from God's sword-wielding angel. Balaam's response is to beat the poor animal. Finally God opens her mouth and she says, "Look, I am the ass that you have been riding all along until this day! Have I been in the habit of doing thus to you?" Balak answers, "No" (Num. 22:30).

Who is the ass, indeed?

This is an important story for all of us to teach. How can we, as rabbis, open up the eyes of human beings to the world around them? How can we raise perceptions, awareness, and gratitude? It is part of our work to nurture humans as they grow in their humanity, to harness their functioning to see what we so readily choose to ignore. We humans are gifted with the ability to sense the world around us. We need to do what Balaam's she-ass does for her master: open our eyes and raise our consciousness of a world that, even without talking animals, is a pretty amazing place to be.

This is an important story for all of us to teach. How can we, as rabbis, open up the eyes of human beings to the world around them? How can we raise perception, awareness, and gratitude? It is part of our work to nurture humans as they grow in their humanity, to help them see what we all so readily ignore.

Chukat
Rabbi Amy Scheinerman, 2013

Three thoughts concerning the copper snakes: homeopathy, retribution, or a lesson on harmful speech.

First: Samuel Hahnemann (1755–1843) is credited with creating the alternative system of medicine known as homeopathy. Based on the doctrine *similia similibus curentur* (like cures like), homeopathic remedies seek to treat the symptoms of disease with highly diluted amounts of the same substances believed to have caused the symptoms in the first place. We find similar phenomena in Exod. 15:25 and in II Kings 2:19–22, where bitter wood and salt are used to sweeten bitter water. In I Sam. 6:1–5, the Philistines craft five golden hemorrhoids and five golden mice to cure infestations of both. Nachmanides tells us, "It is Torah's way that every event in it is a miracle within a miracle. It removes the damage by means of the damager and cures the illness by means of its cause." Perhaps the credit for homeopathic medicine should be given to Moses, who at God's command fashions a *n'chash n'choshet* (copper serpent) to cure the effect of snakebites inflicted on the people by *han'chashim has'rafim* ("fiery serpents") sent by God in response to their complaints against God and Moses (Num. 21:4–9). Abarbanel confirms that the serpent was fashioned of copper in order to imitate poisonous snakes that have red stripes or spots. It has been suggested that the wordplay *n'chash n'choshet* in itself would increase the serpent's homeopathic powers.

Rashi decouples the snakes from Israel's complaints: they are retribution for the spies' bad reports. Why snakes? Rashi understands *han'chashim has'rafim* as retribution for Eve's bad report to Adam: as the snake was punished because of Eve, so these snakes punish Israel because of the ten spies.

Third: King Hezekiah, however, viewed use of the copper snake as idolatry and ordered its destruction (II Kings 18:4). Gersonides suggests that in destroying the copper snake, Hezekiah sought to end harmful speech.

Balak
Rabbi David Novak, 2013

Poor Balak. Rather than allowing Moses and the Israelites to pass freely on the most direct route through Moab to the Promised Land, the Moabite king goes to Bilaam, a known soothsayer, and hires him to curse the Israelites. Rather than curse Israel, Bilaam articulates words the Israelite God places in his mouth: *Mah tovu ohalecha yaakov, mishk'notecha yisrael*, "How good are your tents, Jacob, your dwelling places, Israel" (Num. 24:5).

Our Rabbis found these words astonishing. We begin communal prayer by saying the words uttered by a non-Israelite soothsayer.

One of our many responsibilities as rabbis is to convey the joy in *Mah Tovu*. These words are our collective diving board for what is to come. Our brick and steel, wood and glass sanctuaries are silent rooms until we inhabit them. We can thank Balak. His intentions backfired, and in the place of a curse we received the gift of words we use to reconsecrate physical space, time and again, in the most wonderful way.

Chukat
Rabbi Amy Scheinerman, 2014

"Instruct the Israelite people to bring you a red cow without blemish, in which there is no defect and on which no yoke has been laid" (Num. 19:2).

It is difficult to understand how the ashes effect purification, and even more bewildering to understand how the purified priest who handles them thereby becomes impure with contact. Even King Solomon found the laws of the red heifer recondite and baffling (*Kohelet Rabbah* 7:23).

Mary Douglas (*Purity and Danger*) suggests that *tumah* is about disruption in the proper order, a trespass of proper boundaries and limits, in this case of the body most directly, but by extension, to the world order. The danger impurity presents to the body is mirrored in the society as a whole because the individual's body is a microcosm of society (the social body).

Jacob Milgrom tells us that the ashes of the red heifer purify one from the greatest level of *tumah*, that which comes from contact with a corpse. If *tumah* is a brush with death, *tohorah* is about restoring life.

The (possibly fictional) autobiography of Salomon Maimon uses the laws of the red heifer to ridicule Talmud as a compendium of tedium and irrelevance:

> Take the subject of the Talmud . . . in which the oddest Rabbinical conceits are elaborated through many volumes with the finest dialectic, and the most absurd questions are discussed with the highest efforts of intellectual power; for example, how many white hairs may a red cow have, and yet remain a red cow.

Yet the Talmudic discussion of the red heifer says less about the nature of Talmud than the gulf between our ancestors' notions of order/disorder and life/death and ours. How do we speak about these categories today?

Balak
Rabbi Louis Rieser, 2014

"How goodly are your tents [*ohalecha*], Jacob, your sanctuaries [*mishk'notecha*], Israel" (Num. 24:5).

What is the difference between a tent (*ohel*) and a sanctuary (*mishkan*)? The *Degel Machane Ephraim* (Moshe Chaim Efraim, 1748–1800, a grandson of the Baal Shem Tov) teaches that an *ohel* is something temporary and a *mishkan* is something permanent. This designation remains a bit vague. In the realm of the spiritual, what is it that can be considered temporary and what permanent?

Rav Kook considers a similar question when he contrasts Torah, which he characterizes as *chayei olam* ("The Life in the World"), with *t'filah* (prayer), which he describes as *chayei shaah* ("The Life in Time," Inner Life") *Olat R'ayah*, p. 20). By Torah, he means those durable truths that broaden one's spiritual knowledge. Through Torah study, we enrich our understanding and encounter new revelations. Prayer, on the other hand, does not reveal new information but allows us to connect emotionally with that knowledge we already possess and lets those truths impress themselves on our being. Torah is intellectual, objective, expansive, and eternal. Prayer is personal, immersive, emotional, and fit for this particular moment.

How goodly are your tents, those temporary moments when we need the cover of the Holy One to help us navigate in a world filled with challenges. How goodly are your sanctuaries, those durable institutions where our common truths are publicly proclaimed, where all who wish can ascend God's holy mountain.

Chukat
Rabbi Amy Scheinerman, 2015

The word *chok* ("law"; plural: *chukim*) implies a boundary or limit. The very nature of a *chok* is that it has no apparent rational explanation. Yet the Rabbis struggle with this very concept.

B'midbar Rabbah 19:1–8 offers a string of midrashim struggling to make sense of the *chok* of the *parah adumah* (Red Heifer). Rabbi Levi taught that given that it defiles those who prepare it, yet purifies those who are defiled, it was one of four *chukim* that the *yetzer hara* ("evil inclination") can legitimately criticize as irrational. Rabbi Yosei bar Chanina taught that God promised to reveal its reason to Moses, alone, and intended to do so in the *olam haba* ("the world-to-come"), but Rabbi Akiva deduced its meaning himself. Rabbi Yochanan ben Zakkai explained the purpose of the *chok* to an enquiring idolater as similar in form and function to witchcraft, but when questioned by his disciples who overheard, Rabbi Yochanan claimed that what he had told the idolater was pure nonsense. The truth, Rabbi Yochanan tells his students, is that it is God's decree. Period.

But the Rabbis do not stop here. Later, Rabbi Aibu explained that the *parah adumah*, the only female communal sacrifice, atones for the Golden Calf. This section of *B'midbar Rabbah* seesaws between accepting the law of the Red Heifer as a-rational and doing somersaults to find in it purposeful meaning.

As difficult as it was for the Rabbis to acknowledge and affirm a law without apparent rational basis, so much the more so for us. In our time, just how necessary is it for every ritual and tradition to have a rational basis? Can the a-rational have value and meaning, just as the rational?

Balak
Rabbi Michael Boyden, 2015

The Haggadah tells us, "In every generation there are those who rise up to destroy us." For some reason, it seems, people are frightened by us.

Balak, king of Moab, called on Balaam to curse the Children of Israel. What prompted his action? The Torah tells us, "Moab was alarmed because the people were so numerous," and "Moab dreaded the Israelites" (Num. 22:3). Balak's anxiety is reminiscent of that of Pharaoh, who saw that "the more they were oppressed, the more they increased and spread out, so that [the Egyptians] came to dread the Israelites" (Exod. 1:12).

Interestingly, the same verbal root *tzadi-vav-kuf*, meaning "to dread," is used in both stories. The sixteenth-century Turkish rabbi Moshe Alshich, who made *aliyah* to Safed, pointed out that this root is also used in the word *kotz* (thorn), indicating that we were a thorn in the side of both the Egyptians and the Moabites. It was that same discomfort with the Jews that would lead Haman to declare, "There is a certain people . . . who keep themselves apart. . . . Let an order be made in writing for their destruction" (Esther 3:8–9). Two thousand years later the Nazis would argue, "Die Juden sind unser Unglück" ("The Jews are our misfortune").

Interestingly, though, *Parashat Balak* does not end with the destruction of the Israelites by their enemies. Rather we are told, "While Israel dwelt in Shittim, the people profaned themselves by whoring with the Moabite women, who invited them to sacrifice to their gods" (Num. 25:1). Sometimes losing sight of your own identity can be more diminishing to the Jewish people than the dangers from without.

Chukat
Rabbi Charles Middleburgh, PhD, 2017

In all stages of life, we make a myriad of decisions. Most are inconsequential, but some are highly significant, even life-changing. They not only define us but redefine us; changing, potentially, not only what we become in the world but also how we see ourselves.

Chukat illustrates the power and danger of decision-making: yet again, the Israelites are fed up about something. As their wanderings in the desert have stretched out, they have become more pointed in their disagreements with their leaders and more rebellious, indeed threatening, toward them. In *Sh'lach L'cha*, the people are so furious with Joshua and Caleb that they threaten to stone them to death; in *Korach*, Moses and Aaron's closest relative engages in sedition to deny their leadership.

After these incidents, a row about the lack of water may seem incredibly mundane, but it is disastrous for Moses and Aaron.

Moses seeks guidance from God and he receives it. But when the people assemble in front of the rock, though he knows precisely what he *should* do, Moses makes the wrong decision: rather than speaking to the rock, he hits it in a monumental show of anger.

The punishment for making the wrong decision is devastating: God bans the entire generation present from entering the land of Canaan; they are condemned to die in the wilderness. Without scope for appeal or opportunity for a change of mind, Moses and Aaron have condemned themselves through their own actions. They must await their fate.

Their failure is a timely reminder to us all to decide wisely, and well.

Balak
Rabbi Ruth Adar, 2017

In 1967, at Deir Alla, Jordan, approximately eight kilometers east of the Jordan River, archaeologists found an inscription relating visions of the "seer of the gods Balaam, son of Be'or." It was a startling find, since "Balaam, son of Be'or" is the central figure of *Parashat Balak* in our Torah. However, instead of being a prophet of the Hebrew God, in the Deir Alla inscription he is associated with a number of deities, including "the Shaddai gods" and the goddess Shagar.

In the inscription, the gods tell Balaam that the world will be destroyed. The disaster is explained to him through animals: birds shrieking, animals of the field and herds disrupted. He is able to avert the disaster, although the details are lost due to some damage to the inscription.

While there are many important differences between the Balaam of *Parashat Balak* and the Balaam of the inscription, one striking similarity is the communication with animals. In Torah, the seer has a donkey who speaks to him. In the inscription, birds communicate the news. Yet another similarity is the fact that both stories entail deadly serious subject matter: in Torah, a curse threatens the Israelites; in the Deir Alla inscription, the end of the world is predicted.

In the present time, we also receive messages from the natural world: warnings conveyed by the migration of polar bears, warnings communicated through the shifting of fish in the sea. Like the ancient Balaam, whoever he was, we ignore these messages at our peril.

Balak
Rabbi Charles Middleburgh, PhD, 2017

If we can derive anything from the comedic story of Balaam and his she-ass, beyond its clear statement of Balaam's stupidity and shortsightedness, it is the fact that animals are often much more percipient and quick-witted than humans.

Balaam threatens his ass with violence, but it is she who sees the sword-wielding angel blocking their path. Had she not seen the angel, the "great seer" who communed with God but was blind to what stood before him would have been struck down. Balaam claims to be a prophet, but it is the ass who speaks the wisest words.

All this reminds us of the importance of animals. They sense and become aware of things before we do and, in some cases, exhibit greater intelligence. The story should also alert us to the crimes we perpetrate against them: laboratory experiments, innate cruelty, the quest for food that could just as easily come from other sources, and the lust for their riches (such as ivory or the despicable hunting of whales) are entirely indefensible.

Many famous people have been credited with saying, "The more I come to know people, the more I love my dog."

Seen in this light, Balaam and his ass become nothing less than paradigms: he for the crass myopia of people, she for the suffering of an innocent animal kingdom. As we ponder this thought, I am sure that we should not ignore the fact that in the final analysis it is the beast, and not the man, who is vindicated.

Chukat
Rabbi Charles Middleburgh, PhD, 2018

The dominant themes in *Chukat* are the death of Miriam, the revolt at the waters of Meribah, and Moses's spectacular loss of self-control, which costs him and Aaron the right to cross the Jordan into the Promised Land.

Yet there is an episode all too frequently overlooked: Moses sends messengers to the king of Edom, the country Israel must pass through to reach the Jordan River. He addresses the king in fraternal terms—"Thus says your brother Israel" (Num. 20:14–17)—and requests passage through their land with a promise not to trespass or take water or provisions. Moses's eminently reasonable request is met with a rigidly negative response: "But they replied, 'You shall not pass through!' And Edom went out against them in heavy force, strongly armed. So Edom would not let Israel cross their territory, and Israel turned away from them" (Num. 20:20–21). A direct line may be drawn from this incident to the Edomite collaboration with the Babylonians in the destruction of Jerusalem and its Temple and its exultation at the devastation and exile imposed on their "brother Israel," viciously condemned in Obad. 1:12.

This thread in our tradition reminds us of the depth of bitterness and hatred evident in internecine, intergroup, and international disputes today and of the violence that often results. While many of these clashes are occurring far from where we live, our own societies are growing increasingly polarized, too. If dialogue dissolves and a sense of common purpose is irretrievably corroded, disaster may follow. We should heed the message of our past and build strong bridges in the present.

Balak
Rabbi Michael Boyden, 2018

Was Balaam a good guy or a bad guy? Balaam, sent by Balak, king of Moab to curse the Israelites, ends up blessing them instead. So perhaps he was on our side after all!

Jewish tradition is not wholly unfavorable to him: On the verse "Israel had no prophet like Moses" (Deut. 34:10), *Sifrei Rabbah V'zot Hab'rachah* offers this positive assessment: "Israel had no prophet [like Moses], but the nations of the world did! And who was that? Balaam son of Beor."

Nevertheless, Balaam did not meet with a happy ending. The Book of Joshua recounts that he was put to the sword by the Israelites (Josh. 13:22). According to Rabbi Yitzchak, as related in *Otzar Midrashim* 168, the Israelites were troubled by what they had done to him, but were comforted by a *bat kol* ("voice from Heaven") informing them that they had killed a sorcerer and not a prophet—a negative assessment. *Mishnah*

Pirkei Avot 5:19 tells us, "Whoever has the following three characteristics is a disciple of Abraham our father: . . . a good eye, a humble spirit, and a lowly soul; but three other features characterize the disciples of Balaam the Wicked: an evil eye, a haughty spirit, and a proud soul."

Balaam, after all, had no reservations about setting out to curse the Israelites even though God had told him, "You must not curse that people, for they are blessed" (Num. 22:12).

פינחס *Pinchas*
(Numbers 25:10–30:1)

Pinchas
Rabbi Louis Rieser, 2010

This portion offers two strikingly contrasting descriptions of the qualities we search for in a leader.

Pinchas was a decisive leader: clear and passionate but, alas, murderous. God rewards him with a "covenant of peace" (Num. 25:12). *Mishnah Sanhedrin* 9:6 exonerates him: "One who has sexual relations with an Aramaean woman, zealots beat him up." The *Jerusalem Talmud Sanhedrin* 48b, underscores that Pinchas acted independently. The Kotzker Rebbe suggests that he was Moses's first choice as a successor, perhaps because of his passion and independence. Moses concludes that Pinchas is an unacceptable choice and asks God to appoint an appropriate successor (Num. 27:16–17). God names Joshua and describes him as one "in whom there is spirit" (Num. 26:18). What does that mean?

Sifrei Zuta 26 defines him as "one who walks with the hot-headed ones and with the patient ones, each according to their opinion." He has the intellectual ability to hear and understand the arguments on all sides. In a similar vein, the *Babylonian Talmud Taanit* 25b, recounts a tale of Rabbi Eliezer and Rabbi Akiva. Both went before the Ark to ask God for compassion and for rain, but only Akiva's prayers were effective. A *bat kol* ("voice from Heaven") explained, "It is not because that one is greater than this one, but because that one is forbearing and this one is not forbearing." Leadership requires patience. The Or HaChayim (Morocco, seventeenth to eighteenth century) in his commentary describes this quality in a more spiritual way: "Moses, you have within you [a link to] the root of all the souls [of Israel] and there is within Joshua [a link with] . . . all the souls of that generation." The soul connection allows the leader to understand the needs of the people and the people to accept his leadership.

What qualifies one for leadership: passion, intellectual understanding, patience, or spiritual connection?

Pinchas
Rabbi Janice Garfunkel, z"l, 2011

Parashat Pinchas makes me think about passion. The flip side of passion is fanaticism, but that's for another *d'var*.

Passion is at the heart of Judaism (and perhaps differentiates us from, say, calmer Eastern religions that eschew striving). Passion is why so many Jews are leaders in their fields and why Jewish mothers (and fathers) can be so devoted to their children (who are, as the joke tells us, all either gifted or have special needs). Jews should be *z'rizim* ("zealous") to fulfill mitzvot; as Rashi tells us, Abraham was *zariz* to saddle his donkey and obey God's command.

Many Reform Jews are, indeed, passionate for their own particular calling in life—healing the sick, teaching the young, raising funds for the arts or for medical research, spearheading programs to end poverty or violence.

Food for thought: As rabbis, what can we do to turn some of our people's remarkable "oomph" toward living a more passionately Jewish life? Toward mastering Hebrew and holy texts? Toward a meaningful twenty-five-hour observance of Shabbat, daily prayer, or a novel "Reform" embodiment of Jewish values?

Passion does seem to go hand in glove with certitude. The more ambiguity, the less passion. This might be why liberal religion seems to engender less passion and commitment than Orthodoxy.

Passion is a Jewish gift. May we leaders succeed in turning that energy toward enhancing Judaism.

Pinchas
Rabbi Louis Rieser, 2012

Oy, transitions.

Parashat Pinchas is read in the season of transitions, when new rabbis and presidents take office. This *parashah* also anticipates a transition, as Moses is informed of his impending death and petitions God to appoint an appropriate leader (Num. 27:12–17).

What kind of leader should succeed Moses, or your president, or you? What leadership characteristics do you value most: strength, knowledge, managerial skills, or political savvy?

Ibn Ezra states simply that Moses asks the God of all souls, who knows each soul, to choose one who is worthy. It is a trusting stance.

By contrast, in *Midrash Tanchuma Pinchas* 10, Moses requests a very particular kind of successor. Moses pleads before God, "Master of the Universe, You know the understanding possessed by each individual and that no person is like another. As I depart, I ask You to appoint a leader who can bear all of their varying understandings."

For this stiff-necked people, Moses requests a successor with the fortitude to hear each individual's point of view. This is not to suggest this leader will follow whatever voice is the most vociferous or demanding. Joshua knows the ways of Moses and God. He will, however, honor every individual and his or her particular understanding.

For all leadership, new or old, this is good but difficult advice. Every synagogue leader has suffered the onslaught of freely offered opinions on matters sacred and profane. The best leaders have time for them all, filling each individual congregant with the knowledge that his or her opinion counts. In this season of transitions, it pays to listen to Moses's leadership advice.

Pinchas
Rabbi Stephen Wylen, 2013

"Adonai spoke to Moses, saying, 'Pinchas son of Elazar son of Aaron the priest turned back My wrath from upon the Israelites, when he zealously avenged My vengeance among them so I did not consume the Israelites in My vengeance'" (Num. 25:10–11).

In Jewish tradition, Pinchas has become the archetype of the zealot, the one who acts out of a passion to serve God. Over the centuries, Jewish tradition has become troubled by the figure of the zealot. In the *Babylonian Talmud Sanhedrin* 82a, Rav Chisda states that the government may neither advise nor encourage vigilantes. Had Pinchas requested permission to act zealously against Zimri and Cozbi, it would not have been granted. Further, said the Sages, had Zimri instead killed Pinchas it would have been justified, for he acted in self-defense.

Later commentaries tend to explain away or mitigate the zealotry of Pinchas. He is not upheld as a role model. An exception is in the ArtScroll Stone edition of the *Chumash* (p. 876). There we read:

> The people accused him of wanton murder. . . . In response, God declared that, far from murder, Pinchas had committed an act that had saved countless lives. Indeed, God called him a descendant of Aaron, who was distinguished for his love of mankind and pursuit of peace. And what was more, God rewarded him by appointing him a Kohen, which denoted a covenant of peace, not death.

The trend in Orthodoxy to valorize Pinchas is disturbing. Not that our Orthodox brethren are going to become vigilante killers, but Pinchas comes to represent a certain attitude to the outside world, and it is dangerous to depict this attitude as bringing peace and honor to the inside world.

Pinchas
Rabbi David Novak, 2014

Why does Moses have to turn to God for an answer when the daughters of Zelophehad challenge the laws of inheritance?

There are several possible reasons. First, Moses really does not know what to do in this unique situation. Second, Moses has not been as explicitly instructed by God as he was on so many other occasions. Third, based on Moses's past experience with women, he presumes that they don't count. They were excluded from revelation at Sinai. They don't figure into any census taken.

This is not to suggest that Moses was wrong in turning directly to God in this novel situation. In doing so, God becomes responsible for creating legal precedent for the inheritance rights of women in case there are no male heirs. Zelophehad's daughters, too, recognize the significance of what they were doing in approaching Moses. Perhaps we can give Moses the benefit of the doubt that when turning to God, he knew that it would be best if God, and not Moses, made the direct pronouncement of the legal rights of the women. Still, one wonders if Moses's silence is an expression of his treatment of women in past encounters.

Today, inspired by the daughters of Zelophehad, we strive to live engendered Jewish lives where nothing is prohibited to any Jew based on gender and where the dignity of all is fully respected in our religious and communal practices.

Pinchas
Rabbi Amy Scheinerman, 2015

After reading the account of Pinchas's response to idolatry in Ba'al Pe'or in *Parashat Balak*, *Parashat Pinchas* tells us that Pinchas's action turns back God's wrath, preventing divine genocide, ending the plague, and restoring equilibrium to the Israelite community. Pinchas is granted God's *b'rit shalom* ("covenant of peace;" Num. 25:12), which Torah also calls a *b'rit k'hunat olam* ("covenant of priesthood for all time;" Num. 25:13), because he took "impassioned action" that effected *kaparah* ("atonement") for all Israel.

So much is troubling here:

(1) Pinchas's violent vigilante (in-)justice elicits God's lavish praise and reward. Many commentators, including Hirsch and the Chatam Sofer, chime the champion bell, and even the Chasidic master Tzvi Hirsh of Nadvorna engages in a bizarre textual juggling act to prove that ultimately Pinchas defended Israel in the Mosaic mold.

Talmud, however, takes a far more thoughtful stance: "If [Pinchas] had come to take counsel [with us Rabbis], we do not instruct him to do [as he did]. Further, had Zimri forsaken his mistress and Pinchas slain him, Pinchas would have been executed, and had Zimri slain Pinchas, he would not have been executed, since Pinchas was a *rodeif* ("pursuer;" *Babylonian Talmud Sanhedrin* 82a).

(2) Also disturbing is the motif of dangerous non-Israelite women who sexually induce Israelite men into committing idolatry (see warn-

ings in Exod. 34:16 and Deut. 7:3-4; blame for Solomon's failures in I Kings 11:1–13; and, of course, Jezebel in I Kings 18). Zimri and Cozbi are named in this portion (not in the account of their actions). While "Zimri" has a "musical" lilt, "Cozbi" means "lie" or "deceive" (much as the Rabbis called Bar Kochba "Bar Koziba").

However, we still have women like Tzipporah, Rahab, Yael, and Ruth to hold out.

Pinchas
Rabbi Michael Boyden, 2017

Who would have thought that religious zealotry would still be an issue in the twenty-first century? We are all too familiar with the ruthless violence of the Taliban and ISIS, but religious extremism sadly also exists in other societies—including our own.

This week's *parashah* tells of how Aaron's grandson, Pinchas, impales Zimri and Cozbi, who are involved in coitus. Torah justifies their slaughter on the grounds of the spread of idolatry within the Israelite community.

Indeed, God appears to condone Pinchas's action. "Pinchas . . . has turned back My wrath. . . . Therefore, tell him that I grant him a covenant of peace" (Num. 25:11–12). This episode stands in obvious contrast to Hillel's statement that we should be "Aaron's disciples, loving peace, pursuing peace, and loving humanity" (*Mishnah Pirkei Avot* 1:12).

The Talmud is clearly unhappy with the story. Rav Chisda says that if Zimri had left Cozbi and Pinchas had killed him, then Pinchas would have been guilty of murder. Furthermore, if Zimri had turned over and killed Pinchas, then Zimri would not have been punished, because he would have acted in self-defense (*Babylonian Talmud Sanhedrin* 82a).

Why, then, is Pinchas rewarded with "a covenant of peace"? A closer look at the word *shalom* (Num. 25:12) shows that the letter *vav* is written defectively and is cut in the middle, turning it into *shaleim*. Rabbi Y'hudah comments that the covenant of peace will only be conferred upon Pinchas when he is whole (*shaleim*)—but not when he is deficient (*Babylonian Talmud Kiddushin* 62b).

Peace that is achieved through zealotry cannot be whole and complete.

Pinchas
Rabbi Amy Scheinerman, 2018

The story of Pinchas is deeply disturbing to people with modern sensibilities. God's ebullient approval and praise of Pinchas's violent vigilantism horrifies us. God's pact of friendship with Pinchas and his descendants, specifically a "pact of priesthood for all time, because he took impassioned action for his God, thus making expiation for the Israelites" (Num. 25:12–13) is troubling to explain.

The S'fat Emet is also troubled by the story of Pinchas. He explains that the seemingly extraneous *yod* in his name signifies peace. Referring to the kabbalistic tree, he writes that although Pinchas came from the left side (judgment), God gave him the covenant of peace:

> Priesthood was given to Pinchas as a gift, as though to say that when Israel are deserving, even the left [the quality of judgment] becomes right [the quality of loving-kindness]. Something like this is found in the *Zohar*, to the effect that priesthood had to be given to him, since one who has killed a person is ordinarily disqualified from the priesthood.

Even violent beings are not beyond redemption. Torah does not affirm that Pinchas experienced remorse or did *t'shuvah*, but the S'fat Emet suggests that the *yod* signifying peace in his name implies that he did—and this is why God bestowed upon him the covenant of peace. Such is the power of repentance.

מטות/מסעי   *Matot/Mas'ei*
(Numbers 30:2–32:42 and Numbers 33:1–36:13)

Matot/Mas'ei
Rabbi Amy Scheinerman, 2010

Matot/Ma'sei close out Torah's chronicle of four decades in the wilderness. Tz'lophechad's daughters, whom we meet in Numbers 27 when they appeal to Moses to amend the laws of inheritance, reappear at the very end of *Sefer B'midbar* (Book of Numbers). Although the right of daughters to inherit land from their father when there are no sons remains intact, now male relatives express the concern that if Mahlah, Tirzah, Hoglah, Milcah, and Noah marry men outside the tribe of M'nasheh, tribal land holdings will be lost to the tribe. In response, Moses limits their marital choices to men within the tribe.

Have the daughters' gains been reversed or diminished? If the women continue to own and control the land they inherited, and it does not pass into the control of their husbands, then their gains have been diminished, but not reversed. Our proclivity to champion the just and egalitarian cause of Tz'lophechad's daughters, however, seems to be in conflict with the established Jewish priority of community over individuality. How do we reconcile two competing priorities?

Tamara Cohn Eskenazi and Elizabeth Goldstein, in *The Torah: A Women's Commentary* (p. 1014), note that the five women who close the wilderness narrative mirror the five women who open the account of the Exodus: Shifrah, Puah, Miriam, Yocheved, and Pharaoh's daughter.

This observation, coupled with the seeming diminution in Numbers 33 of the inheritance rights won in Numbers 27, reminds us of the glacial pace of cultural change, often needed in its own right, and crucial for movement toward social justice. We who are impatient can take heart that although slow, those who are courageous and persistent—as these ten women attest—enjoy success.

Matot
Rabbi Michael Boyden, 2011

Perhaps one of the reasons why democracy has a bad name is because politicians have a nasty habit of not carrying out their promises. Israel's third prime minister, Levi Eshkol, is reported to have remarked, "I know I promised, but I didn't promise to carry out my promise!"

Included in this week's *parashah* are the laws relating to making vows. The clear implication is that the commitments we take upon ourselves have consequences. Perhaps that is why Maimonides wrote, "A person should not make few vows and promises. However, when he does make them, he should make a point of keeping them" (*Mishnah Torah Hilchot N'darim*).

Our *parashah* commences with the words, "Moses spoke to the heads of the Israelite tribes" (Num. 30:2). The purpose behind this is to emphasize that leaders have a special responsibility to remember that words count.

Perhaps it was because the Torah viewed the taking of vows so seriously that our Rabbis showed disdain for the practice. Rabbi Natan said, "A person who makes a vow is like someone who builds a pagan altar. And a person who fulfills it is like someone who offers up incense on it" (*Babylonian Talmud N'darim* 59a).

The Talmud also teaches us that "a person should never promise a child that he will give him something and then not give it to him, because, in doing so, he teaches him to lie" (*Babylonian Talmud Sukkah* 46b).

The message is clear—and not only for politicians. Don't make promises unless you really intend to keep them.

Mas'ei
Rabbi Stephen Wylen, 2011

"These are the journeys of the Israelites" (Num. 33:1). The Torah records forty-two places Israel stopped in their forty years of wandering in the desert. Generations of commentators have asked: What possible relevance has this to the generations that followed, that it is included in Scripture? One principle of Torah interpretation is that *maasei avot*, the experiences of our ancestors, are repeated in the lives of the Jewish people. Throughout our history, Jews have been wanderers. We have gone to Babylon, Rome, Spain, Germany, Poland, Morocco . . . Whenever civilization has peaked around the Mediterranean, Jews have played a part.

The remarkable mobility of the Jews has been powered by our unique perspective on "place." The world is divided into only two realms: *Eretz Yisrael* and *Galut* ("exile"). As long as a Jew is in *galut*, one place is no different from another. We are exiled from one place and settle in another, but nothing has changed. Whenever the Jew has become too comfortable in any land—medieval Spain, Enlightenment Germany—it has not gone well for us. Our mobility has afforded us not only safety, but prosperity as well. We do not linger in suffering out of attachment to any forsaken place in the exile. The Yiddish folk song "Dona Dona" tells of our acquired wisdom: "Calves are easily bound and slaughtered, never knowing the reason why. But all those who treasure freedom, like the swallow has learned to fly."

Matot/Mas'ei
Rabbi Janice Garfunkel, z"l, 2012

Why list all these waystations? Perhaps to remind us that life is rarely the smooth journey we would hope or expect. Those who left Egypt never made it to the Promised Land. What started out as a year's march from point A to point B ended up being a lifetime's march from one random place to another random place, not even making progress toward the ultimate goal.

Even icons of success experience many failures along the way. Just some of Abraham Lincoln's failures: In 1831, he failed in business. Then he ran for the state legislature—and lost. He wanted to go to law school but couldn't gain admittance. So he borrowed money from a friend but lost it all in another failed business venture, which took seventeen years to pay off. In 1835, he had a nervous breakdown and was in bed for six months. He ran for speaker of the state legislature—and lost. He ran for Congress—and lost. Finally, in 1846, he was elected to Congress, but when he ran for reelection, he lost yet again. He lost in his bid for senator as well. He received fewer than one hundred votes for the vice-presidential nomination in 1856. In 1860, he was finally elected president of the United States.

Lincoln wrote, "The path was worn and slippery. My foot slipped from under me, knocking the other out of the way, but I recovered and said to myself, 'It's a slip and not a fall.'"

We have too much shame around failure, and our culture practically requires us to rewrite history on our resumes to "spin" our missteps into successes they were not. Perhaps we can relieve our congregants of their unnecessary shame by acknowledging that failure is an inevitable part of life. Alvin Fine wrote that we go from "defeat to defeat to defeat, until we realize that life is not some high point along the way, but in making the journey, stage by stage, a sacred pilgrimage."

Matot/Mas'ei
Rabbi Pamela Wax, 2013

The Baal Shem Tov is reputed to have said that "forgetting is the true exile." We are therefore enjoined to remember the forty-two stages of our journey through the desert, just as we recall the forty-two towns that were given to the Levites. God's mystical name, derived from the *Ana B'Koach* prayer, is said to have forty-two letters and is used to assist us in transitions.

Do you remember Marah? The Sea of Reeds? R'fidim? Chatzerot? Some of those places have clear memories attached; some are now forgotten. *Midrash Tanchuma* likens this travelogue to a king whose son was ill. "He brought him to a distant place for treatment. When they returned, the father recounted, 'Here we slept; here we cooled ourselves; here your head ached.'" We are nothing if not a people of memory, honoring people, places, and events. My personal observance as I light candles each Friday is to silently recall one highlight from each day gone by in order to honor the week now past: *shamor v'zachor* ("keep in your heart and remember").

If we remove the first and the last years of the journey when the Israelites were, indeed, constantly on the march, Rashi calculates that there were only twenty stations during thirty-eight years. This means that there were long periods of normalcy at one oasis or another. Some of us have had the luxury of a long rabbinate in one location; others have moved numerous times. How do you recall and honor your personal journey? Since we are taught that "Moses recorded the starting points of their various marches, as directed by Adonai" (Num. 33:2), to what extent do you believe that your own travel itinerary was planned and directed by God?

Perhaps you have already reached your ultimate destination, your Promised Land; if not, wishing you a *n'siah tovah* ("a good trip")! *Chazak chazak v'nitchazeik* ("from your strength to ours").

Matot
Rabbi Amy Scheinerman, 2014

Matot is a not a happy *parashah* for the status of women.

Matot opens with a discussion of vows, with special emphasis on how vows made by women living in or coming into the domain of a man can see their vows annulled by their father or husband. Talmud limits his authority to annul her vow to those of self-denial and those affecting the marital relationship (*Babylonian Talmud N'darim* 79a), but it is not difficult to extend the latter to anything of which he disapproves or that run contrary to his interests. Only widows and divorcees are independent agents vis-à-vis their vows; attachment to a man makes a woman subject to his authority. In turn, these laws evoke the most infamous vow of the Bible, that of Jephthah concerning his daughter, which led to the murder of an innocent under religious pretense (Judges 11).

Also in this *parashah*, we read about Moses's final retribution against the Midianites in a campaign of annihilation commanded by God. Torah records that "the Israelites took the women and children of the Midianites captive and seized as booty all their beasts, all their herds, and all their wealth" (Num. 31:9), but after the fact, it appears, Moses expresses his anger that they spared the lives of non-virginal women, who "are the very ones who, at the bidding of Balaam, induced the Israelites to trespass against Adonai in the matter of Peor, so that Adonai's community was struck by the plague" (Num. 31:16).

Given reproductive politics here in the United States and conflicts rife around the globe, perhaps this *parashah* might serve as a reminder to consider and evaluate the position of women here and abroad at this juncture in history.

Mas'ei
Rabbi Michael Boyden, 2014

Parashat Mas'ei not only brings us to the end of the Book of Numbers, but leads us, in effect, to the conclusion of a journey that began early in the Book of Exodus. Just as we read then, "The Israelites journeyed from Ramses to Sukkot" (Exod. 12:37), so now we read, "These were the journeys of the Israelites" (Num. 33:1).

Our *parashah* mentions no fewer than forty-two stations on the Israelites passage from Egypt to the Promised Land. The list of place names initially makes for boring reading. In a world in which we travel much, we tend to note the hour of departure and arrival but have little time for the journey. On a long flight, we count the hours and minutes until it will end. However, names and places are important, for they are what make up life's journey.

We read this *parashah* at a time of beginnings and endings, at the very time of year that we mark the three weeks that culminated in the destruction of the First and Second Temples and the beginning of our exile as a people.

In our own lives, we also mark beginnings and endings. We make a great fanfare when a child is born and gather together with our family and friends for funerals, but what really counts is what takes place on the way. It is not only what has been and what will be, but more especially what is.

Rabbi Sholom Schwadron quotes the view that "Each generation in which the Temple is not built is as though it was destroyed in their lifetime and can be perceived as delaying the redemption" (*Jerusalem Talmud Yoma* 1:1). Our lives and our personal journeys are what count.

Matot
Rabbi Louis Rieser, 2015

In the opening verses of Numbers 32, Reuven and Gad note four times that the land east of the Jordan River is good land for cattle and that they are cattlemen. They ask that this land be granted them in lieu of their portion in the Land of Israel. They parry an initial objection that they are not supporting their fellow tribes by agreeing to serve as shock troops. But other objections are not so easily set aside.

The Sages teach, "Better a handful of satisfaction in this land than both hands full of trouble on the other side of the Jordan" (*Vayikra Rabbah* 3:1). On the eve of receiving the divine gift of *Eretz Yisrael*, they opt out in favor of land of their own choosing.

For these tribes, cattle are primary. Children are not mentioned until verse 16; wives, until verse 26. Their quest for material benefit precedes family, their fellow tribes, and the divine gift of the Land. Their satisfaction trumps all other concerns. Their quest for material benefit overtakes any notion of spiritual inheritance.

Moses accepts their offer. *Midrash HaGadol* teaches, however, that "one who is ungrateful cannot accept the Kingdom of Heaven," perhaps with these tribes in mind. In the end, the tribes of Reuven and Gad are the first to be exiled (*Eichah Rabbah*, proem 5).

Deuteronomy will remind us that we entered a rich land. The richness lay not in the material of the land, characterized elsewhere as a land that consumes its inhabitants, but in its spiritual promise. How often do we opt for material good rather than spiritual promise?

Mas'ei
Rabbi Stephen Wylen, 2015

The Torah says, "These are the journeys of the Israelites who started out from the land of Egypt" (Num. 33:1). It is well-known that according to midrash the forty-two journeys of the Israelites during their forty years of wandering in the desert are symbolic of the many exiles and wanderings of the Jewish people, who have been driven from one place to another during our two millennia of exile. Of old, our people understood the exile as Israel's way of atoning for all the sins of the world until the days of the Messiah should arise.

It has also been said that this verse symbolizes those who lift up their feet to go and study Torah, voluntarily exiling themselves from their hometowns and their families to go to a place of Jewish learning. This journey also counts as one of the "journeys of the Israelites by the command of God." The great Jewish scholars of old used to leave their homes and go to a place where there was a great yeshivah. Rashi went to the Rhineland to learn Torah, and when he established an even greater yeshivah, the scholars of Germany came to France to study in his school. Jews in Eastern Europe would depart their shtetl to go to a great yeshivah, perhaps in the vicinity of Vilna.

Reform rabbis of today undertake a similar journey. Once they are ordained, they go to the community where they are called and where a rabbi is needed. It could be a small town or a region of America distant from one's birthplace. The rabbi seldom has the opportunity to observe Pesach or the Yamim Noraim (Days of Awe) in the company of extended family. These are journeys that are at the command of God, and they function as atonement for the Jewish people to bring closer the messianic age.

Matot/Mas'ei
Rabbi Amy Scheinerman, 2017

Two eighteenth-century Chasidic views on the opening of *Parashat Mas'ei* and its peculiarly worded account of the Israelites' journey through the wilderness provide food for thought and discussion in the twenty-first century: "Moses wrote of their departures and their journeys according to Adonai," and then, "These are their journeys according to their departures" (Num. 33:2).

First view: The Ishbitzer Rebbe, Mordechai Yosef Leiner (1765–1827), in *Mei HaShiloach*, associates the first mention of Israel's journeys—"according to Adonai"—with God's viewpoint by which the Israelites, regardless of their moral behavior, "all live in an existence coming from God's essence.... There is no advantage in one's actions." Accordingly, every Israelite "found grace and goodness with God" and experienced redemption. "Their journeys according to their departures" reflects the human perspective where "one acquires goodness by means of actions and trials." How do we balance the two?

Second view: The Chozeh of Lublin, Yaakov Yitzchak Horowitz (1745–1815), in *Divrei Emet*, learns from Rabbi Bachya ibn Pakuda that the same two phrases in Num. 33:2 allude to two rungs on the spiritual ladder. Abraham exemplifies the higher rung: "[He] attained the entire Torah before it was given." Abraham was able to perceive the depth of Torah's spiritual qualities and adhere to God without its laws. Concerning the lower rung, "In the exile of Egypt, our ancestors became coarsened. We needed to receive the Torah first, in order to become attached to God." Moses, the prophets, and the Israelites needed both the Written and the Oral Torahs to teach Abraham's spiritual level.

Matot/Mas'ei
Rabbi David Novak, 2018

Arriving at the end of *Sefer B'midbar* ("Book of Numbers") we find what might be a fitting conclusion to Torah. The vagaries of the travel recounted, the tribes' portions divvied up, blessings and warnings given, it is time for the Israelites to take up residence in the Promised Land. The text leaves us primed for the people to embrace their covenantal responsibilities to the God who made their freedom possible. They are ready to "dispossess" the inhabitants of the land.

In words that strike many moderns as disturbing and problematic, God warns the Israelites preparing to displace people who had long lived in the land: "But if you do not dispossess the settled-folk of the land, those who are left of them shall be as barbs in your eyes, as spines in your sides; they will assault you on the land that you are settling in, and it shall be: as I planned to do to them, so I will do to you!" (Num. 33:55–56).

Why? Torah is both of God and profoundly human. It understands how, in general, people are seduced by the cultures around them and how easy it is, in this instance, to descend into the idolatrous practices of Canaanite culture. Throughout history, time and again, Jews have encountered both overt and subtle pressure to internalize the cultures of hegemonic host societies. In our time, as rabbis who sometimes find ourselves "going against the grain" of our dominant culture's values, we must repurpose Torah's warning to preserve Jewish values and priorities.

Deuteronomy

Deuteronomy

דברים *D'varim*
(Deuteronomy 1:1–3:22)

D'varim
Rabbi Stephen Wylen, 2010

Abraham ibn Ezra comments on "across the Jordan" (Deut. 1:1):

> If you will understand the mystery of the twelve [final] verses [in the Torah], "and also Moses wrote" (Deut. 31:22), "and the Canaanites were then in the Land" (Gen. 12:6), "and on the mountain Adonai is seen" (Gen. 22:14), "and his bedstead of iron is now in Rabbat Amon" (Deut. 3:11), then you will comprehend the truth.

Ibn Ezra's comment is sparked by his recognition that the directions to the Plains of Moab are given from Jerusalem, not from Sinai. This prompts Ibn Ezra to recall the most obvious textual evidence that the Torah was written at a later time. This comment was not hidden away by later generations. Ibn Ezra's commentary is included in all of the *Mikraot G'dolot*. This demonstrates that *torah l'moshe misinai* ("Moses received the Torah at Sinai") was not a required belief in premodern Judaism. It was a common belief (see Rashi on *B'har*), but a faithful Jew could believe otherwise.

Do you sing *v'zot hatorah* ("this is the Torah") when you raise the Torah scroll? If you do, it is probably because it is a fun little ditty. But should Reform Jews be affirming a belief so contrary to historical facts and our own religion of science and reason?

D'varim
Rabbi Stephen Wylen, 2011

"Moses spoke all these words . . . across the Jordan" (Deut. 1:1).
Ibn Ezra comments:

> If you understand the secret of the twelve verses [that conclude the Torah] and the secret of "Moses wrote" (Deut. 31:32) and "the Canaanites were then in the land" and "on the mountain of God it is seen" and "his iron bedstead is now in Rabbat Ammon" (Deut. 3:11), then you will know the truth.

These words of Ibn Ezra are published in every standard edition of the *Mikraot G'dolot*. What this means is that the belief that the entire Torah was given to Moses at Mount Sinai was not an obligatory belief of premodern Judaism. It was a common belief. It was an expected belief. But Spinoza stated openly that the Torah was written by men over a period of time. That truth had already been published in the second most famous Torah commentary of all time.

It is often said that all Jews were Orthodox until Reform Judaism came along. That is not true. Orthodoxy is, if anything, the youngest of all the modern Jewish movements, arising as a negative response to the challenge of the movements that incorporated modern beliefs and methods.

It is common among postmoderns to claim that there is no such thing as truth; there is only perception. The Torah, however divine, has been filtered through human understanding. Is this a perception, or is it, as Abraham ibn Ezra says, the truth?

D'varim
Rabbi Bill S. Tepper, 2012

Recently, I have been engaged in different kinds of transitions. I attended school graduation ceremonies, signposts in the transition from youth to maturity. Our congregation installed its new board, signaling a renewed sense of commitment to our temple and larger community. I traveled again to Israel, crossing over, if only for ten precious days, to reconnect with the spirit of our remarkable Jewish tradition in the Land.

In *Parashat D'varim*, the Israelites are *b'eiver hayardein*, "on the other side of the Jordan" (Deut. 1:1). Their journey through the wilderness is over; it is time to cross the water and enter their promised land. Years earlier, the Israelites stood on the shore of the Sea of Reeds. Their crossing was one from servitude to freedom. In *D'varim*, crossing the water shall once again transform them as a people. Like the Sea of Reeds, the Jordan River represents a demarcation between Israel's past and future and between dream and reality.

At the turn of the twentieth century, so many of our forebears, propelled by the vision of religious, economic, and political freedoms, crossed the ocean to create new lives in America.

Thus, as Jews and Hebrews (*ivrim*, "the travelers") we possess a special understanding of what it means to cross over: from old to new, from fear to hope, and from uncertainty to promise. May all our transitions—over all our Jordans—facilitate our desire to enrich and enhance our world and everyone with whom it is our blessing to share it.

D'varim
Rabbi David Novak, 2013

This is it: Moses's last chance to wrestle with God and the People of Israel, the parties sharing in the covenant freely accepted at Mount Sinai. This is what we, as rabbis, do to this day—we wrestle, as did Moses, with our inheritance that is Torah. We are teachers of the best tradition of Moses, whom we call *Moshe Rabbeinu*, "Moses our teacher." Like Moses in *D'varim*, we use all of our human tools and faculties to persuade, cajole, teach, argue, and lovingly expose our people to Torah's multifaceted meanings. Like Moses, we deal with people who come to us from many backgrounds—who believe what the text says, never looking beneath the surface; who don't affirm that they are part of the covenant; who affirm the covenant but do not know what it means. Like Moses, it becomes our job to expose our fellow God-wrestlers with all of the means we have as teachers.

Moses never gives up on the people—and neither should we. As rabbis, this is our job: to make text meaningful and relevant, to build bridges, and to never give up on the holy pursuit of making our traditions meaningful.

D'varim
Rabbi Amy Scheinerman, 2014

Rabbi Menachem Nachum Twersky of Chernobyl (1730–97), writing about Moses's speech on the steppes of Moab, draws a direct line from Israel's wilderness wanders to our personal life journeys:

> The Torah was given to Israel only after seven weeks of wandering through the Sea of Reeds and . . . through various deserts until they came to Mount Sinai. All this was in order to cut off the outer shells [*k'lipot chitzoniyot*], the superficialities that formed a curtain dividing them from the Written Torah. . . . By traveling through those deserts . . . as well as by witnessing the miracles . . . faith in the Blessed One became rooted in their hearts. . . . This is the case today as well. The challenges we have regarding Torah are there because of our *k'lipot*. . . . Now that the collective shells have been defeated and set aside, it is up to every person who studies Torah to defeat one's own inner harsh places, so that we not be separated from the faces of Torah (*M'or Einayim*).

Mordecai Kaplan drew a distinction between "transvaluation" and "revaluation." The former "consists in ascribing meanings to the traditional content of a religion or social heritage, which could neither have been contemplated nor implied by the authors of that content." Kaplan speaks of the ongoing interpretive process whereby "the teachers and sages of a later period did not hesitate to read their own beliefs and aspirations into the writings . . . of an earlier period." Kaplan termed his method "revaluation," which "consists in disengaging from the traditional content those elements which answer permanent postulates of human nature, and in integrating them into our own ideology" (*The Meaning of God in Modern Jewish Religion*, p. 6).

M'or Einayim seems to circle around Kaplan's concepts both clockwise and counterclockwise: He certainly sees himself as within the uninterrupted chain of interpretive tradition. And while we might see his interpretation as discontinuous with all that came before, the very fact that he doesn't suggests that Kaplan's "revaluation"—however conscious his interpretative method—is indeed "transvaluation."

D'varim: Shabbat Chazon
Rabbi David Novak, 2015

Parashat D'varim opens with Moses's long and eloquent review of the wilderness journey. What begins on a positive note devolves in rebuke for the Israelites' response to the report of the ten spies: "You refused to go up, and flouted the command of Adonai your God. You sulked in your tents" (Deut. 1:26–27).

Parashat D'varim coincides with Shabbat Chazon, on which we read the third haftarah of rebuke leading to Tishah B'Av. Rebuke—whether from Moses in the twelfth century BCE or Isaiah in the eighth century BCE, or, as we encounter it today, from our internal voice or the voice of others—challenges who we are. None of us embrace rebuke. We are often inclined to perceive it as being ill-considered or thoughtless, perhaps correctly, but perhaps out of self-defense. Even more difficult to accept is the kind of rebuke that is offered in a rude or even harmful manner.

Does rebuke serve any meaningful purpose? It may help us to become aware of behaviors that are deleterious to us and to others. However, already the Rabbis knew that in order to be effective, *tocheichah*, "rebuke," must be offered in the appropriate manner to enable the recipient to hear it. Offering criticism requires nuance and often gentleness.

It is our responsibility, when warranted, to offer thoughtful rebuke. In so doing, we may catalyze change, small or large, to create more successful communities and more effective human beings. Disturbing the surface veneer, even when uncomfortable, often leads to promising outcomes.

D'varim
Rabbi Stephen Wylen, 2016

"These are the words that Moses spoke to all the Israelites across the Jordan" (Deut. 1:1).

Abraham ibn Ezra says, "You will understand 'across the Jordan' if you understand the secret of the final twelve verses in the Torah [which describe the death of Moses] and certain other verses such as 'the

Canaanites were then in the land' (Gen. 12:6). And if you understand this you will know the truth."

It is commonly believed that before the Enlightenment all Jews believed that God gave the entire Torah to Moses at Mount Sinai (*torah l'moshe misinai*), as Orthodox Judaism today affirms. This is not the case. Every Jew of even moderate education had the *Mikraot G'dolot* on the shelf that included the "Big Three" commentators: Rashi, Ibn Ezra, and Ramban. If they studied the *parashah* with commentaries, they learned Ibn Ezra, who taught that the Torah was given over a period of time.

The secret of "across the Jordan" is that these are instructions to get to the place where the author of Moses's final speeches was: Jerusalem, not Mount Sinai. These words could only have been written after the time when King David conquered Jerusalem and made it the capital of his kingdom. *Torah l'moshe misinai* was a common belief; it was not a required belief. One could argue over how many centuries it took to write the Torah, but the essential difference is between a static Torah and a dynamic Torah. Ibn Ezra taught that the Torah is dynamic, evolving. We Reform Jews, then, are just as traditional as Orthodox Jews in our belief about the origins of Torah. Not only that, but we know the truth. Yes, religion is not just all about how you feel; it is also about affirming that which we know to be true on the basis of firm evidence.

D'varim: Shabbat Chazon
Rabbi Michael Boyden, 2017

At one time or another, we all (both individuals and societies) have to contend with the dissonance between our hopes and how things actually turn out. Both in the United States and Israel, reality is often different from what our founding ancestors envisaged.

Moses was filled with optimism. "Adonai, the God of your ancestors, will increase your numbers a thousandfold and bless you as [God] promised you" (Deut. 1:11).

Fast-forward six hundred years to the period prior to the destruction of the First Temple, and Isaiah rebukes his people in God's name with the admonition, "I have raised and brought up children, but they have sinned against Me" (Isa. 1:2), part of the haftarah for the Shabbat preceding Tishah B'Av.

The *parashah* (Deut. 1:12) and haftarah (Isa. 1:21), as well as *Eichah* (Lam. 1:1), traditionally read on Tishah B'Av, each contain the word *eichah*, an expression of desperation and despair. However, the word can also be pointed as *ayekah*—"Where are you?"—the question that God addresses to Adam in the Garden of Eden (Gen. 3:9).

At times of disillusionment we need not only to look at external circumstances. We also need to look at ourselves. We need to move forward and maintain our optimism, as does Isaiah in the concluding words of his prophecy: "Zion shall be redeemed with justice, and those who return to her with righteousness" (Isa. 1:27).

D'varim: Shabbat Chazon
Rabbi Ruth Adar, 2018

On Shabbat Chazon, we read the last of the famous haftarot of warning before Tishah B'Av. The text describes Isaiah's vision of the destruction of the Temple and ends with a *nechemta* ("a word of consolation"): "Zion shall be redeemed with justice, and those among her who repent, with righteousness" (Isa. 1:27).

Parashat D'varim is well suited to be read before Tishah B'Av because it expresses a similar warning. *D'varim* ("Deuteronomy") famously retells the story of *Sh'mot* ("Exodus"), *Vayikra* ("Leviticus"), and *B'midbar* ("Numbers"). However, Moses's oration begins after Sinai. *Parashat D'varim* contains a three-part warning about the penalties for failure to trust the God of Israel. Part one focuses on the failure first recounted in *Sh'lach L'cha*, the story of the spies. In *Parashat D'varim* the focus is on the failure of the people rather than the spies. Because they did not trust in God, they will spend thirty-eight more years in the desert before their children take possession of the Land. Part two of the *parashah* focuses on the victories of the new generation. When the old generation passes away, God directs their offspring to turn toward the Land. They make a triumphal march past other nations and prevail against them. In part three, God apportions land to each tribe. One generation fails a test and dies in exile. The next generation passes the test and takes possession of the land.

This *parashah* has the same message as the haftarah: failures to trust God will be punished, but those who have faith will possess the Promised Land.

ואתחנן   *Va-et'chanan*
(Deuteronomy 3:23–7:11)

Va-et'chanan
Rabbi Joshua Minkin, DMin, 2010

"Honor your father and your mother" (Deut. 5:16).

A man approaches me in the hospital. His seventy-five-year-old mother is close to death, her body riddled with cancer. "Rabbi," he begins, "my mother is dying and I feel responsible. Six years ago, she discovered a lump in her breast. After a lumpectomy, radiation, and chemo treatments, she got involved with natural healing methods. She became fanatical about it. She took an enormous number of vitamins. She ate only organic foods. I let her do this. I gave her the money."

He pauses to dab tears from his eyes. "I did this even though I did not believe in it. I am a man of science. I teach in a university. A few months ago, she began complaining of a loss of energy. It suddenly occurred to me a few days ago that it might be cancer. Even then she would not go to the hospital until she received an okay from her nutritional advisor. I should have made her come earlier. I feel so terrible."

I found myself very much in agreement with him. In his place, I would have felt the same way. However, I realized that his mother had her own sense of values. He chose to respect them, even though he disagreed with them.

"Each of us creates a narrative as we live our lives," I responded. "Your mother's included a belief in these organic methods. You allowed her to live her life with integrity according to these beliefs. Even more, you have given her the gift of allowing her to die with this integrity intact. There is no way to know that this way of living did not give her more years, rather than fewer. Your intentions were those of love."

"I suppose you are right," he replied. We are not commanded to love our parents, but to honor them—honoring their wishes, even when we despise their choices. We are the only creatures that have free will, that can make choices. This is one way in which we are *b'tzelem Elohim* (in the image of God). Our will is a reflection of the divine essence within us. Honoring that essence brings honor to God.

Va-et'chanan
Rabbi Joshua Minkin, DMin, 2011

Sh'ma yisrael, adonai eloheinu, adonai echad, "Hear O Israel, Adonai is our God, Adonai is One" (Deut. 6:4). The kabbalists believed that before Creation, the entire universe was God. God needed to perform an act of *tzimtzum* ("contraction") to make room for Creation. Until God created—all was God. But in the act of creating, was the Creation separate from God? Can there be anything that is not God? I read the *Sh'ma* as an appeal for unity. Believing in a completely transcendent God destroys this unity. Our entire known universe, you, and I are part of God. We pray to the Divine that is within Creation, as well as beyond Creation.

We claim to be created *b'tzelem elohim*, "in God's image." We can also create; and our creations can have drastic consequences for the world we live in: acid rain, global climate change, and radioactive leakage—perils that threaten to make our world inhabitable. We are commanded to choose life. Efforts that promote life—all life—are God-affirming. The *Sh'ma* tells us that God and the world we live in are one. In caring for the world, we worship God; caring for the world is therefore a divine commandment. *Kohelet Rabbah* reminds us that God has given the world to us. We are now its custodians. *V'ahavta et adonai elohecha*—"Love Adonai your God."

Let us choose life.

Va-et'chanan
Rabbi Amy Scheinerman, 2012

Parashat Va-et'chanan includes the first paragraph of the *Sh'ma*. The Torah depicts a powerful God who commands, rewards, punishes, and emotes. The God of Torah is coercive and demanding.

But the God of my experience is nothing like this. Everything in the universe is in God, and God is the ground of Being and makes possible the dynamism of everything in the universe through creativity, novelty, and freedom.

I hear in the paragraph:

- Love God with every aspect of your being.
- Internalize and assimilate this love.
- Make it so much a part of your being that your children inherit it.
- Make it part of you at all times and places—fundamental to who you are.
- Let it guide your actions in the world (your hand) and your perceptions, thoughts, and emotions (your forehead).

Read this way, the first paragraph of the *Sh'ma* is not only about adherence to laws and regulations. Rather, it might be understood this way: God alone is the ground of Existence and Becoming in the universe. Therefore, everything is part of a larger tapestry whose threads are inextricably interwoven. Raise your children to understand this so that their lives, too, are a blessing. Everything you do—your thoughts and feelings, your very life, your strengths and abilities to effect change—all will have a ripple effect in this universe. Know this at all times and in all places, lest you separate yourself from the universe. Remind yourself night and day—as you lie down at night and consider what you have become that day, and as you rise up in the morning and ponder what you will do and become that day. Let God's love and your continual becoming ground you always—let it be your home base.

Va-et'chanan
Louis A. Rieser, 2013

"And I pleaded with God at that time, saying . . ." (Deut. 3:23).

Rabbi Levi Yitzchak of Berditchev, in *K'dushat Levi*, notes that the word *leimor* ("saying") is superfluous because we already know that Moses pleads. He explains that Moses needs to make sure that God is, as it were, "in a receptive mood for the prayer that would follow." It is a fascinating thought. Since prayer is a two-way street, it requires that both the pray-er and God be prepared for the exchange.

Truth is that it is hard enough to prepare oneself to pray. Maimonides reminds us that "prayer without devotion is no prayer at all" (*Mishneh Torah, Hilchot T'filah* 4:15). We often place the phrase "Know before whom you stand" (derived from *Babylonian Talmud B'rachot* 28b) above the synagogue ark, but how often do we focus on how to present ourselves in prayer? When do we begin the transition from dealing with the mundane to addressing the Holy: as we begin to dress, as we enter the synagogue, or as the first strains of *Mah Tovu* begin to calm the chatter? And what of God?

It is beyond our power to prepare the Holy One to receive prayer, but there are things we can do to tip the scales. The *Babylonian Talmud B'rachot* 7a reveals that God's own prayer is "May My mercies overpower My anger." Similarly, Rabbi Akiva reminds us that the most basic rule of Torah is to "love your neighbor as yourself." If we can enter the synagogue with a mix of *chesed* and *rachamim* ("love" and "mercy"), perhaps we can succeed in preparing God to hear our prayers.

Va-et'chanan
Rabbi Joshua Minkin, DMin, 2014

"I stood between Adonai and you" (Deut. 5:5).

There is a Chasidic teaching (*Iturei Torah*, vol. 6, p. 43) that says, "The 'I' of man is the barrier that cuts off man from his Creator. As long as he thinks about his 'I' it is difficult for him to approach Holiness."

As humans, we experience the world in the state of "I"-ness. We are at the center of all that we perceive. Our natural tendency is to view these perceptions as "truth." However, our interpretations of what we perceive are informed by culture and experience. To wit: A fifty-five-degree day feels cold in the middle of a simmering summer, but wonderfully warm in the frigid depths of winter.

God is the source of morality and ethics. We mistake our being created in God's image as giving us the understanding of good and evil. Chaim Vital and Moshe Cordovero suggest that each of the six hundred thousand souls present at Sinai received its own version of the Torah. Relying exclusively on our own interpretation of morality prevents us from truly approaching holiness.

The Chasidic teaching above applies to the collective "I," as well. Thinking that our way is the only way interferes with doing what is truly right. American exceptionalism and Jewish chosenness should be understood as positive commandments to act ethically as nations, not loopholes to permit immoral acts perpetrated against other people or even our own.

Ben Zoma taught, "Who is wise? The one who learns from everyone. Who is honored? The one who honors others" (*Mishnah Pirkei Avot* 4:1).

Va-et'chanan
Rabbi Louis Rieser, 2015

Moses's prayer for permission to enter the Land was denied, and Moses prays again. What kind of prayer does Moses choose for this vulnerable and all-important moment in his life?

Prayer is difficult to practice and to explain. *Sifrei* lists ten styles of praying: chant, meet, groan, distress, cry, anguish, plead, entreat, stand, implore, and graciousness; each is reflected in Torah and deserves its own explanation.

Sefer Baal Shem Tov (*Parashat Noach* 159) considers the style of Moses. The Baal Shem Tov assumes that Moses is praying to change God's decree. In asking whether a divine decree can ever be changed, the Baal Shem Tov shifts our notion of grace. Moses pleads God to be *chanun* (gracious); he prays for graciousness. This style of prayer appeals to God's compassion.

Rashi (to Deut. 3:23, echoing Exod. 33:19, "I will be gracious to whom I will be gracious") states that the divine response changes not because of our accomplishments, but rather thanks to a freely given act of grace—but the decree, once issued, cannot be changed.

The Baal Shem Tov disagrees. A decree was given for a specific individual possessing a specific character. If that individual changes from bad to good and becomes a different person, that different person deserves a different decree.

Prayer, introspection, and *t'shuvah* ("repentance") aid us in better knowing ourselves and knowing before whom we stand. Moses's plea serves as a model for all who desire a different decree in their own lives.

Va-et'chanan: Shabbat Nachamu
Rabbi Louis Rieser, 2016

The destruction of the Temple launched our communal journey into exile. Isaiah's response is to repeat the term *nachamu, nachamu* ("comfort, comfort!"; Isa. 40:1). I understand this doubling of the word to signify the multiple responses individuals may have of exile.

On *erev* Shabbat Nachamu 2015 I was diagnosed with a brain tumor. This week is the anniversary of that diagnosis—*nachamu, nachamu*. In advance of my anniversary, I contemplated some meanings of *nachamu*. My goal was not to clarify the term, but to contrast different points of view.

It is crucial to remember that exile exists in many forms: there are political, social, psychological, and emotional exiles, and more. For me, exile stems from illness, as Paul Cowan, z"l so brilliantly and honestly described in his article "In the Land of the Sick."

One understanding of *nachamu* could point to the loss of the previous state of being and the grief that loss precipitates. We often maintain the belief that an unfortunate episode will one day be resolved and life will return to normal: "Renew our days as of old" (Lam. 5:21).

Upon hearing my diagnosis, the first words my wife Connie and I uttered were that our lives will never be the same, a common response of those who are members of the club. The future is irreversibly changed. It is difficult to fathom our future reality. I do not expect the old normal to return. This is an alternate understanding of *nachamu*. It is disturbing, but real.

Our work puts us in touch with those who experience many forms of exile: political, social, psychological, and emotional exile = and illness. On this Shabbat Nachamu and throughout the year, how can you guide yourself and your congregants to an appropriate response to their experiences of exile?

Va-et'chanan: Shabbat Nachamu
Rabbi Joshua Minkin, DMin, 2017

"Comfort, oh comfort My people," says your God (Isa. 40:1).

Deutero-Isaiah speaks to the leaders of the people of Israel after years of exile. The times for chastisement are over. Now is the time for healing and encouragement. He wants to rouse the people who are comfortably ensconced in Persia and Babylonia, to shake off their torpor and look to a future beyond exile. The theology of a universal God who uses other nations to punish Israel's sins preserved the people in their ignominy. Isaiah, however, believed in redemption. God is forgiving and punishment is not eternal.

Comfort My people: let them know they are not powerless.

At times, anyone may need to hear this message. It is all too easy to fall into despair after a tragedy or traumatic experience—to ask, "What is the point? There is nothing to be done." Like Israel in exile we cry, "My way is hidden from Adonai; my cause is ignored by my God" (Isa. 40:27).

As rabbis, we are not immune to despair, yet we are still called upon to comfort our people. We seek to help them overcome despondency and believe in the power of justice. Yet, we must also learn from the prophets. Theirs was the voice. They led by courageous example. But they knew when to step aside. Their success, and ours, is when our people themselves commit to the work and take the lead. When the work is intimidating and exhausting, we must remind all, "[God] gives strength to the weary, fresh vigor to the spent" (Isa. 40:29).

Va-et'chanan
Rabbi Stephen Wylen, 2018

Sh'ma! Hear! An act that our tradition teaches is an essential and foundational commandment for every Jew because everything follows from

Sh'ma! Rabbi Pinchas of Koretz went to spend Shabbat with a certain sage. Rabbi Pinchas asked this sage to speak on a certain topic in which he was known to have some expertise. The sage humbly suggested to Rabbi Pinchas that to truly learn this topic he should read a specific chapter in a certain book. Rabbi Pinchas replied, "It would please me greatly to hear this matter directly from the lips of the tzaddik. One who learns from a book gains knowledge, but one who hears with his own ears from the lips of the teacher has acquired the soul of the teaching" (*Otzar HaChasidut* in *Iturei Torah* 6:33).

For most human beings, learning is far more readily absorbed by hearing than by reading. In my years of teaching college and giving final exams, I observed that students had difficulty responding to questions drawn from assigned reading but readily responded to questions based on matters I had discussed in class. There is no substitute for Hear! What is more, spoken words convey far more than knowledge: the teacher's passion for the subjects moves the souls of the students, transmitting the "soul of the teaching."

A rabbi is not only a repository of Torah; a rabbi is meant to be a living embodiment of Torah. This aspect is best realized when we speak with our entire souls, and people Hear! with their whole souls.

עֵקֶב *Eikev*
(Deut. 7:12–11:25)

Eikev
Rabbi Janice Garfunkel, z"l, 2010

Had I been asked before my children were born what qualities I wanted in a child, I am sure I would not have thought to include "obedient." When I thought of "obedient," I thought of Milgram's experiments and Nazis saying, "I was only following orders."

But then the good Lord wisely blessed me with a child who was, shall we say, not the most compliant. I went through a shamefully long period of time battling mightily (and unsuccessfully) to instill in her this quality that I never really admired to start with. I began to think about my own relationship with compliance, realizing that I, myself, had been an overly compliant child, and still, today, am overly sensitive to the criticism of others (a common characteristic of rabbis?).

God's attempts at gaining compliance do not seem to have worked out well, either—not with Adam and Eve, and not since then. Reading the opening lines of this week's *parashah*, I can certainly see why some Christians see the "Old Testament" God as conditional and controlling, versus the "New Testament" God as loving unconditionally. But, ironically, Judaism, as practiced, tends to focus much more on "What does God want of us, and how can we do it?" and not at all on the reward and punishment.

We seem to have chosen to be "wrestlers with God" rather than "submitters to God." I suppose I want that for my children, too.

Eikev
Rabbi Amy Scheinerman, 2011

"For your God is bringing you into a good land, a land with streams and springs and fountains . . . a land of wheat and barley, of vines, figs, and pomegranates, a land of olive trees and honey . . . a land whose rocks are iron [*avaneha varzel*] and from whose hills you can mine copper" (Deut. 8:7–9).

Simple enough: the Land will supply everything the Israelites need to create new lives and a new nation.

For *Chazal*, there is another lesson to be learned. In *Babylonian Talmud Taanit* 4a, Rav Ashi tells us that a scholar should be as hard as iron. He cites Jer. 23:29. Rabbi Abba tells him that Deut. 8:9 is another source for this lesson: "Do not read *avaneha* ["rocks"] but rather *boneha* ["builders"]. Rav Ashi and Rabbi Abba are promoting "minds of steel" that are like "steel traps." One is reminded of Rabbi Yochanan ben Zakkai's description of Rabbi Eliezer: "A plastered well that never loses a drop" (*Mishnah Pirkei Avot* 2:11).

This point is not the last word. Ravina responds, "Despite this, a person should train oneself to be gentle."

I often hear rabbis deplore the ignorance of so many Jews. Ravina is reminding us that when we have such students we have to be especially gentle. Teaching is not a venue to demonstrate our intellectual acumen and mastery of Torah—our "minds of steel"—but rather an opportunity to connect with people, to help them connect with Torah, with God, and with the community.

Eikev
Rabbi Michael Boyden, 2012

Our *parashah* begins *V'hayah eikev tishm'un*, often translated "And if you do obey" or "If you listen." The English unfortunately misses the subtlety of the word *eikev*, which is from the same root as *akeiv* ("heel") or the Modern Hebrew *maakav* ("follow-up," "sequence"). The noun *eikev* appears in Ps. 19:12: *b'shomram eikev rav*, "in keeping them much follows." Our *parashah*, therefore, is about consequences.

No Frenchman or American ever considers whether she or he is entitled to live in her or his country or whether it even has the right to exist. Nationhood is taken for granted. However, for us as Jews, whose collective memory includes the destruction of two Temples, who live in a world in which many Palestinians deny our historical connection to the Land of Israel, and whom Iranians threaten to wipe off the map, the existence of a Jewish state is always conditional.

Our right to a land of our own is ultimately not dependent upon our military prowess or the intent of our enemies but, in the words of Martin Luther King Jr., "the content of [our] character." That was, after all, the justification for the Israelite conquest of the land in the first place—"It is not because of your virtues and your rectitude that you will be able to possess their country; but it is because of their wickedness that Adonai your God is dispossessing those nations before you" (Deut. 9:5)—as well as the cause of our exile.

Nevertheless, our haftarah concludes on a positive note: "For Adonai has comforted Zion, comforted all her ruins. He has made her wilderness like Eden, her desert like the Garden of Adonai" (Isa. 51:3).

Eikev
Rabbi Amy Scheinerman, 2013

"Hear, O Israel! You are about to cross the Jordan to go in and dispossess nations greater and more populous than you: great cities with walls sky-high; a people great and tall, the Anakites, of whom you have knowledge; for you have heard it said, 'Who can stand up to the children of Anak?' Know then this day that none other than the Eternal your God is crossing at your head, a devouring fire; it is [God] who will wipe them out. [God] will subdue them before you, that you may quickly dispossess and destroy them, as the Eternal promised you" (Deut. 9:1–3).

When the Israelites have crossed the Reed Sea, their crossing transformed them from slaves into free people. Now they stand poised to cross the Jordan River and become a sovereign nation in their ancestral homeland.

Our lives are filled with crossings. We are dynamic beings, continually changing. The motivation to change may come from within, or change might be foisted on us. There are times when change is needed, but we resist.

To cross our rivers, we need to dispossess the powerful feelings that we are incapable, inadequate, and uncomfortable: they are giant Anakites. We need to focus on the divine spark within—the devouring fire—which can subsume our weaknesses and fears. Perhaps we can wipe them out, perhaps we can only subdue them, but either is sufficient to fulfill our promise. The trick to crossing is to privilege the devouring fire over the Anakites.

Eikev
Rabbi Amy Scheinerman, 2014

Birkat HaMazon is rooted in Deut. 8:10: "When you have eaten your fill, give thanks to the Eternal your God for the good land that [God] has given you."

This verse is followed immediately by a prescient warning not to forget God and God's mitzvot when

> [you] have built fine houses to live in, and your herds and flocks have multiplied, and your silver and gold have increased, and everything you own has prospered, beware lest your heart grow haughty . . . and you say to yourselves, "My own power and the might of my own hand have won this wealth for me." (Deut. 8:11–14, 8:17)

Torah describes the danger of affluence, which we observe often. Deuteronomy 11:16 warns that when Israel feels sated they may be lured by other gods, gods that are easy enough to identify in our age. The S'fat Emet tells us:

> The ARI, z"l, explained that the life-energy of God's word within the food is that which sustains the soul, just as the corporeal food sustains the body. It is by means of blessings we recite that we find the inner food to nourish the soul. Surely, since God made the food that nourishes humans, there is sustenance in it for the inner self, as well. By means of Torah we find that inward food.

The interweaving of the concrete physicality of food with the spiritual nourishment of God goes back to the Pharisees' insistence that the table is the altar and we are the priests. We need this perspective even more today. However comfortable and well versed in science, our people need the soul nourishment that only Torah provides.

Eikev
Rabbi Ruth Adar, 2015

In *Parashat Eikev*, God warns that in good times we may be inclined to forget the true source of our prosperity, thinking, "My power and the might of my hand have produced all this wealth for me" (Deut. 8:17). Indeed, when we have worked hard and toiled for many years to reach a place of security, it is only natural to give ourselves credit for what we have accomplished. But this portion warns us never to forget that no matter how well we have done, humility still applies.

The word usually translated as "wealth" in Deut. 8:18 is *chayil*, the same word we know from *Eishet Chayil*, usually translated as "a woman of valor." Brown-Driver-Briggs offers a four-part definition of *chayil*: "strength, efficiency, wealth, army." If *chayil* means "strength," it implies strength like that of an army, like that of the woman at the close of the Book of Proverbs: interconnected, efficient, valorous. The Deuteronomist's choice of words reminds us that whatever wealth we have is not simply our own doing, but the result of a complex mix of effort, energy, valor, persistence, and good fortune—all from God and, perhaps, interconnected with other human beings, too.

Many people work hard all their lives and have little to show, even though they have done nothing wrong. Others, through no fault of their own, are disabled by physical or mental illness and unable to work. We must hold any wealth we have with humility.

Eikev
Rabbi Ruth Adar, 2016

Parashat Eikev offers us a path to deeper understanding of *b'rit milah* with its command to "circumcise the foreskin of your heart and be no more stiff-necked" (Deut. 10:16). What is the connection between circumcision and a stiff neck? The *Babylonian Talmud Sukkah* 52a, offers a clue, saying that Rav Avira (or some say Rabbi Y'hoshua ben Levi) taught, "Uncircumcised is one of the names of the *yetzer hara* [evil inclination]."

B'rit milah is the consecration of the male body to the covenant and to the behaviors associated with the covenant. The penis is the locus of male sexuality and a symbol of male power in a patriarchal world. Removing the foreskin in the context of the *b'rit milah* ritual is an expression of dedication to the behaviors associated with Torah and the will to control the human inclination to selfishness.

However, that dedication should not end on the eighth day, nor is it limited to males. Jews of all genders are commanded to live out the promise implied in *b'rit milah*, to control our *yetzer hara*. We do not modify the body lightly or thoughtlessly. This outward sign of the covenant is not easy, but it is an expression of seriousness about Jewish identity.

Eikev
Rabbi Amy Scheinerman, 2017

"[God] subjected you to the hardship of hunger and then gave you manna to eat, which neither you nor your ancestors had ever known, in order to teach you that a person does not live on bread alone, but rather a person lives on all that comes forth from the mouth of Adonai" (Deut. 8:3).

This verse is commonly understood to say that people need more than bread to survive.

But Torah does not support this interpretation. The *p'shat* ("simple meaning") suggests the opposite. The Israelites survived on manna—less than bread—proving they could survive on whatever they had. What is more, the manna (like the other wilderness privations and hardships) was designed both to test Israel's strength and loyalty and to cultivate their dependence on God.

Rabbi Tzvi Hirsch of Nadvorna advises us:

> Understand this through a parable: A servant is fed from the king's own food, taken right out of the ruler's mouth. More than the servant takes pleasure in the food itself, he rejoices that the king in all his glory gives

it directly to him, from his own mouth. Even if the food is a delicacy, this pleasure sustains him more fully than the food itself.

Nourishment is provided when we understand our blessings as coming from God. Perhaps this is why just a few verses later (Deut. 8:11–17) Torah warns the Israelites of the danger of forgetting God when they enter the Land and find their standard of living considerably elevated.

Eikev
Rabbi Joshua Minkin, DMin, 2018

"[Lest when] all that you have is multiplied . . . you say in your heart, 'My power and the might of my hand have gained me this wealth'" (Deut. 8:13, 8:17).

In the eighteenth century, Rabbi Tzvi Hirsch Berliner, commenting on the verse above, cites Prov. 22:2, "The rich and the poor have this in common [literally: meet together]: Adonai made them both":

> The rich man generally thinks that he attained his wealth because of his brilliance, while the poor are generally looked down upon as ne'er-do-wells who cannot succeed because of a lack of ability. However, when "the rich and poor meet together," when they happen to be in the same place at the same time, one can in most cases see that the poor man is no less intelligent than the rich one. (Torah Gems, pp. 212–13).

It is important to expose the myth that rich people are smarter, better, and more talented than poor people. In addition to anecdotal evidence to counter this myth, *Forbes* (October 6, 2016) estimated that one-third of the four hundred richest Americans inherited their wealth, noting, "It helps to inherit a couple billion." Luck also plays a large role, as with Bitcoin millionaires. Just as inheritance and luck account for a significant percentage of the wealthy, poverty does not signal a lack of intellect or talent. To those who claim investing in the education of poor people is a waste, Rabbi Tzvi Hirsch would say, "Bring the rich and poor together in one place and you will find that intelligence and talent cannot be determined by one's financial condition."

ראה *R'eih*
(Deuteronomy 11:26–16:17)

R'eih
Rabbi Louis Rieser, 2010

R'eih opens with a challenge. "See, I set before you this day blessing and curse" (Deut. 11:26). Open your eyes and see the multiple options before you. If only every option were tagged: blue for blessing, red for curse. At any moment you could simply choose the tag that fit your mood. But it is never that easy. It depends where you choose to look, what you choose to see.

When Balaam blesses the Israelites in defiance of Balak's order to curse them, he describes himself as a true prophet: "one who beholds visions from the Almighty, prostrate, but with eyes unveiled" (Num. 24:4). By contrast, we often view the world with blinders and veiled vision. How often do we physically see the poor, hungry, or homeless in our own town? Does where we look limit our opportunities to bring blessing into the world?

The final paragraph of the *Sh'ma* counsels us to look at the tzitzit, reminders of the path of blessing, rather than following "after your heart or your eyes, which can lead you astray" (Num. 15:39). Sight is not foolproof, but requires a reality check. If you see the world only through one type of lens, you will miss opportunities for holy action, occasions of blessing, and moments of wonder. Or you may find yourself straying in ways that bring a curse to you and/or your community.

In truth, we do not have two separate realities before our eyes: one side blessing and the other curse. Rather, at every moment, we are challenged to extract the blessing from what we see before us while we avoid the curse. It is the hard work of being human.

R'eih
Rabbi Amy Scheinerman, 2011

Yogi Berra said, "When you come to a fork in the road, take it."

"See, this day I set before you blessing and curse: blessing, if you obey the commandments of Adonai your God that I enjoin upon you this day; and curse if you do not obey the commandments of Adonai your God, but turn away from the path that I enjoin upon you this day and follow other gods whom you have not experienced" (Deut. 11:26–28).

Who is this God who commands, rewards, and punishes?

Those who do not view God this way can interpret the words "command" and "obey" differently. C. Robert Mesle explains the philosophy of Alfred North Whitehead. In Process-Relational Philosophy, God is the source of Being, free will, and emergent possibility. Mesle writes:

> God is the only one who has the strength, the ability, to be open to every single experience in the world. God is the only one who can take everything in, integrate it with God's own infinitely ancient wisdom, and create God's self out of that relationship in each moment. God is the only one who can then feedback to every creature in the world a lure and call toward those possibilities that are best for it. (*Process-Relational Philosophy*, p. 87)

In this framework, God lures us to make the right choices but does not and cannot prevent us from making bad choices. "To obey" then means that we respond to God's ethical lure and avoid the alluring "gods" that draw us to lesser choices. It is we who bring blessing and curse upon ourselves by our choices. As Rabbi Berra said, "When you come to a fork in the road, take it."

R'eih
Rabbi Stephen Wylen, 2012

The Torah says, "See, I set before you today blessing and curse" (Deut. 11:26)—that is, the blessing and the curse come together, not separately. The blessing comes from obedience to the mitzvot of God. What kind of curse accompanies a mitzvah? According to Rabbi Levi Yitzchak of Berditchev, it is the curse of pride, which is the same as self-awareness. When one performs a mitzvah, one is proud and pleased to perform the mitzvah. While the mitzvah brings us close to God, the pride removes us from God. When we are full of ourselves, there is no room within for God.

One must therefore perform a small act of *t'shuvah* with each and every mitzvah, to make the mitzvah an act of pure service. Through *bitul hayeish*, the negation of self, we reach a state of *d'veikut*, "intimacy with the Divine." This is the greatest joy.

Rabbi Levi Yitzchak raises an intriguing paradox in relation to this teaching: Because we are by nature "something," we rise to a higher level when we make ourselves "nothing." Because God is by nature "nothing," being infinite, God responds to us by rising to the level of "something"—by being a presence in our lives.

R'eih
Rabbi Amy Scheinerman, 2013

"There shall be no needy among you—since the Eternal your God will bless you in the land that the Eternal your God is giving you as a hereditary portion. . . . If there is a needy person among you, one of your kin in any of your settlements in the land that the Eternal your God is giving you, do not harden your heart and shut your hand against your needy kin. Rather, you must open your hand and lend whatever is sufficient to meet the need" (Deut. 15:4, 15:7-8).

Torah here (and in many other places) instructs us to open our hands, hearts, and wallets to help others. Talmud elaborates elegantly in the *Babylonian Talmud K'tubot* 67b: "'What he needs' includes even a horse to ride upon and a slave to run before him." Gemara supplies principles and a wealth of examples of *tzedakah* and *chesed* ("love") done right.

Many of our congregations have a *chesed* or *bikur cholim* ("visitng the sick") committee. I have a Christian friend who loves the New Testament verse "It is more blessed to give than to receive" (Acts 20:35). But let's be honest: it's easier to give than to receive.

It can be exceptionally difficult and painful to be in need, especially when one is a rabbi and public figure. What happens when we are the one in need, be it emotional, physical, or financial need? Are we capable of reaching out when the need requires more than rides, dinners, babysitting, and the like? When the need is deep inside us, do we know how to turn to someone, and do we even have someone to turn to?

R'eih
Rabbi Michael Boyden, 2014

Parashat R'eih revisits almost word-for-word the laws found in Lev. 11:44 concerning permitted and forbidden animals, including the reasoning behind these laws. Leviticus instructs us to be holy (*v'hitkadishtem*), while Deut. 14:2 explains that the reason for observing these mitzvot is "because you are a holy people to Adonai your God." In other words, kashrut is not about health or hygiene, but about *k'dushah*.

Emphasizing our uniqueness will not appeal to everyone. However, it should be recalled that the Maccabees resisted Antiochus Epiphanes's law forbidding circumcision and that Hannah's seven sons were prepared to die rather than bow before an idol and eat pork.

The use of the pig as an anti-Jewish symbol first appears in German churches in the thirteenth century in the form of the "Judensau" ("Jewish sow") and runs through history into modern times. Kashrut is a matter of personal choice. However, eating pork demonstrates, at least to my mind, a lack of historical sensitivity. Those who are desperate for a ham sandwich may be comforted by the words of Rabbi Yom Tov ibn Ashvili (thirteenth century): "Why is the pig called *chazir* [i.e., from the verbal root *chazar* = to return]? Because the Holy One blessed be God will restore it to Israel in the world-to-come."

R'eih
Rabbi Louis Rieser, 2015

Can you see blessings or curses (Deut. 11:26)? Since a mixture of good and bad is embedded in all things, M'or Einayim (Menachem Nachum Twersky of Chernobyl, 1730–1787) teaches that clear sight, which is a matter of analysis, is needed if one is to discern the difference and choose the good.

Even the gift of the Land presents temptations and opportunities. In the Land, this portion notes, the people will be able to present offerings, feast on plentiful food, interact with neighbors, and learn from prophets. But these opportunities might also lead one astray. The Land's wealth brings temptations. Keen (in)sight is needed to avoid being seduced. It is a contemporary problem, too.

M'or Einayim underscores this challenge by commenting on the paired words *aseir t'aseir* (Deut. 14:22), referring to wealth and to tithing. Twersky contrasts the acquisitive teaching of *Kohelet Rabbah* 1:32, "Nobody departs from the world with even half his desire gratified. If he has a hundred, he wants to turn them into two hundred," with *Mishnah Pirkei Avot*'s assertion (4:1) that one who is satisfied with his portion is considered wealthy. Wealth is not ultimately a matter of the outward accumulation of money, but rather of the inner cultivation of satisfaction.

One who is satisfied, who feels no lack in his world, has no problem sharing his wealth. That is not an anti-materialist philosophy, but one of seeing the good in what one possesses. The goal, Twersky teaches, is to behave "as if": to give generously and with a holy intent in order to rise to the level of satisfaction, seeing blessing in all one has.

R'eih
Rabbi Ruth Adar, 2016

"There will always be poor people in the land. Therefore, I command you to be open-handed toward your kin and toward the poor and needy in your land" (Deut. 15:11).

With this statement, *Parashat R'eih* begins its explanations of the rules of *Sh'mitah*, the "Sabbatical year." With an economic fact—"There will always be poor people in the land"—and the comnclusion following—which could be paraphrased as "And you have responsibilities to them"—the Written Torah undergirds the huge body of Oral Torah addressing *tzedakah* and economic justice.

When Maimonides set out for a systematic study of our responsibilities to the poor in *Mishneh Torah Hilchot Mat'not Aniyim*, he looked into this passage and its commentaries, as well as the commandments and commentaries for tithes and the corners of the field. The collection of verses from the Torah seems to be a motley collection of agricultural laws, tax law trivia, and the law for the Sabbatical year. However, by Maimonides's day the Oral Torah had developed these raw materials into a well-reasoned program for the care of the poor. This public welfare program of Jewish tradition is not a war on poverty. Grounded in gritty realism, it is a relatively modest program that accepts the existence of poverty without sending messages, teaching lessons, or punishing the poor for their poverty.

R'eih
Rabbi Michael Boyden, 2017

Exodus recounts that the night before the Israelites departed Egypt every household sacrificed a lamb and ate it in its entirety. "They shall eat it roasted over the fire, with unleavened bread and with bitter herbs" (Exod. 12:8). By the time we reach the Book of Deuteronomy, the rules of the game have changed: "Look only to the place that the Eternal your God will choose . . . to establish [God's] name there. There you shall go, and there shall you bring your burnt offerings. . . . Together with your households you shall feast there" (Deut. 12:5–7).

When the Torah prohibits kindling fire "throughout your settlements on the Sabbath day" (Exod. 35:3), the original purpose may well have been to confine the sacrificial cult to the Temple alone, where "a fire shall constantly burn on the altar, not to go out" (Lev. 6:6).

As if to emphasize the point, *Parashat R'eih* instructs us not to offer up sacrifices anywhere you see (Deut. 12:13). However, *Sifrei R'eih* points out that exception to this rule can be made whenever a prophet, such as Elijah at Mount Carmel, says otherwise!

Ultimately, the question is: who determines the way Jews should practice their Judaism? In Israel, the Orthodox rabbinate oversees marriage and divorce, holds a monopolistic jurisdiction over kashrut supervision, and controls the operation of municipal cemeteries. They would have sympathized with the centralization of the cult—but the centralization of the cult stifles creativity and leaves little room for each of us to express our Jewishness in our own ways.

R'eih
Rabbi Mark Levin, 2018

Deuteronomy 13 contains laws separating Hebrews, or Israelites, from idolaters. Why? Clearly, we tend to duplicate the beliefs and actions of the communities in which we live. Contrasting with the idolaters, Deut. 13:5 commands, "It is your God Adonai alone after [or: behind] whom you should walk, whom you should revere, whose commandments you shall observe, whose voice you shall heed, and whom you shall serve and cling to." Five verbs in rapid succession: walk, revere, observe, heed, and serve—five actions to feel God's presence within.

In the *Babylonian Talmud Sotah* 14a, we read:

> Rabbi Chama bar Chanina asks, "What does 'walk after Adonai your God' mean? Is it possible to walk after [or: behind] the Shechinah? . . . It means to walk after God's ethical traits. As God clothes the naked, so you shall clothe the naked. As God visits the sick, so you shall visit the sick. As God comforts mourners, so you shall comfort mourners. As God buries the dead, so you shall bury the dead."

We know that philosophical proofs for God's existence ipso facto cannot work. Through action within a community of like-minded people we arrive at a strong internal affirmation of God's presence in our lives, validated by the community in which we live. Every action for God's sake is building the sanctuary in every generation and in every community, so that God may live within us, as Exod. 25:8 states. (See *Torah T'mimah* to Exod. 25:8.)

R'eih demonstrates our predicament. We, too, live among idolaters. *Imitatio dei*, acts connecting us to God, not faith affirmations, bring God's self-selecting people from Egypt, again and again.

שפטים   *Shof'tim*
(Deuteronomy 16:18–21:9)

Shof'tim
Rabbi Janice Garfunkel, z"l, 2010

Do you like being evaluated? Being judged? Mostly, we say we don't, but maybe that is all we really want. So says Julian Barnes, in his book *A History of the World in 10½ Chapters*. Toward the end of this collection of loosely related short stories, a man discovers he has died and gone to heaven, where he is free to do whatever he wants for all eternity. He indulges in earthly pleasures for a very long time but eventually becomes bored. He tries joining the heavenly chorus to praise God, but that, too, doesn't keep him happy for eternity. Eventually, he realizes, "I want to be judged." So, arrangements are made, and his entire life is scrutinized. The moment of judgment arrives, and God declares the verdict: "You were OK." I agree with Barnes—I think we do want to be judged. We hope that an Ultimate Judge, the True Arbiter, is numbering, measuring, and counting, that everything is seen and weighed against a true and absolute scale of justice. We want to be known, we want to be seen.

This reminds me of the movie *Avatar*, where the standard greeting is "I see you." Author Jay Michaelson writes, "As the Na'Vi explain in the film, though, 'I see you' doesn't mean ordinary seeing—it, like *Namaste*, really means 'the God in me sees the God in you.' I see Myself, in your eyes."

Maybe what we really want most of all is to be seen, to be known, to be valued—which is to be judged.

Shof'tim
Rabbi Stephen Wylen, 2011

"According to the Torah that they shall instruct you and according to the judgments they speak to you, you shall do, not turning from the word they pronounce to the right or to the left" (Deut. 17:11)

Why do we say the blessing *asher kid'shanu* when we light the Chanukah candles? Where are we commanded in the Torah to light the *chanukiyah*? This verse contains the commandment, for all the teachings of the Sages are commandments of the Torah.

When Rabbi Y'hoshua did not wish to acknowledge the date that Rabban Gamliel had set for Yom Kippur, Rabbi Akiva urged him to submit, for as Rabbi Akiva told him, "We have no Torah at all except for the one we receive from the interpretation of the leaders of Israel in every generation" (*Babylonian Talmud Rosh HaShanah* 24b–25a).

Some say we should obey the Sages even if they tell you that right is left and left is right. Others say that we should obey the Sages only so long as they say that right is right and left is left. Are we obligated to obey a nonsensical tradition? Opinions differ.

As Reform Jews, children of the Enlightenment, we have the right to make our own decisions.

Shof'tim
Rabbi Amy Scheinerman, 2012

Parashat Shof'tim is about law and order, necessary to maintain a just society. *Shof'tim* articulates two overarching principles of justice: (1) justice is blind or it is not just (Deut. 16:19); (2) the king is to possess his own scroll of Torah (Deut. 17:18–19).

Is the point that everyone—even a king—is beholden to Torah, in which case Torah is simply a book of rules to be obeyed? Or is the point that by internalizing the process of Torah, everyone—including a king—can find divine guidance and values for living a life of meaning and creating a just society ("Justice, justice shall you pursue" [Deut. 16:20])?

Rabbi Shlomo Ephraim of Luntschitz, the sixteenth-century Polish author of *K'li Yakar*, commenting on *minchah chadashah* (Lev. 23:16, which Gemara calls *sh'tei halechem*, the two loaves brought on Shavuot), says, "The Torah must be new for each person every day as the day that it was received from Mount Sinai." As the loaves must be new, so Torah must be fresh to each of us. "For the words of Torah shall be new to you, and not like old matters, which the heart detests. For, in truth, you are commanded to derive novelty each and every day." The Kli Yakar is not talking about rules, because rules don't change "each and every day." He is talking about insight, truth, and guidance—which the process of Torah provides in abundance.

What are the implications for how we teach Torah?

Shof'tim
Rabbi Joshua Minkin, DMin, 2013

The concepts of justice and judgment are central to Judaism. The High Holy Days revolve around the theme of God as a just and true Judge. The Reform Movement has taken the verse, from our *parashah*, *Tzedek, tzedek tirdof*, "Justice, justice shall you pursue" (Deut. 16:20), as its rallying cry.

A fundamental requirement for justice is that there be judges to determine wrongdoing and administrators to punish offenders. We see this in the opening words of our *parashah*, "You shall appoint judges and officials . . . [who] shall govern the people with righteous justice" (Deut. 16:18).

However, due to partisan bickering in Washington, over 10 percent of all federal judgeships remain vacant. Appointments are being held hostage by the minority party through parliamentary tactics intended to delay confirmation votes, sometimes by more than a year. Yet when confirmation votes are finally allowed to occur, most judges are approved by lopsided majorities and sometimes even unanimously. In the past, judicial nominees have been rejected, but in such cases, votes were taken expeditiously. This has led to unconscionable delays in the courts. People are languishing in prison waiting for their appeals to be heard, contrary to the Sixth Amendment. *Mishnah Pirkei Avot* 5:8 equates justice delayed with justice denied.

Our verse further demands that officials be appointed to administer laws, as well as enforce judicial decisions. Here the confirmation process has been even slower. There has been a deliberate attempt to achieve through filibuster what was impossible to achieve through the ballot box.

We are commanded, "You shall not pervert justice" (Deut. 16:19). We must condemn this injustice that is being done in our name.

Shof'tim
Rabbi Louis Rieser, 2014

A gatekeeper determines who or what may pass through a gate. When Torah instructs us "to appoint judges and offices for yourself at all of your gates" (Deut. 16:18), it establishes civil law.

For the Chasidim, however, this teaching concerns personal piety. Two examples illustrate possible understandings.

The Mei HaShiloach (Mordechai Yosef Leiner of Izbica, 1801–54) identifies the gates with seven physical apertures through which we apprehend the world: two eyes, two ears, two nostrils, and a mouth. Through our senses we receive or give good—or its opposite. The information we acquire through these organs excites our emotions and leads us to act for holy purposes—or not. Our internal judges and officers can control our passions and lead us to choose the holy.

Levi Yitzchak of Berditchev (1740–1809) identifies the gate as our heart. He teaches that it is "within our power, down here on earth to 'open' the gates of loving kindness, the source of God's blessing for mankind" (*K'dushat Levi*, trans. Eliyahu Munk, p. 760). The heart-gate connects our life with that of the Holy One. God desires the world to experience goodness, but divine will is enacted through our deeds. Each of us is our own gatekeeper, the judges and officers who decide to open the gate—or not. Each of us has the power to open the gate and allow *chesed* ("love") nd *b'rachah* ("blessing") to enter the world.

However we conceive the "gates"—as the boundary through which we encounter the outside world or by which we meet the divine will—we are our own judges and officers, bearing responsibility for what we keep out and for what we send out into the world. May our choices always be for good.

Shof'tim
Rabbi Michael Boyden, 2015

Parashat Shof'tim refers to the prerequisites for a civilized and orderly society. Not surprisingly, it begins with the words "You shall appoint judges and policemen for yourself in all of your gates" (Deut. 16:18).

The fact that our portion chooses to start here is not coincidental. Rabbi Chanina advised us to "pray for the welfare of the government, because but for the fear that it inspires people would swallow each other up alive" (*Mishnah Pirkei Avot* 3:2). At a time when the misuse of power so easily leads to mob violence and indiscriminate looting, we must do what we can to make sure that law and order are administered fairly and justly.

Rabbi Abraham Sabba (1440–1510) noted that Torah instructs us to "appoint judges for yourself." At first sight, the words "for yourself" seem superfluous, but Sabba observed, "A person must first of all judge himself and only afterward will he be capable of judging others. How could one judge others before one has judged oneself?"

No less valuable is the observation of Rabbi Moshe Alshich (1508–93) concerning the words "for yourself": we should appoint judges to judge ourselves, because no one is above the law.

When we occasionally see policemen taking the law into their own hands, we would do well to remember the Talmudic warning that "whoever appoints a judge who is unworthy is as though he had planted an *asheirah* [pagan cultic object] in Israel" (*Babylonian Talmud Avodah Zarah* 52a). The ultimate onus of responsibility lies, therefore, not with the judges and the police officers, but with those who appoint them.

Shof'tim
Rabbi Joshua Minkin, DMin, 2016

"To keep all the words of this law and these statutes, to do them; that his heart be not lifted up above his brethren, and that he turn not aside from the commandment" (Deut. 17:19–20).

There is general agreement among traditional commentators that to "lift one's heart above his brethren" refers to haughtiness, which, in turn, leads to a neglect of the commandments. In our own time, we are all too aware of good people who become corrupted by power, money, sex, or fame. Clergy are certainly not immune. One wonders if those working hard for the public good say, "Because I do so much holy work in other areas of my life, God will overlook these small sins I commit." This mode of justification has no end. Small sins graduate to more serious ones, without the person even realizing it. We learn, "The evil impulse is at first like a spider's thread, but ultimately becomes like cart ropes" (*Babylonian Talmud Sukkot* 54b).

Rabbi Israel Joshua Trunk of Kutno (1820–93), however, warns that excessive humility opens one to being swayed by the crowd, which can also lead to a neglect of the commandments. He comments in *Iturei HaTorah* (vol. 3, p. 264) on I Sam. 17:9–24, where Saul allows his troops to take Amalek booty: "Saul turned from God's commandments because . . . he obeyed what the people told him."

Maimonides urges balance: "The two extremes of each quality are not the proper and worthy path for one to follow or train oneself in. . . . The upright path is the middle path of all the qualities known to man" (*Mishneh Torah Hilchot Dei-ot* 1:3–4).

Shof 'tim
Rabbi Joshua Minkin, DMin, 2017

"You shall appoint judges and officers" (Deut. 16:18).

According to Rashi, judges issue verdicts, and officers compel people to accept judges' decisions.

Rabbi Simcha Bunim of Pshischa further proposes that whenever we make a decision, we must appoint internal judges to weigh carefully whether the decision is correct, and officers to carry out that decision, just as an officer enforces the decisions of the court. Too often many of the best intentions are wasted because of our failure to carry them out (*Torah Gems/Iturei Torah*, p. 252).

Elul, the month dedicated to personal *cheshbon nefesh* ("self-assessment"), has just begun. How often do the same items reappear on our list of resolutions? At Rosh HaShanah our will to change is strong, but as the year goes by, our perseverance dwindles. It may be a diet, and the temptation of a delicious dessert just this one time. Sometimes our concentration falters, and before we realize it, we are doing just what we had resolved to change.

Is self-commitment enough? Our tradition is suspicious of an affected party. Being both judge and defendant gives our officers incentives to look the other way. However, by asking for help, whether a group or just friends, our officers must now report to others as well. Our commitment is to them as well. This increases the stakes and makes following through a matter of honor and reputation.

Shof'tim
Rabbi Amy Scheinerman, 2018

Looking ahead to the High Holy Days, the S'fat Emet offers us a wonderful reading of Deut. 16:18 he learned from his grandfather, who pointed out that *v'lo anachnu* can be read as "and not we ourselves" and heard as "and we are [God's]"—two understandings in accord with "[God] has made us and not we ourselves" (Ps. 100:3).

The S'fat Emet expounds:

> The more a person can negate his own self ("and not we ourselves"), the closer that person can draw to God ("we are [God's]"). These are two parts of the service of God. First we have to negate the body and the corporeal world. For this we need officers, who can force the body to change its ways, to turn from evil (Ps. 34:15). Then we can draw near to the Creator and do good. For this we need to be judges, to take hold [of God] with our minds."

Rosh HaShanah and Yom Kippur afford us the opportunity to engage in "we are God's" alongside "and not we ourselves": Yom HaDin (the Day of Judgment) calls us to deep introspection, as we fully embrace being our own officers "who can force the body to change its ways," reminded of our agency to do good and promote justice. Yom HaKippurim (the Day of Atonement) encourages a temporary neglect of the body while we focus on elevating other aspects of our being, perception, and experience to the fore. Both happen in the context of community, reminding us that they should not be merely yearly experiences, but repeated experiences throughout the year.

כי תצא *Ki Teitzei*
(Deuteronomy 21:10–25:19)

Ki Teitzei
Rabbi Michael Boyden, 2010

This week's *parashah* includes, at first sight, what appears to be a simple statement: "When a man takes a wife" (Deut. 24:1). However, the *Babylonian Talmud Kiddushin* 2a, interprets this to mean that "a wife is purchased . . . by money, by a legal document, or by intercourse." However harmless the giving of a ring by the groom to the bride beneath the chuppah may seem, halachically this transaction, in the presence of witnesses, constitutes a purchase.

Our *parashah* likewise views divorce as a unilateral act. "If she fails to please him, because he finds something obnoxious about her, he shall write her a bill of divorce" (Deut. 24:1). While, in the Mishnaic period, our Sages sought to protect women's rights by introducing the *ketubah*, and determining that in order to be valid, a divorce required the acceptance of the *get* by the wife, such measures fail to bring about true equality. There could be no clearer example of the values that lie behind such one-sidedness than in the laws of *yibum* and *chalitzah* ("laws regarding the re-marriage of a widow"), with which our *parashah* also deals. These laws may not generally affect Jews in the Diaspora. However, the reality of a Jewish state, in which the chief rabbinate holds sole jurisdiction over marriage and divorce, shows how out of step with contemporary norms the halachah can be.

At a time when the folksy, seductive approach of Chabad attracts many, we would do well to remind ourselves of the ethical blemishes of Orthodoxy and why its way is not ours.

Ki Teitzei
Rabbi Louis Rieser, 2011

Ki Teitzei includes more mitzvot than any other *parashah*—74 of 613—offering a wonderful opportunity to discuss the experience of being commanded. Liberal Judaism is challenged by the notion of obligation. While our teachers—Eugene Borowitz, Abraham J. Heschel, Arthur Green, among many others in the academic world—outline rationales by which liberal Jews ought to consider themselves commanded, we who work in the congregational world know that it can be a difficult job to convince *amcha* ("our people").

D'varim Rabbah Ki Teitzei 3, commenting on Deut. 22:8 ("When you build a new house then you shall make a parapet for your roof"), offers what I consider a soft sell. The midrash does not dwell on the rationale of the mitzvot. Neither does it consider the consequences of disregarding them. Rather, it lists a series of mitzvot that begin at your front door and touch every aspect of your life, adding a simple note that you should live this way if you wish holiness to constantly accompany you:

> If you have made for yourself a door. . . . If you have put on a new garment. . . . If you have gone to cut the hair of your head. . . . If you have a field and you have gone to plow it. . . . If you are about to sow your field. . . . If you reap your field. . . . God said: Even if you are merely journeying on the road, the mitzvot accompany you.

The message is simple but elegant. We can choose to make our every act holy, and therefore to imbue every aspect of our lives with holiness. If not for God's sake, then perhaps we can act for our own.

Ki Teitzei
Rabbi Louis Rieser, 2012

"If, along the road, you chance upon a bird's nest . . . let the mother go and take only the young, in order that you may fare well and have a long life" (Deuteronomy 22:6).

Nachmanides reminds us that this is an extension of an earlier commandment (Lev. 22:28) against slaughtering any animal on the same day as its young. He notes (in his commentary on Deut. 22:6) that these commandments teach "that we should not have a cruel heart, but should be compassionate." The commandment helps human beings to improve their character.

Alan Morinis, who sparked renewed interest in *musar*, teaches that we each have a lifelong spiritual curriculum, which is to refine our character, and that compassion is one of the topics on that curriculum. He cites Rabbi Moshe Cordovero's teaching that "one's compassion should extend to all creatures, and one should neither despise nor destroy them, for the wisdom above extends to all of creation—inanimate objects, plants, animals, and humans." This is a commandment to extend compassion toward a mother bird specifically, with the broader goal of training us to act with compassion in every possible situation.

If we train our soul to feel compassion with a mother bird, we will be more compassionate with those who anger us, those who challenge us, or those who simply make us uncomfortable. When we act with compassion, we improve our lives and the lives of others so that we may all fare well and enjoy a long life.

Ki Teitzei
Rabbi Janice Garfunkel, z"l, 2013

Parashat Ki Teitzei includes practical advice for living. We should take our cue from this for our own congregational work.

Someone who lives in an area with many Jews told me she goes to an AA meeting once each month at a synagogue, and that is her primary "synagogue attendance." To my surprise, she told me that approximately six hundred people attend this meeting every month, attesting to the deep and important need of so many of our people. Jews, like everyone else, have needs—practical needs. To thrive, our congregations should be addressing those needs. Do Jews have rebellious and disobedient children, as mentioned in our *parashah*? Indeed, the challenge of parenting well is a paramount need that is very poorly supported in our society, leaving room for synagogues to fill that gap, to provide terrific and wise leadership and camaraderie in the art of parenting.

Sometimes we seem to enjoy blaming the people for their lack of participation; but if we do an even better job of addressing their needs, they are more likely to come in greater numbers to our shuls. I believe that if our focus is on filling the varied unmet needs of our people, they will fill our buildings and see the relevance and value of Judaism.

Ki Teitzei
Rabbi Stephen Wylen, 2014

The Torah teaches us to build a parapet around the roof of our house, lest we incur guilt should someone fall accidentally from our roof (Deut. 22:8). Our Sages taught that the person who fell from the roof deserved to fall and that good things are brought about by good people and bad things are brought about by bad people (*Babylonian Talmud Shabbat* 32a).

I wish that I could share the faith of our Sages in the ultimate justice of chance events, but even without such faith our Sages teach an important lesson. Even if someone deserves punishment, the pious fervently wish that punishment should not come about through one's own self. If you find yourself in the position of being the avenging arm of God, be assured that this is a punishment that has been placed upon you because you have been found wanting in the heavenly court of justice.

We should strive to be more like Moses and less like Nebuchadnezzar.

Ki Teitzei
Rabbi Joshua Minkin, DMin, 2015

"When your military goes into battle, be on your guard against everything evil" (Deut. 23:10).

Freud believed that the survival of civilization depends upon the ability to control human aggressive and sexual instincts. He wrote, "Culture has to call up every possible reinforcement in order to erect barriers against the aggressive instincts of men and hold their manifestations in check" (*Civilization and Its Discontents*, p. 86).

In war, those barriers tend to break down. Soldiers are required, as a matter of course, to violate the fundamental prohibition against killing other human beings. Even the killing of civilians, which is prohibited, may be accepted as "collateral damage." "Commandeering supplies" (stealing) is a regular occurrence.

Concerning the tenth plague, the slaying of the firstborn, *M'chilta D'Rabbi Yishmael* comments, "Once permission has been granted to the destroyer to terrorize, it no longer distinguishes between the righteous and the wicked." Ismar Schorsch (*Canon Without Closure: Torah Commentaries*, p. 229) observes, "The Torah substitutes the word 'destroyer' twice for God's name in reference to the tenth plague (Exod. 12:13, 12:23), as if to suggest that when God's fury is fully unleashed all moral distinctions collapse."

Our verse recognizes that a different code of conduct is presumed in battle. Yet it does not absolve us from moral behavior, even when faced with an immoral enemy. Knowing how easy it is for our aggressive instincts to overcome our moral boundaries, we must be on our guard not only against major crimes but, as our verse says, against everything evil.

The destruction of a dam begins with a crack that grows until the dam collapses. By ignoring small cases of injustice, it becomes easier to rationalize larger ones.

Ki Teitzei
Rabbi Michael Boyden, 2016

The notion that anyone could be practicing "biblical Judaism" in the twenty-first century is absurd. Were that the case, we would be stoning our "stubborn and rebellious sons," as enjoined upon us in this week's *parashah* (Deut. 21:20). Already in the *Babylonian Talmud M'nachot* 29b, we read the famous story of Moses getting "beamed down" into one of Rabbi Akiva's *shiurim* ("lessons") and not understanding at all what was going on there! We appreciate the audacity of Rabbi Y'hudah, who was implying that Judaism had moved on since Moses's time.

Mishnah Sanhedrin 8 goes into immense detail in order to ensure that no child could ever be categorized as a "stubborn and rebellious son." Torah speaks of sons, but not of daughters. The son must have pubic hair, but not yet a beard. He must have eaten meat and drunk wine—but no other alcoholic beverage. Both parents must be physically fit and agree to bring their son to be tried by the city's elders. *Mishnah Sanhedrin*

11:6 concludes, "There has never been a 'stubborn and rebellious son' and there never will be one!" and claims that Torah includes this mitzvah only for exegetical purposes!

Most of us would find it difficult to accept that contention and would be more inclined to believe that the Rabbinic authorities of the second century simply did not share all of the values of biblical law. We would argue that Judaism's ability to evolve and redefine itself is precisely what has enabled it to remain relevant throughout the ages to this very day.

Ki Teitzei
Rabbi Amy Scheinerman, 2017

The prohibition against cross-dressing (Deut. 22:5) is comprehendible in its historical and cultural context, but highly problematic in the twenty-first century. We could explain the prohibition as an innocent relic of the ancient world, but knowing that it can still be found in many cultures around the globe today belies the notion that it is so innocent a relic.

The Chasidic master Rabbi Avraham Chayim of Zloczow (1750–1816) provides an alternative. He treats the prohibition to cross-dress as an allegory. In *Orach L'Chayim*, he points out that the "giver" of *tzedakah* ultimately receives more than the "recipient" of his largess because "the pauper does more for the householder than the householder does for the pauper" (*Vayikra Rabbah* 34:10). He then evokes Rabbi Chanina, who said that he learned much from his teachers, more from his colleagues, and most of all from his students, making the point that the same is true for Torah: the "receivers" give the most (*Babylonian Talmud Taanit* 7a).

"Giving," he then tells us, means to wear men's clothing; wearing women's garb is "receiving." He writes, "Although you are in the 'male' role, you must not think of yourself as superior to the passive 'female' receiver in this interaction. Rather think, as you give either of thought or of money, that you are receiving more than you give . . . taking pride over the one receiving is considered despicable, as our Sages taught [in *M'chilta Yitro* 9] concerning "Every haughty person is an abomination to Adonai" (Prov. 16:5)."

The stereotyping of active and male giver and female and passive receiver is certainly problematic, but if we understand the message in its historical context, it is still valuable.

Ki Teitzei
Rabbi Charles Middleburgh, PhD, 2018

It is easier to identify which topics to avoid in this *parashah* than which to embrace. Among the available topics are sexual ethics, the rebellious son, an array of capital and corporal punishments, bodily hygiene while on military maneuvers, and these gems: safeguarding the welfare of farm animals, being neighborly, and showing compassion to a slave who has run away from a cruel master.

Thrown into the mix are the mitzvot of *shaatneiz* and *tzitzit* (Deut. 22:11–12). At first sight, these two laws do not seem to be connected. In Torah's first iteration of *shaatneiz* (Lev. 19:19), only the mixing of threads is prohibited; here the wool and linen are specified. Numbers 15:38 instructs us to add fringes to a *beged* ("garment," but also connotes dishonesty), and here to add them to a *k'sut* ("covering" or "clothing"), too.

Therein lies the reason for the juxtaposition of these verses with everything else: the injunctions about *tzitzit* refer to inner and outer piety.

Parallel to the *shaatneiz* rules, the *beged* refers to one's outer garment, to outward displays of piety that can mislead others; and the *k'sut*, which covers our skin, to the private domain—challenging us when we are alone to see who and what we truly are. It is not the public commandments that reveal our true selves; it is those done far from the public gaze, even those unknown to anyone but ourselves, that truly represent the person we are.

כי תבוא *Ki Tavo*
(Deuteronomy 26:1–29:8)

Ki Tavo
Rabbi Amy Scheinerman, 2010

Fear is a motivating and paralyzing. Reward can provide irresistible incentive. The fifty-four-verse *tocheichah* ("rebuke") of *Ki Tavo* is a double-barreled delivery of fear and incentive. It is also a deeply troubling passage. It paints the picture of a God who is as vindictive and punishing as loving and rewarding. What is more, our ancestors knew, no less than we do, that the world does not work as the *tocheichah* suggests.

Threatening and intimidating sermons are part and parcel of human religious and literary experience. Recall the sermon on Jonah in Herman Melville's *Moby Dick* or the one delivered in a Jesuit school in James Joyce's *A Portrait of the Artist as a Young Man*. Is this merely a way to induce humans to make the right choices? Or is it a means of manipulating their behavior?

Two thoughts come to mind. First, this *tocheichah* is an expression of the conviction that what we do matters deeply, not only to ourselves, but to the broader community and indeed to the world. We often experience ourselves as separate, unique, encapsulated. But everything is intertwined.

Second, as Rambam pointed out, fear influences behavior initially, but in the long term, love is far more powerful and yields a richer harvest. Perhaps that is why this *tocheichah* is preceded by the ceremony of first fruits, which affords the people an opportunity to show the signs of God's love in their lives.

Ki Tavo
Rabbi David Novak, 2011

One of the most famous passages in our Passover Haggadah is found in *Ki Tavo*. When we bring the first fruits of the new land to the priest in charge, the Torah tells us:

> You shall then recite as follows before YHVH your God: "My father was a fugitive Aramean. He went down to Egypt with meager numbers and sojourned there; but there he became a great and very populous nation. The Egyptians dealt harshly with us and oppressed us; they imposed heavy labor upon us. We cried to YHVH, the God of our ancestors, and YHVH heard our plea and saw our plight, our misery, and our oppression. YHVH freed us from Egypt by a mighty hand, by an outstretched arm and awesome power, and by signs and portents. The Redeeming One brought us to this place and gave us this land, a land flowing with milk and honey. Wherefore I now bring the first fruits of the soil which You, O YHVH, have given me. (Deut. 26:5–10)

How wonderful is this affirmation of our freedom to be in a land, to cultivate it, to offer its bounty to God, and to provide for the Levite, the stranger, the orphan, and the widow. Our liberation story inspires us to give in order to enhance the well-being of others. Through generosity we were freed. Through generosity we, if only temporarily, free others from what binds them.

Ki Tavo
Rabbi Amy Scheinerman, 2012

The dreaded *tocheichah* ("rebuke") of *Ki Tavo* presents a host of theological quandaries, but also the recognition that our lives are variously blessed and cursed. The most terrifying curse of the *tocheichah* is that enemies will invade and ravish the Land, devouring both cattle and crops, causing the starving population to resort to cannibalism: they will eat their own children and even hoard the flesh. Could there be a more devastating curse than this?

Torah tells us that the ultimate blame lies not with the marauding enemy, but with Israel herself: "But if you do not obey Adonai your God to observe faithfully all the commandments and laws which I enjoin upon you this day, all these curses shall come upon you and take effect" (Deut. 28:15). This verse may be another way of saying that we are our own worst enemy.

Judaism was, from the beginning, a countercultural movement: Torah is predicated on rejecting the idolatries and wrong values of surrounding cultures in favor of a monotheism built on human dignity, compassion, and justice—all summarized in a covenantal package. How countercultural are we today? Surely there are elements of the broader culture well worth inviting in, but how successfully do we push away materialism that threatens spirituality, consumerism that compromises the integrity of Creation, and the tendency to value form over substance, which forces us to invest more energy into ceremonies than learning?

Ki Tavo
Rabbi Michael Boyden, 2013

Ki Tavo is a challenging *parashah*. It is full of curses—in a world in which we seek blessings. However, it contains important messages, such as "Cursed be the one who misleads the blind" (Deut. 27:18). And blindness need not only be a physical impediment. Commenting on the verse "You shall not place an obstacle before the blind" (Lev. 19:14), *Sifra* expounds, "If a person seeks your advice, don't tell him something that is unfitting for him. Don't tell him to go out at dawn when thieves could rob him, or at noon when he could become dehydrated. Don't tell him to sell his field and buy a donkey when you intend to purchase it yourself." Just as blessings are real, so are curses. Sometimes, however unpleasant it may be, we need to be reminded of that.

The opening verses of our *parashah* are also about remembering. "My father was a fugitive Aramean and went down to Egypt" (Deut. 26:5). And when do we need to say those words? Precisely when we have come into the Land and settled down. Certainly looking optimistically toward the future is important and good, but the future we shape should be informed by the lessons of our past.

In a post-Zionist world where only few of the witnesses of the horrors of the Holocaust are still among us, we need to be reminded of the importance of a Jewish state. It must never be taken for granted.

Ki Tavo
Rabbi Israel Zoberman, DMin, 2014

For the Israelites, reentering the Promised Land is more than a physical act. At the core of their great adventure is a spiritual drama of heartfelt thanksgiving to God who led Israel from Egypt's confining House of Bondage to freedom's open promise and Sinai's responsibility.

The offering brought to the priest from the bounty of a land flowing with milk and honey, in recognition of divine benevolence, should be internalized for generations to come. It is a humbling acknowledgment of an individual's, along with a people's, limitations, particularly for a nation covenanted to be a kingdom of priests and a holy nation.

However, given the human proclivity to take blessings for granted and ignore the true record of one's accomplishments and failings for short-term self-aggrandizement, the Israelites' offering of earth's produce is grounded in a remembrance of the gifts' divine origin. This assumes even fuller significance when reciting the liberation saga, because doing so liberates one from petty narrowness and pagan blindness and opens one's eyes to the larger scene of the human enterprise, in which God is a senior partner.

It is precisely in the moment of peak rejoicing over the harvest's fruitful yield that the celebrating Israelites are commanded to recall their people's trying sojourns and subsequent suffering in the crucible of Egyptian tyranny, lest a journey of forgetfulness ensues, with disastrous consequences.

It is difficult to reconcile the lyrically tender words "Behold from the heights of Your holy abode in heaven and bless Your people, Israel" (Deut. 26:15) with the harsh punishments yet to come for straying from God's covenant.

Ki Tavo
Rabbi Ruth Adar, 2015

Ki Tavo contains the famous formula for bringing the first fruits to the Temple, the same formula that we recall in the Passover Haggadah, beginning: "A wandering Aramean was my father." This line was later the subject of a question sent to Maimonides by a man known to us only as Obadiah the Proselyte. He wanted to know if it was permissible for a convert to Judaism such as himself to talk about "my father" when, in fact, Jacob was not his biological ancestor. He extended the question to phrases such as "our God" and others that suggest full membership in the Jewish people.

Maimonides's gracious answer has been a comfort to ever since. "Yes!" he writes in return. "You may say all this in the prescribed order and not change it in the least."

Maimonides reminded Obadiah that Abraham brought many souls into the covenant and that ever since, all those who have adopted Judaism are counted among the disciples of Abraham. Maimonides concludes by admonishing Obadiah, "Do not consider your origin as inferior!"

So, too, do the blessings, curses, and commandments in this portion apply to the whole people of Israel, not only to some. We are one people, whether we became Jewish in the waters of the womb or in the waters of the *mikveh*.

Ki Tavo
Rabbi Amy Scheinerman, 2016

The famous first fruits ceremony of *Ki Tavo* places the land's fertility into the context of the Israelites' journey into the Land under God's direction and protection. The declaration is highly personalized—uttered by individuals, couched in the first-person singular, emphasizing one's personal relationship with God: "I acknowledge this day before Adonai your God that I have entered the land. . . . My father was a fugitive Aramean. . . . Wherefore I now bring the first fruits of the soil which You, O Adonai, have given me" (Deut. 26:3, 26:5, 26:10).

The declaration then turns to tithes. One is required to formally attest before God that one has paid the required tithes to the Levites and to the poor. Failure to do so constitutes *maal* ("trespass"), since the harvest belongs to God, first and foremost. "I have cleared out the consecrated portion from the house; and I have given it to the Levite, the stranger, the orphan, and the widow, just as You commanded me" (Deut. 26:13). Imagine the power of making that declaration publicly in the Temple.

Imagine there were a moment set aside during Rosh HaShanah services for making a similar declaration silently and privately—"I have fulfilled my obligation of *tzedakah* by sharing the blessings You have bestowed upon me with those in need in the past year, or I will complete the fulfillment of my obligation before Yom Kippur"—and then another on Yom Kippur to confirm that the mitzvah had been fulfilled.

Ki Tavo
Rabbi Ruth Adar, 2017

Chapter 27 of Deuteronomy begins with a command: upon crossing the Jordan the people are to set up large stones, cover them with plaster, and inscribe on them all the words of the Torah. Imagine stones large enough to inscribe the Torah upon them!

As magnificent an image as this is, how could the people cut such large stones, write the Torah on them, and then transport the stones to Mount Ebal? Verse 8 further complicates matters by seeming to say that the unhewn stones of the altar should have the words of Torah inscribed upon them as well. Both ancient and modern commentators wrestle awkwardly with these verses.

But what if we frame this as an act of transformative magic or, better yet, as metaphor? Both *matzeivot* ("stone pillars") and idolatry are strictly forbidden in Deut. 16:22. Here, in chapter 27, the people are told to make several such pillars—and perhaps an altar too—and cover them with the words of the Torah. These *matzeivot* are permitted, indeed commanded, because they take the old idolatrous form of worship and transform it into a uniquely Israelite form.

In much the same way, our people have often adopted and adapted the customs, foods, and ways of other nations, reworking them in accordance with Torah. Thus, we need not approach new things with trepidation or fear—we need only make sure that they are transformed, like the stelae, by the truth of Torah.

Ki Tavo
Rabbi Stephen Wylen, 2018

"Cursed is the person who will make an idol or graven image, which is an affront to God, the work of human hands, and serves it in privacy, and the people shall respond: Amen" (Deut. 27:15).

Rabbi Samson ben Pesach of Ostropol (d. 1648), wondering why this curse alone is stated in the future tense while all the others are in the present, speculates that even the intention to make an idol is prohibited. Idolatry is one of the three sins for which a Jew should accept death rather than transgress. In the story of the Maccabees, this command was taken seriously, and many Jews in that time chose death.

Today we are more tolerant of dabbling in syncretistic religious practices. Many Jews do not quail from placing a rose before a statue of Buddha before meditating or placing a Christmas tree in their home. Rabbi Yochanan ben Zakkai's attitude toward idols was pragmatic. When challenged about why he attended a bathhouse with a statue of Aphrodite, he responded that the gentiles walked naked in front of it (*Mishnah Avodah Zarah* 3:4). If it is not treated with reverence, it is a decoration, not an idol. Many Jews hold that unless we worship something, it is not an idol.

The *M'chilta* (to the Ten Commandments) disagrees: "You shall not worship them nor serve them. Not worship—if you believe in them. Not serve—if you do not believe in them." What is serving without believing? "A Christmas tree in our home is acceptable because we don't believe in Jesus."

How do we take the prohibition of idolatry seriously without being improperly judgmental?

נצבים/וילך   *Nitzavim/Vayeilech*
(Deuteronomy 29:9–30:20 and Deuteronomy 31:1–30)

Nitzavim/Vayeilech
Rabbi Joshua Minkin, DMin, 2010

"You are all standing this day before Adonai your God, the leaders of your tribes, your elders and your officers . . . to your woodcutters and your water-drawers" (Deut. 29:9). God is making the covenant with all of Israel, the wealthy and powerful, as well as those who are not. Torah does not make reference to the poor and powerless, but rather to woodcutters and water-drawers. Tradition holds that these people came from the "mixed multitude" that left Egypt with the Hebrews—people who had no standing among our community, except through petition. Who are today's "woodcutters and water-drawers"? It is clear from Joshua 9 that these people are held in very low esteem. When those who were to be assigned these roles came to join the Hebrews, it was not out of a commitment to our God or the revelation, but out of a fear of being destroyed.

    All too often rabbis complain that their temples seem to fill up only on Rosh HaShanah and Yom Kippur and that the real congregation consists of those who fill the pews every Shabbat and festival. High Holy Day Jews are denigrated and viewed as if they were second-class citizens. Sometimes their motives are questioned, with some claiming they are only motivated by guilt or by fear generated by the *Un'taneh Tokef*. Yet those are the people whose dues pay our salaries, run our schools, and allow the temple to serve the entire community. We need to be reminded that even the woodcutters and water-drawers were included in God's community, regardless of their motivation.

Nitzavim/Vayeilech
Rabbi Michael Boyden, 2011

Our *parashah* is traditionally assigned to the Shabbat preceding Rosh HaShanah. Although the purpose behind this, according to the *Tosafot*, is to conclude reading the curses before the start of the New Year, another explanation might be that *Parashat Nitzavim* is about personal accountability. All of you stand today before Adonai your God. There is even a special mention of "your policemen," as if to emphasize that they too are not above the law.

And why the reference to those who draw water and cut down trees? Rashi explains that this refers to those who converted in the time of Moses. The Torah, then, is inclusive, not exclusive. One recalls the well-known letter that Maimonides wrote to the convert Ovadiah, who questioned whether he was entitled to say "our God and God of our ancestors." Rambam's response was unequivocal: "Do not think that your background makes you inferior. If we are descended from Abraham, Isaac, and Jacob, you are descended from the One who spoke and the world was created."

The Torah refuses to distinguish between Jews-by-choice and those born Jewish, adults and children, women and men; between the privileged few and those lacking the mere necessary.

As Rashi puts it, "It is not in heaven or on earth, neither in the mountains nor on the hills, but within you." Jewish living, then, is the responsibility of each and every individual. As we prepare ourselves for the High Holy Days, we are reminded of the ultimate challenge: "I have set before you this day life and death, the blessing and the curse. Choose life that you may live" (Deut. 30:19).

May it be God's will that we be inscribed in the Book of Life!

Nitzavim
Rabbi Joshua Minkin, DMin, 2012

"I command you this day, to love Adonai . . . that Adonai your God may bless you in the land. . . . But if . . . you are lured into the worship and service of other gods . . . you shall certainly perish; you shall not long endure on the soil" (Deut. 30:16–18).

What is the connection between loving God and "enduring on the land"?

Our mystics teach that if we shut out the world and look beyond ourselves, we realize God pervades our entire world, living and inanimate. Everything is inextricably interconnected, extending far beyond human relationships. It includes the earth itself—its air, water, soil, flora, and fauna. Exploring this web of connections reveals imminent threats to the well-being of everything on earth: global climate change, rising seas, chemicals that poison our planet.

Torah doesn't just warn us of the problem. It proposes the solution: "[If] you return to Adonai . . . heed God's command with all your heart and soul . . . God will restore your fortunes and take you back in love" (Deut. 30:2–3). Truly loving God—the God inherent in everything—requires forsaking the gods of consumption, acquisition, luxury, and entitlement, returning to our covenant with God. Our mission is stewardship. We must restore and protect the finely balanced network of life. By loving God, the land regains balance and fertility.

"I have put before you life and death. . . . By loving Adonai . . . you shall have life and shall long endure upon the soil" (Deuteronomy 30:19–20).

Vayeilech
Rabbi David Novak, 2012

Vayeilech links Moses, Joshua, Ezra, and us in a chain of transmission. Yet on Shabbat Shuvah, nestled between Rosh HaShanah and Yom Kippur, many of us experience a sense of absence. Seats filled only days earlier are empty. How do we sustain ourselves this Shabbat as we experience the visible emptiness? How do we who love Shabbat, who keep and remember this "palace in time," find strength after experiencing the vitality of Rosh HaShanah?

We go back to this teaching, entrusted to us: *Chazak ve-ematz*, "Be strong and resolute" (Deut. 31:7). Spoken long ago and repeated time and again, *chazak ve-ematz* can resonate in our rabbinic lives today. The Torah repeats words for special emphasis; now, as then, *chazak ve-ematz* is a powerful message in the face of life's many complex, difficult realities.

As Moses prepares to take his leave of the people at God's command, he entrusts the Torah to his successor Joshua and to the people. In the Book of Ezra we find: "the teaching of Moses, the man of God" (Ezra 3:2). This teaching, so central to our identities, motivated us all to choose service to the Jewish people. Now we are the ones alive, and our voices foster understandings of this teaching.

The seats will soon be filled again and then return to the pattern of the regular year. We will rely on our inner strength and innate courage to go on in all the ways that we rabbis embody *chazak ve-ematz*.

Nitzavim/Vayeilech
Rabbi Stephen Wylen, 2013

The Torah says, "Gather the people—the men, the women, the children, and the foreigners in your gates—to hear, to learn, to revere Adonai your God and to do all the words of this Torah" (Deut. 31:12).

Rashi says, "Why include the children? To give a reward to those who brought them." It is well-known that little children interfere with and diminish the attention of adults. One might say, "It is better to leave the kids at home." That is why Rashi raises the question. The reward for bringing children is greater by far than the deficit of disruption caused by their presence. Children are very open to the holy atmosphere of a sacred gathering, and it makes a great impression upon them.

As Rabbi Nathan Adler, in *Iturei Torah* (ad loc.) points out, as a general rule, it is better to pass on the opportunity for personal fulfillment in order to educate the young in the ways of Torah and good deeds.

This has broad implications for monthly children's services on Shabbat. They drive away regular worshipers, while ghettoizing children and limiting them to only monthly attendance. Children who regularly attend Shabbat services prefer the adult worship. It is preferable to tolerate disruption caused by the presence of children and to challenge the children to grow and to nurture in them an appreciation of adult Judaism.

Nitzavim/Vayeilech/S'lichot
Rabbi Louis Rieser, 2014

Nitzavim addresses our contemporary malaise. So many people identify as Jews without ever consciously performing any Jewish act. This portion reminds us that despite complaints that the Torah is too hard—hidden over the sea or beyond the heavens—it is "very close by, in your mouth and in your heart, to observe it" (Deut. 30:14).

The problem is certainly not new. The S'fat Emet offers a reading that places the responsibility for action on the individual, but with a spiritual bonus. He begins by noting that Rashi identifies the mouth and the heart as the oral and written Torah. *D'varim Rabbah* 8:2 uses this verse to teach that one recites a blessing before and after opening and closing the Torah.

Using these two sources, S'fat Emet moves to a more personal conclusion: the Torah is written on the heart of every Jew, but it is closed, sealed. Being a Jew means that you possess a spark of holiness, but it is locked away in your heart, inaccessible until you find the key. In much the way some people possess personal gifts that go unused and neglected, so may our Torah remain locked away and inaccessible.

The key is speech. The movement that comes from speaking words of Torah awakens the mind and opens the seal upon the heart. Can you recall the inspirational words of Torah that led you to the rabbinate, to perform acts of *g'milut chasadim* ("deeds of mercy"), or to move through the world with compassion? This is the oral Torah that S'fat Emet calls us to speak for ourselves and for our communities, a Torah of awakening and holiness that is very close by—in your heart and in your mouth.

Nitzavim
Rabbi Stephen Wylen, 2015

"You are standing here today, all of you before Adonai your God . . . to enter into the covenant and the oath of Adonai your God which Adonai your God makes with you today" (Deut. 29:9–11).

Nachmanides asks: What does Moses mean when he speaks of entering a covenant "today"? The Jews have been party to a covenant with

God since Mount Sinai. He presents three possibilities for "today": (1) Moses is going to teach and explain the details of the Torah to the assembly on this day; (2) the people will gather in front of the Ark to gaze upon it, and the meaning of the Ark and the tablets that it contains are the covenant and the oath; (3) the people are going to perform a ritual of covenant, just as they did at Mount Sinai when they first entered the covenant, with sacrifices and ceremony.

Nachmanides raises a question: How does a Jew of "today" confirm the covenant that God made with the Jewish people at the beginning of our history? He shares with us three possibilities for how a Jew might renew the covenant:

1. Learn the Torah! Education!
2. Show reverence for the symbols of Judaism, which are found in the home and the synagogue, for example, mezuzah, ark, *ner tamid* ("eternal light").
3. Hold a ceremony of commitment to the covenant, for example, a bar mitzvah observance. The ceremony of confirmation, at the time of Shavuot, is designed to reaffirm in the younger generation the covenant of Mount Sinai.

It is always "today."

Vayeilech
Rabbi Amy Scheinerman, 2015

Moses tells the Israelites that, at the age of 120, *lo uchal od latzeit v'lavo*—he "can no longer be active" (Deut. 31:2). He publicly hands over the reins of leadership to Joshua, who will take them where Moses cannot go: across the Jordan River into *Eretz Yisrael*. Moses implores them to be strong and resolute in their faith in God and Joshua. Yet it is God who tells Moses, "The time is drawing near for you to die" (31:14), and again, "You are soon to lie with your fathers" (31:16). It would seem that it is one thing to relinquish duties one can no longer fulfill, but quite another to face relinquishing life itself.

During these *Aseret Y'mei T'shuvah* (Ten Days of Repentance), as we approach Yom Kippur, the unavoidable reality of mortality weighs heavily upon us. Awareness, however, does not mean that we are prepared.

An alarmingly low percentage of Americans have adequate retirement funds. More than half of those between fifty-five and sixty-four do not have wills. An even higher percentage of parents of young children lack wills that stipulate custody of their offspring in the event they die. Approximately three in four Americans do not have advance directives; most of those who do suffer from chronic illnesses. Equally important are the open and honest conversations with loved ones who might be in the position of making health care decisions should one be incapacitated.

Just as we gather the community to engage, together, in the painful and difficult work of *t'shuvah*, perhaps we can gather the community at this time of year—when mortality hangs in the air—to learn about and hold painful and difficult conversations about preparations we all need to make. If congregations brought in experts to help people begin the process of financial planning, preparing wills, and writing advance directives, perhaps many could enter the new year breathing more easily—how life-affirming!

Nitzavim
Rabbi David Novak, 2016

When two people learn Torah together it is said that the *Shechinah* dwells between them.

This is one of the many ways the instruction from *Nitzavim* is realized in our lives. Here we are told that Torah's insights are *lo nifla* for us to observe (Deut. 30:11). *Nifla* means "wondrous," "miraculous," "stupendous," or "baffling"—Torah is not beyond our capacity to keep or comprehend. We know *nifla* for its use in other contexts: for God's healing of all flesh, for the wonder of the parting of the sea. In telling us that it is *lo nifla* Torah tells us, "No, this thing is very close to you, in your mouth and in your heart to do" (Deut. 30:14).

This is our reminder that we do not need to experience miracles to make Torah real in our lives. It uses the straightest of straight talk to emphasize our widely held understanding that we were all at Sinai when Torah was first revealed. Torah's insights sometimes are complicated to realize, but life, as we live it, is also complex. Just because there are complexities does not mean that the pursuit of Torah should be set aside. It should be embraced.

We are privileged to bring people from diverse Jewish experiences into Torah's abundance. In our invitation to Torah, we are able to demonstrate that all of us have equal access, whether we experience it in Hebrew or English. As lovers of Torah, who make it our life's work, we are able to deepen people's experiences of Torah, revealing time and again Torah's many profound and pleasant pathways.

Vayeilech
Rabbi Amy Scheinerman, 2016

"Moses went and spoke these words to all Israel. He said to them, 'I am now 120 years old. I can no longer go out and come in. Adonai has said to me, 'You shall not go across the Jordan'" (Deut. 31:1–2).

The language of "go out" and "go across," as well as the dual meaning of *teva* ("ark" and "word") reminded Levi Yitzchak of Berditchev of the language used to describe a *sh'liach tzibur* who "goes down in front of the ark" (*Babylonian Talmud Shabbat* 24b) and "passes before the ark" (*Babylonian Talmud B'rachot* 34a). With this connection to the verse in mind, he says, "The tzaddik who prays to God must become attached to the words of the prayer. The holy words themselves take the lead. But there are some great tzaddikim who are on a higher rung than this: they lead the words. This was the rung of Moses, husband to the *Shechinah* according to the *Zohar*."

We who are called upon to lead others in prayer, cannot always "lead the word." Often the "word leads" us, and sometimes even that is a stretch—and not because we are approaching the age of 120.

Bachya ibn Pakuda's reminder that "words are the shell, meditation the kernel. Words are the body of the prayer, and meditation its spirit" (*Chovot HaL'vavot*) may provide spiritual motivation to reach higher, but there is also another route. When we focus on the mitzvot and experiences we have shared with those before us who have come to pray—through *bikur cholim, nichum aveilim* ("visiting the sick," "comforting the mourners"), life-cycle events, pastoral counseling, Shabbat and holy day celebrations, private conversations, jokes exchanged—we may find the spiritual energy we need to ascend to a higher rung.

Nitzavim/Vayeilech
Rabbi Amy Scheinerman, 2017

"Surely this Instruction which I enjoin upon you this day is not too baffling for you, nor is it beyond reach" (Deut. 30:11).

The eighteenth-century Chasidic master Rabbi Yisachar Dov Baer of Zloczow, in *M'vaseir Tzedek*, writes of the joy and pleasure that come from fulfilling Jewish obligations. He notes that Rabbi Y'hoshua ben Levi teaches (*Babylonian Talmud Eiruvin* 22a):

> Moses specifies "this day" to teach us mitzvot should be not delayed until tomorrow, but rather performed today and without consideration of a reward, just as food simmering in preparation for Shabbat should be tasted on Friday—the mitzvah should be enjoyed as soon as possible. What is more, since Shabbat is a taste of *haolam haba* ["the world-to-come"], one should engage in Jewish living with the clarity and pure intention one invests in the pleasures of this world, knowing the pleasure will be far greater in *haolam haba*.

For those who do not believe in a world-to-come, there is nonetheless a wonderful message here about the joys and pleasures—both immediate and unforeseeable—of Jewish traditions and rituals.

Imagine we could teach liberal Jews the traditions and rituals of Judaism not only from the perspective of identity and obligation, but as acts that will generate joy and bring pleasure to us and those with whom we share them—and that joy and pleasure are legitimate motivations for engaging in mitzvot. Imagine helping them find genuine joy and self-sustaining pleasure in wearing a tallit, hanging a mezuzah, eating kosher food, prayer and meditation, and *talmud torah* ("Torah study").

Nitzavim
Rabbi Ruth Adar, 2018

In *Parashat Nitzavim*, Moses foresees that there will be times when the covenant seems a useless burden to its inheritors. "One who hears the words of these sanctions may fancy himself immune, saying, 'I will be safe, though I follow my own willful heart' [with disastrous results]" (Deut. 29:18). Like the *rasha* ("evil child") at the seder, some Jews are tempted to say, "What do promises made by my ancestors have to do with me? I cannot see any advantage in keeping this covenant." Sometimes they convert out, but more often they merely assimilate.

The German Jewish philosopher Franz Rosenzweig asked, "Why be Jewish?" He wrote to his parents that he was thinking of converting to Christianity because "we live in a Christian state, we go to Christian schools, read Christian books." What point was there to the covenant?

He gave Judaism one last look by participating in the High Holy Day observances of 5672. Famously he reached the end of *N'ilah* with a renewed sense of Judaism as a precious inheritance and spent the rest of his life reclaiming that inheritance for himself and for other Jewish adults. Rosenzweig called for a "new learning" that begins in the modern world and leads into Torah. "From the periphery back to the center; from the outside, in."

May 5779 be a year of return; may all of us charged with teaching adults find ways to make Torah speak to our learners in the lives they live.

האזינו *Haazinu*
(Deuteronomy 32:1–52)

Haazinu
Rabbi Michael Boyden, 2011

Many fear death rather than accept that it is a natural occurrence in the cycle of life. Those who do not view this world "as a corridor to the world beyond" see death as the end rather than as a transition. Vast sums are poured into anti-aging treatments and into preserving life beyond the proverbial "three score years and ten, or even four score years," as if life were the measure of all things. Believers invest their leaders with immortality and visit their graves or shrines in search of succor and inspiration.

Fortunately for Judaism, Moses's burial place remains unknown, and all we are left with are his final words in the form of an ancient poem. "Give ear, O heavens, let me speak; / Let the earth hear the words I utter" (Deut. 32:1). As *Midrash Tanchuma* puts it, Moses turns to the heavens and the earth to write his eulogy. And how does he want to be remembered? "Recall me as though I were still alive and entreating mercy for Israel."

How typical that even in his death, Moses is concerned not for himself but for his people. Such is the nature of a true guide. Unlike so many of today's leaders, Moses is described as meek and humble.

Sifrei D'varim observes that there are those who say that Moses never died. Indeed, his ongoing presence, like that of the heavens and the earth, gains expression through our living lives of Torah and by the mercy that God bestows upon us.

Haazinu
Rabbi Michael Boyden, 2012

Parashat Haazinu is not an easy poem to read because the language is archaic and difficult to understand. However, its articulation of the challenges that we face as Jews makes the effort worthwhile.

Those who "make it" in life all too frequently forget their roots. Material comforts are to be welcomed and enjoyed, but only as long as they leave room for matters of the spirit.

"So Jeshurun grew fat and kicked. . . . [You] forgot the God who labored to bring you forth" (Deut. 32:15, 32:18) reminds us how easily we are enticed by prosperity. As Rabbeinu Bachya ben Asher (thirteenth-century Spain) put it, "They replaced the service of God with that of another."

No less threatening to our lives as Jews is the plague of ignorance. Today's generation is probably better educated than any in history, yet when it comes to seder night, all too many resemble the child who does not know how to ask the question and the parent who does not know how to answer.

My late father-in-law, Moshe Ariel, z"l was a Torah scholar and had a novel interpretation for the statement "Ask your father, he will tell you; your elders will give you the answer" (Deut. 32:7). He saw this as a parallelism: "Ask your father, and he will tell you that your elders [i.e., your grandparents] will give you the answer." In other words, rather than each new generation knowing more, each generation knows less.

Parashat Haazinu, coming immediately after Yom Kippur, reminds us of the challenge to return to our heritage and remember God's words: "See, then, that I, I am the One. There is no god beside Me" (Deut. 32:39).

Haazinu
Rabbi Amy Scheinerman, 2013

Haazinu, often called *Shirat Moshe* (the "Song of Moses"), expresses God's tender love and unceasing devotion to Israel, despite her willful rejection of God in favor of idols. God therefore determines to destroy her but has a change of heart when it occurs to God that other nations will take credit for Israel's dissolution. In the end, God decides to avenge Israel's enemies. Phew, that was a close one.

Or was it?

Haazinu certainly reflects a messy situation. God's love is unrequited, Israel's disloyalty evokes divine anger, and revenge against Israel is considered, rejected, and transferred to the nations. This is hardly a kiss-and-make-up poem. Yet the poem offers us hope that what has gone awry can be set aright even when strong feelings of resentment and even bitterness remain—perhaps not perfectly, not with a Hollywood ending, but in time effectively.

What a wonderful poem to read as we conclude the High Holy Days. As Tikva Frymer-Kensky, z"l wrote, "[This poem] offers hope for the people of Israel in the time of their greatest suffering, for it carries with it a sense of anticipatory forgiveness and the end of suffering, the promise of an eternal bond that remains unbroken even through difficult times" (*In the Wake of the Goddesses*, 1992, pp. 162–63).

Repentance and forgiveness are a continuing cycle in our lives because that is the nature of human relationships and of our relationship with God: ups and downs, closeness and distance, bubbling enthusiasm and withering disinterest. There is something comforting in this: repentance and reconciliation are always offered us.

Haazinu: Shabbat Shuvah
Rabbi Michael Boyden, 2014

There could not have been a more devastating blow for Moses than to be instructed by God to ascend Mount Nebo to "view the land of Canaan" only then to be informed, "You shall die on the mountain that you are about to ascend."

Moses is told that this is a punishment for his having broken faith with God at the waters of Merivat-kadesh and for his having failed to uphold God's sanctity.

The fifteenth-century commentator Rabbi Isaac Karo has God say, "Because you did not honor Me, neither will you be honored when you lead the Children of Israel."

There may be a clue in the final words of last week's *parashah* to the harsh treatment that Moses receives. There Moses tells the Levites, "I know how defiant and stiff-necked you are. Even now, while I am still alive in your midst, you have been defiant toward Adonai; how much more, then, when I am dead!" (Deut. 31:27). Moses has lost faith in his people, and a leader who has no respect for his flock will ultimately lose his own authority and be unable to guide them.

The tragedy for Moses is that he cannot make amends. This stands in stark contrast to Shabbat Shuvah, with its message of repentance and forgiveness.

However, we are not children whose bumps and bruises can be kissed and made better. Some things—at least in this world—will sadly never be forgotten or forgiven.

Haazinu
Rabbi Louis Rieser, 2015

Haazinu—give ear. Moses instructs the people to listen carefully. "When I proclaim God's name, then [you] praise God's greatness" (Deut. 32:3). Rashbam imagines Moses telling Israel, "When I tell you of the great deeds that God did for you, the kindnesses God granted to you, and that God is just in whatever will happen to you, [then] you, too, should praise God's greatness, testifying to the truth." It is as if Moses is saying, "Let my words stir a memory within you so that you can respond wholeheartedly to God."

This verse, which is the source of certain call-and-response phrases in our liturgy, suggests a tension residing behind thee antiphonal prayers. *Haazinu*, after all, anticipates Israel at a time of spiritual crisis. The call seeks to awaken us to God's power in our lives. The response to such a call should be intentional, not an unconscious reflex.

Given that background, I want to consider the way we recite the *Bar'chu* and its response, *Baruch Shem*. I have attended services where, driven by music or custom, the two halves of the prayer have merged into one, losing the flavor of the call-and-response. What might change if we pause before *Baruch Shem* and perhaps invite worshipers, "Please first call to mind one instance of holy kindness or divine goodness in your life. Then speak the words *Baruch shem* . . . to confirm that you accept the call to prayer and are wholeheartedly present." Could this be a pause that refreshes, reminding us that prayer that evokes God's presence is spiritually essential?

Ha'azinu
Rabbi Amy Scheinerman, 2016

"Rising like an eagle from its nest, hovering over its young" (Deut. 32:11).

Dov Ber Friedman, the Magid of Mezeritch (1704–72) envisions God as an eagle hovering over her nest: "There is in everything the divinity that gives life to all, and it is the essence of life because it is connected with the beginning of thought. And the essence of that connection is that nothing exists without that life, and all existence is nothing but that life, which is connected to the beginning of thought, an inseparable unity." For the Magid, mystical merging with God is the realization that we are not separate from God, that our being derives from God's being. Yet he offers the image of the eagle "'hovering over its young,' touching but not touching" because he understands that try as we might to merge with God, we will never entirely succeed, but rather have moments of insight among times of disconnect.

For those of us who are not mystics, this is still a helpful teaching on several levels. How often do we experience a sense of aloneness and vulnerability, like an eaglet, not yet able to fly, in a nest attached to a high cliff? The image of the hovering, nurturing, protecting mother eagle is a powerful one. The image of "touching but not touching" mirrors the experience of many of us in our attempt to reach a spiritual connection with God that is all too ephemeral, transient, fly-by-night. Yet we try again, and connect again, and again lose the connection. The Magid reminds us that this is normal; that mother eagle will return to her nest.

Haazinu
Rabbi Stephen Wylen, 2017

The Torah says, "You neglected the Rock that begot you; forgot the God who brought you forth" (Deut. 32:18). The nineteenth-century commentator Jacob Kattina, in *Korban HeAni*, suggests that the rock in this verse refers not to God but to one's own parents. He says, "If you forget the ways of your parents, then the second half of the couplet comes into play: you forget God."

As Jews secularize, the laws and rules become less important to many Jews. However, the traditions that are handed down—if not from Abraham and Sarah, then from Grandma and Grandpa—are the foundations of Judaism. Judaism is a very traditional way of life.

One story that became central in every generation of Sunday school textbooks is the story of how Abraham found God by smashing his father's idols. Every Jew with even a smattering of religious school education has learned that midrash. Ironically, the foundation text suggests that the essence of Judaism may be the radical rejection of the parental path.

How did this midrash become so central to American Jewish education, and why? What meaning do our students carry away from this part of their Jewish education?

וזאת הברכה V'zot Hab'rachah
(Deuteronomy 33:1–34:12)

V'zot Hab'rachah
Rabbi Joshua Minkin, DMin, 2016

"Hear, Adonai, the voice of Judah, and restore him to his people" (Deut. 33:7).

The Chidushei HaRim, Rabbi Yitzchak Meir Rothenberg (1799–1866), wrote, "Judah's quality was to bring holiness to his everyday pursuits—and bring him to his people—while that of Joseph was to be holy and separate: 'They [blessings] shall be on the head of Joseph . . . him that is separate from his brethren' (Gen. 49:26). That is also the difference between Hasidic leaders . . . some who wish to have very few Hasidim . . . while others want [many] . . . even if it results in a dilution of holiness" (*Torah Gems*, p. 300).

Our society too often equates size with quality—valuing larger as greater and more important. Often people will leave a good situation, one that offers them meaningful work and where they are happy, to pursue dreams of grandeur, thinking that status and high pay will bring substantially greater happiness. Each of us has a different temperament and different skill set. No one situation can make everyone happy.

We who serve the Jewish community are vulnerable due to the human proclivity to assign value based on size. Some of us work in large institutions with many people (like Judah), while others work with few (like Joseph). We work in congregations, schools, hospitals, prisons, and a variety of other communal institutions. A congregation may consist of thiry households or three thousand—but they all need a rabbi. Nurturing Jewish lives is important whether a handful or hundreds—everywhere, the ripple effect will reach many, both in this generation and beyond. Time invested in comforting and supporting one suffering soul is priceless.

The work we do is not quantifiable. But it *is* meaningful and it *is* holy.

V'zot Hab'rachah
Rabbi Louis Rieser, 2018

Why does Deuteronomy end here and not include the first chapters of Joshua that tell more of the wilderness story? Perhaps Torah ends with the death of Moses to ensure that we think of Torah as the Book of Moses. And perhaps it ends with Moses's blessings of the twelve tribes of Israel, which invites a comparison with the blessings Jacob bestowed on his twelve sons, to teach some wonderful Mussar (system of "Jewish ethics").

The blessings Jacob bestows on his deathbed (Genesis 49) are fraught through and through with negativity. He points out his sons' faults. He issues stern warnings. Perhaps Jacob feels compelled to offer guidance and direction one last time, but given how little of that he has offered until now, one wonders where in all this his sons can feel his love and devotion to them.

In contrast, and even though Moses has cause to criticize, excoriate, and warn Israel, his blessings focus on the tribes' strengths and positive traits. His final address to Israel is filled with affirmation and love.

Rabbi Eliezer taught, "Repent one day before your death." His disciples asked him, "Does a person know precisely on which day they will die?" "All the more reason to repent today," he replied (*Babylonian Talmud Shabbat* 153a). If this advice applies to repentance, how much more so to blessing our loved ones with messages of pure love while we can.

I don't want my last words to my children to be an expression of disappointment or criticism. I want my last words to convey, "I love you, wholly and completely." I want to end life positively.

Additional
Readings

הימים הנוראים   *The High Holy Days*

Rosh HaShanah
Rabbi Michael Boyden, 2011

Our prayers refer to Rosh HaShanah as Yom HaZikaron, the Day of Memorial. The association between the New Year and remembrance is first expressed in the Book of Leviticus, which describes the day as *shabbaton zichron t'ruah* ("the Day on which we remember the Sound of the Shofar," Lev. 23:24).

Our commentators are divided as to what precisely that means. In most cases it is understood as indicating that through our sounding the shofar, God will remember the Binding of Isaac and forgive our sins. However, Maimonides approaches *zichron t'ruah* from an anthropocentric perspective with the appeal "Awaken from your slumber. . . . Search your deeds, repent, and remember your Creator" (*Mishneh Torah Hilchot T'shuvah* 3:4).

Memory is bittersweet. There are episodes that we like to remember and those that we would prefer to forget. We must recall the past. George Santayana wrote, "Those who cannot remember the past are condemned to repeat it" (George Santayana, *The Life of Reason: Reason in Common Sense*, p. 284). That is an important message for us, both as nations and as individuals, as we survey our deeds and do *t'shuvah* (repentance). We build museums and memorials lest what has been be forgotten but, in doing so, run the risk of becoming trapped in the past and being unable to move on.

Our Rosh HaShanah greeting looks to the future: *L'shanah tovah tikateivu*, "May you be inscribed for a good year." What has been has been. Our purpose in acknowledging the past, and in seeking to make amends, is to prepare us so that we are able to commence a new chapter and seek a better tomorrow.

Rosh HaShanah
Rabbi Amy Scheinerman, 2013

Avinu Malkeinu is arguably the most emblematic prayer of the High Holy Days because it expresses the essence of our prayers and aspirations for the coming year. It joins forces with that powerful image of *Sefer HaChayim* (the "Book of Life"), in which there are two kinds of inscriptions, though we usually don't much distinguish between them.

The first inscription is what is written about us, the text that we imagine God to be reading on Rosh HaShanah. This is compelling because it reminds us that everything we do and say—not to mention everything we neglect doing and fail to say—makes a difference. Nothing hovers meaninglessly in the air; all those looks, gestures, words, and comments find a landing spot in someone's head or heart.

The second kind of inscription is God's inscription (more like prescription) for us in the coming year. We implore God to write us down for life, redemption, and sustenance, implying that it's mostly in God's hands, not in ours.

We acknowledge responsibility for the first kind of inscription—but do we always accept responsibility for the second, the potential blessings and curses we can be to those we know and love?

We are each God's manifestation in the world: God's eyes, ears, hands, feet . . . and mouth. If words are like arrows, here are some to keep in the quiver and shoot generously in the coming year: "I feel good when I'm around you." "I love your sense of humor." "It's fun to do things with you." "You're easy to talk to." "I always know I can count on you to listen." "You always have something interesting to say." "I appreciate your caring." And most of all: "You're important to me."

Rosh HaShanah
Rabbi Amy Scheinerman, 2014

Jeremiah remonstrates his people: "Can an Ethiopian change [the color of] his skin, or a leopard his spots? So, too, can you, in whom evil is engrained, do good?" (Jer. 13:23). An apple once spoiled cannot again be ripe.

But is it true that people cannot fundamentally change? Surely, we make scores of resolutions in our lives that come to naught, but the High Holy Days are predicated on the belief that people can change in deep and profound ways.

At the age of twenty-two, Cornealious (Mike) Anderson participated in an armed robbery, for which he was sentenced to thirteen years in prison. Due to a clerical error, he was not picked up to serve his sentence until last July—thirteen years later. In the interim, Anderson turned his life around, became a master carpenter, married, had four children with his wife LaQonna, and by all accounts led a model life. Judge Terry Lynn Brown, who released Anderson, said, "You've been a good father. You've been a good husband. You've been a good tax-paying citizen of the State of Missouri. That leads me to believe that you are a good man and a changed man." For his part, Anderson says he turned his life over to God. He told a reporter, "If you do the right thing, good things will happen in your life and in the law, as well."

Anderson's story includes traditional elements of reward and punishment, repentance and forgiveness, and bids us to ask: What does it take to truly change? Why do some people succeed where others fail? What will it take for us to change?

Rosh HaShanah
Rabbi David Novak, 2015

What is left to say about God's command to Abraham to immolate Isaac on an altar?

According to biblical scholar Phyllis Trible, this is a text of terror.

Midrash Tanchuma and others wonder why Sarah is silent: Sarah, who demanded that Abraham toss out Hagar and Ishmael in order to defend

Isaac's status, is silent even when the Adversary (Satan) approaches her in the guise of Isaac and tells her what Abraham is about to do. She dies on the spot.

Perhaps the text could not stand, as it does, if she and Abraham had an angry encounter, as is known to happen among married couples. Perhaps she would have used her own body to protect her son, and Abraham would have been forced to physically move her while she shouted in angry protest.

Sarah's silence continues to vex us. Given what we know about the bond that forms between mother and child, what mother would not do everything in her power to protect her child, even from God and her husband?

Pamela Greenberg writes in her translation of Psalm 137, "One day you, too, will see your brightest future shattered against a rock." Babies (and children) are their parents' brightest future. No wonder Sarah's silence is louder than words.

Rosh HaShanah
Rabbi Michael Boyden, 2016

The two traditional Torah readings for Rosh HaShanah are disturbing. On the first day we read how Abraham expelled Hagar and Ishmael from his home. It is a tale of jealousy and hard-heartedness. Although Ishmael is Abraham's firstborn, he and his mother are cast out into the wilderness and left to fend for themselves. While Isaac's name appears no fewer than six times in the first twelve verses of the Torah reading, Hagar and Ishmael are simply referred to as the "maidservant" and the "maidservant's son." When you obliterate people's names, as the Nazis did by assigning their victims numbers in the concentration camps, you rob them of their identity and individuality, making it far easier to ignore their humanity.

In the traditional second-day reading, after having disposed of Hagar and Ishmael, Abraham is prepared to take Sarah's only son, Isaac, and offer him up as a sacrifice on Mount Moriah. Where is Abraham's inner voice, the voice that pleaded with God for justice in order to save Sodom and Gomorrah? How could he be willing to slaughter Sarah's only son?

Both tales demonstrate how easy it is to justify the unforgivable and be indifferent to the needs and rights of others. When we label people "refugees" or "illegal immigrants" they become mere statistics, robbed of a human face. How sad that it takes a dramatic image, like that of the drowned Syrian child, Aylan Kurdi, to sensitize us—for at least for a moment—to the suffering of others.

Rosh HaShanah
Rabbi Charles Middleburgh, PhD, 2017

This Rosh HaShanah will be the thirtieth *yahrzeit* of my father, z"l, who died in 1987. This year on the Yamim Noraim (Days of Awe), I will also mention my mother, who died in March, for the first time. A milestone *yahrzeit*, a recent bereavement, and a sixty-one-year-old orphan!

Remembering is a paramount theme on Rosh HaShanah. Midrash tells us that the shofar reminds God to exercise forbearance when we attempt to atone. The *Zichronot* verses recall occasions when God remembered Israel and acted on our behalf. The root *zayin-chaf-reish* has an intriguing duality to it that encompasses both remembering and naming, as when God tells Moses that YHVH is God's name, how God will forever be named, and how we should think of God (Exod. 3:14–15).

The death of parents, pivotal figures in our life story, removes two of our most powerful anchors and reconnects us with some of our most formative experiences, both positive and negative. When we remember our parents, we remember far more than their personalities, traits, and foibles . . . we remember our own.

The High Holy Days also facilitate remembering of the most challenging kind—remembering our own failings and weaknesses. Through remembering and atoning, we have the opportunity to redirect our lives and forge a better self.

This Rosh HaShanah especially I will remember both my parents, and through that memory commit to being what they would expect of me, now that I no longer have their presence in my life.

Rosh HaShanah
Rabbi David Novak, 2018

Rosh HaShanah culminates a seven-week ascent from the chasm of God's seemingly complete rejection of Israel conveyed in Lamentations, read on Tishah B'Av, through seven reassuring haftarot of consolation read each Shabbat between Tishah B'Av and Yom HaZikaron. These seven weeks help us prepare ourselves for Rosh HaShanah's profound spiritual opportunity to align ourselves with God's reassurance, trust, and acceptance. In so doing, we arrive at Rosh HaShanah prepared for the spiritual excavation of our beings.

Rosh HaShanah's spiritual heft can represent so much more for rabbis than just the massive preparations many of us do for the people we serve. If we develop our own spiritual practices to complement the seven-week ascent, we will be ready to both lead others and do our own work of *t'shuvah* ("repentance") when Rosh HaShanah arrives.

What other practices might we adopt? As a daily reminder we could sound the shofar at the beginning of our workday. We could read Alan Lew's magnificent *This Is Real and You Are Completely Unprepared* or the superb book *Preparing Your Heart for the High Holy Days: A Guided Journal* by our colleagues Rachel Sabath Beit-Halachmi and Kerry Olitzky. A few minutes of meditation each day will allow clarity to enter our minds. We could read one of the prayers or poems in *Mishkan HaNefesh* each day to reflect on the *machzor*'s deep riches. Given how busy rabbis are in Elul, it is important that we carve out sacred moments for ourselves to experience the spirituality of the Yamim Noraim (Days of Awe).

Shabbat Shuvah
Rabbi David Novak, 2018

Our human sense of guilt can easily separate us from God, and so the prophets proclaim: God's abounding and forgiving love is freely given. (It is not earned, as in some other traditions.) The understanding of God's freely given love and forgiveness goes a long way to alleviate some of our sense of guilt and promotes reconciliation. Shabbat Shuvah is our annual invitation to experience clarity in our relationships with God, especially when we feel we have mucked it up. No matter what we may have done, Shabbat Shuvah's clarion message is that the God of Israel will take us back in love when we turn our attention to our relationship with God and pursue change, even if it is infinitesimal or incremental change.

Our triptych haftarah makes God's attitude explicit. The prophets promise that God will accept our repentance, taking us back in love, removing God's anger and our shame and guilt from the relationship: "Generously will I take them back in love, for My anger has turned away from them," says Hosea (14:5). "And you shall know that I am in the midst of Israel, that I Adonai am your God and there is no other. And My people shall be shamed no more," proclaims Joel (2:27). "Who is a God like You, forgiving iniquity and removing transgression!" concludes Micah (7:18). These are intimate, strong, and forgiving messages. Giving voice to these words on the Shabbat preceding Yom Kippur allows us to regain solid footing in our relationship with God in the ongoing process of repentance and atonement.

Yom Kippur
Rabbi Amy Scheinerman, 2011

The process of *cheshbon nefesh* ("self-assesment"), which done right is a long and grueling step in the process of *t'shuvah* ("repentance"), culminates in Yom Kippur. We repent, ask forgiveness, atone, wipe the slate clean, and begin again.

It has long troubled me that we focus exclusively on our sins, transgressions, failings, and faults. The rites and prayers of Yom Kippur are intended to facilitate our self-effacement, even rehearse our death, as if we are scaring ourselves into dropping our bad behavior.

If the goal is to improve, should not examining what we have done well and right, where we have been compassionate and loving, patient and forgiving, be a significant part of the process? Recognizing our strengths and successes encourages more of the same, and that is a sure road to improvement.

Perhaps our spiritual work on Yom Kippur should include an assessment of the good, not toward the end of resting on our laurels or expanding our self-image, but toward the clearly prescribed end of doing more of the same with the knowledge we can.

Yom Kippur
Rabbi David Novak, 2013

No sooner do we conclude Yom Kippur than we pray *Maariv* and include a prayer for *t'shuvah* ("repentance"). So soon? In reciting the blessing for *t'shuvah* right after Yom Kippur, we can't possibly imagine having done anything in the moments since the service ended and a speedy *Maariv* begins.

What are we praying for? Perhaps we might see this prayer as a prayer of aspiration, for the ability to create an ever-present *t'shuvah*-consciousness, a spiritual tool we can use to tinker with ourselves not just on Yom Kippur, but on all of our days.

T'shuvah is a powerful concept. When we look at ourselves, when we make adjustments, when we bring to the surface what we'd rather suppress deep inside, we are giving ourselves the opportunity to use *t'shuvah* for self-improvement and greater self-awareness. Whether we pray daily or not, the power of *t'shuvah* is always available to us, 365 days a year.

What the Mussar Institute says of *musar* applies also to *t'shuvah* as a practice and aspiration: "The goal of Mussar practice is to release the light of holiness that lives within the soul. The roots of all of our thoughts and actions can be traced to the depths of the soul, beyond the reach of the light of consciousness, and so the methods Mussar provides include meditations, guided contemplations, exercises and chants that are all intended to penetrate down to the darkness of the subconscious, to bring about change right at the root of our nature."

Yom Kippur
Rabbi Amy Scheinerman, 2014

A story is told of the Chasidic rabbi Aharon of Karlin: In desperation and despair, parents of an incorrigible boy brought their son to the great rabbi. The child loved roaming the woods outdoors, and the more the parents insisted he spend his time indoors studying Torah, the more defiant he became. The great rabbi listened to their story and growled, "So he won't study Torah. Leave him here for two hours and I will give him a talking-to he will never forget." The parents were nearly too frightened to leave their child with the fierce man, but no sooner had they left than Rabbi Aharon got up, went over to the child, put his arms around him, and tenderly hugged him to his chest. For two hours, the boy sat in the embrace of the great rabbi listening to his heartbeat.

In the days to come, the parents noticed that the boy was becoming increasingly empathetic. He helped others resolve their differences, and the love of study was ignited in his heart. In time, he became a rabbi. If people asked how he came to learn Torah, he would tell them he learned Torah when Rabbi Aharon of Karlin held him silently against his breast.

What is Torah study about? What is Torah about? For many of the Chasidic masters, it is about developing in ourselves empathy and love for others. For Levi Yitzchak of Berditchev, the *shefa* ("divine flow") itself is compassion. How can this understanding influence the spiritual work we do on the High Holy Days in general and on Yom Kippur in particular?

(Martin Buber's version of this story appears in *Tales of the Hasidim*, vol. 1, p. 200. Doug Lipman's version is found in Penninah Schram's *Chosen Tales*, p. 207.)

Yom Kippur
Rabbi Amy Scheinerman, 2015

The term *cheit*, often translated as "missing the mark" based on its origin in the realm of archery, carries a different meaning and connotation than the term "sin" in English, which is often defined in dictionaries as "willful transgression" or "reprehensible action." Leviticus 4:2 explains that a *cheit* is an act committed *bishgagah* (unintentionally). Therefore, one may bring a *chatat*, a sin offering, to the *Mishkan*. There is a way to make up for a *cheit*: try again. There is always another arrow in the quiver because life affords us more chances to aim for the target.

Ronald L. Eisenberg writes, "The purpose of the sin offering was not to bribe God to overlook the sin or to balance it with an act of generosity. Rather, its goal was to make the donor aware of his more generous side, so that he would not see himself as merely weak and rebellious" (*The 613 Mitzvot*, pp. 54–55).

The *Babylonian Talmud B'rachot* 26b, discussing the time parameters for *Shacharit*, *Minchah*, and *Maariv*, takes up the question of what to do if one has missed reciting an *Amidah*. The answer: say another the next time you pray. The Gemara expresses concerns about prayers that cross the boundaries between one day to another, and Shabbat to *chol* ("profane time"), but in each case, there is a solution that assumes people mean well and can do what is right.

Does repeating the *Amidah* twice in the afternoon make up for missing it in the morning? That depends upon how you choose to view it.

For the Rabbis, the important thing was to assure people that their mistakes were correctable and their efforts were acceptable and even precious to God. This perspective is valuable amidst the many confessions and mentions of sin on Yom Kippur.

Yom Kippur
Rabbi Ruth Adar, 2016

Two Days of Atonement I shall never forget.

The first was my first as a rabbi. I officiated at my first funeral on the afternoon before *Kol Nidrei*. The deceased woman and I shared a first name. Although I did my best to focus on the deceased and her family, I could not shake the feeling that I was officiating at my own funeral. That feeling clung to me that evening and all the next day.

The second memorable Yom Kippur was last year. The morning before *Kol Nidrei* I was short of breath. As it worsened, I lay across my kitchen table, gasping for breath. It crossed my mind that I might be dying, and as we sped toward the hospital, all I could think was that I was not ready, definitely not ready. The ER staff ascertained that my lungs were riddled with blood clots; they administered medicine and treated my family gently. Later I learned that the survival rate for pulmonary embolisms is low; I am fortunate to be alive.

Every Yom Kippur we rehearse for our own deaths, eschewing physical pleasures to focus on the meaning of our mortality. *Un'taneh Tokef* reminds us that life is frighteningly unpredictable. Those two Days of Atonement drove these messages home in a way even prayer and fasting cannot. I felt heaven saying, "Pay attention!" Perhaps it takes a brush with mortality to help us fully appreciate the time we have and value life's potential. May we each rise from prayer with a renewed sense of the urgency of life, the preciousness of every moment.

Yom Kippur
Michael Boyden, 2017

There is something symbolic about reading the Book of Jonah in the middle of the afternoon on Yom Kippur. Just when the fast begins to bite and we are feeling at our very lowest, Jonah is on a downward spiral. First, he goes down (*vayeire*, Jonah 1:3) to Jaffa. Then he descends (*vayeired*, 1:3) into the boat. When the storm breaks, he goes down (*yarad*, 1:5) into the very recesses of the vessel and falls asleep (*vayeiradam*, 1:5). Although *vayeiradam* comes from a different verbal root, the alliteration cannot be coincidental.

Jonah is the anti-prophet, who does not want to fulfill his mission. He doesn't care about the Ninevites. Contrast Jonah with Moses, who entreats God, pleading, "Forgive this people's sin according to Your great kindness" (Num. 14:19)! Jonah cares only about himself: he falls asleep in the storm while the sailors struggle to save the ship, and he sits comfortably in the shade under a gourd awaiting Nineveh's destruction. What a stark contrast with the heathen mariners, who cried out to God to save them, and the gentiles of Nineveh, who proclaimed a fast and donned sackcloth!

In a world where Jews can often be self-centered, the Book of Jonah is a reminder that God cares for all humankind "and much cattle" (Jonah 4:11). As the medieval commentator David Kimchi put it, "It was written as a moral lesson for Israel . . . to teach them that God . . . has pity on the penitents of every people."

Yom Kippur
Rabbi Stephen Wylen, 2018

"Yom Kippur atones for transgressions between a person and God; Yom Kippur does not atone for transgressions between one person and another until the transgressor has appeased the other" (*Mishnah Yoma* 8:9). These words are part of the confessions in the *machzor*.

Emanuel Levinas directs our attention to a common misunderstanding of this passage by modern liberal Jews ("Toward the Other," in *Nine Talmudic Readings*). The modern Jew reads into this passage his or her secular leanings: one does not have to be a religious person; it is sufficient, and in fact superior, to be an ethical person.

We understand the automatic nature of the forgiveness of religious sins to be an indication of their insignificance. Only a sin that requires appeasement is to be taken seriously. Ergo, if we make amends with our fellow human beings, our obligation is fulfilled.

Levinas teaches us that just the opposite is the case. Appeasement is the simpler case because it can be achieved without introspection or transformation. I get the parking ticket; I pay the fine; no admission of guilt is required. The sin between a person and God is more serious because no appeasement is possible. Therefore, nothing less than the total transformation of the person is required to fulfill one's obligation.

Through the observance of Yom Kippur I must make myself a new person. Only in this way can I be right with God. The hardest thing is to look honestly at one's own self and admit the need to change one's ways.

סוכות, שמיני עצרת, ושמחת תורה
Sukkot, Sh'mini Atzeret, and Simchat Torah

Sukkot
Rabbi Amy Scheinerman, 2011

The Talmud records a disagreement between Rabbah and Rava concerning fastening a holder onto the *lulav*: "Rabbah said: . . . When you bind the *hoshanas* of the house of the *reish galuta* ["exilarch"], leave a place for the hand to hold [i.e., some of the *lulav* protruding from the bottom] so that [the holder] should not interpose. Rava said: Anything whose purpose is to beatify [the mitzvah of the *lulav*] is not an interposition" (*Babylonian Talmud Sukkah* 37a).

Rabbah wants us to grasp the *lulav* directly—to hold it with our hands and feel its components directly, rather than separate ourselves from the branches for the convenience of a holder. Rava says that if the purpose of the holder is *hidur mitzvah* ("the beautification of a mitzvah") then it is not considered an interposition, because the holder becomes an accessory to the *lulav*. Rabbah tells us that a fancy piece of technology removes us from the natural, earthy roots of the celebration of Sukkot. Rava agrees, except in the case where the technology becomes integral to the very *lulav*.

The use of technology in religious life—visual *t'filah* ("prayer"), video, audio, PowerPoint, instrumental music using many instruments—has long been a subject of discussion. Do these technologies enhance our experience through heightened visual and auditory sensory input, greater musical complexity, and the dynamism of the experience? Or do they remove us from the symphony of human voices alone, the feel of a worn prayer book in our hands, the freedom to pray at our own pace and grapple with the words? Do the images in visual *t'filah* enliven our imaginations or diminish our ability to conjure up our own images?

There is no right or wrong answer, but it is worthwhile to recognize the varying sensibilities in our communities.

Sukkot
Rabbi Amy Scheinerman, 2014

The S'fat Emet likens the sukkah to a chuppah, within which the marriage of Israel to God is consummated (Lev. 23:43).

He then connects the phrase *poreis sukkat shalom* ("who spreads a sukkah of peace") in the evening prayers with Jacob's erection of *sukkot* for his cattle (Gen. 33:17), noting that *poreis* can mean "divide" or "set apart" as well as "spread forth." Why has God set us apart (Deut. 32:9)?

The S'fat Emet arrives at this:

> This is the real meaning of "who spreads a sukkah of peace": The inner point is that everywhere is wholeness [i.e. God]; Israel represents this among God's creatures. On Sukkot seventy bullocks are offered for the seventy nations. The water libation is also interpreted by the Talmud to mean that Israel should pray for God's kingdom to spread over all Creation. This is the meaning of "Do not be like servants who serve the king only to receive a reward" (*Mishnah Pirkei Avot* 1:3).

The S'fat Emet reminds us that Israel's mission is to serve all Creation —all people—and not just our own interests, and not merely for the sake of reward, but out of love for God. Ironically, we are "set aside" in order to interact with, and transform, the world.

This prompts us to ask: Does the Jewish people have a mission beyond the borders of our own communities? What is the purpose of our being a people? How can we best fulfill that purpose?

Sukkot
Rabbi Michael Boyden, 2015

Coddled in our air-conditioned homes and provisioned with packaged food purchased at liberally stocked local stores, most of us live lives that are largely detached from agriculture and the harsh realities of nature. It takes a storm or a severe winter with power outages to remind us of the frailty of the human condition.

Therefore, *Chag HaAsif* (the "Festival of Ingathering") is a time to make a conscious attempt to sensitize ourselves to nature and celebrate its miraculous abundance, because we have successfully gathered in the harvest before the winter rains.

Even the *arbaah minim* ("four species") connect us with the changing seasons. We shake them in the four cardinal directions (*arba haruchot*) and up and down, symbolizing our hope that the winds (*ruchot*) will blow, presaging the rains that will fall from the heavens upon the earth. If there is no rain, then we shall have nothing to drink, and we shall be unable to irrigate the land on which we grow our food. The Mishnah tells us that on Sukkot we are judged for water (*Mishnah Rosh HaShanah* 1:2).

However, Sukkot is more than that, for we are not only subject to the vagaries of nature but also the victims of our own species' inhumanity. The sukkah is a refugee tent because we fled from the land of Egypt. When one looks at the mammoth Syrian refugee camps in Jordan, Lebanon, and Turkey, one comprehends the plight of our ancestors.

Being conscious of these realities, Sukkot is a time for celebration because we have brought in the harvest and have roofs over our heads. Therefore, the Torah instructs us, "You shall rejoice in your festival . . . and you shall have nothing but joy" (Deut. 16:14–15).

Sukkot
Rabbi Stephen Wylen, 2016

The height of a sukkah must be at least ten *t'fachim* ("hand-breadths")"— a little less than a yard. This is sufficient to get one's head and upper body into the sukkah. The sukkah may be no higher than twenty *amot* (cubits)—about thirty feet. A sukkah higher than this is not considered to be a sukkah.

While the tradition does not explicitly state why a sukkah may not be higher than twenty cubits, it is easy to understand this limitation when you think about human perception. If you look up and see the s'chach ("the covering of the sukkah"), then you know you are in a sukkah. If the sukkah has a cathedral ceiling, then you do not feel you are in a sukkah but rather in some sort of wide, open space.

From the dimensions of the sukkah we learn an important principle. Religion is human-sized. Religion is made for people, not for God. Since God is infinite, a sukkah of any size would not be large enough or too small to contain God. But the sukkah must fit both the physical and psychological dimensions of a human being. The same can be said, in a more abstract sense, for worship, for beliefs, and for every aspect of religion. They are sized for human beings. Maimonides points out that while our belief in the One-ness of God points to something beyond human perception, our comprehension of God is limited by our human minds. It is therefore true to say that we humans created God in our own image, inasmuch as our concept of God is bounded by the limits of human consciousness.

Sukkot
Rabbi Michael Boyden, 2017

Sukkot is the only holiday in the Jewish calendar on which we are specifically commanded to rejoice. The mitzvah is referred to no fewer than three times: "You shall rejoice before God for seven days" (Lev. 23:40); "You shall rejoice on your festival" (Deut. 16:14); and "You shall indeed be happy" (Deut. 16:15).

We are told to rejoice because "Adonai your God has blessed you with all of your produce" (Deut. 2:7). In a world in which we drive down to the local supermarket and pick our food off the shelves, we have become desensitized to the frailty of human existence. It takes a drought, a flood, or a power outage to remind us that we should take nothing for granted. Therefore, if we have been blessed, we should be joyful!

Nevertheless, our celebration should not be self-centered. The Torah itself commands us to include our servants, the Levite, the stranger, the orphan, and the widow. Indeed, Maimonides warns us in his *Mishneh Torah*: "Anyone who locks the doors of his home and eats and drinks with his children and his wife but does not feed and provide liquid refreshment for the poor and the bitter is not rejoicing in the performance of the mitzvah but simply indulging his stomach" (*Hilchot Yom Tov* 6:18).

The kabbalistic custom of *ushpizin*, in which we symbolically invite each of seven biblical figures to join us in our sukkah during the days of the holiday, emphasizes the importance of hospitality and sharing our joy and blessings with others.

Sukkot
Rabbi Michael Boyden, 2018

Living in centrally heated and air-conditioned homes and shopping in local supermarkets and convenience stores, we have become insensitive to the true meaning of Sukkot. The sukkah too easily becomes an adult playhouse. We decorate it and invite our friends to visit. But that is not what the sukkah was really about.

Sukkot, like Pesach and Shavuot, is connected both to history and to nature: "You shall dwell in sukkot for seven days . . . because I caused the Children of Israel to dwell in sukkot when I brought them out of Egypt" (Lev. 23:42–43). The sukkah is a refugee tent. It is home for those who have no home. We would do well to google "Syrian refugee tents" to learn what a sukkah is really like. It's about frailty, exposure to the elements, and suffering.

Sukkot is also *Chag HaAsif*, the Festival of Ingathering, because winter is fast approaching and we need to bring in the harvest before the rainy season. We wave our *lulav* and other species in the four cardinal directions, up, and down in a ritual whose meaning may well be connected to our prayers for rain, which traditionally start immediately following Sukkot. Farmers know only too well how crucially important rain is. We in our concrete jungles are insulated and isolated from so much of nature.

We can rejoice on Sukkot as the Torah commands us to do, because we thankfully have roofs over our heads and food in our kitchens. This Sukkot our thoughts and hearts might turn to the many refugees around the globe whose tents are not playhouses.

Chol HaMo-eid Sukkot
Rabbi Amy Scheinerman, 2012

Moses pleads with God to accompany Israel in their wilderness travels. The plague that God wrought in the aftermath of the Golden Calf has subsided, and God's anger has diminished, but Moses is worried that God will abandon Israel. God assents, saying, "I will make all My goodness pass before you, and I will proclaim before you the name Adonai, and the grace that I grant and the compassion that I show. . . . But you cannot see My face, for a human being may not see Me and live" (Exod. 33:19–20). This should come as no surprise, since the second commandment, recorded in Exod 20:4, makes clear that creating images of God is prohibited.

Yet if humanity is created in the image of God, are we not seeing facsimiles of God's countenance?

Arthur Green, in his book *Ehyeh: A Kabbalah for Tomorrow*, writes that the most important teaching he received from Rabbi Abraham Joshua Heschel was in response to the question "Why are we forbidden to make images of God?" The answer is not because God is beyond all images and therefore no image could depict God. If that were the case, Heschel argued, images of God would be harmless because they would be meaningless. Rather, "God has an image, and that is you." Arthur Green elaborates: "You may not *make* the image of God because you *are* the image of God. The only medium in which you can make God's image is the medium of your entire life, and that is precisely what we are commanded to do" (p. 121).

Perhaps Exod. 33:20 is reflecting that God, who permeates and saturates the entire universe, cannot be fully known by any one person. But we get many glimpses every day through everyone we encounter.

Chol HaMo-eid Sukkot
Rabbi Janice Garfunkel, z"l, 2013

HeChag, "THE Holiday." We all know that, historically, the first Chanukah was a belatedly celebrated Sukkot. But more than two thousand years later, there are additional reasons to think of Sukkot as "the Jewish Christmas," the antidote to Christmas-envy.

The primary reason is *gashmiyut*, "physicality." Sukkot provides us with so much to do physically. As a child, I was envious not only of the *gifts* of Christmas, but of the trees, ornaments, miniature crèches, lights, and decorations. We humans like to do physical things, especially after all the introversion and soul-searching of the Ten Days. As an adult, I can indulge my desire for *gashmiyut* during Sukkot.

Imagine the mass commercialization of Sukkot! I buy great sukkah decorations such as glittery plastic wheat sheaves and acorns at craft and hobby stores. I adorn my sukkah with Christmas lights. But I can imagine far more: decorations produced specifically for Sukkot, and heirloom sukkah decorations that are passed from generation to generation. (Imagine the adorable possibilities for "Baby's First Sukkot.")

The religious themes of Sukkot are rich and deep, but too few Jews even acknowledge the existence of this, one of my favorite holidays. Perhaps this is no more than a fantasy, but imagine millions of gentiles setting up sukkot (and keeping up with the Joneses)! Jews would follow suit! The larger market will make it economically more viable to produce fabulous Sukkot merchandise.

Chol Hamo-eid Sukkot
Rabbi Michael Boyden, 2014

There are few stranger customs in Judaism than the shaking of the *lulav*, which is not done on Shabbat due to the prohibition against carrying. What is this custom all about?

The Torah (Lev. 23:40) tells us to "take" the four species but does not explain what precisely we are meant to do with them! Interestingly, Neh. 8:15 instructs the people to take a variety of leafy branches to build the sukkah. The list isn't exactly the same as that in Leviticus. Nevertheless, the Karaites use the four species for that purpose.

Mishnah Sukkah 3:9 gives instructions as to when precisely we are meant to wave the four species, but the question still remains: Why?

Rabbi Isaac Abarbanel understood the waving to be an expression of joy and thanksgiving at the ingathering of the harvest.

However, there is the inkling of a different understanding in a baraita in the *Babylonian Talmud Taanit* 2b. There it is asked, "When do we start mentioning rain?" (That is, when do we start praying for it?) Rabbi Eliezer's answer is "From the time we take the *lulav*. . . . The reason for the four species is to make intercession for water. Just as these four species could not exist without water, so the world would not exist without water."

So we take hold of the four species and shake them in the four cardinal directions from which the wind blows, then raise and lower the *lulav* in the hope that the rains will fall from the heavens above and water the earth below.

Simchat Torah
Rabbi Amy Scheinerman, 2011

On Shavuot, we celebrate the existence of Torah—its very being. That Torah exists is a fact. Certainly we can ponder who the authors were, when various parts were written, and examine variant manuscripts, but Torah is a fact.

On Simchat Torah, we celebrate our intimate relationship with a sacred text. We bring it down off the bimah and into our midst for a sustained visit, cradle it, sing and dance with it. Simchat Torah, therefore, affords us an opportunity to ask: What is Torah to us—to this community, in this place, in this generation? Simchat Torah also invites us to ask: What is Torah to me? How can Torah serve as my guide?

To answer either question, we need to dig deep. But we have encouragement to freely do so from Rabbi Shlomo Ephraim of Luntshitz (1550–1690), a poet and commentator best known for his Torah commentary *K'li Yakar*. He teaches, "The Torah must be new for each person every day as the day that it was received from Mount Sinai. . . . For the words of Torah shall be new to you, and not like old matters which the heart detests. For, in truth, you are commanded to derive novelty each and every day."

Rabbi Shlomo Ephraim's teaching speaks to the meaning of Simchat Torah. He not only invites us, but he expects us to bring our own questions and find our own answers in Torah. His teaching suggests that Torah is relational. It is discovered and experienced anew in every generation and in every soul.

Sh'mini Atzeret / Simchat Torah
Rabbi Amy Scheinerman, 2013

Hillel's humility is legendary, a model for all generations to come. It is surprising, then, to read a saying attributed to him in the Talmud that, on the surface, sounds "like an" antithesis.

Each year, Jews from throughout the nation assembled in Jerusalem to celebrate Sukkot. On each night of the festival until Sh'mini Atzeret, they performed *Simchat Beit HaSho-eivah*, the water-drawing ceremony. *Mishnah Sukkah* makes the bold claim that one who has not seen the rejoicing of the water-drawing ceremony has never seen rejoicing in his life. So many lamps were lit in the courtyard of the Temple that all of Jerusalem was illuminated; there were dancing, singing, musical instruments, juggling, and *shofarot* blasting. Then water libations were poured on the altar. By all accounts, it was a spectacle of peerless joy.

The Talmud also tells us that during the ceremony, Hillel would declare, "If I am here, everyone is here!" (*Babylonian Talmud Sukkot* 53a). On the surface, the statement seems far from the humility of Hillel. In fact, it sounds vain, egotistical, conceited. But understood in context, something rather different emerges. Hillel was concerned that all the "I's" (i.e., every individual) attend. With everyone present, he invested himself—his time, his effort, his essence—in the festivities of Sukkot, into creating a celebration in response to the mitzvah of God to rejoice. As a result, his joy was complete—nothing was lacking, and no one was missing.

Simchat Torah
Rabbi David Novak, 2015

We are a people who sanctifies time. Reading Torah helps us mark the passage of time. By reading the Torah according to a prescribed cycle, texts grab us with new insights each time we read them anew. It is easy to experience Torah as an *eitz chayim*—a "tree of life." This is a tree with multiple small "t" truths.

We experience the collapsing of time vividly in that special moment on Simchat Torah when we quite merrily read the last word of *Sefer D'varim* ("Book of Deuteronomy")—*yisrael*—and then launch into the first word of *Sefer B'reishit* ("Book of Genesis")—*b'reishit*. There is no transition from the end to the beginning. The old is made new again.

When we live through cycle after cycle of the Torah's reading, we come to see that Torah reflects our lives. Returning to the familiar to glean new realizations is a great gift that the cycle of reading, and, particularly, the transition from *D'varim* to *B'reishit* again, affords us. It is well worth rejoicing.

Simchat Torah
Rabbi Amy Scheinerman, 2016

Somewhere in the fog of history, the Pilgrimage Festival of Sh'mini Atzeret was overlaid with Simchat Torah so that in *Kiddush, Birkat HaMazon*, and *K'dushat HaYom* we add *HaSh'mini, chag HaAtzeret hazeh, z'man simchateinu*, "Atzeret–Simchat Torah, season of rejoicing," or a similar formulation.

On first glance, Simchat Torah's placement in the festival cycle seems anticlimactic. By the time Simchat Torah comes around, who isn't worn out by all the *chagim*?

Yet the layering of Simchat Torah on top of Sh'mini Atzeret, and its position in the cycle of festivals, enhances its meaning. Tishrei is a time of religious and spiritual renewal that affords us the opportunity to chart a new or corrective course for our lives, unburdened (we hope) from some of our past, refreshed and invigorated. The intense introspection and spirituality of the High Holy Days, and the emotions evoked by the process of *t'shuvah* ("repentance") and *kaparah* ("atonement"), then give way to the equally intense experience of physicality and the world around us when we live for a week in our sukkot, eat in abundance (rather than fast), and observe the seminal mitzvah of Sukkot: being joyous. If the period from Rosh

HaShanah through Yom Kippur guides our spiritual preparation, Sukkot enhances our sense of re-creation in seven days of celebration. The eighth day, the day of completion, is Simchat Torah, a day dedicated to completing, but also to beginning anew our annual reading.

Completion, re-creation, and renewal—all come together in Torah. Perhaps we might celebrate Simchat Torah with another *tikkun* ("a nightlong ritual"), as we do on Shavuot.

Simchat Torah
Rabbi Michael Boyden, 2017

For a Jew, there is no ritual object that is more sacred than a *sefer Torah*. The Mishnah lays out the priorities: "A town's citizens who sold its open space may purchase a synagogue with the proceeds; [if they sold] a synagogue, they may purchase an ark; an ark, they may purchase mantles; mantles, they may purchase [sacred] books; books, they may purchase a Torah scroll" (*Mishnah M'gilah* 3:1). However, the process may not be reversed: "If they have sold a Torah scroll, they may not purchase [sacred] books." The Talmudic principle is clear: *maalin bakodesh v'lo moridin*—"one may ascend in holiness but not descend" (*Babylonian Talmud M'gilah* 9b).

When we dance with the Torah scroll, we recall how the Nazis rounded up Torah scrolls from the synagogues they destroyed, but also how nearly sixteen hundred of them were later rescued from the former Czechoslovakia and transported to England to be painstakingly restored and distributed to Jewish communities throughout the world.

The Torah accompanied us throughout the lands of our dispersion. Israel Defense Forces chief rabbi Shlomo Goren held it in his embrace when he blew the shofar at the Kotel in a reunited Jerusalem in 1967. Fifty years later the Women of the Wall struggle for the right to read Torah at that same spot.

All of these thoughts and many more accompany us as we, like our ancestors before us, celebrate Simchat Torah, marking our joy at having once more completed reading the Torah and having returned to its beginning.

Simchat Torah
Rabbi Michael Boyden 2018

Although the Torah is replete with holidays, it makes no mention of Simchat Torah. It appears that the name was used for the first time by Rabbi Isaac ibn Ghiyyat in eleventh-century Spain.

So why do we celebrate? On the one hand, it is an occasion for thanksgiving, because we have lived another year and successfully completed the reading of the entire Torah. However, we not only complete the Torah cycle but also immediately commence once again in order to reinforce the importance of Torah study.

There is no symbol more central to our heritage and identity than the Torah. The Talmud asserts that the Romans knew that when they wrapped the scroll around Rabbi Chananya ben T'radyon and burned him at the stake (*Babylonian Talmud Avodah Zarah* 18a) and when Titus had sex with a whore on an open Torah scroll in the Holy of Holies as the Second Temple was being destroyed (*Babylonian Talmud Gittin* 56b).

Nearly two thousand years later, the Nazis gathered up Torah scrolls from the Jewish communities they had destroyed in Bohemia and Moravia with the intention, so it is believed, of establishing a permanent exhibition of relics of a defunct culture. Those *sifrei torah*, which came to be known as the Czech Memorial Scrolls, now serve Jewish communities across the globe.

Simchat Torah is, then, an occasion to celebrate the survival of our heritage and the Torah study that nurtures our continuation. And so, as we dance our *hakafot*, we sing, "Rejoice and be happy on Simchat Torah and give honor to the Torah."

Sh'mini Atzeret
Rabbi Joshua Minkin, DMin, 2018

Perhaps it would be helpful to rabbis if Sh'mini Atzeret preceded the High Holy Days. In the pre–High Holy Day race against time to produce scintillating sermons, brilliant explanations, and inspiring commentary, with the fear of writer's block hanging over us, we may focus on what we need to do and forget what we need to be. Sh'mini Atzeret can help.

The Talmud compares the offerings made on Sukkot with those made on Sh'mini Atzeret:

> Rabbi Elazar said: To what do these seventy bullocks [offered throughout Sukkot] correspond? To the seventy nations. To what does the single bullock [offered on Sh'mini Atzeret] correspond? To the singular nation. A parable is told of a king of flesh and blood who said to his servants, "Prepare for me a great feast." On the last day, he said to his beloved friend, "Prepare for me a small meal so I may enjoy your company alone."
> (*Babylonian Talmud Sukkah* 55b)

Imagine sharing a private meal with God—in spiritual peace and quiet—prior to the *chagim* (the "Festivals").

First and foremost, we are *k'lei kodesh* ("holy vessels") dedicated to helping those we serve access the Divine. This is difficult to keep in mind in the face of deadlines. *Atzeret* symbolizes our need to stop (*laatzor*) and pay attention to what is essential. This year, let us each try to prepare a small meal with God, one that affords us one-on-one quality time, not only after the onslaught of the *chagim*, but also before.

חנוכה　　*Chanukah*

Chanukah
Rabbi Michael Boyden, 2010

My colleague and teacher Lionel Blue tells the story of how he decided to take advantage of a free day on December 25 to call on congregants. He turned up unannounced at one home and succeeded in thoroughly embarrassing the members of his synagogue, who were in the middle of their Christmas celebrations, paper hats and all! At that point, he decided it would probably be more prudent for him to go home.

The Books of the Maccabees relate the story of the Jewish rebels, who managed to seize control of part of Israel, which was at that time a client state of the Seleucid Empire. By contrast, a baraita in Tractate *Shabbat* relates the well-known tale, absent from the Books of the Maccabees, of the miracle of the oil that lasted for eight days.

Whichever aspect we prefer, the primary message of Chanukah is surely about the Kulturkampf (struggle of cultures) between two civilizations: Judaism and Hellenism. The fact that Jews underwent painful and risky operations to remove signs of their circumcision, in order to participate naked in athletic and sporting events as was the Greek custom in those days, only goes to show what steps they were prepared to take to be like everybody else.

Perhaps one of the greatest challenges facing Jews today—and Israel is not immune from the problem—lies in deciding who we are. As the prophet Elijah put it in a different context, "How long will you waver between two opinions? If Adonai is God, follow God. If Baal is god, then follow him" (I Kings 18:21).

Chanukah
Rabbi Stephen Wylen, 2014

How important is Chanukah? Chanukah is a "minor" festival. "Minor" is a technical term. It means first of all that the observance of Chanukah is not commanded in the Torah. Secondly, it means that it is permitted to work during Chanukah. One thing "minor" does not mean is "less important."

Arguably, in American Jewish life there are three major holidays: the Yamim Noraim (Days of Awe), Pesach, and Chanukah. These are the holidays that Jews actually observe and that give meaning to Jewish existence.

If one wishes to argue that Sukkot and Shavuot are more important than Chanukah, that's fine, but who is listening to you? Are we Israelite farmers?

It makes sense that Chanukah is an important holiday to American and Israeli Jews because its theme, as interpreted by us since the Enlightenment, resonates with our own lives. For American Jews, Chanukah is about the fight for religious liberty and the pride of a religious minority group. For Israelis, Judah Maccabee is a Zionist hero.

Rabbis, if you are yelling at Jews to stop making such a big deal out of Chanukah, what is to be accomplished? Is Chanukah the Jewish Christmas? I would say no; rather, both Chanukah and Christmas are secular holidays that resonate in a secular society.

Chanukah
Rabbi Louis Rieser, 2015

In *K'dushat Levi*, Yitzchak Levi of Berditchev observes that Rosh HaShanah occurs on the "dark moon" and Pesach falls on the "light moon." Rosh HaShanah marks God's first emergence into our world, and Pesach, God's manifestation in our world.

Chanukah lies in between the two: the moon on 25 Kislev is visible but not full. This middle zone, between God's emergence and God's manifestation, is where we exert our power and influence on the world, making God's potential a reality, doing the work God would have us do in this world.

There are at least two implications. First, in contrast to the legendary cruse of oil and *Al HaNisim*, which invest all power in God, both the male story of Chanukah (the Maccabees) and the female story of Chanukah (Judith) are stories of power, of humans acting to make God manifest.

Second, Yitzchak Levi's thinking implies that the notion of halachah as a fixed set of divine rules is all wrong: halachah must be a process employed to bridge Rosh HaShanah (the emergence of the Divine) and Pesach (the manifestation of the Divine).

In both regards, the gritty history of Chanukah is far more spiritually meaningful than the rabbinic legend.

Chanukah
Rabbi Joshua Minkin, DMin, 2017

Why eight nights of Chanukah?

I cringe each time I hear of the miracle of the oil, thinking, "That's Talmudic propaganda to prevent another suicidal Jewish rebellion against Rome. Rather, it's to celebrate a missed Sukkot festival, as soon as possible." "They celebrated joyfully for eight days, as on the Feast of Booths, remembering how, not long before, they had spent the Feast of Booths living . . . like wild beasts" (II Macc. 10:6).

Eyal Regev, of Bar-Ilan University, in "Hanukkah and the Temple of the Maccabees" reminded me of classes with Dr. Martin Cohen. Regev suggests that to legitimate their power (in Cohen's terms: P2 becoming P1), the Hasmoneans needed to be seen as the only bearers of the Temple traditions. They created Chanukah to link their re-consecration of the Temple to earlier, symbolically potent religious and political (re-)consecration ceremonies (*miluim*), which often lasted eight days and occurred around Sukkot.

The inaugurations of the Tabernacle (Leviticus 8–9) and Solomon's Temple (II Chron. 5:3) lasted eight days, as did Hezekiah's Temple rededication (II Chron. 29:17). Regev notes, "Just as Solomon inaugurated the First Temple, the returning exiles consecrated the altar [Ezra 3], and Nehemiah concluded the covenant [Nehemiah 8]—Judas Maccabeus and his men reinstated the Temple rites . . . around the time of Sukkot" (p. 97).

Nonetheless, currently, our most important connection is that Sukkot is *z'man simchateinu*, "our season of happiness." We are commanded to have nothing but joy (Deut. 16:15), which II Maccabees affirms. May your Chanukah be full of rejoicing.

Chanukah
Rabbi David Novak, 2018

With their account of Chanukah, our Sages transform a Jewish civil war into a miracle tale of one day's worth of oil burning for eight days in the re-consecrated Temple. Not entirely masked is the fact that Chanukah involved a Jewish civil war between the dominant Jews who adopted and assimilated into Hellenistic culture and a minority who fought to preserve Temple worship.

That ancient battle is reflected in one of our most pressing challenges today: the internecine struggle for Jewish sustainability against assimilation. As the 2013 Pew study on Judaism and our own anecdotal evidence demonstrate, Chanukah's conflict lives in the present, and many of us feel it acutely especially in North America. This is much more than a "December Dilemma." It exists year-round. Most of the Jews we serve live in and are deeply influenced by the dominant culture.

I wish we all had large advertising and marketing budgets to fill the seats. Lacking that, there are online tools to send pithy weekly e-mails to congregants and constituents. These are written from the heart, certainly touching, and take but a minute to read. Many use social media to "touch" congregants and constituents with messages that show up in their newsfeed (once you get folks to sign up). Like the flame on the *chanukiyah*, these are small ideas that may assist us in the project of sustaining Jewish identity in our seductive mainstream world. *Chag urim samei-ach!* Happy Chanukah!

ט"ו בשבט   *Tu BiSh'vat*

Tu BiSh'vat
Rabbi Amy Scheinerman, 2010

A wonderful aspect of the Tu BiSh'vat seder is that, like the Pesach seder, its rituals can be interpreted on so many levels. There are four categories of fruits consumed at many Tu BiSh'vat sedarim.

The first category is fruits or nuts that have hard, inedible outer skins or shells and a soft edible inner core (such as pineapples, oranges, or walnuts). These can symbolize:

- The protective shield of the earth for all life
- The innate healing power of our minds and bodies
- God's healing presence in our lives
- Our capacity to act with compassion and justice to better the lives of others

The second category is the inverse: fruits with a soft, fleshy outer covering, but a hard, inedible core (such as olives, dates, or apricots). These can symbolize:

- The life-giving and self-renewing power of the earth
- The untapped and hidden—but fertile—spiritual capacity within us

- The spark of the Divine within each of us waiting to be planted in fertile soil

The third category is fruits that have a tough outer skin and a pit within (such as avocado, mango, or pomegranate). These can symbolize:

- The resilience of earth's ecosystem to generate and sustain life
- The resilience of the human soul to weather challenge and affirm life
- Our ability to pursue justice for others, to protect their rights, and to nurture their dignity

The fourth category is fruits that are edible inside and out (such as grapes, figs, or apples). These can symbolize:

- The symbiotic relationship possible between earth and humanity
- The loving relationship between God and Israel
- The dynamic and loving relationships we are capable of in our own lives

Tu BiSh'vat
Rabbi Amy Scheinerman, 2015

From the very beginning—*Gan Eden* (Garden of Eden)—people were surrounded by extraordinary delights. The foundation of Judaism is joy. We are even commanded to be joyful: God gives us abundant blessings with the full expectation that we will enjoy them—and this gives God pleasure ("More than the calf wants to suck, the cow wants to suckle" [*Babylonian Talmud P'sachim* 112a).

Receiving the gifts of life with gratitude brings us closer to God. According to the kabbalists, the problem in Eden was the fact that Adam and Eve decoupled physical pleasure from spiritual joy in God. Pleasure was enjoyed for its own sake rather than as a means to connect with the Ultimate. Tu BiSh'vat is viewed as a *tikkun* ("repair") for the sin in the Garden of Eden. The *tikkun*, of course, is in us: Tu BiSh'vat affords us the opportunity to feast on fruit and nuts and wine and more, and to celebrate with *b'rachot* ("blessings"), *kavanah* ("intention"), and gratitude in a way that the very act of pleasure brings us closer to God. We see, touch, smell, and taste the fruits.

It is said that the Baal Shem Tov was once visiting Rabbi Yaakov Koppel and saw him dancing around his Shabbat table for a full hour. The Besht asked the meaning of his dancing, and Rabbi Yaakov replied, "Before I taste physical food, I digest its spiritual essence. This makes me so excited that I feel compelled to sing and dance!"

Tu BiSh'vat is a new year—may it set a spiritual standard for the year to come.

Tu BiSh'vat
Rabbi Michael Boyden, 2016

Tu BiSh'vat is a perfect example of Judaism's ability to adapt to changing circumstances and thereby remain relevant. The New Year for Trees started off, in the *Babylonian Talmud Rosh HaShanah* 2a, as the cutoff date for assessing the age of a fruit tree for the purposes of tithing. However, with the destruction of the Second Temple and the exile that followed, this New Year lost all practical relevance. Fifteen hundred years later, Tu BiSh'vat underwent a revolutionary mutation when Rabbi Yitzchak Luria instituted the kabbalistic Tu BiSh'vat seder.

Diaspora Jews in the Middle Ages would eat dried fruits from Israel to signify their connection with the Land. Today, given modern transportation, we could eat fresh fruit at our seder, but we continue with the old custom, even if most of the dried fruits come from Turkey!

However, this is not the end of the story. At the end of the nineteenth century Rabbi Ze'ev took his students out to plant saplings in Zichron Yaakov. This practice was later adopted by the Jewish Teachers Union and the Jewish National Fund in order to encourage afforestation in Israel.

Tu BiSh'vat has also become a holiday with an ecological message emphasizing the need for environmental awareness. As *Kohelet Rabbah* 7:13, which is quoted in many sedarim, puts it, "If you destroy [My world] there will be nobody to repair it after you."

Tu BiSh'vat
Rabbi Amy Scheinerman, 2017

"When in your war against a city you have to besiege it a long time in order to capture it, you must not destroy its trees, wielding the ax against them. You may eat of them, but you must not cut them down. Are trees of the field human to withdraw before you into the besieged city? Only trees that you know do not yield food may be destroyed; you may cut them down for constructing siegeworks against the city that is waging war on you, until it has been reduced" (Deut. 20:19–20).

Torah's sensitivity to trees as an integral and essential element of the natural environment may seem obvious but is easily forgotten, as we see in the news. Rambam noted, "Not only one who cuts down a fruit tree, but anyone who destroys household goods, tears clothing, demolishes a building, stops up a spring, or ruins food deliberately, violates the prohibition *bal tashchit* ["do not destroy"]" (*Mishneh Torah Hilchot M'lachim* 6:10).

The Center for Sustainability and Commerce reports that, on average, each of us generates 4.3 pounds of trash each day—that amounts to more than 1,500 pounds per year. How many times a day do we violate *bal tashchit*?

Many people seem to believe that once they have converted to reusable beverage bottles, shopping bags, cloth napkins, and fabric cloths for cleaning, they've done their share. Tu BiSh'vat can be our yearly reminder to continually up our game: read newspapers and magazines online and avoid paper waste; wash and recycle aluminum foil; kick the gift-wrap habit; clean and reuse ziplock bags; buy products with less packaging; use public transportation; shop at secondhand and thrift stores; join with several neighbors and compost.

Tu BiSh'vat
Rabbi Michael Boyden, 2018

Tu BiSh'vat is the only holiday in the Jewish calendar—if we discount Shavuot and several fastdays—that actually has no name, but is rather known by a date. Hillel tells us that the fifteenth of Sh'vat is the New Year for Trees (*Mishnah Rosh HaShanah* 1:1), whose original purpose was the collection of tithes. Rashi explains in his commentary to Tractate

Rosh HaShanah that "in terms of the tithe, one does not tithe the fruit of a tree that ripened before Sh'vat together with that which ripened after Sh'vat, because trees [are tithed] according to ripening."

Tu BiSh'vat lost all practical relevance with the destruction of the Second Temple and the exile of our ancestors from their land. It was only in the Middle Ages that the date obtained new significance when Jewish mystics developed the Tu BiSh'vat seder, eating dried fruits to reinforce their sense of connection with the Land.

At the beginning of the twentieth century this became an opportunity for schoolchildren to plant saplings as part of a program of reforestation. The great forests of the Galilee and Carmel mountain range had become denuded of trees during the period of the Ottoman Empire, and swamp and desert had encroached on agricultural land. In that sense, Tu BiSh'vat became a holiday associated with ecology. Many sedarim include these words from *Kohelet Rabbah* 7:19: "Do not ruin and destroy My world, because if you ruin it, there will be no one after you to set it right."

There could not be a clearer example of Judaism's ability to adapt and reinvent itself to meet the challenges of changing circumstances.

פורים   *Purim*

Purim
Rabbi Michael Boyden, 2010

One never knows quite what to do with Purim. On the one hand, it is a joyous festival. Students and even teachers in Israel attend school replete with costumes, wigs, and vulgar makeup. Children in B'nai B'rak can be seen wandering the streets dressed up as gangsters and puffing on their first cigarettes.

They say that Yom Kippur is "like Purim" (*ki-Purim*). On Purim the pious put on costumes and pretend to be wicked, while on Yom Kippur the wicked pretend they are pious.

Yet we cannot easily dismiss the carnage in *M'gilat Esther*; seventy-five thousand enemies of the Jews are slain, and Haman and his entire family are hanged on the gallows. Maybe that is why we are enjoying drinking so much that we cannot discern between "cursed be Haman" and "blessed be Mordecai" (*Babylonian Talmud M'gilah* 7b). Then, in our stupor, at least we won't have to confront the moral and theological dilemmas in *M'gilat Esther*.

How could Mordecai let the king's people take Esther away and make her participate in Ahasuerus's orgy in search of a new wife? The Talmud tells us that Esther was *karka olam* (*Babylonian Talmud Sanhedrin* 74b), that is, she submitted to the embraces of the heathen king without participating actively; but this argument is hardly convincing. Imagine her misery!

One way to deal with these dilemmas is to view the story as fantasy. Rather than depicting fact, *M'gilat Esther* reflects a very different reality in which Jews are the underdogs and perpetual victims of antisemitism. It requires wishful thinking and a world of make-believe for the Jew Mordecai to be led triumphantly on horseback through the streets of the city.

Perhaps that is why the midrash (*Eichah Rabbah* 3) tells us that "the days of Purim will never leave the Jews or their memory be forgotten by their seed." The twin themes of the memory of suffering and the dream of a better tomorrow continue to accompany us to this day.

Purim
Rabbi Janice Garfunkel, z"l, 2012

Should our Purim *shpiels* include a beauty contest scene?

I'd like to propose that they should not, because (1) it is not accurate to the text; and (2) the actual head-wife selection scene is richer, more nuanced, much more interesting for adults, and shows off Esther's strengths.

Purim *shpiels* are another form of biblical commentary. I am confident our talented congregants can write something just as funny, frivolous, and family-oriented for the *shpiel* while remaining closer to *M'gilat Esther*.

What is valuable about the selection of the queen as it appears in the *M'gilah*? Purim makes light of tragedy. The gathering of maidens for lifetime imprisonment in a harem is tragic. Ahasuerus is a buffoon, but not a harmless one. (Purim is a sort of "Springtime for Hitler and Germany" or *Hogan's Heroes*.) What if the women swooned melodramatically about being taken into the king's harem, never to see their families again, while Esther remains calm and brave? After all, she is already an orphan but has not been defeated by that adversity. In their fear, the women vie for Vashti's old estate as head wife, but Esther does not. Is it God who arranges for her to be chosen nonetheless? Or is it that she is her authentic self with Ahasuerus, when no one else is?

Share your nuanced versions of the selection of a new queen scene online!

Purim
Rabbi David Novak, 2016

It is no surprise that the Jewish people have embraced Purim with love and enthusiasm: *M'gilat Esther* is an epic and classic story of redemption. A cruel and vindictive advisor to the venal king issues an edict for the destruction of the Jewish People because Mordecai refused to bow before him. Our heroine Esther unravels with each yearly retelling, and we celebrate our redemption again and again.

This redemptive moment is visited not only once each year on Purim, but also once each week during our most sensual ritual, the *Havdalah*. The liminal situation of the Jews in Persia is paired with the liminal moment when Shabbat gives way to the new week as we repeat these words from *M'gilat Esther*: "For the Jews there was light and gladness, joy and honor," to which we add, "so may it be for us." Through this line, *Havdalah* brings the redemptive spirit of the Purim story into the concluding moments of Shabbat. How wonderful that, in celebrating Shabbat each week we envision redemption, a time when the world will be wholly Shabbat. Until then, Shabbat is a taste of that future redemption, a promise of a time when there will be no more evil plotting and all will live as one. So may it be for us.

Purim
Rabbi Charles Middleburgh, PhD, 2017

It's behind you!

The phrase "It's behind you," a staple audience shout at a UK winter pantomime, has always struck me as being particularly well-suited to Purim, whose pantomime dimension is never fully plumbed. We have pantomime villains, overblown bit-part characters, and a plucky hero and heroine who beat all the odds in the final act. If we choose to play the more serious side, we talk about the prefiguration of classical antisemitic tropes in Haman's words to the king in Esther 3:8–9.

It is at this point that our previous ability to speak about Jew-hatred as a thing of the past smacks hard into the brick wall of twenty-first-century reality. Antisemitism has not just reared its ugly head; it has metastasized through the use of political issues in the Middle East and radicalized

Islam. It is more prevalent now than at any time in my recollection. The post-Shoah proclamation "Never again!" is proven sadly empty, and if we kid ourselves that the latest incarnation of the oldest hatred is nothing about which to be too concerned, I fear we make a grave error.

Purim reminds us every year that when Jews unite, the odds against us may be beaten; but the comforting thought that Jew-hatred is behind us, a relic of the past, no longer seems true. We need to show resolution and a far greater capacity for uniting to face the threat modern Jew-hatred presents to us all.

Purim
Rabbi David Novak, 2018

In our time we celebrate the miracle of Purim with all of the trappings of a carnival: costumes, drinking, and abundant merriment. This is how we understand our obligation to "publicize the miracle" of Purim, so important that our Sages required even women to hear the *M'gilah*, even as they asserted that the women who heard it would not understand it. We are fortunate to live in a time when women are empowered to read, hear, and understand *M'gilat Esther*, especially because it is graced with a female heroine who courageously saves her people.

The Sages included *M'gilat Esther* in the biblical canon because its story is empowering for a small people living in foreign lands and experiencing an acute absence of God.

In our day, we are able to recognize that the first eight chapters compose an exquisite and literarily ingenious novella: A Jewish woman goes undercover, marrying the dim and malleable king, who is manipulated and duped by his prime minister, the personification of pure evil. Enjoined by her uncle, the Jewish queen outsmarts and outlives the Jewish people's (and her own) nemesis.

Yet the impact of Esther is marred with the verses that portray Jews exacting revenge by killing tens of thousands of their enemies. Even as we joyously embrace the many mitzvot of Purim—sending one another gifts, giving charity to the poor, abundant feasting and merriment— we should also acknowledge the text's turn toward bloodlust. It is an all-too-human impetus that diminishes the miracle of *hesteir panim*, the unnamed and hidden God working in the background.

פסח, ספירת העומר, יום השואה, יום הזיכרון, יום העצמאות, ושבועות
Pesach, the Time of the Omer, including Yom HaShoah, Yom HaZikaron, Yom HaAtzma-ut and Shavuot

Pesach
Rabbi Amy Scheinerman, 2010

The *rasha* ("evil child") asks, "What does this service mean to you?" Because he says "you" and not "us," the Haggadah concludes that the *rasha* has excluded oneself from the community and its foundational narrative, and thus from the possibility of redemption.

Perhaps the *rasha* is merely reflecting an insecure identity. Perhaps the *rasha* is asking a sincere question: "What does this mean to you? I want to learn from your experience of the tradition." Or perhaps the *rasha* is disillusioned or distanced from Jewish tradition, and the seder experience of "back to the future" fails to impress as meaningful. Perhaps this is the time to help the *rasha* see the deep and continuous connection that leads back to a set of seminal events: Exodus/revelation/covenant—redemption/Torah/commitment.

Perhaps one response to the *rasha* is found in *Sh'mot Rabbah* 24:1. Reuven and Shimon, wading through the muddy Reed Sea and stumbling over rocks, complain that the Exodus feels just like Egypt. "There we had clay, here we have clay. There we had mortar and bricks, here too." They do not understand that they were free. They do not experience the miracle. They miss redemption.

The importance of the historicity of the Exodus pales in comparison with the meaning of redemption, the firm belief that it is both a possible and worthy goal and that we are God's partners in bringing redemption to the world. If we do not believe in the possibility of redemption, we cannot make it real. If we do not taste redemption (physically, emotionally, spiritually)—and Pesach allows us to do this—we cannot make it our agenda. The very goal of redemption is the inheritance of Israel.

Pesach: Yizkor
Rabbi Amy Scheinerman, 2010

In his seminal work *Haggadah and History* (2005), Yosef Hayim Yerushalmi refutes the criticism that the celebration of Pesach is an exercise in Jewish nostalgia:

> However dimly perceived, in the end it is nothing less than the Jewish experience and conception of history that are celebrated here. . . . For Passover is preeminently the great historical festival of the Jewish people, the Haggadah is its book of remembrance and redemption. Here the memory of the nation is annually renewed and replenished, and the collective hope sustained.

He suggests that in the celebration of the seder, Jewish memory and Jewish history unite, a surprising claim inasmuch as he contends that the Rabbis had no interest in history qua history.

Harold Bloom writes in the foreword to Yerushalmi's *Zakhor* (pp. xvii–xviii):

> Judaism kept its belief in the meaning of history while teaching habits of thought that were and are profoundly ahistorical. A Jew might be a poet or a philosopher or a kabbalist speculator as well as a rabbi, but for fifteen centuries [following Josephus] he would not think of being a historian.

Yerushalmi himself felt that in the modern age, history has replaced Scripture as the validating arbiter of Jewish ideas and values, and the trade has not been a profitable one for us. Torah tells us that remembering is a sacred obligation. We are taught to search for meaning when we observe the mitzvah of remembering. Historiography need not conflict with that goal, but it should not replace remembering: the study of our sacred texts, the observance of our festivals, and recalling our loved ones during *Yizkor*.

Pesach
Rabbi Joshua Minkin, DMin, 2015

Y'mei chayecha hayamim; kol y'mei chayecha l'havi y'mot hamashiach—"The days of your life" indicates this world. "All the days of your life" indicates the days of the Messiah. (Haggadah)

Shlomo Yosef Zevin, in *A Treasury of Chassidic Tales on the Festivals* (vol. 2, p. 366) writes, "The word *l'havi* literally means to bring in. . . . All the days of our lives ought to be directed to bringing in the Messianic era." Zevin further quotes Reb Yosef Yitzchak of Lubavitch, who explains the word *l'havi* this way: "The Torah obliges us to . . . bring life into our contacts with all material things of This World, so that our This World should be the world of a Torah observant Jew."

I find two lessons in the words of Reb Yosef Yitzchak. First, no Jew may ignore the problems of this world. We are commanded to help make messianic times a reality—a time of peace and justice, in which hunger and homelessness are eliminated and the dignity of all people is respected. Through our work for social justice and *tikkun olam*, we bring fruition to the concept of the Messiah. As our colleague Robert Levine said so well, "There is no Messiah . . . and you're it."

Second, "bring life into . . . This World": *Eitz chayim hi*—Torah is life. We must infuse the everyday with holiness and not be blind to the miracles and blessings in our lives. These too are Torah and allow us to truly say *shehecheyanu v'kiy'manu v'higianu laz'man hazeh*.

Pesach
Rabbi Amy Scheinerman, 2016

Our story of redemption entails three types of bread: fancy yeast breads of Egypt, matzah, and manna. Ancient peoples ate flatbread (examples: lavash, tortillas, naan, johnnycake, tortilla, injera). Our matriarchs and patriarchs ate something like matzah or pita. People have been baking bread for thirty thousand years, but Egyptians may have been the first to bake yeast breads five thousand years ago. (Hieroglyphs depict the process; archaeologists have uncovered grinding stones, baking ovens for yeast bread; and yeast cells have been detected in ancient loaves.)

Our colleague Howard Kosovske makes a compelling argument that *s'or*, which we often translate as "leavening," refers specifically to sourdough. He posits that it is the sourdough, key in a bread-based diet, that the Israelites are commanded to destroy.

I've thought a lot about this idea. Destroying the *s'or* constitutes an enormous act of faith in God. After redeeming Israel from Egypt, will God redeem Israel/the Jews from the threat of starvation? (It takes a week to produce a new sourdough from wild yeast.) Without *s'or*, the Israelites are limited to eating the flatbread of their ancestors, expressing a rejection of, and independence from, the slave culture of Egypt that produced luxurious breads but dehumanized people.

The third bread in the Exodus story is manna. In the wilderness, between the pyramids and yeast breads of Egypt and the traditional flatbreads of *Eretz Yisrael*, God provides manna, ephemeral bread that appears in the morning and disappears within hours, teaching the Israelites that God's presence in their lives is constant and dependable. It weans the Israelites off "Egypt" and prepares them to make their own way in *Eretz Yisrael*.

Ironically, it seems like yeast bread is the bread of affliction, and flatbread is the bread of freedom.

Pesach
Rabbi David Novak, 2017

Chad Gadya, that melodious Aramaic tune sung at seder's end, has a cumulative lyric. A small animal—a goat—suffers from being eaten by a cat that the dog bit, each stanza expanding, until God slices the throat of the Angel of Death. As Joseph Tabory in *The JPS Commentary on the Haggadah* (p. 67) notes, "The basic idea of the version of the song in the haggadah is that every deed will find its retribution and for every strong thing there is something stronger."

As an allegory for the Jewish people, *Chad Gadya* expresses the conviction that God will ultimately intervene in Jewish suffering, especially collective suffering. Our people's ongoing suffering is one of our most profound questions—a question with no good answer (perhaps that is why Job is included in our biblical canon: to remind us that there are questions with no good answers).

Perhaps we sing *Chad Gadya* simply because those who came before us sang it. We join our voices to theirs to affirm the hope that there will again be a redemptive moment, a time when God will once again hear our cry.

At the same time, we sing it to remind ourselves that in a world badly in need of redemptive acts, we need our liberation narrative that reminds us of those liberating and redemptive acts that remain in our hands to perform.

Pesach
Rabbi Michael Boyden, 2018

Ask anyone what Pesach is about and they will tell you that it is the festival of freedom. It was not by chance that the American civil rights movement of the 1960s and the subsequent struggle to release *refuseniks* trapped in the former Soviet Union adopted the slogan "Let My people go."

However, that's not the end of the sentence. The call to Pharaoh to release the Israelites from slavery is followed no less than seven times by *v'yaavduni*, "that they may serve Me." In the Egyptian cultural context of the time, where Pharaoh ("great" or "high") was viewed as the gods' representative on earth, the call to worship the One God was a threat to Pharaoh's legitimacy in the same way religious faith challenged the supremacy of the Soviet empire and its credo.

Interestingly, the word *chofesh* ("freedom") does not appear even once in the Exodus story, but only later in connection with the release of Hebrew slaves in the seventh year. Furthermore, the Modern Hebrew term for "freedom," *cheirut*, does not appear in the Torah even once, but is used in the well-known interpretation of Exod. 32:16 in *Mishnah Pirkei Avot* 6:2: *Al tikra charut ela cheirut*, "Do not read 'engraved' but rather 'freed.'"

What is the difference between "Let My people go" and "Let My people go that they may serve Me"? We all need frameworks. Without them, we are rudderless ships on a tempestuous sea. Pesach, then, is not primarily about liberty, but about direction and freedom for a purpose.

S'firat HaOmer
Rabbi Amy Scheinerman, 2016

Pesach is incomplete without Shavuot. Freedom is not an end in itself, but rather a means to justice, peace, and fulfillment. The season is about our journey from *avdut* to *avodah*, from being involuntary slaves to Pharaoh to becoming covenanted servants of God. The period of the Omer is the bridge, and each day is a paving stone along the way. How appropriate to count the steps.

In a way, the season of the Omer mirrors the High Holy Days. At a six-month remove, it affords another opportunity for introspection and spiritual growth. The goal on the High Holy Days is purely personal and relational: we try to repair our relationships and ourselves. During the Omer, our frame is more communal: redemption and revelation were experienced by the entire nation of Israel together.

The kabbalists encouraged their followers to focus on one of the seven lower *s'firot* during each of the seven weeks of the *s'firah* ("Omer Counting")—*Chesed, G'vurah, Tiferet, Netzach, Hod, Y'sod,* and *Malchut*—and in any given week, devote one day to each quality. The *s'firot* are interpreted in many ways, so returning to each of them seven times need not be redundant, but rather expansive, with abundant options and opportunities to learn and teach.

Seven is the number of Creation. Seven squared implies a higher order: the Omer affords us an opportunity to re-create ourselves, to renew ourselves.

S'firat HaOmer
Rabbi Michael Boyden, 2017

Rabbi Chaim Paltiel (thirteenth-century France/Germany) compared the period of the *S'firat HaOmer* to a person counting the days until his loved one would be freed from prison and receive a great gift. The prison symbolizes the time of slavery in Egypt, while the gift was the giving of the Torah.

Since the counting of the Omer relates to the seven weeks between the beginning of the barley harvest at Pesach and the harvesting of wheat at Shavuot, this period would have lost all significance in the Diaspora had it not been for the statement in the *Babylonian Talmud* (*Y'vamot* 62b) that twelve thousand pairs of Rabbi Akiva's students died from a plague between these two holidays "because they did not respect one another." As a consequence, the period of *S'firat HaOmer* ("Counting of the Omer") became a time of mourning. However, many would argue that if we are to mourn for twenty-four thousand of Rabbi Akiva's students who died nearly two thousand years ago, we should mourn throughout the entire year for those who perished in the Holocaust.

Of more relevance to us is the comment by the fourteenth-century Spanish rabbi David Abudraham, who wrote, "Every Jew was busy with his own harvesting. . . . They were commanded to count so that they would not forget when to make their pilgrimage (to Jerusalem on Shavuot)." Many Jews are so busy making a living these days that they leave little time for being Jewish. *S'firat HaOmer* is about remembering who you are even when you have a busy schedule.

S'firat HaOmer
Rabbi Amy Scheinerman, 2017

Forty years of wandering in the wilderness was a formative experience that still resonates in the Jewish soul. *B'midbar Rabbah* 1:7 offers two expositions of "Adonai spoke to Moses in the wilderness of Sinai" (Num. 1:1). First, *Chazal* explain that Torah was given together with fire, water, and wilderness because just as these three are free to all humanity, so, too, are the words of Torah free. Second, only those who make themselves an ownerless wilderness can acquire wisdom and Torah.

As we spend seven weeks preparing to ascend Mount Sinai and receive again God's Torah, we might contemplate the multiple messages in this midrash: Wisdom is "free." It is not the province or possession of one class or group or people. Torah was not given in *Eretz Yisrael* that we might claim a larger portion than anyone else or to be the sole source of wisdom. Hence, we can learn from anyone. That being said, we have our own unique wisdom—tried and true—and it is not enough to enrich ourselves with it. The wisdom we glean from Torah tradition is to be shared with everyone who is interested. "If I am not for myself, who will be for me? If I am for myself alone, what am I? If not now, when?" (*Mishnah Pirkei Avot* 1:14).

Finally, to acquire wisdom, from any source, we must clear away preconceived notions and beliefs that erect barriers against wisdom. In an age when Stephen Colbert's "truthiness" was Merriam-Webster's 2006 Word of the Year (and the Oxford Dictionary's 2016 Word of the Year was "post-truth"), at a time when news is bundled to fit people's ideologies, opening our minds is more important than ever.

S'firat HaOmer
Rabbi Amy Scheinerman, 2018

Commenting on Lev. 23:10, the Ishbitzer Rebbe, Mordechai Yosef Leiner, notes that the Arizal pointed out that *omer* is numerically equivalent to *yakar* (310), hinting to the fact that while God's precious divine light is available to Israel on the first night of Pesach, afterward the temporary illumination is subsequently concealed.

> Therefore, on the second night of Pesach, longing for a return of God's light, a great cry remains in the hearts of all Israel, and they cry out to the blessed God, "How precious [*yakar*] are Your kindnesses, God!" This is what King Solomon spoke of: "Those who love Me I love, and those who seek Me will find Me [*yimtza-un'ni*]" (Prov. 8:17).

The extra *nun* in *yimtza-un'ni* "represents the fifty gates of wisdom in the Torah and on Shavuot" that the mitzvah of the Omer opens to us. *S'firat HaOmer* (Counting of the Omer) thus facilitates the pull of each person's heart toward God. One way for us—whether or not we resonate with Kabbalah—to understand the Ishbitzer Rebbe's message is to recognize that a wonderful Pesach seder lights a spiritual fire in people and that it is difficult to maintain its flame. With the next opportunity for a spiritual high fifty days away, *S'firat HaOmer* can be the bridge (leading through fifty gates) that keeps people on an upward spiritual journey.

While many have produced wonderful materials for the counting the Omer, the Ishbitzer's insight suggests we invest even more heavily in this endeavor.

Chol HaMo-eid Pesach
Rabbi Amy Scheinerman, 2013

Among the many Talmudic conjectures concerning *haolam haba* ("the world-to-come"), we find that of Sh'muel in the *Babylonian Talmud B'rachot* 34b: "There is no difference between our time and the messianic age except that in the future time, *am yisrael* [the People of Israel] will be free from subservience to other nations."

Sh'muel's perspective on slavery is encapsulated in the paragraph *Avadim Hayinu* in the Haggadah, where he pinpoints the beginning of our history of enslavement to the time of our enslavement in Egypt (Deut. 6:21). Much later, Rambam concurs with Sh'muel: redemption is a matter of physical and political freedom.

Rav, however, sees enslavement as a spiritual state of mind. He famously pinpoints the history of our enslavement back to our idolatrous ancestors.

We might consider Sh'muel's interpretation of slavery "physical" and Rav's interpretation "psychological" (encompassing spirit and emotion).

Which comes first? Do we need to desire freedom in order to secure it? Or must we experience freedom to truly think like free people? We have ample examples of people who freed their minds and spirits long before they gained physical freedom; in fact, it was the ideal of freedom that inspired their struggle to be extricated from whatever forms their enslavement took. However, there are people who need someone to "free them" before they can truly understand what it means to be free (something to ponder as we consider what type of approach is appropriate for those who come to us for help).

Moreover, is it in freedom of the spirit or freedom of the body that we, like Moses, glimpse God? "[God] answered [Moses]: I will make all My goodness pass before you, and I will proclaim before you the name Adonai, and the grace that I grant and the compassion that I show. . . . I will take My hand away and you will see My back" (Exod. 33:19–23). Perhaps it is in both.

Chol HaMo-eid Pesach
Rabbi Amy Scheinerman, 2014

The Torah reading for Chol HaMo-eid Pesach includes the passage in which Moses asks to see God and, in Exod. 33:12–23, glimpses God's back. If seeing is believing, then even a glimpse fortifies Moses for the trials and tribulations to come. So, too, the Israelites: *M'chilta Bachodesh* tells us that the Israelites see God as a warrior at the Reed Sea and as a wise elder at Mount Sinai. We do indeed create our own images of God.

How do we gain a sense of God's presence? Rebbe Nachman of Bratzlav, in *K'dushat Levi*, tells us that miraculous transformations of nature bespeak God: "There are two ways of serving our blessed Creator. One comes about as we behold miracles and wonders, the transformation of nature. When God makes natural forces do His bidding, we understand that God rules over all and that all His creatures are obliged to serve Him in awe...The second path is that of true awareness, knowing that He has created all things by the word of His mouth, and that He is able to transform them." This is the better way. In an age where ideas and intellectual pursuits are often steered by scientific thinking, where miracles belong to the realm of myth and legend, and people don't expect a glimpse of God, the *M'chilta* and Rebbe Nachman pave the way for Abraham Joshua Heschel's "radical amazement," the conscious awareness of God as the source of being.

The people we teach, serve, and lead want to find a way to "see" God. Happily, tradition offers many paths to walk.

Seventh Day of Pesach
Rabbi Joshua Minkin, DMin, 2016

"The Eternal is a warrior" (Exod. 15:3).

Torah often employs language that is uncomfortable and even offensive to modern ears. Anthropomorphisms and issues of gender are examples that come to mind. There are also inherent messages that are hard for us to accept. For me, *Shirat HaYam* (the "Song at the Sea") is one of them because it glorifies war and rejoices at our enemy's annihilation. How can I find a way to accept and even rejoice in the message of *Shirat HaYam*?

For me, God is the embodiment or manifestation of my *yetzer tov* ("the good inclination"), not an all-powerful deity that controls events in our world. God is the idealized aspect of me that calls me toward everything positive. Egypt is my wayward, undisciplined, hedonistic self—my *yetzer hara* ("the evil inclination"). In the battle between right and wrong, I root for the good guys.

Athletes and public speakers often use visualizations and affirmations to enhance their performance. By imagining success, their actual performance approaches their virtual performance. Numerous scientific articles attest to the reality of this effect. *Musar* uses these same techniques to shape moral behavior.

I have found that I can use *Shirat HaYam* to visualize my *yetzer hatov* conquering my *yetzer hara*. The unitary force for good vanquishes my myriad shortcomings represented by Pharaoh's soldiers and charioteers being thrown into the sea that comes crashing down around them, obliterating them forever.

While I will never be wholly without faults, aiming high helps me progress.

Seventh Day of Pesach
Rabbi Joshua Minkin, DMin, 2017

All of us are familiar with the midrash about Nachshon ben Amminadab taking the initiative of walking into the Reed Sea until the water rose to his nose. At that moment, the sea splits and the Children of Israel are able to walk safely across.

But there is another midrash that tries to reconcile the account of crossing the Reed Sea in Exodus with the description in Ps. 106:7:

> "But they were rebellious at the sea, at the Red Sea." The Rabbis ask: Why does the text repeat "at the sea" twice? Their first rebellion was their refusal to go into the sea. However, when they descended into the midst of the sea, they found it was full of clay, because it was still wet from the water. . . . Reuven then said to Shimon, "In Egypt we had clay, and now, in the sea, again we have clay. In Egypt, we had mortar and bricks, and now, in the sea, once again we have mortar and bricks." (*Sh'mot Rabbah* 24:1)

This was a second rebellion. Something extraordinary had just happened, but Reuven and Shimon's eyes were closed to the miracle that had just occurred. The sea may have split, but they saw only the clay lining the bottom of the seabed. All they noticed was how much the mud inconvenienced them. Freedom didn't feel any different from slavery. The Rabbis want us to see that focusing only on ourselves and being blind to the infinite wonders God creates every day is a form of rebellion against God.

Yom HaShoah
Rabbi Janice Garfunkel, z"l, 2010

I propose that we never use phrases like "Nazi beasts." I know that survivors themselves often refer to Nazis this way. However, it is morally wrong to deny the humanity of even Nazis. More importantly, it is unwise and an act of self-deception. They were not beasts; they were, alas, human beings created in God's image, no less than you or I.

One devastating lesson from the Shoah is that human beings, created *b'tzelem elohim*, are capable of a degree of cruelty toward other human beings that is simply incomprehensible to most of us. As far as we know, these *b'nei adam* ("human beings") were not aberrant, not created differently, and did not possess some genetic defect. What is appalling is that under certain circumstances, normal people—at least some normal people—are capable of abnormal cruelty, and the large majority of people are capable of tolerating and ignoring indescribably cruel acts committed by others.

Only a tiny minority actually stood up against the Nazis and risked their own lives to save Jews. Could any person become either a Nazi perpetrator or a righteous gentile? Is it possible that you or I could have done such evil things? Is it the teachings of Judaism, including the fundamental lesson that every human being is created *b'tzelem elohim*, that make it impossible for me to imagine myself descending to such depths of cruelty? If so, what a powerful image for the truth of Torah is indeed "a Tree of Life to those who hold fast to it."

Yom HaShoah
Rabbi David Novak, 2011

The method to Claude Schwartzmann's artistry in his 1985 film *Shoah* is to let the evil of the Shoah unspool slowly, never using archival footage, and only letting the people speak for themselves. These people are the victims who are brought to tears as if it were only yesterday that they were in the camps, having to disentomb parents and children, including their own. These people include the train operators who drove the people to the camps, who were given vodka to drown out the screams behind them. These people include the locals who claim to have warned the people, but talk is cheap when it is always someone else's fault.

Shoah is nine and one-half hours long, a speck in time when one thinks about the Nazis' and their collaborators' killing machine. It is tough to watch, but watch it one must, remembering that our people experienced genocide just for being Jewish.

Yom HaShoah
Rabbi Charles Middleburgh, PhD, 2018

Avram Shlonsky's oath to "remember it all, remember and never forget" is always on my mind at this time of the year.

The anaphora is striking; it is as if Shlonsky tells us first to remember for the sake of remembering and then to never forget (by itself an insufficient response).

The world in which we live, the context in which we still bear the pain of the Shoah, is one in which the Shoah has not only been forgotten, but actively denied. We can fulfill our moral duty, as Shlonsky frames it, by doing two vital things: we must never forget the cruelty with which the world has visited us, but we must also remember the heights we have attained, the contributions to human civilization that we have made.

We must never forget, in the midst of that remembrance, that as much as we have been treated with bestial cruelty, we have also been showered with acts of decency and kindness; that during the worst moments of the Shoah, there were those who risked everything for a Jewish family, a Jewish child. The stories of these righteous, when they are known, become a tapestry of remembrance, a rejoinder to denial, of the capacity of men and women for extreme bravery and compassion even at a mortal risk.

On Yom HaShoah the statistics still haunt us. We will always remember those who are gone. Let us never forget those who manifested human decency, who saved lives and in so doing helped preserve the Jewish people.

Yom HaZikaron
Rabbi Michael Boyden, 2010

Many have mixed feelings about Yom HaZikaron being observed in Israel on the day before Independence Day. There are those who contend that it is difficult to cope with the rough transition from a day of national mourning to one of celebration. Others argue that it is precisely the onset of Yom HaAtzma-ut that enables them to transcend the deep emotions of Yom HaZikaron.

Israel's first president, Chaim Weizmann, is quoted as having said, "No country is given to its people on a silver platter." The Israeli poet Natan Alterman reinterpreted that notion when he had two weary soldiers, unclear whether dead or alive, declare in his poem "The Silver Platter," "We are the silver platter on which the Jewish state was given to you."

Yom HaZikaron is the day on which we remember the more than twenty-two thousand members of the Israel Defense Forces who gave their lives in defense of the State of Israel. Without their sacrifice, there would be no Israel. In a world in which there are those, including not a few Jews, who question our very right to exist in a Jewish state, students of history know only too well the suffering that we endured when we were powerless.

Nevertheless, the existence of our country comes with a price tag. There are few families in Israel who have not been touched in one way or another by the loss in battle of those closest and dearest to them. Our beloved son Jonathan z"l was killed by the Hezbollah in Lebanon while defending Israel's northern towns and kibbutzim.

Yom HaZikaron is a reminder that Israel's survival cannot be taken for granted. Our soldiers, sailors, and airmen and airwomen are the silver platter that makes it possible.

Yom HaZicharon
Rabbi Michael Boyden, 2018

Israeli poet Natan Alterman wrote:

> Dressed in battle gear, dirty, shoes heavy with grime, they quietly ascend the path to change their clothes, to wipe away the traces of a gruesome day and night on the front line. . . . Yet the dew of their youth is still visible on their brows. Thus they stand at attention, giving no sign of life or death. Then a nation in tears and amazement asks: "Who are you?" And they silently reply: "We are the silver platter on which you were given the Jewish state" ("The Silver Platter").

We all celebrate Israel's Independence Day, but it comes with a price. Eighteen-year-olds in other countries are at college, savoring independence and enjoying the experiences of a new chapter in their lives. Not so our children, who face the harsh discipline of military service and are sent to the front line in defense of their country.

Zelda wrote, "Each of us has a name given to us by God, and given to us by our father and mother. . . . Each of us has a name given to us by the sea, and given to us by our death."

When the sirens sound at 11:00 a.m., everything stops. People get out of their cars even on Israel's busiest highways and stand at attention for two minutes in memory of our fallen, who gave their lives so that there could be an Israel.

Israel's military cemeteries are packed with those who come to pay their respects and identify with those of us who mourn. Their presence is a reminder that the sacrifice of our children is not to be taken for granted.

Yom HaAtzma-ut
Rabbi Amy Scheinerman, 2010

There was a time when we were a landed people and our covenant with God seemed inconceivable without the Land. It played a central and pivotal role. Our formative stories, from Avraham onward, revolved around coming into the Land, leaving the Land, being exiled from the Land, and returning to the Land. For more than two millennia, the messianic vision was inseparable from the Land. Over the past several generations, many lives have been sacrificed to secure Jewish sovereignty over land to build and protect a Jewish state.

For some of us, the State of Israel is a refuge should calamity again strike. But for many, it is far more: it is *reishit tz'michat g'ulateinu* ("the beginning of our redemption"), tinged with redemption. It is home to many vibrant expressions of Judaism and exciting approaches to Jewish living.

However, there is a considerable gap between vision and reality. For all Israel's diversity, Jewish religious rights remain in the hands of a narrow and narrow-minded minority, rather than the province of all. Events this winter at the Kotel have driven that home.

For some, this is reason to surrender to despair: if Israel cannot meet our expectations, perhaps it is not worth our emotional investment. Yet the vision is worthy, and therefore it is our responsibility to bring it to reality. While it is sad that our struggle is internal, it is still a sacred struggle. *Lo alecha ham'lachah ligmor, v'lo atah ben chorin l'hibateil mimenah,* "You are not required to complete the task, yet you are not free to withdraw from it" (*Mishnah Pirkei Avot* 2:16).

Yom HaAtzma-ut
Rabbi Michael Boyden, 2011

More than half of American Jews under the age of thirty-five interviewed in a survey conducted by sociologists Stephen Cohen and Ari Kelman (*Beyond Distancing: Young Adult American Jews and Their Alienation from Israel*), declared that they would not view the destruction of Israel as a personal tragedy. Indeed, the historian Jonathan Sarna wrote, "Young Jews today often view Israel through the lens of contemporary media. They fixate upon its unloveliest warts." (Jonathan Sarna, *The Gap Generation*).

These observations attest to the growing gulf between much of Diaspora Jewry and the State of Israel and should serve as a wake-up call for all Jewish leaders at a time when the Jewish state is celebrating its sixty-third birthday. Young Jews on whose radar screens Israel does not even appear or those who are alienated by consistent attempts to delegitimize her do not, of course, remember the days when Jews all over Europe were fleeing for their lives while most of the world turned its back on them. At a time when the Arab world yearns for Al-Quds and there is even a special unit of the Iranian Revolutionary Guard bearing that name, it would indeed be a strange stroke of fate were much of the Jewish People to sever ties with the State of Israel.

To distance ourselves from Israel means to split the Jewish world in two. To leave Israel out of our collective consciousness means to reduce our Jewish identity to that of a religious or ethnic experience.

One of the challenges that we face as Jewish leaders today is to ensure that this does not happen. It begins with us.

Yom HaAtzma-ut
Rabbi Michael Boyden, 2018

If you had told a Jew in Auschwitz in 1944 that there would be a Jewish state four years later, he or she would have told you that you were dreaming.

Since Israel's independence was declared, its Jewish population has increased elevenfold. There are more Jews living in Israel today than in any other country. Israel's GDP stands at over $300 billion. Life expectancy is among the highest in the world. Israel ranks as the second most important high-tech center, and its shekel is the world's second strongest currency.

For two thousand years we prayed, "Next year in Jerusalem" and "Gather in our exiles from the four corners of the earth to our land." Those heartfelt sentiments are now an option dependent not upon divine providence, but upon personal choice.

Nonetheless Israel has its problems. The messianic aspirations of Jewish zealots, coupled with Palestinian obstinacy, harm efforts to achieve a two-state solution. The Iranian threat to wipe Israel off the map remains a constant challenge for our defense forces. The power exercised by religious political parties has given the Orthodox establishment the means to discriminate not only against Reform Jews, but also against all those who do not share their worldview. As we celebrate Israel's achievements and seventieth birthday, we are painfully aware of its shortcomings. We recognize that the *y'rushalayim shel matah* ("the Wordly Jerusalem") falls far short of the *y'rushalayim shel maalah* ("the Heavenly Jerusalem").

There are many challenges, but there is also much for which to be grateful.

Lag BaOmer
Rabbi Stephen Wylen, 2010

There is a kabbalistic tradition to celebrate Lag BaOmer as the *hilula* (*yahrzeit*) of Rabbi Shimon bar Yochai. While RaShBY is renowned as the central character of the *Zohar*, in a broader sense, he represents all of the Rabbinic Sages.

The connection between Rabbi Akiva and Lag BaOmer is already well established, based on the legend that Judaizes the prohibitions of the month of May, which originate in Roman superstition.

We Reform Jews, if we still cherish rational religion, may not wish to return to prohibiting weddings during the loveliest of months. We can find enduring meaning in Lag BaOmer if we develop the kabbalistic tradition of the *hilula*.

The sacred concepts of Judaism are encapsulated in holidays that celebrate archetypal events: Pesach is redemption; Shavuot is revelation. The greatest innovation of Judaism was made along after the Torah holidays were already set: the central place we accord to Torah learning, and our fateful decision to replace the priesthood with the scholars of Torah. *Talmud torah k'neged kulam*, "The study of Torah outweighs them all." Shavuot and Simchat Torah celebrate Torah as a heavenly gift.

Yet no sacred day commemorates Torah scholarship. Lag BaOmer may fill this gap.

Lag BaOmer
Rabbi Amy Scheinerman, 2011

We commemorate the *yahrzeit* of Rabbi Shimon ben Yochai on Lag BaOmer. The *Babylonian Talmud Shabbat* 33b, tells us that having voiced sharp criticism at the cultural values of the Roman Empire, Rabbi Shimon hid in a cave for thirteen years until the emperor died, annulling the edict against him. His son-in-law Rabbi Pinchas ben Yair escorted him from the cave to a bathhouse.

[Rabbi Pinchas] took [Rabbi Shimon] into the baths and massaged his flesh. Seeing the clefts in his body, he wept, tears streaming from his eyes. "Woe to me that I see you in such a state!" [Rabbi Pinchas] cried out. "You should be happy to see me like this," [Rabbi Shimon] retorted, "for if you did not see me in such a state you would not find me so [learned]." Rabbi Shimon had neglected his health in favor of learning.

Must an elevated soul or intellect come at the expense of health? Rabbi Shimon expresses contempt for the vulgar materialism of Roman culture. But is neglecting our bodies—the very ones that make Torah study possible—a religiously responsible response? We have such a complicated and fraught relationship with our bodies. Our tradition promotes health, but also learning at the expense of health.

Avot D'Rabbi Natan tells us that Hillel partook of the Roman baths because he considered it a mitzvah to care for the image of God. So should we.

Americans are growing increasingly unhealthy, at great cost to everyone. We should teach that doing our best to stay healthy—physically and psychologically—is a religious obligation. Some of our congregations now have a social worker or nurse on staff. *Kol hakavod* to them. Respect.

Lag BaOmer
Rabbi Joshua Minkin, DMin, 2017

A rebbe lay dying. His Chasidim surrounded his deathbed singing his praises: his vast learning, his great works of charity, his fervent spirituality. When they finally stopped, the rebbe sat up and asked, "And does no one comment on my great humility?"

What's wrong with this picture? It is clear that the rebbe's motivation for being humble (if he truly was) did not exemplify the dictum of Antigonos of Socho: "Do not be like servants who serve their master in order to receive a reward" (*Mishnah Pirkei Avot* 1:3). Rather, he feigned humility for the sake of his reputation.

The *midah* ("attribute") of humility has special importance for Lag BaOmer.

Kabbalists associate each week of the Omer with one of the lower seven emanations (*s'firot*). Each day of the week is also assigned a *s'firah*. The fifth emanation, *Hod*, represents humility. Lag BaOmer is the fifth day of the fifth week. Double *Hod*. What does it mean to be humble in one's humility?

Alan Morinis writes in *Everyday Holiness* (p. 53), "Proper humility means having the right relationship to self, giving self-neither too big or too small a role in one's life." Too large an ego results in arrogance, too little leads to self-abasement.

Lag BaOmer is a good time to take stock of our humility, which differs from other *midot*. If you are doing it right, no one notices, not even you, because you are humble in your humility.

Lag BaOmer
Rabbi Amy Scheinerman, 2018

There is an irony to the joy of Lag BaOmer: Amidst an extended period of mourning commemorating a plague that ravaged the students of Rabbi Akiva, we joyously celebrate the thirty-third day of the Omer, the *yahrzeit* of Rabbi Shimon bar Yochai. The legend that the plague was lifted on the thirty-third day of the Omer would seem to account for the brief cessation of mourning, but the story of Rabbi Shimon's *yahrzeit* seems also to hold sway as the reason for bonfires, symbolizing the light of his mystical revelations. Yet when is a *yahrzeit* a day for festive celebration?

Among kabbalists, the *yahrzeit* of a tzaddik is a *yom hilula*, a day of festive rejoicing. Ovadia Bartenura (1445–1515) wrote, "On the eighteenth of Iyar, the *yahrzeit* of Rabbi Shimon bar Yochai, people from areas surrounding [Meron, north of Tz'fat, the site of Rabbi Shimon's tomb] gather and light huge bonfires in addition to candles. Many barren women have been helped and the sick have been healed when they made a promise and donation for this holy site." To this day, huge crowds gather in Meron in anticipation of Lag BaOmer and joyously celebrate his *yahrzeit* in accord with the assertion by Chaim Vital (1542–1620) that Rabbi Shimon referred to the day of his death as *yom simchato* ("the day of his joy," *Shaar HaKavanot*), because on his last day, he revealed all the mystical secrets he had learned, many during his years in a cave (*Babylonian Talmud Shabbat* 33b–34a).

Beyond mentioning their accomplishments and reciting *Kaddish*, might we consider celebrating the *yahrzeit* of those we consider to be tzaddikim?

Yom Y'rushalayim
Rabbi Mark Levin, 2018

JPS Hebrew-English Tanakh translates Ps. 122:3 as "Jerusalem built up, a city knit together." We've likely all struggled with interpreting the Hebrew of the latter phrase, *k'ir shechub'rah lah yachdav*.

Robert Alter approximates the political reality more closely with his translation: "Jerusalem built like a town that is fastened together."

Targum Yonatan offers a *d'rash* rather than a translation: "Jerusalem that is built in heaven [*bir'kiah*], a city that is joined together as one on the earth [*b'arah*]."

Rashi elaborates further: "And our Rabbis said, 'There is a Jerusalem built in the heavens [*bashamayim*], and in the future the Jerusalem below will be like her.'"

Brown-Driver-Briggs connotes Jerusalem with "City" or "Foundation of Peace," and Onkelos on Gen. 14:18 associates Melchizedek's city called "Peace" (*Shalem*) explicitly with Jerusalem, becoming the "City of Peace."

Consider this paradox: the more central Jerusalem becomes, the more divisive the city. Not only is the walled Jerusalem divided into four separate quarters, but the three Abrahamic religions, each with its essential shrine, fight for control of so-called holy places. Where is the *k'ir shechub'rah lah yachdav*? No wonder only the Religious Zionists in Israel care about Jerusalem Day.

How magnificent would it be if we Reform Jews, in celebrating Jerusalem Day, pursued the ideal Jerusalem, cooperating in creating means by which to bring the heavenly Jerusalem closer to the earthly? Perhaps *Targum Yonatan* foresaw the future already two millennia ago (forgive my paraphrase): "Jerusalem that is built in heaven is the city brought together as one on the earth." Would such a city transformed not be heavenly?

Shavuot
Rabbi Janice Garfunkel, z"l, 2010

In Leonard Fein's *Where Are We?* (p. 26), he tells a story of a man in Haifa smiling at a Chasid he passes, causing the Chasid to ask, "Do I know you?" "Yes, we met at Sinai" was the quick-witted reply. Smacking his forehead, the Chasid answers, "Oh, yes! Forgive me, it was so hot and crowded that day. How have you been?"

Fein goes on to write that the question whether or not Sinai actually happened is irrelevant. What matters is that he was there. This is a deliciously complex and (maybe?) Reform point of view. Whether or not the event happened in history, what we Jews have in common is that we choose to share the metaphor. We live as if it did happen. We are shaped and molded in our very being by the reality of Sinai, by the covenant into which our ancestors entered, and by which we are bound.

For thousands of years our people has been shaped by a narrative, by a story of redemption: first the physical redemption from Egypt, then the spiritual redemption at Sinai. I don't really believe that God gave the Torah word for word to Moses at Mount. Sinai. But I do believe that every Jew should now be living as if there was a Mount Sinai moment and that each of our lives today must be an answer, a response, to that encounter.

Shavuot
Rabbi Amy Scheinerman, 2011

Why eat dairy foods on Shavuot?

Doesn't the divine taste of cheesecake suffice as explanation? Perhaps *Shir HaShirim* (Song of Songs) 4:11—"Like honey and milk are under your tongue"—is the original recipe for cheesecake.

More conventional commentators understand *Shir HaShirim* 4:11 as Rabbi Akiva understood it: "Like honey and milk [the Torah] are under your tongue." Milk is likened to Torah because it sustains us. I hasten to note that the context of the verse is marriage—evoking the covenant between God and Israel forged at Sinai on Shavuot.

The *Babylonian Talmud B'chorot* 6b, supplies perhaps the most traditional explanation. The Torah given at Sinai includes the laws of kashrut. The Israelites did not have kosher pots and pans, nor did they yet know how to do *sh'chitah* ("ritual slaughtering"), so they ate dairy, which requires no advance preparation.

One more golden oldie: the gematria for *chalav* (milk) is forty, mirroring the forty days Moses spent on Mount Sinai.

Shavuot is the culmination of a spiritual process that is initiated on Pesach, when we retell and relive our redemption from Egypt. For seven weeks we march toward Sinai and record our progress as we count the Omer. For seven weeks we contemplate our covenant with God and our relationship to Torah. Each year we take the same journey because our relationship with God and our understanding of Torah change as we change. What remains constant, however, is that Torah is God's gift of spiritual nourishment to us—mother's milk—that we might grow in our capacity for insight, compassion, and love.

Shavuot
Rabbi Joshua Minkin, DMin, 2015

Shavuot is a holiday with an inferiority complex. I suggest that Shavuot, sandwiched between Pesach and the Yamim Noraim (Days of Awe), should be a time of formulating new resolutions and recommitting to old ones.

It has been eight months since we formulated our last resolutions on the High Holy Days; six months since our resolutions for the secular year. Our fortitude may be flagging. The word *shavuot* pointed slightly differently means "oaths." An oath is a serious promise. This is the perfect opportunity to reexamine the oaths we made and see in what way we are off target and what we need to do to get back on the right track. Shavuot marks the time when God and Israel exchanged vows. We can take this opportunity to review and renew our own vows to God and to ourselves.

Shavuot has long been a time when we hold confirmation ceremonies, at which our youth consciously recommit themselves to the responsibilities they assumed when becoming bar/bat mitzvah. Why shouldn't we take the same opportunity to reassess and recommit ourselves to the projects we took on to improve ourselves? A collective social action project on Shavuot afternoon would help fulfill resolutions to do more *tikkun olam*. How many of us made a resolution to study more? *Tikkunei Leil Shavuot* allow us to make good on that resolution.

For those who have broken resolutions to diet, we have an opportunity to have one last piece of cheesecake before starting our resolution anew (a small piece for those still dieting). *Chag samei-ach!*

Shavuot
Rabbi Amy Scheinerman, 2017

We often joke about the Jewish obsession with food. But for the Chasidic master Dov Ber Friedman of Mezeritch, ingesting food can be tantamount to ingesting Torah. He draws a beautiful connection between the physicality of eating and the spirituality of Torah learning, quoting from *Tanchuma B'shalach* 20 where the two are fused: "Torah was given only to those who ate the manna."

Just as it took Moses forty days to learn Torah from God, Dov Ber tells us, so it takes a student forty years to learn Torah from a teacher. For this reason, God needed to provide supplemental spiritual sustenance to keep the people going in the form of manna and Shabbat.

With what do we need to provide ourselves and others to promote the digestion of Torah throughout people's lives?

Dov Ber also quotes the Torah: "A person does not live by bread alone, but by all that comes forth from the mouth of Adonai" (Deut. 8:3). Hence, as *Mishnah Pirkei Avot* 3:4 asserts, "Three who sit at a table and speak words of Torah, it is as though they ate at God's table." Dov Ber concludes, "Everything contains Torah . . . the true sage can attain Torah through food. Eating itself is engaging with Torah."

Is Shavuot the commemoration of a mythical event? Are we looking back to some moment in the past? Or is it a stopping point on our ongoing, forward-looking journey to Mount Sinai?

Shavuot
Rabbi Ruth Adar, 2018

In ancient times Sukkot was the most beloved holiday of the year, so much so that it was referred to as *HeChag*, "The Holy Day." The people of Israel loved Sukkot and celebrated it with the enthusiasm we today bring to Passover.

Passover celebrates part one of the great drama of the Jewish people—the Exodus from Egypt. It is currently the *chag* (festival) celebrated by the greatest number of Jews around the world. On Shavuot, we celebrate part two of the great drama. Fifty days following Passover, deep in the wilderness of Sinai, the Israelites stand at the foot of Horeb, and in a final act of accepting the freedom God won for them, they agree to accept the Torah and its 613 mitzvot. They freely bind themselves to God. That covenant will shape their lives—as well as our lives and destiny—forever.

Why is this *chag* practically a secret holiday to modern-day Jews? Perhaps Shavuot sits in the shadow of the work and the drama of Passover, despite the seven weeks of the Omer. Perhaps the American rhythm of life—school is letting out and people are leaving for vacation—conflicts with the Jewish rhythm of the year. As we celebrate Shavuot today, it certainly lacks the drama of Passover.

But I wonder: If Sukkot was *HeChag* (The Festival) in the past, and Passover is *HeChag* today, perhaps Shavuot will be *HeChag* at some time in the future. Perhaps some years from now its message will come to the fore and we will come to fully appreciate its meaning.

Can we imagine the circumstances under which Shavuot would come into its own as a beloved festival?

ט' באב Tishah B'Av

Tishah B'Av
Rabbi Amy Scheinerman, 2010

Avot D'Rabbi Natan depicts Rabbi Y'hoshua ben Chananya in deep mourning over the loss of the Temple:

> One time Rabbi Yochanan ben Zakkai was walking in Jerusalem with Rabbi Y'hoshua and they beheld the Temple in ruins. "Woe to us," cried Rabbi Y'hoshua, "for this House where atonement was made for Israel's sins now lies in ruins!" Rabban Yochanan answered, "We have another source of atonement, the practice of *g'milut chasadim*, as it says, 'I desire loving-kindness and not sacrifice' (Hosea 6:6)" (*Avot D'Rabbi Nathan* 4).

The *Babylonian Talmud Bava M'tzia* 60b, however, portrays Rabbi Y'hoshua as criticizing those who engaged in ascetic mourning practices in the aftermath of the destruction of the Second Temple:

> My sons, come and listen to me. Not to mourn at all is impossible, because the blow has fallen. To mourn overmuch is also impossible, because we do not impose on the community a hardship that the majority cannot endure.

Many today forgo Tishah B'Av altogether because they do not mourn the loss of the sacrificial cult. But Tishah B'Av is about the massive loss of Jewish life, sovereignty over the Land, and many other catastrophes that have checked our history. Perhaps the advice of Rabbi Y'hoshua—

not to mourn overmuch—is helpful here, but he also states that "not to mourn at all is impossible." Much of our strength lies in our ability to maintain continuity and connection with the generations who came before. The destruction of the Second Temple was an unprecedented crisis—politically, socially, religiously, and spiritually—and ultimately gave birth to Rabbinic Judaism, which we can acknowledge in commemorating the day, reminding ourselves that even in crisis and catastrophe there is hope.

Tishah B'Av
Rabbi Janice Garfunkel, z"l, 2011

Some Jews feel very uncomfortable about having real power. We were powerless for over two thousand years, and we got used to it. Being on the outside can feel, ironically, like a safe place to be. When things go wrong in a society—and they always do—the outsider can say, "It is not my fault!" It is easy to be the critic. The outsider can feel both powerful and righteous.

When the power is placed in our own hands, however, we discover that even the right actions have negative consequences, especially when there is an enemy trying to destroy us. We also learn that (as in our individual lives) we can control what we do, but no matter how powerful we may be, we cannot control what others do. So even when we do the right things, bad things can still happen to us and to others.

Tishah B'Av is so very rich in themes! How amazing our history is! We were powerless for so long. We are still bent, somewhat, into the stooped shape of an exiled and battered people. We are still *dor hamidbar* (the generation of the wilderness). Or, as some Zionists would say, some of us are still bowed over by our Diaspora mentality, while Zionists stand erect and proud with a gun and a plow in their hands, courageously embracing power and responsibility.

On this day of memory and commemoration, we can explore the theme of a homeland lost and regained, of power lost and power regained. Having power is better! But it takes some getting used to.

Tishah B'Av
Rabbi Louis Rieser, 2014

In the 1970s I observed Tishah B'Av at the Kotel. I saw people for whom the *chorban* ("destruction") possessed a palpable immediacy. They wailed and beat their breasts as if the destruction had just occurred. I could not experience the loss in any emotional sense.

In the 1980s, following the lead of friends, I blended Tishah B'Av with the observance of Hiroshima/Nagasaki Day. The words of the survivors, recorded by Robert Jay Lifton in *Death in Life: Survivors of Hiroshima* eerily echo those of Lamentations. These modern words provided me with an analogy through which to understand our ancient disaster.

One example: "He has worn away my flesh and skin; he broke my bones. He besieged and encircled me with bitterness and travail. He has placed me in darkness like the eternally dead" (Lam. 3:4–6).

> I had the sensation that my whole body had been split. . . . But I didn't know what had happened, and everything seemed strange. . . . I asked my friend whether anything had happened to my face. . . . She cried out to me and said that I too had been burned and should go home. . . . I touched my face and the skin stuck to my finger. That frightened me. And when I touched my nose, I had no sensation of my nose but my finger felt something swollen and hot (Lifton, *Death in Life*, p. 175).

I wish I could feel the destruction of the Temple, the place where God caused The Name to dwell, deep in my *kishkes*. But it is not my experience, and *Eichah* does not lead me to that understanding. The atomic catastrophe, which still threatens our world, affords me a brief glimpse into the dimensions of that earlier destruction. Through analogy, I can begin to feel our two-thousand-year-old loss.

Tishah B'Av
Rabbi Michael Boyden, 2015

"How solitary lies the city, once so full of people!" So begins the Book of Lamentations, traditionally read on Tishah B'Av.

But now things are different. More Jews live in Jerusalem today than at any time in recorded history.

For many, the Temple that once stood in Jerusalem was never God's house. As even King Solomon acknowledged in God's name, "The heaven of heavens cannot contain You; how much less this house that I have built" (I Kings 8:27).

The destruction of the Temple was and is, of course, a tragedy for many. However, the sacrificial cult was, in Maimonides's words, "a deeply ingrained and universal practice with which people were brought up" (*Guide for the Perplexed* 3:32).

On Tishah B'Av, we mourn not only the destruction of the Temple and the cessation of that cult, but perhaps primarily the loss of Jewish sovereignty.

While there are many who pray for the establishment of a Third Temple and prepare for that eventuality, most of us see the sacrificial cult as belonging to the past. We do not mourn for the destruction of the Temple, but rather yearn for the day when, in the words of the prophet Zechariah, "The fast of the fourth month and of the fifth, the seventh and the tenth shall become festivals of joy and gladness" (Zech. 8:19).

Today Jewish sovereignty is once again established in our ancient land. However, the fact that Jerusalem still remains a divided city and the day has yet to come when, in Isaiah's words, "My house shall be called a house of prayer for all peoples" (Isa. 56:7)—that is still a reason to mourn.

Tishah B'Av
Rabbi Amy Scheinerman, 2016

For the early Chasidim, our world mirrored the cosmic realm. The Tabernacle, and after it the Temple, was not only the nexus between heaven and earth, but reflected the very structure of the cosmos. The eighteenth-century Chasidic master Ze'ev Wolf of Zhytomir extends the parallels to include the human body as a reflection of the Temple. He draws a line from our souls to God. That line goes directly through the Temple, and specifically through the Holy of Holies that is our heart.

In *Or HaMeir*, Ze'ev Wolf writes:

> The Sages taught (*Babylonian Talmud B'rachot* 4:5): "Align your heart toward the Holy of Holies [during prayer]." Their intent was to teach

us that a person's form and its limbs correspond to the structure of the Tabernacle and the number of its holy vessels. It follows that you must put your midot in order and build yourself up as a complete structure from head to toe, in order to align yourself with the Temple. Then doing something repugnant will not even occur to you because you have become mindful of the great sanctity of the Holy of Holies. No impure forces may come into that space. Even the High Priest entered it only once a year to perform the service. This is how you sanctify your heart, which corresponds to the Holy of Holies. Your heart is a *mishkan*, a dwelling place for holiness.

For Ze'ev Wolf, the health of our souls has cosmic significance beyond our personal lives. For liberal Jews struggling with the meaning of Tishah B'Av, this might be a helpful teaching.

It will have to suffice.

Tishah B'Av
Rabbi Stephen Wylen, 2017

When the Temple was destroyed, asceticism increased.

> Rabbi Y'hoshua debated with the ascetics, saying, "Perhaps you should refrain from bread, since the grain offering is no longer offered." They replied, "We will stop eating bread." He said, "The first fruits are no longer offered." They replied, "We will stop eating produce." He said, "The water libation is no longer offered. Will you cease from drinking water? Rather, this is the way: Build a home and plaster the walls, but leave a corner unfinished. Hold a feast but leave out one ingredient. A woman may wear her jewelry, but leave aside one ornament. And those who mourn for Jerusalem will merit seeing her joy renewed" (*Babylonian Talmud Bava Batra* 60b).

The Rabbis saved Judaism after the destruction. Had Judaism depended upon the *aveilei tziyon* ("Zion mourners") it would have been its end. Encapsulated in the fifth of the *Sheva B'rachot*, our Sages taught us one of Judaism's most important lessons: even in our happiest hour, we take a moment to mourn the incompletion of the world. We mourn in measure, and we celebrate life.

For too many Jews today, Judaism has become a sentimental occasion for mourning the Holocaust and, when they attend synagogue, to recite

Kaddish for their entire list of deceased ancestors. For these Jews, Judaism is not a way of celebrating life. There is no future in such a Judaism.

We place all of our sorrows into one day of the year—the ninth day of the month of Av. The rest of the year we rejoice.

Tishah B'Av
Rabbi Louis Rieser, 2018

Forty-four years ago, on Tishah B'Av, I stood in the Kotel Plaza watching a dozen American teenage girls approach the Western Wall. They watched as an older woman passionately wailed with grief, as if the Temple had only just been destroyed and she were standing amidst its wreckage. The teenagers looked bewildered. Clearly, this was beyond their experience and comprehension. The older woman looked at them and said in Yiddish, "What kind of Jewish girl doesn't pour out her heart to the wall?" Seeing that the girls did not comprehend a word, she repeated her question in Hebrew, which they understood no better.

How different are we from these girls? How many languages—culturally, historically, religiously—removed are we from fully understanding the question and having a response? Many of us have ignored the question long enough. It is time for us, as liberal Jews, to sort out our relationship to Tishah B'Av so that we can find the right modality or modalities to respond to the old woman's question. Perhaps the Rabbis got it right: Tishah B'Av can serve us, as it did them, as a framework to mourn every catastrophe that feels earth-shattering, from terror attacks to school shootings to natural calamities. What is more, we survived Tishah B'Av, found ways to draw close and comfort one another, and went on to live and thrive and again feel hope.

ט"ו באב   *Tu B'Av*

Tu B'Av
Rabbi Amy Scheinerman, 2017

The Mishnah ends Tractate *Taanit* (4:8) on a high note: "Rabban Shimon ben Gamliel said, 'Never were there more joyous days for Israel than the fifteenth of Av and Yom Kippur.'" On both occasions, young women went out dressed in white and danced in the vineyards to attract the eye of a suitable young man. Imagining the young women going out in the evening—when the moon would be full—paints a romantic picture, and everyone loves romance. Thus, Tu B'Av has recently been dubbed the "Jewish Valentine's Day," at least in English-speaking countries.

One might suspect Tu B'Av of being as frivolous as Valentine's Day until one reads the entire mishnah. There are several elements of Rabban Shimon ben Gamliel's account that are often ignored: The young women did not go out in their own white dresses; they borrowed dresses "in order not to cause shame to those who did not have their own." No doubt, this also masked the wealth of the woman's family, making gold digging harder. The mishnah reports that the women would recite the last two verses of Proverbs 31, adjuring the men to consider not grace and beauty, but rather character and reverence for God.

While harkening to an ancient, patriarchal, far-from-egalitarian society, the holiday preserves three important and timeless Jewish values: First, avoid bringing shame to the poor. Second, ensure that the poor can participate fully in society. Third, genuine romance must be grounded in character and integrity in order to blossom into enduring love.

אלול   *Elul*

S'lichot
Rabbi Amy Scheinerman, 2016

Ze'ev Wolf of Zhytomir, the eighteenth-century Chasidic master, recalls a parable he heard from the Magid of Mezeritch on Rosh HaShanah about a king who sent his children to a faraway country. After many years in exile, recalling how happy they had been in their father's court, they longed to return. They sent loving messages to their father in advance, but once they returned to the royal court, they could see that their father had changed. Despite their pleas for mercy, he was silent and expressed none of his former love and mercy for them. How could this be? They came to realize that in the time they had been away, they had become so used to the ways of the other nations that they had forgotten the king's language. They could only speak the language of the other nations. Their words had not even been heard by the king. They stopped using words altogether and simply called out, a universal cry for mercy.

    Many Jews return to synagogue for *S'lichot* or Rosh HaShanah after a hiatus. Some feel distant from the idiom of the *machzor* and Jewish prayer. Yet their emotional and spiritual needs are universal. Our task is to find a way to help them connect in whatever language they speak so they can be part of the homecoming and renewal of the High Holy Days.

Glossary

Adam—"human being;" name of the first human being.

Adamah—"earth."

Adonai—one of God's names.

Adonai Yimloch—"God will reign." Liturgical line.

Ahavah—"love."

Akarah (bibl.)—"barren woman."

Akeidah (bibl.)—"binding." Refers to Genesis 22, the story of the binding of Isaac.

Aliyah—"rising." Refers either to the ritual honor of Torah reading, or to the concept or process of Jewish immigration to Israel.

Amcha—"our people."

Amidah—central prayer consisting of a number of rabbinic blessings.

Am Yisrael—"the People of Israel."

Amora—(plural: *Amoraim*) the composers of Talmudic teachings.

Ana B'Koach—prayer for Shabbat evening.

Arbaah minim—"four species." Refers to the four plants relevant to the festival of Sukkot.

Aron—Torah Ark.

Aveirah—"transgression."

Avinu Malkeinu—"Our Father, Our King." Liturgical text, prayed predominately on the High Holy Days.

Avodah—"service;" "prayer service."

Avot D'Rabbi Natan—rabbinic text; one of the Minor Tractates.

Avot v'Imahot—lit. "Patriarchs and Matriarchs." Liturgical line.

Balagan—"chaos."

Bal tashchit—"do not destroy." Rabbinic law.

Bat—"daughter."

Bat kol—"voice from Heaven."

Bavli—Babylonian Talmud.

Beged—"clothing."

Bein adam lachaveiro—"between humans and humans."

Bein adam LaMakom—"between humans and God."

Beit k'neset—"synagogue."

Ben—"son."

B'gidah—"treachery."

Bigdei kodesh—"sacred clothing."

Bikur cholim—"visiting the sick." Rabbinic law.

Birkat HaMazon—blessing after eating.

Birkat Shalom—"blessing of peace."

Bitachon—"trust."

(Sefer) B'midbar—(the Book of) Numbers.

(Midrash) B'midbar Rabbah—Midrash on the Book of Numbers.

B'rachah—"blessing."

(Sefer) B'reishit—(the Book of) Genesis.

(Midrash) B'reishit Rabbah—Midrash on the Book of Genesis.

B'rit—"covenant."

B'rit milah—"the covenant of circumcision;" circumcision.

B'rit shalom—"covenant of peace."

B'tzelem Elohim—"in God's image."

Chachamim—"sages."

Chag—(plural: *chagim*) "festival."

Chag HaAsif—"Festival of Ingathering;" Sukkot.

Chag samei-ach—"Happy Holiday!"

Chag urim samei-ach!—"Happy Festival of Lights!;" Happy Chanukah!

Chalav—"milk."

Chalitzah (bibl.)—ritual process to avoid levirate marriage. See: *yibum*.

Chas v'chalilah—"God fordbid."

Chayil—"strength."

Chazak chazak v'nitchazeik—"from your strength to ours."

Chazak ve-ematz—"Be strong and resolute" (Deut. 31:7).

Chazal—the Sages.

Cheirut—"freedom."

Cheit—"sin;" often translated as "missing the mark."

Chesed—"love, benevolence, kindness, grace."

Cheshbon nefesh—"self-assessment."

Chochmah—"wisdom."

Chofesh—"vacation;" "the right to do whatever one chooses."

Chok—(plural: *chukim*) "law."

chol—"profane."

Chuppah—wedding canopy.

Davar Acheir—"another thing;" introducing another topic or divergent perspective.

Degel Machane Ephraim—written by Moshe Chaim Efraim, 1748–1800.

Derech Eretz—the way things are; acts of decency.

Derech Eretz Zuta—non-canonical rabbinic tractate.

Divrei Emet—written by Yaakov Yitzchak Horowitz (1745–1815).

Dor Hamabul—"the generation of the flood."

D'rash—Explanation or interpretation of the Bible; also refers to a short speech or article that teaches about the Bible and applies its lessons to daily life; the homiletic interpretation of the biblical text.

D'var (Torah)—Explanation or interpretation of the Bible; also refers to a short speech or article that teaches about the Bible and applies its lessons to daily life.

(Sefer) D'varim—(the Book of) Deuteronomy

Eichah—the Book of Lamentations.

Eichah Rabbah—Midrash on the Book of Lamentations.

Ein od milvado (kabbalistic)—"there is nothing else [but God]."

Eirev rav—"mixed multitude."

Eitz chayim—"a tree of life."

El Shaddai—one of God's names.

Eretz Yisrael—the Land of Israel.

Frum—"religious."

Galut—"exile."

Gan Eden—"Garden of Eden."

Ger—(plural: *gerim*) "stranger," "one who is not a member of the community. Abraham uses this term to introduce himself to the group of Hittites in Genesis 23:4.

Get—certificate of divorce.

Hashkiveinu—"let us lie down in peace." Liturgical line.

Heichalot literature—early mystical literature.

Hidur mitzvah—"the beautification of mitzvot."

Hachnasat orchim—"hospitatlity." Rabbinic law.

Hakafah—(plural: *hakafot*) ritual dancing or walking in a circle.

Hakodesh—"the Holy."

Hashgachah—"divine providence."

Havdalah—ritual separation between Shabbat or a festival and the following day.

Histapkut—"satisfaction;" "simplicity." Chasidic principle.

Ish—"man."

Ishah—"woman."

Kaddish–liturgical text. Usually: prayer for mourners.

Kahal—"congregation."

Kaparah—"atonement."

Kavanah—"intention."

K'dushah—"holiness."

K'dushat HaYom—"the sacredness of the day." Liturgical text.

K'dushat Levi—written by Levi Yitzchak of Berditchev (1740-1809).

Kein y'hi ratzon—"may it be God's will."

Ketubah—marriage certificate.

Kiddush—"sanctification;" ritual blessing over a cup of wine.

Kiddushin—marriage.

K'lei kodesh—"holy vessels."

K'li Yakar—written by Shlomo Ephraim of Luntschitz (1550-1609).

Kohein—(plural: *kohanim*) bibl. "a priest;" also one who descends from priestly lineage.

Kohein Gadol (bibl.)—the High Priest who has special privileges and responsibility on the Temple service.

Kohelet—(the Book of) Ecclesiastes.

(Midrash) Kohelet Rabbah—Midrash on the Book of Ecclesiastes.

Kol hakavod—"Respect!"

Korban—(plural: *korbanot*) "sacrifice."

K'tonet passim—"coat of many colors."

L'shanah tovah tikateivu—"May you be inscribed for a good year."

Lulav— one of the four species used during the Jewish holiday of Sukkot. See *arbaah minim*—"four species."

Maamarei Admor HaZakein—written by Shne'ur Zalman of Lyady (1745-1813).

Maftir—closing verses of the Torah reading; final person called to the Torah.

Malshinut—"slander."

M'chilta (d'Rabbi Shimon)—halachic midrash on the Book of Exodus.

M'gilah, M'gilat Esther—(the Book of) Esther.

Mei HaShiloach—written by the Ishbitzer Rebbe (1801-1854).

Meise—"story."

Meit mitzvah—"mitzvot on behalf of the deceased."

Mi Chamochah—"Who Is Like You." Liturgical line.

Midah k'neged midah—"measure for measure."

Midah (kabbalistic)—(plural: *midot*) "personal attribute."

Midrash B'reishit Rabbah—Midrash on the Book of Genesis

Midrash B'midbar Rabbah—Midrash on the Book of Numbers.

Midrash HaGadol—medieval compilation of Midrashim.

(Midrash) Kohelet Rabbah—Midrash on the Book of Ecclesiastes.

Midrash Rabbah—rabbinic compilation of Midrashim.

Midrash Sh'mot Rabbah—Midrash on the Book of Exodus.

Midrash Sifra—Midrash on the Book of Leviticus.

Midrash Tanchuma—rabbinic compilation of Midrashim.

Midrash Vayikra Rabbah—Midrash on the book of Leviticus.

Midrash Yalkut Shimoni—medieval compilation of Midrashim.

Mikdash—"sanctuary;" the Temple in which the Israelites worshipped God.

Mikraot G'dolot—rabbinic commentary on biblical texts.

Mikveh—"ritual bath."

Milah—see *b'rit; b'rit milah*.

Min hashamayim—"straight from heaven."

Mishkan—the Tabernacle that the Israelites built in order to worship God in the wilderness.

Mishnah—early rabbinic compilation of legal material.

Mishneh Torah—written by Maimonides (1135-1204).

Moreh Nevuchim—("Guide for the Perplexed") written by Maimonides (1135-1204).

M'or Einayim—written by Menachem Nachum Twersky of Chernobyl (1730-1797).

Moshe Rabbeinu—"Moses our teacher."

M'tzaveh—"the One who gives commandments."

Musar—modern school of ethics.

Naar (bibl.)—"young man."

Naaseh v'nishma—"We will do and obey." Refers to Exodus 24:7.

Nasi—"the head of the community."

Neis—"miracle."

Nefesh—"soul, spirit."

Ner tamid—"eternal light."

Nichum aveilim—"comforting the mourners." Rabbinic law.

Nidah (bibl.)—ritual impurity.

Nigun—Chasidic melody.

N'ilah—closing service of Yom Kippur.

Ohel Mo-eid—"Tent of Meeting;" a place in the Israelite wilderness camp where Moses, the priests, and the people would communicate with God.

Olam haba—"the world-to-come."

Orach L'Chayim—written by Avraham Chayim of Zloczow (1750–1816).

Panim el panim—"face to face."

Parashah—weekly Torah portion.

Pirkei Avot—early rabbinic text; part of the Mishnah.

Pirkei D'Rabbi Eliezer—medieval compilation of Midrashim.

P'shat – the plain sense of the biblical text.

P'sikta D'Rav Kahana – rabbinic compilation of Midrashim.

Purim *shpiels*—"Purim plays."

Rachamim—"mercy, compassion."

Rasha—"evil person;" "evil child."

R'chilut—"gossip."

Remez—a "hint" to a deeper layer of meaning of the biblical text.

Seder—(plural: *s'darim*) ritual meal with liturgical readings.

Sefer HaYashar—medieval Midrash.

S'firah—(plural: *s'firot*) "heavily sphere"

S'firat HaOmer—"the counting of the Omer;" liturgical time between Pesach and Shavuot

Shaah—"hour."

Shaar HaOtiot—written by Isaiah Horowitz (1565-1630).

Shaatneiz (bibl.)—(the prohibition of) mixing of threads. Refers to Lev. 19:19.

Shabbaton zichron t'ruah – "the Day on which we remember the Sound of the Shofar," Rosh HaShanah. Refers to Lev. 23:24.

Shalshelet hamasoret—"the chain of transmission."

Sh'chitah—"ritual slaughtering." Rabbinic law.

Shechinah—one of God's names.

Shehecheyanu v'kiy'manu v'higianu laz'man hazeh—"for giving life, sustaining us, and enabling us to reach this season." Liturgical line.

Shirat HaYam—Song at the Sea.

Sh'ma—central prayer consisting of a number of biblical quotes.

Sh'ma Yisrael, Adonai Eloheinu, Adonai Echad—"Hear O Israel, *Adonai* is our God, *Adonai* is One" (Deut. 6:4).

Sh'mitah—"Sabbatical year for the land."

Sh'moneh Esreih—see *Amidah*.

(Sefer) Sh'mot—(the Book of) Exodus

(Midrash) Sh'mot Rabbah—Midrash on the Book of Exodus.

Sh'nei Luchot HaB'rit—written by Isaiah Horowitz (1555-1630).

Shulchan Aruch—written by Joseph Karo (1488-1575).

(Midrash) Sifra—Midrash on the Book of Leviticus.

Simchat Beit HaSho-eivah (rabbinic)—the water-drawing ceremony performed on Sh'mini Atzeret, the eighth day of Sukkot.

Sod—the mystical meaning of the biblical text.

Sukkah—(plural: *sukkot*) "booth."

Sulam—"ladder."

Tahor (bibl.)—"ritually pure."

Talmid chacham—"Jewish scholar."

Talmud—rabbinic compilation of laws and Midrashim.

Talmud Torah—"Torah study."

Tamei (bibl.)—"ritually impure."

Tanach—the Hebrew Bible.

(Midrash) Tanchuma—rabbinic compilation of Midrashim.

Tanna—(plural: *Tannaim*) early rabbinic authorities; compilers of the Mishnah.

Targum Onkelos—early rabbinic Aramaic translation of the Torah.

Targum Yonatan—early rabbinic Aramaic translation of the Hebrew Prophets.

T'filah—"prayer."

t'fillin—"phylacteries."

tiferet—"splendor."

Tiferet Yehonatan—written by Jonathan Eibeschitz (1690–1764).

tikkun (kabbalistic)—"a night-long ritual;" "repair."

tikkun olam (kabbalistic)—"repair of the world."

tocheichah—"rebuke."

Tohorah—"cleansing, purification."

Torah l'Moshe miSinai—the belief that that God gave the entire Torah to Moses at Mount Sinai

Torah T'mimah—by Baruch Epstein (1860-1941).

Tosafot—medieval commentators on the *Talmud*.

Tov—"good."

T'shuvah—"repentance."

Tumah—"defiled."

Tzaar baalei chayim—"not to cause an animal undue pain." Rabbinic law.

Tzaraat (bibl.)—leprosy.

Tzedakah—"justice;" "charitable giving."

tzimtzum (kabbalistic)—[God's] "contraction."

tzitzit—prayer fringes.

Un'taneh Tokef—"Let us proclaim the power of this day." Liturgical text, prayed on the High Holy Days.

Ushpizin (kabbalistic)—biblical guests to the sukkah.

Vayikra—(the Book of) Leviticus.

Vayikra Rabbah—Midrash on the Book of Leviticus.

Yahrzeit—day of death.

Yamim Noraim—"Days of Awe;" High Holy Days.

Yetzer hara—"the evil inclination."

Yetzer tov—"the good inclination."

Y'hudi—(plural: *y'hudim*) "Jew."

Yibum (bibl.)—levirate marriage.

Yirah—"fear."

Yod-Hei-Vav-Hei—Tetragrammaton; one of God's names.

Yoveil (bibl.)—"Jubilee year."

Y'rushalayim shel maalah—"the Heavenly Jerusalem."

Y'rushalayim shel matah—"the Worldly Jerusalem."

Y'rushalmi—Jersualem / Palestinian Talmud.

Zeicher tzaddeket livrachah—"May her memory be a blessing."

Zichronot verses—liturgical texts prayed on Rosh HaShanah.

Zohar (kabbalistic)—mediaeval kabbalistic text.

www.ingramcontent.com/pod-product-compliance
Lightning Source LLC
Chambersburg PA
CBHW050546160426
43199CB00015B/2556